The editors

Hazel Heath MSc, BA(Hons), DipN(Lond), FETC, CertEd, ITEC, RGN, RCNT, RNT
Independent Nurse Consultant, and Editor, *Nursing Older People*

Roger Watson BSc, PhD, CBiol, FIBiol, ILTM, FRSA
Professor of Nursing, University of Hull, and Editor, *Journal of Clinical Nursing*

The authors

Mark T Bevan MSc, BSc(Hons), PGCert (Advanced Practice),
CertEd, RN (Chapter 37)
Nursing Lecturer, University of Leeds

Mark Bevan is the lead educator for renal nursing modules and has been involved in renal nursing for 20 years. He is currently undertaking research into dialysis satellite units as well as the incidence of depression and anxiety in a pre-dialysis population. His other work includes management and teaching of advanced nursing practice for nurses in primary and secondary care.

Jan H Beynon BSc(Hons), DRCOG, MRCP (Chapter 24)
Consultant Geriatrician, Department of Medicine for Older People, Queen Alexandra Hospital, Portsmouth

A consultant geriatrician working in a large district general hospital, Jan Beynon's main areas of interest are osteoporosis and falls; she is actively involved in developing these services in Portsmouth and southeast Hampshire.

Emma Briggs PhD, BSc(Hons), RN, PGCert (Research)
(Chapter 42)
Lecturer in Nursing, Florence Nightingale School of Nursing and Midwifery, King's College, London

Emma Briggs teaches across pre-registration, post-registration and postgraduate courses on pain management, wound care and research methods. In 2004 she completed her PhD in Nursing Studies, which explored nursing care and postoperative pain management in hospitals.

Mary Clay MSc Advanced Clinical Practice (Older People), RGN, RM, PGCEA (Chapter 34)
Consultant Nurse for Older People, Kensington and Chelsea Primary Care Trust

Mary Clay currently works across the Trust to help improve the services that older people receive, including supporting community hospitals and care homes.

Kate Davidson RGN, RHV, BSc(Hons), PhD (Chapter 6)
Lecturer, University of Surrey, Guildford

Kate Davidson lectures on the Sociology of Later Life and Social Policy and Welfare, and she is a Co-Director of the Centre for Research on Ageing and Gender (CRAG) at the University of Surrey. She is President Elect of the British Society of Gerontology, to assume office in 2006.

Jan Dewing RGN, MN, BSc, DipNursEd, RNT, DipNurs (Chapter 8)
Senior Fellow, Practice Development, Royal College of Nursing Institute, and Independent Consultant Nurse

Jan Dewing's work with the RCNI centres on developing work-based learning resources to support practitioners explore and utilise 'emancipatory' practice development in order that they might develop more effective cultures for service users. Much of her work is with older people's services and she has a specialist interest in dementia care.

Peter Draper RN, BSc, PhD, CertEd (Chapter 40)
Senior Lecturer in Nursing, Faculty of Health and Social Care, University of Hull

Research interests include quality of life of older people and spirituality in the context of health care. He is also an ordained Minister in the Church of England.

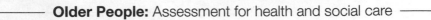

Christine Eberhardie TD, MSc, RN, RNT, ILTM, MIHM
(Chapter 33)
Senior Lecturer in Nursing, St George's Hospital Medical School, London

Christine Eberhardie teaches nutrition support in relation to neuro-science and palliative care nursing.

Jon Glasby BA, MA/DipDW, PhD (Chapter 1)
Senior Lecturer, Health Services Management Centre, University of Birmingham

Jon Glasby is a qualified social worker and an academic with inter-ests in community care services for older people and in health and social care partnerships.

Sue M Green RN, BSc, MMedSci, PhD, PGCert (Chapter 36)
Senior Lecturer, University of Southampton

Sue Green teaches nutritional care to pre-qualifying nurses and those undertaking programmes of study following qualification.

Nicky Hayes RGN, BA(Hons), MSc, PGCert(HE) (Chapters 19 and 21)
Consultant Nurse for Older People, King's College Hospital NHS Trust, London, and the Care Homes Support Team, Southwark Primary Care Trust

Nicky Hayes' clinical work currently spans both acute hospital care for older people and NHS support for older residents of care homes in southeast London. The focus of her clinical work is the assessment of continuing care needs but she also has specialist interests in falls and in Parkinson's disease.

Hazel Heath MSc, BA(Hons), DipN(Lond), FETC, CertEd, ITEC, RGN, RCNT, RNT (Chapters 9 and 10)
Independent Nurse Consultant, and Editor, *Nursing Older People*

Hazel Heath's independent commissions include projects with the Department of Health, Nursing and Midwifery Council, Help the Aged and the Royal College of Nursing. She has been the Senior Teacher in Nursing Theory and Practice at St Bartholomew's in London, Chair of the RCN's Forum for Nurses Working with Older People and the RCN's Adviser on Nursing and Older People.

Sharon E Maher BSc(Hons), RGN (Chapter 41)
Part-time staff nurse, who currently works on a medical ward at the Leicester Royal Infirmary

Sharon Maher's special interest has always been working with older people, in both hospital and community settings.

Jill Manthorpe MA (Chapters 7, 22 and 27)
Professor of Social Work and Co-Director of the Social Care Workforce Research Unit, King's College London

Jill Manthorpe has researched and taught in the areas of social and health care for older people for many years and has been involved in local Age Concerns and in other voluntary and community sector activities. Recent studies include looking at unmet need for low-level services, intermediate care and older people's champions. She has recently published books and articles on early recognition of dementia, dementia care, elder abuse, risk, rural services and older people's strategies. She is currently working with the Healthcare Commission on its joint inspection of older people's services.

Brendan McCormack BSc, DPhil, RNT, RGN, RMN, PGCEA (Chapter 3)
Professor of Nursing Research, University of Ulster, and Director of Nursing Research and Practice Development, Royal Hospitals Trust, Belfast

In his current post, Brendan McCormack is Director of Nursing Research and Practice Development in the Royal Hospitals Trust, Belfast, and manages these activities across all specialities while maintaining his specialist practice focus on gerontological nursing. In addition he is the leader of the School of Nursing's 'Working with Older People' Recognised Research Group, co-ordinating research and development activity in this area. Brendan has written extensively on gerontological nursing and is co-editor of a new journal, *The International Journal of Older People Nursing*.

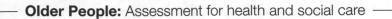

Tina McDougall BSc, SRD (Chapter 36)
Head of Nutrition and Dietetics Services, Hull and East Yorkshire Hospitals NHS Trust

Tina McDougall is an experienced nutritional support dietitian who strives to raise awareness of the importance of early identification and treatment of the malnourished acutely ill hospitalised patient.

Henry A Minardi MSc, BSc, DipN, DipCounselling&Supervision, CertEd, RGN, RMN (Chapters 19 and 21)
Consultant Nurse, Liaison Psychiatry for Older Adults, Central and North West London Mental Health NHS Trust

There are several strands to Henry Minardi's work as a consultant nurse: clinical, local and national strategic planning, research and education. Clinical work involves seeing older adults on general hospital wards either for a 'one off' psychiatric assessment or for assessment and follow-up. His teaching and research interests are in using counselling skills, prevalence of depression with older adults and emotion recognition in others by people with Alzheimer's.

Ian Norman BA, MSc, PhD, RMN, RGN, RNMH, CQSW, ILT, FEANS (Chapter 2)
Professor of Nursing and Inter-disciplinary Care and Head of the Mental Health Section, Florence Nightingale School of Nursing & Midwifery, King's College, University of London, and Editor-in-Chief of the *International Journal of Nursing Studies*

Ian Norman is a social scientist with a professional background in mental health, general and learning disability nursing and social work. His research programme is concerned with evaluation of workforce-related initiatives for improving the delivery of health and social care and the outcome of these initiatives for staff, patients and services. He has a particular research interest in inter-professional education and working among health and social care professionals, and the care of older people, particularly those with mental health problems.

Lynne Phair MA, BSc(Hons)Nursing, RMN, RGN, DPNS
(Chapter 10)
Consultant Nurse Older People, Crawley Primary Care Trust, and
Fellow of the University of Brighton

Lynne Phair has always worked with older people, including in NHS
mental health services, primary care, the voluntary sector and as
an expert witness. She has led practice and service development
projects, has advised the Department of Health on older people
issues, and was a member of the RCN Older Persons Steering
Group.

Karen Rawlings-Anderson RN, BA(Hons), DipNEd, MSc
(Chapter 5)
Senior Lecturer, City University, St Bartholomew School of Nursing
and Midwifery, London

Karen Rawlings-Anderson is currently the Programme Director for
the MSc Nursing at City University. Her main areas of teaching relate
to professional and theoretical issues in nursing practice, and she
has particular interest and expertise in cultural aspects of care.

Irene Schofield MSc(Gerontology), CertHlthProm(Open), CertEd,
RGN, RNT (Chapters 17 and 20)
Research Fellow in Gerontological Nursing, Glasgow Caledonian
University

Irene Schofield works on research and practice development projects
involving older people and older people's nursing.

Julie Tillotson RGN, BSc(Hons), Nurse Practitioner and
Ophthalmic Nursing Diploma (Chapter 18)
Advanced Nurse Practitioner at Bournemouth Eye Unit

Julie Tillotson's work focuses on assessing, diagnosing and treating patients with urgent or emergency eye problems. She frequently
attends local meetings for persons newly registered blind or partially
sighted, giving talks and learning about the ways in which people
overcome their difficulties.

Roger Watson BSc, PhD, CBiol, FIBiol, ILTM, FRSA (Chapters 11, 12, 13, 14, 23, 25, 26, 28, 31 and 35)
Professor of Nursing, University of Hull, and Editor, *Journal of Clinical Nursing*

Roger Watson's clinical experience was gained working with older people with dementia, and he has a particular interest in the assessment of eating difficulty and the measurement of competence and caring in nursing.

Diane Wells (formerly **Macklin**) MPhil, BA, DipSocStud, DipRes, CertEd, RN, DipNurs, RNT, Cassel Certificate in Psychosocial Nursing (Chapter 4)
Lecturer, Faculty of Health and Social Care Sciences, Kingston University and St George's Hospital Medical School, London University; freelance Balint Seminar Leader and Researcher

Diane Wells' particular interest is the practitioner–client relationship. In courses, such as 'Biographical Approaches to Working with Older People' and 'Chronic Illness and Ageing', she uses Balint-style seminars to study examples of practitioner–client interactions and to promote skills in psychosocial care.

Isabel D White MScNursing, P/GDiploma Psychosexual Therapy, BEd(Hons)Nursing Education, DipLScNursing, RGN, RSCN, RNT, OncCert (Chapter 9)
Cancer Research UK Nursing Research Training Fellow

Isabel White has worked in cancer care since 1984, and has a specialist interest in the psychosexual impact of cancer and its treatment on people living with cancer and other chronic or life-limiting illnesses. As the majority of those affected by cancer are older adults, she is particularly interested in the assessment and support of couples facing sexual and relationship adjustment in later life.

Lesley Wilson BNSc(Hons), RGN (Chapter 39)
Clinical Manager, Southampton City Primary Care Trust

Lesley Wilson has worked in continence promotion for 12 years as a Continence Adviser and Continence Services Manager, and now maintains her links as an expert adviser to the service. She served on the Committee of the RCN Continence Care Forum for seven years and now edits their newsletter.

Philip Woodrow MA, RGN, DipN, GradCertEd (Chapters 16, 29, 30, 31, 32 and 38)
Practice Development Nurse for Critical Care, East Kent Hospitals NHS Trust

Philip Woodrow has published widely in nursing journals, and is author of three books: *Intensive Care Nursing: a framework for practice* (Routledge, 2000), *Ageing: issues for physical, psychological and social health* (Whurr; 2002) and *High Dependency Nursing: observation, intervention and support* (Routledge, 2004).

Mary Woolliams BNurs(Hons), RGN, PGDip Geratology (Chapter 15)
Lecturer in Adult Nursing, Oxford Brookes University

Mary Woolliams has worked in acute general medicine and as ward manager on a rehabilitation unit for older people. She now teaches pre-registration students on the Adult Nursing Programme.

Contents

Foreword

This is a comprehensive book on the assessment of older people. The material covers a broad range of issues from the biographical and cultural and religious to the physiological; as such, it is probably unique.

The book is set within the context of current health and social care policy and includes the Single Assessment Process, one of the planks of the National Service Framework for Older People. Despite the wide range of material that is covered, the book is written in an accessible style. Whilst clearly aimed primarily at professionals, it may well have a wider audience. The authorship of the chapters demonstrates a wide range of expertise across the health and social care spectrum, and many of the authors will be 'household names' in their own disciplines.

Age Concern has shown considerable foresight in commissioning this book and I hope that it finds use in the many settings where older people are cared for.

Ian Philp
Professor of Health Care for Older People, University of Sheffield
National Director for Older People and Neurological Conditions,
Department of Health

Introduction

Assessment is the foundation for health and social care and is integral to all areas of policy and practice with older people. Sound assessment is essential for competent practice; it establishes the grounding for an older person's relationship with services and, even within a single assessment encounter, the decisions can be life-changing.

Assessment takes an infinite range of forms for an enormous variety of purposes and, when working with older people, a great deal of practitioner time is spent in assessing. Assessment can be a single event for a specific purpose or a feature of an ongoing relationship between an older person and a care professional. If it is to be effective, wherever it is undertaken, whatever its purpose and whoever assesses, a sound understanding of older people and the influences on their lives and health is essential.

This book aims to support assessment for health and social care, in all its diversity, by offering a knowledge base to underpin assessment practice and the decisions that result from this. It offers an easy-to-use guide to assessment that practitioners can carry with them and consult when specific issues arise. While with an older person, a care professional can encounter concerns about, for example, pain, hearing or continence. The relevant sections in the book offer information on age-related changes, how these manifest, how to assess them and what conclusions could be drawn. The text offers succinct explanations of the evidence-base underpinning assessment practice alongside frameworks, tools, checklists and trigger-points for further assessment or onward referral.

The book can also be used as a basis for systematic learning, and care professionals may wish to study some of the sections before they enter an assessment situation: for example, values underpinning assessment, biographical and developmental approaches, or cultural and religious needs.

To encompass all aspects of assessment comprehensively would require many volumes; this book offers a foundation and includes guidance on additional resources that readers can access.

- Part 1 sets out the current health and social care context and identifies frameworks for interagency and interdisciplinary assessment. It also explores the values underpinning assessment and how these manifest in practice.
- Part 2 focuses on individuality in later life and the influences upon this. It considers individual biography, culture and religion, lifestyle, coping strategies, sources of support and sexuality. It clarifies the concept of consent and the implications of this for assessment.
- Part 3 details a range of foundations for care and support, including the influence of environment, the effects of normal ageing, communication and risk.
- Part 4 covers essential elements for life, including physiological functioning, eating and drinking, and elimination.
- Part 5 explores key contributors to quality of life.

The principles, evidence and frameworks in this text are broadly applicable. The legislation and policy initiatives are those currently operating in England, although some of these are adopted more widely. This book does not attempt to debate policy issues in detail, to discuss funding or to deal with specific assessments (eg for intermediate or continuing care). As readers will appreciate, health and social policy constantly evolves, and assessment titles, terminology and the criteria that determine the outcomes constantly evolve accordingly.

Assessment can be challenging. Whilst it basically determines what help might be most appropriate for individuals and what support they will receive, it is increasingly becoming a means of determining the most effective use of limited resources. When assessments establish eligibility for services or funding, practitioners can be faced with the dilemma of identifying needs while, at the same time, rationing the resources that could meet these.

The complexity of assessment with older people should not be underestimated. As this book identifies, older people who encounter care professionals commonly have complex, coexisting and interrelated health and social issues. Many aspects of assessment can be subtle, particularly those concerning rights, risks, consent and abuse. Along with the skills to observe, question, make decisions and achieve mutual understanding, sound knowledge is essential if assessment is to result in support that is timely, co-ordinated, appropriate, acceptable and effective.

Assessment can also be highly rewarding. It offers opportunities for professionals to build relationships with older individuals and to learn more about their lives, experiences, perspectives and aspirations for the future. Sound and effective assessment can identify, anticipate and prevent needs or problems. Also, in the hands of skilled practitioners, assessment in itself can be therapeutic.

In the realities of health and social care today, where older people frequently move through many different services, even within a single episode of care, assessment can offer a unifying continuity. As an integral element within the cycle of support, older people's assessed needs and choices can determine the planning, provision and continuing evaluation of care services. Ultimately, regardless of boundaries between health and social services, the various sectors of care provision or the disciplines of practitioners, the most important outcome of assessment is that older individuals are offered the support they want and require in the manner that is most helpful to them.

Hazel Heath and Roger Watson
May 2005

Part 1
Concepts and Context

1 The health and social care policy context

Jon Glasby

Each year, health and social services in the UK assess millions of older people with a view to establishing their eligibility for statutory services and deciding what sort of support may best meet the individual's needs. In social care, the assessment process is subject to statute and to detailed regulations under the NHS and Community Care Act 1990, and a range of different statistics are collected to capture the considerable activity that is undertaken in social services departments across the country. For example, just over one million people received community care assessments in 2002/2003, around 600,000 of whom were over 75 (Department of Health/National Statistics 2004). In health care, the assessment process is not necessarily set out in such a centrally defined and legally mandated way but it is just as important:

- In primary care, a GP assessment is the starting point for older people with health needs, making a preliminary diagnosis and deciding whether to prescribe medication or to refer on for more specialist assessment.

- In hospital, an older person may receive a range of different assessments with regard to manual handling, mental health, activities of daily living, risk of pressure sores, nutrition and a number of other aspects of their physical, social and psychological functioning.

- In nursing, assessment is the first stage of the nursing process (assess, plan, implement, evaluate).

In other areas, too, assessment is the focus of a significant amount of activity. In mental health, for example, detailed responsibilities are set out in the Mental Health Act 1983 for psychiatrists and approved social workers involved in the 'sectioning' process for people who need to be admitted to inpatient care. Elsewhere, family members, friends and neighbours providing regular and substantial care to others are entitled to an assessment of their needs under the Carers and Disabled Children's Act 2000, while children in need are assessed under the Children Act 1989. Whilst we can probably never be sure, it is possible that health and social care practitioners spend more of their time assessing service users and patients than they do engaged in any other activity. Certainly, previous government guidance suggests that the proper assessment of need should be 'the cornerstone of high quality care' and a central feature of policy and practice (Department of Health 1990: 3).

Why does assessment matter?

According to the Department of Health (1989: 18–19), assessment is a crucial activity in shaping the way services respond to need, should include a wide range of relevant services/professionals and should be based on the active participation of the individual and, where appropriate, their family:

> 'The objective of assessment is to determine the best available way to help the individual ... All agencies and professions involved with the individual and his or her problems should be brought into the assessment procedure when necessary. This may include social workers, GPs, community nurses, hospital staff ..., nurses, physiotherapists, occupational therapists, speech therapists, continence advisers, community psychiatric nurses, staff involved with vision and hearing impairment, housing officers ..., home helps, home care assistants and voluntary workers. Assessments should take account of the wishes of the individual and his or her carer, and of the carer's ability to continue to provide care, and where possible should include their active participation. Effort should be made to offer flexible services which enable individuals and carers to make choices.'

In recent years, the centrality of assessment has been most strongly asserted in the community care reforms of 1990–1993. Prior to this, older people entering an independent sector care home were entitled to support from the social security system if they qualified on financial grounds. Although this policy evolved over time in a relatively unplanned way, it meant that people could enter very expensive services with state financial support without any assessment of their care needs to determine whether this was the best way of supporting the person concerned. As a result, the number of independent sector homes and the amount of public money being spent in this manner rocketed (Means and Smith 1998: 50):

- The number of places provided by the private sector rose from 46,900 (1982) to 161,200 (1991).
- Expenditure increased from £10 million (1979) to £1,872 million per annum (1991).
- The number of people receiving such payments increased from 12,000 (1979) to 90,000 (1986).

In response, the Government introduced the NHS and Community Care Act 1990, making social services departments the lead agency responsible for assessing the needs of individual people and of the local community, and arranging care packages to meet these needs within available resources. Arguably, this could be both a good thing and a bad thing, ensuring that services are appropriately tailored to the needs of the individual but at the same giving local authorities an implicit rationing role and making them responsible for bringing a rapidly escalating budget under control. As a result, subsequent debates about assessment have tended to focus on how best to promote the positive features of the community care reforms (the emphasis on the appropriate assessment of individual need) and to minimise some of the more negative features (an emphasis on strict eligibility criteria, rationing and managing scarce resources).

Different types of assessment

Central to the community care reforms and to subsequent assessment policy and practice have been the notions of needs-led and service-led assessment:

- Traditionally, health and social care have been accused of offering very service-led approaches (ie failing to assess the true needs of the individual and simply assessing with a view to slotting the person into an often fairly narrow menu of in-house services). As an example, it is still possible to hear some practitioners talk about assessing someone for day care or for residential care. Arguably nobody should be assessed as needing these services: people may require support with their personal care needs, social stimulation and support with meals, but these needs can be met in a variety of ways. This might include day care or residential care but could equally include a range of other approaches that some people might prefer.

- In contrast, post-1993 policy has emphasised the importance of needs-led assessment (ie separating out the functions of assessment and service provision). This means that an assessor or care manager helps to identify an individual's needs and that this process is separate from the decision about which services may best meet these needs. This is often described in terms of a purchaser–provider split, the care manager purchasing services to meet the individual's needs from a range of potential providers (including the public, private and voluntary sectors).

In addition, different commentators identify different types or styles of assessment. In a key early publication following the Community Care Act, for example, Smale and colleagues (1993) sought to distinguish between: a questioning model, where the assessor sets the agenda and is perceived as the 'expert'; an administrative model, where pro formas are drawn up by managers to constrain both users and professionals; and an exchange model, where the assessment process is a shared enterprise and the service user is respected as an individual. More recently, there has been much greater emphasis on a number of different approaches to ensure that assessment is as person-centred and individualised as possible. These include:

- The notion of self-assessment (often associated with younger people with physical impairments). Clearly, the person most likely to know about someone's needs is the person themselves, and disabled campaigners have been crucial in developing notions of self-assessment and self-managed services whereby organisations of disabled people support the service user to assess their own needs and devise their own care packages (often using Direct Payments – cash payments made to disabled people for their social care needs in lieu of directly provided services) (for further discussion, see Priestley 2004).

- The concept of person-centred planning (practised particularly in services for people with a learning difficulty), which seeks to discover what is important to a person from their own perspective through a process of continual listening and learning, and acting upon this in alliance with the person, their family and friends (Department of Health 2001) (see Chapter 3 for further discussion of person-centred approaches to assessment).

- The notion of a single assessment process to ensure that all relevant health and social care agencies share information about the older people they meet and that service users have to give their personal (and sometimes very private, sensitive) information only once instead of, at present, to a range of different professionals, none of whom seems to share this information with the others. Such an approach raises a range of issues about data protection, confidentiality and the role of information technology, but also offers an important mechanism for delivering more joined-up services to people with needs that may often span the boundaries of traditional service provision (see Chapter 2 for a further discussion).

From policy into practice?

Although many people initially welcomed many of the community care reforms with cautious optimism, there has since been a range of studies that question the extent to which current assessment practice lives up to the ideals of official guidance (see, for example, Davis et al 1997; Challis 1999; Glasby and Littlechild 2004). In particular, a number of commentators question the extent to which assessments can be said to be:

- genuinely needs-led;
- genuinely person-centred;

- genuinely multi-agency;
- genuinely participative.

Ultimately, recent policy developments offer an opportunity to improve assessment practices and to deliver truly integrated, responsive and person-centred care. However, it is up to the people reading this book to make sure that they hold true to these principles in practice and deliver official aspirations to make the proper assessment of need 'the cornerstone of high quality care' (Department of Health 1990: 3).

2 The Single Assessment Process: a framework for interdisciplinary and interagency assessment

Ian Norman

In the UK, assessment of need has become one of the key elements in the Government's strategy to implement community care policy, for ensuring both appropriate placement and cost-effective high-quality care. The emphasis is now on the development of comprehensive multidisciplinary assessment involving both health and social care agencies (Department of Health 1997a,b) and local implementation of the Single Assessment Process (SAP), which provides the most comprehensive framework hitherto for interprofessional and inter-agency assessment of older people.

This chapter points to the difficulties of achieving collaborative interdisciplinary and interagency assessment of older people and describes the SAP, which is expected to lead in time to convergence of assessment methods and results nationally. Successful implementation of the SAP requires health and social care professionals to think and work in new ways, which is why it is the main focus of this chapter.

Barriers to collaborative assessment

It is widely held that collaborative interprofessional working between different health and social care disciplines and different agencies is a prerequisite of good assessment practice, and indeed of high-quality community care. But there are many obstacles to collaboration and it is rarely totally achieved in practice. Frequently cited obstacles include:

- ambiguous roles and responsibilities of staff;
- conflicting power relationships arising from the different culture, philosophy and educational requirements, status and backgrounds of health care disciplines; and
- different health and social care organisations having different structures, competing priorities and differing agendas (Vanclay 1997).

The research evidence suggests that the process of assessment is rooted in and reflects the professional identities of assessors with the result that it is limited and partial. This is nicely illustrated by an experiment described by Runciman (1989) in which she showed different groups of professionals a three-minute video of an older woman talking to an assessor and asked them to list her needs. There was considerable agreement between and within groups about her problems, but proposed solutions varied widely. For example, most professionals noted that the woman had difficulty rising from her chair but the solutions offered varied across professional groups – ranging from physiotherapists suggesting a programme of hand exercises to improve her grip, health visitors suggesting a higher chair, to general practitioners suggesting a hip replacement. The health professionals also made diverse value judgements about the woman: she was described variously as cheerful, depressed, anxious, stubborn, apathetic, dogmatic, proud, lonely, neat and unkempt, and her room as cluttered and uncluttered.

Twigg and Atkin (1994) argue that, in the absence of clear and explicit agency, policy or practice guidance on assessment, practitioners rely on their implicit knowledge, which helps to explain adherence of different professionals to their particular perspective, as in Runciman's study. Twigg and Atkin suggest three sources of implicit knowledge:

- professional training and values;
- the culture of the office; and
- assumptive worlds.

Professional training

The most obvious of these three sources of implicit knowledge is professional training and values, which result in professionals operating with different conceptual models of care, from which they derive their assessment procedures, objectives and working methods. An attempt to categorise these conceptual models was made by Baraclough and colleagues (1979), who located occupations drawn from primary health, medical specialities and psychiatry along two axes (Figure 2.1).

The horizontal axis is the focus of concern and/or intervention and ranges from: holistic (where the patient/service user is considered as a whole person, member of a family, or a social group or part of a community) to reductionist (where the system, organ, cell or molecule is seen as the target for assessment and intervention). The vertical axis is the designated status of the patient/service user, which ranges from autonomous (where autonomy, independence and self-realisation are seen as of primary importance) to dependence (where autonomy and independence are relinquished or suspended in favour of control).

Baraclough and colleagues (1979) suggested that medical specialists work mostly in the bottom right corner (they are reductionist and protective), social workers mostly in the top left-hand corner (they are holistic and enabling). Health visitors, district nurses and general practitioners move between these two positions, depending on the needs of their patients and their preferred mode of working. Psychiatrists work mostly in the bottom left-hand quadrant. They adopt a holistic perspective but are controlling. This model was developed more than 25 years ago but it still provides a useful way of categorising different professional perspectives, which explains to some extent their different ways of assessing and working with patients/service users.

Whilst differing conceptual models of care held by members of a multiprofessional care team may in some cases provide patients/service users with the benefit of a broad range of professional perspectives on their problems and care, these conceptual models may be expressed more negatively. Nolan (1994) points to professional protectionism (the tendency to defend an area of practice to which a

Figure 2.1 Classification of conceptual models of care held by members of the primary care team and medical specialists and psychiatrists (Baraclough et al 1979)

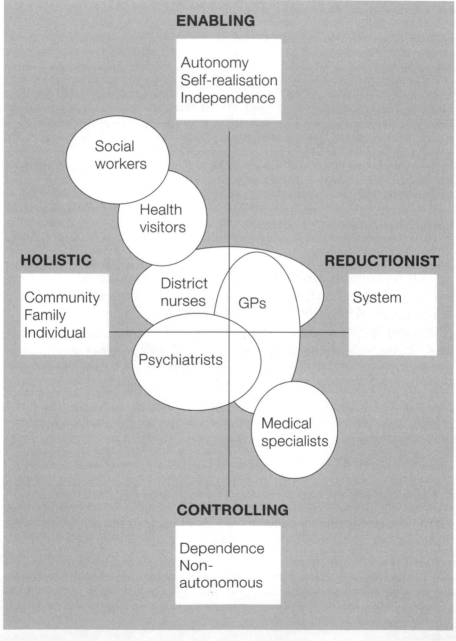

profession lays claim) and professional reductionism (the tendency to reduce the focus of assessment to a set of problems consistent with the professional's conceptual model) as two major factors, which inhibit collaborative assessment practice.

Office culture and assumptive worlds

The culture of the office, Twigg and Atkin's (1994) second source of implicit knowledge, refers to local accepted methods of working and intervention that develop, often in the absence of a strong professional socialisation and conceptual frameworks. Twigg and Atkin give the example of social work departments in which work with some major groups, such as older people, is accorded low status and so tends to be left to unqualified practitioners.

The assumptive worlds of assessors, Twigg and Atkin's third source of implicit knowledge, exist at a subconscious level and so are more difficult to challenge or change than assessment practices arising from the other two sources. Such assumptive worlds incorporate moral judgements about deserving and less deserving cases, for example. A study by Ellis (1993) found that such judgements were often a major factor in determining which individuals received services and which did not, and also that the more difficult the case, the more likely it was that moral judgements would inform assessment decisions; Nolan and Grant (1992) reported a similar finding. Inadequate resources to develop service options can also hamper collaborative assessment (Baldwin and Woods 1994). Assessors are often in a paradoxical situation, because they are, *de facto*, also rationers of care who have little incentive to probe too deeply and risk uncovering needs that cannot be met.

In sum, there are many obstacles to interagency and interprofessional assessment practice because assessors rely on their implicit knowledge. Sources of such knowledge include professional socialisation and training, accepted local practices, and underlying assumptions, which may operate at a subconscious level. In addition, assessors are frequently in a paradoxical situation in their role of both uncovering people's needs and rationing care.

Interprofessional education

Collaborative assessment practice requires that professionals from different agencies and disciplines understand each other's roles and responsibilities and establish a common dialogue. One key to this is thought to be interprofessional education, which is now widely perceived as a potentially effective method for enhancing collaborative practice (World Health Organization 1988) because it provides opportunities for professionals or those in training to meet and interact, whereas uniprofessional education does not.

The UK Government sees interprofessional education as having a central role in the development of the 'new' NHS. For example, the third of six principles underpinning the 1997 White Paper *The New NHS* (Department of Health 1997b) is 'to get the NHS working in partnership'. Expanding on this later, the document states:

> *'In an NHS based on partnership it will be increasingly important for the staff of NHS Trusts to work efficiently and effectively in teams within and across organisational boundaries. Integrated care for patients will rely on models of training and education that give staff a clear understanding of how their own roles fit with those of others within both the health and social care professions.'* (Department of Health 1997b)

In the NHS Plan published three years later, the Government's objectives for interprofessional education are more ambitious than simply learning about each other's roles. The Plan states:

> *'There will be new joint training across the professions in communication skills and in NHS principles and organisation. They will form part of a new core curriculum for all education programmes for NHS staff ... A new common foundation programme will be put in place to enable students and staff to switch careers and training paths more easily.'* (Department of Health 2000a: 86)

> *'We believe it is important that the NHS ... should work with higher education providers and accreditation bodies ... to develop education and training arrangements which are*

genuinely multi-professional and which will enable students to transfer readily between courses without having to start their training afresh.' (Department of Health 2000b: 7)

Finch (2000) points out that these policy statements imply any or all of the following outcomes for students: that they should:

- know about the roles of other professionals;
- be able to work with them in the context of teams where each member has a clearly defined role;
- substitute for roles traditionally played by other professionals, when this may be more effective; and
- switch training pathways to enhance career progression.

Finch argues that universities need a clear view about what interprofessional working really means before curricula can be developed to underpin it.

The first two of Finch's outcomes could improve assessment practice by promoting multidisciplinary teamwork and complementary roles across different agencies. The third and fourth objectives are more radical, because they blur the boundaries between disciplines and so point to common assessment practice.

In sum, interprofessional education may have substantial benefits for interprofessional collaboration but the current evidence base is too weak to know one way or another (Zwarenstein et al 2004). However, forms of joint training alone are unlikely to improve collaborative assessment practice unless practitioners and agencies have explicit assessment frameworks within which to operate and a clear view of what constitutes a good assessment.

Assessment frameworks

Early efforts at framework development focused on local assessment forms, which, however, were inclined to supersede their function. Nolan and Caldock (1996), among others, point to the tendency of common assessment forms with tick-box type formats to be used to justify decisions that have already been made. An analysis of 50 documents used in the assessment of older people by UK social services agencies (Stewart et al 1999) found that they also tended to focus assessment largely on the obvious, physical functioning or activities of daily living, for example, but the reason for collecting such information was often unclear and information was seldom interpreted in a meaningful way. Moreover, there was enormous variability between documents, thus hampering their ability to generate standardised information.

Nolan and Caldock (1996), in endorsing an assessment framework based on Rolland's (1988) therapeutic quadrangle, suggest that any such framework for multidisciplinary/multiagency assessment of older people should be:

- flexible and, therefore, adaptable to a variety of circumstances;
- appropriate to the audience it is supposed to address;
- able to incorporate the views of the key players – users, carers, agencies;
- able to bring diverse views together, while providing scope for the expression of diversity and variability within individual circumstances.

The most ambitious framework for interdisciplinary and interagency needs assessment of older people so far is the Single Assessment Process (SAP), which was introduced by the National Service Framework for Older People with the aims of ensuring that older people 'receive appropriate, effective and timely responses to their health care needs, and that professional resources are used effectively'. It is to a consideration of the elements of this framework that this chapter now turns. (Full details can be obtained from the Department of Health, Single Assessment Process website.)

The Single Assessment Process

In a press release issued in January 2002, Jacqui Smith, the Health Minister, introduced the SAP thus:

> *'All too often assessment is done to older people rather than with them and is often duplicated by professionals because information is not shared.*

'Single assessment aims to change this by placing the older person at the centre of the process and recognising that a good assessment is based on the older person's account of their needs and wishes. It acknowledges that older people, not the various professionals they encounter, are the real experts.

'It will ensure that health and social services profession-als work better together in assessing older people's needs and planning their care. This should lead to a more uniform approach to assessment across the country, less duplication and paperwork, more emphasis on looking at older people's needs in the round and getting the service right first time.'
(Department of Health Press Release, 28 January 2002)

The SAP is designed, in particular, to ensure that:

- the scale and depth of assessment is in proportion to the older person's needs;
- agencies do not duplicate each other's assessments;
- professionals contribute to assessments in the most effective way; and
- information is obtained to determine the provision of funding to support residents in care homes that provide nursing care.

The SAP provides an overall framework of key attributes, values, domains and stages of assessment, which is expected to result in convergence of procedures, outputs and outcomes over time. Thus, whilst local assessment processes may vary, all assessment systems should be able to generate a single assessment summary, comprising sets of standardised assessment information.

The main elements of the SAP as a framework for multidisciplinary assessment are outlined below.

Key attributes and common values

Local approaches to the SAP must be:

- *Person-centred* – which involves, for example, professionals and agencies working together in what the older person, or those close to them, regard as their best interests; building a comprehensive picture of their needs to a level of detail that is proportionate to their needs; and ensuring informed consent with regard to the circumstances under which the needs and circumstances of older people may be collected and shared.

- *Standardised* – which involves, for example, producing a single assessment summary (of which more later) for each individual case, which incorporates contributions to assessment by different professionals and agencies that are trusted and accepted; and generating information for strategic planning and performance monitoring.

- *Outcome-centred* – which translates assessment information into effective care plans and services, and promotes the older person's health, independence, quality of life and potential for rehabilitation.

In addition, all agencies and professionals involved should work to a common set of values, which are concerned with:

- person-centred care and independence;
- carers and family members, and the importance of supporting them;
- integrated and responsive services; and
- training, development and support of staff.

Domains and stages of assessment

The SAP identifies nine domains, and associated sub-domains, within which assessment may take place. These are: the user's perspective (including their expectations, strengths, ability, motivation and perceived needs); clinical background (including health history and medication); disease prevention (including blood pressure, nutrition, alcohol use, smoking); personal care and physical well-being; senses;

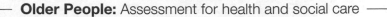

mental health; relationships; safety; and immediate environment and resources (including housing, finances, access to local facilities).

The SAP identifies seven stages to comprehensive needs assessment, as follows.

Stage 1: Publishing information about services

This stage involves review and development of the types of information provided to older people and other groups about available services and what they might expect of the SAP.

Stage 2: Case finding

Although not mandatory, agencies are invited to develop case-finding systems to identify, and invite for assessment, older people who are not referred to them for help. Examples of case-finding methods include postal questionnaires and the over-75s health check.

Stage 3: The four types of assessment

The SAP identifies four types of assessment, which together are designed to identify the actual and potential needs of an individual, evaluate their impact on independence, daily functioning and quality of life, and inform action planning.

Contact assessment. This refers to a contact between an older person and health or social services 'where significant needs are first described or suspected'. It involves collecting basic personal information, establishing the presenting problem and exploring the potential for wider health or social care needs.

Contact assessment may be carried out by a trained and competent, but not necessarily professionally qualified, member of staff. It involves simple questions to enquire about health status, stamina and energy, for example; the Department of Health's current advice is that there are no other systematic and reliable methods of contact assessment currently available.

Overview assessment. This form of assessment may be carried out by a single professional, from either health or social services (depending on local agreements about interagency working), in cases where it is judged that the individual's needs are such that a fuller assessment is required and will involve exploration of all or some of the assessment domains identified previously. Assessment tools are recommended (mentioned later) that are evidence-based and include 'signposts', which might indicate the domains that should be explored. For example, if the older person is found to be incontinent of urine, assessment of mobility, medication and access to the toilet would be indicated. Some of these tools include scales, which can identify the presence or severity of particular problems.

Specialist assessments. This type of assessment involves detailed exploration, by a qualified and competent professional, of specific needs to confirm the presence, extent, cause and likely development of a health condition or problem.

Comprehensive assessment. This involves specialist assessment of all or most of the domains of the SAP when this is indicated by the person's needs and circumstances. Almost by definition it will involve a range of different professionals with relevant knowledge and skills. In many cases geriatricians and old-age psychiatrists and their teams will play a prominent role, using appropriate assessment tools.

In some cases an overview assessment may be considered unnecessary and delay provision of appropriate help. In others an overview assessment may have been carried out to explore areas of concern. Comprehensive assessment is likely to be indicated for people whose needs are intensive or prolonged, including older people requiring permanent admission to a care home or receipt of a substantial package of community care.

Stage 4: Evaluating assessment information

Some assessment tools provide protocols to help professionals to interpret the meaning of the assessment and guide them towards appropriate service responses; the Department of Health provides some examples on the SAP website. Assessment information may be drawn on to identify risks and needs.

Risk assessment. Evaluating assessment information involves the professional and older person evaluating the risks to independence in the immediate and longer term that arise from identified needs, taking account of the likely outcome if help is not provided. Risk assessment should take account of the older person's:

- autonomy and freedom to make choices;
- health and safety factors;
- ability to manage personal and other daily routines; and
- involvement in wider and community life.

A judgement needs to be made about which risks cause serious concern and which are a natural part of independent living (see Chapter 22, 'Rights and risks').

Needs. The SAP uses the term 'presenting need' to refer to needs that are reported by older people themselves or by those close to them. The term 'eligibility need' is used to refer to the needs that fall outside the local council's eligibility criteria, and so should be met; eligibility needs are set according to the council's resources. The SAP requires that presenting and eligibility needs be clearly distinguished in the assessment summary and subsequent care plans.

Stage 5: Deciding what help should be offered

This stage of the SAP involves making decisions on whether or not to provide support and treatment, and, if appropriate, what help to provide. The SAP draws attention to Standard 1 of the NSF for Older People (Department of Health 2001), which points out that, if a person's assessed needs fall within the council's eligibility criteria, it becomes an 'eligible need' that the council should meet.

Stage 6: Care planning

Under the SAP, care planning should build on the strengths and abilities of individuals and the part they can play in addressing their own needs, and should lead to effective service delivery. Care plans, which should be realistic, are required for all older people who receive services, and should be in proportion to their level of need and service provision. With the consent of the older person, they should be shared across agencies and service providers as fully as possible, to prevent unnecessary duplication of assessments.

This stage of the SAP highlights the importance of older people and those close to them being informed clearly of which agency is responsible for which aspect of assessment and service, and to whom complaints should be directed, if necessary.

Stage 7: Monitoring and review

The final stage of the SAP involves arrangements to monitor the older person's needs and the effectiveness of services provided, to guide adjustments in the care package over time. Reviews should: determine how far the interventions provided have achieved the outcomes set out in the care plan; reassess individual needs; help determine users' continued eligibility for support and treatment; amend the care plan in response to changing need; and comment, where appropriate, on how users are using Direct Payments.

It is recommended that care plans be scheduled and reviewed routinely; this is often after the first three months, at least annually thereafter and also when unexpected major changes occur.

The single assessment summary

A requirement across all local agencies is that sufficient information is collected to complete the single assessment summary for older people, which will be made available to identified professionals in the NHS and social services. Three sets of standardised assessment information must be collected in a standardised format from every locality and incorporated into the local single assessment summary; software is being developed to support the development of electronic care records. The three sets of information cover:

- basic personal information;
- needs and health (which will comprise all assessment domains of the SAP, an account of how conclusions were reached, threats to independence and, if appropriate, scores for activities of daily living and cognitive function on a recognised scale); and
- summary of the care plan (incorporating all care aims, the needs that they address, a list of services received and the name of

the care co-ordinator). Aggregation of data from single assessment summaries locally and nationally will show what sorts of help are received by older people with particular needs and circumstances. This information can be drawn on to plan future service provision.

Assessment tools

Past experience suggests that adherence to a common assessment document or tool can result in assessment that is mechanical and is likely to limit rather than increase the scope of assessment. Rather than requiring adherence to any one single assessment tool, the Department of Health has opted for a more encompassing framework for the SAP, which is designed to lead to convergence of assessment methods and results over time irrespective of the tools chosen for local use. The Department of Health has established an accreditation process for off-the-shelf tools that have been developed by independent bodies for national use in the overview assessment of older people's needs.

To be accredited a tool must:

- be structured and worded so as to facilitate a person-centred conversation;
- make explicit the contribution of older people to their own assessment;
- emphasise older people's views and their wishes, strengths and abilities;
- make explicit the impact of older people's environments, relationships and other factors on their needs;
- support professional judgement and help professionals link together different parts of the assessment, evaluate risks and refer to other agencies;
- take account of age, gender, race, disability and other factors that influence need and care planning;
- cover adequately the SAP domains;
- be suitable for use by a variety of health and social care professionals.

In addition, any instructions for use of the tool must be clear and the tool cannot be contractually bound to any single software solution. It must respect consent and confidentiality, use national standard datasets where appropriate as they become available, and be capable of producing information for the single assessment summary.

To date (early 2005) the Department of Health has accredited three off-the-shelf assessment tools for use during overview assessment of the SAP:

- the Minimum Data Set Home Care Version 2.3, developed by the Personal Social Services Research Unit, University of Manchester (Challis);
- FACE for Older People V.3, developed by FACE Recording and Management Systems (Clifford); and
- EASYcare Version 2004, which has been developed by the University of Sheffield in collaboration with European partners (Marriott).

Implications of the Single Assessment Process for professionals

The SAP is an important initiative, which will however require professionals to begin to work in different ways if its potential benefits are to be realised. Implementation requires that local protocols on joint working be established that set out professional involvement in contact and overview assessments and promote responsible team working and flexibility. These must be underpinned by a strategy for staff development across the different agencies involved to agree shared values, establish a common language and understand the organisational and cultural changes needed for successful implementation. In addition, front-line staff need to become competent in multiagency work and to widen their knowledge base to encompass both health and social care needs in old age.

It is envisaged that involvement of different professionals in the assessment will be along a continuum and will vary across cases. For example, involvement for one professional might be restricted to receiving a telephone call to check whether the older person is in receipt of services or, at the other extreme, it might involve making a joint assessment visit with others. Agencies are asked to map out involvement of their staff in relation to different types of cases and to monitor this in practice. In addition, the NSF for Older People (Department of Health 2001) requires local councils to establish joint teams to provide assessment, care planning and service delivery for older people suffering from stroke, falls and mental health problems. This is based on clinical experience, which suggests that specialist teams can improve joint working across disciplines and agencies.

For individual older people with complex needs who need help from different agencies and disciplines, one professional will be nominated to act as a care co-ordinator; community nurses or social workers, who may often have a long-term role with older people, are often best placed to take on this function. Local agencies are urged to agree local protocols for care co-ordination that take account of their statutory duties with regard to assessment, including who should do it, the tasks involved and how access to these individuals can be readily secured. As with joint working, flexibility in the interests of the older person is preferred to rigid rules.

Conclusion

This chapter has outlined impediments to interdisciplinary and interagency assessment and has described the Single Assessment Process (SAP), which aims to provide a national framework designed to eliminate duplication of assessment and to ensure that professionals and agencies work together in assessment in the most effective way.

Reports in 2003 from local councils to the Department of Health indicate variable progress towards implementing the SAP locally (letter from Anthony Sheehan to Chief Executives of Strategic Health Authorities, April 2004). 1 April 2004 marked a key milestone in the implementation of the SAP by which the systems and processes underpinning the SAP were to be in place across England; at the time of writing it is too early to know whether this milestone has been reached.

The SAP goes well beyond previous interdisciplinary and interagency assessment frameworks, most of which have emphasised adherence to a single assessment tool. It holds much promise and may deliver substantial benefits to older people if: practitioners and agencies shun the lure of a single (albeit Department of Health accredited) off-the-shelf assessment tool as a quick fix to the challenges of multidisciplinary and multiagency assessment for older people; and adherence to the SAP is accompanied by changes in working practices and an increase in trust between professionals and agencies. It is these changes in interprofessional relations that are likely to be the most difficult to deliver.

3 Underpinning values

Brendan McCormack

From the many debates in the literature about assessment, it would not be difficult to believe that, as long as we use the right assessment tools, the outcome of assessment will be satisfactory for all concerned. This view is built on the belief that human beings are 'flawed' and thus incapable of making dispassionate decisions without using an assessment tool that has been well tested in practice. Whilst there is some legitimacy in this argument, it is equally true that the essence of person-centred assessment is the relationship between the assessor and the person being assessed. This means that we have to explore our own values and those of others when deciding what is important to the lives of those we care for and to ourselves.

It is well recognised that timely high-quality assessment can have a significant impact on the care outcomes that older people experience (Department of Health 2001a). But what does 'high-quality' assessment mean? Person-centred assessment entails getting to know the person in order to undertake an effective assessment, and when we talk about getting to know another person, we are essentially talking about understanding their values. But to know someone also requires us to understand our own values. In any relationship, we make judgements about another person through our own established views, beliefs and values.

What are values?

Our values are a collection of beliefs or attitudes about what is good, right, desirable or worthwhile. Each of us has a *value system*: the way we organise or prioritise our values in order to make a decision.

Essentially, our values and our values system act as the foundation on which we make judgements and choices in our personal and professional lives. Values are underpinned by 'beliefs' – the things we consider important in life. Values either guide our behaviour (to tell the truth, to be honest, to be kind, etc) or they shape our ambitions in life (to be famous, to earn a lot of money, to gain seniority in a career, etc). Whilst there are all kinds of values that underpin the way we live our lives, in the context of assessment, we are talking about *moral values* – beliefs about what is important in order to respect another person (in this case, the person we are assessing). If assessment is going to be person-centred, the values of the assessor are as important as those of the person being assessed. For example, if I do not think that knowing your beliefs about your relationships with members of your family is important to your care, I will not consider it necessary to assess this.

Person-centredness and person-centred assessment

Person-centredness is concerned with our right to have our values and beliefs as individuals respected – our personhood. It is argued that it is these values that give us our uniqueness and our authenticity (McCormack 2001). Respect for others reflects commitment to having a deep understanding of the other person as a thinking and feeling human being with potential to change and develop. Person-centred assessment is thus based on the value of personhood. It requires us to know the values held by another in order to treat them as persons. It requires us to work with individual beliefs, values, wants, needs and desires, and to adopt approaches to work that enable flexibility, mutuality, respect, care and being with another in an interconnected relationship (McCormack 2001). So how does such a philosophy have an impact on the way we assess older people's need for care and what values are important to consider when undertaking person-centred assessment? I suggest that the following values are core to the conduct of person-centred assessment.

Respecting life stories

The meaning of life for older people is not demonstrated through the tedium of superficial daily life (Katz 1990). Latimer (1997) and Agich (1993), for example, warn against the exclusive reliance on general and functional abilities as the way to assess an individual's capacity and potential. Assessment that includes a 'biographical account' using narrative and story is one method of establishing a baseline value history and establishing a life-plan. Biographical approaches emphasise an understanding of older people's own definition of their needs through their accounts of their lives and planning services to meet these definitions of need. The purpose of the story is to make sense of the present in the light of the past. This approach can be seen in the approaches to reminiscence and life review that attempt to aid an understanding of the meaning of life, through a wish to find in the experience of older people elements of strength and positive affirmation.

Even though life around them may have little meaning or significance, through individual life review the person may discover meaning in *their* own life. Assisting the individual to find this meaning may help them to tolerate the incongruity of their current situation and create a future. As Moody (1991) has asserted, if my life is intelligible, my life has purpose and my hopes and desires ultimately can be satisfied, and happiness can be found. Finding out what is important to the person prevents paternalism (ie making decisions on another's behalf based on the decision-maker's view of what is 'best') and provides a foundation for collaborative decision-making between the person and the carer. Working with people's values allows individuals to have the relationship that they want to have with care workers. However, as the research indicates, professional carers need to be open to listening and hearing the stories of older people and valuing this activity as an important part of care giving (Goldsmith 1996, for example).

Commitment of time

Person-centred assessment requires a sustained commitment in order to ensure that the value of the person remains central. For many practitioners, balancing competing workload pressures can seem to make sustained commitment to an individual person un-realistic. However, there is clearly a moral issue of 'means and ends' here: a thorough assessment is the means to generating a person-centred care plan (the end). For example, if we are committed to planning care that values older people as individuals, is it ethical to undertake an isolated or one-off assessment of their needs with-out a long-term commitment to their ongoing assessment? The key issue is that practitioners should consider a long-term vision for their assessment before undertaking the first step and, in doing so, have a clear understanding of the need to commit time to get to know the person over time.

The preparation of the environment

Research into person-centred practice highlights the importance of the environment of care in enabling and sustaining a person-centred approach (McCormack 2001; Nolan et al 2001). Issues such as team–patient relationships, interprofessional relationships, the organisation of practice, systems and approaches to work and the quality of leadership are all key factors in delivering person-centred practice. Person-centred assessment requires careful attention to the preparation of the environment. Every effort should be made to ensure that the environment is conducive to the person being able to talk about themselves without fear of being overheard, misunder-stood or judged by others. This value goes beyond taking the person to a quiet place to undertake the assessment (although this is a good place to start!). Other key issues to consider include:

- *Team structures and processes:* does the team structure within which I work enable me to establish a picture of the person over time – does our team structure promote continuity?
- *Team relationships:* do the relationships established in the team enable me to draw on others' expertise if I need help and support?
- *The organisation of work:* when conducting an assessment, am I anxious about the rest of my case-load or will the team sup-port me in managing my work?

- *Communication systems:* do the established documentation systems enable the recording of information in a person-centred way?

- *Attitudes to person-centred assessment among team members:* do we as a team value the importance of person-centred assessment? Do we have a flexible approach to the organisation of work that supports the planning of care on an individual basis?

These issues are complex and cannot be put in place without a commitment to person-centred practice from the whole team. A person-centred environment is one that openly discusses these issues and strives to find ways to maximise opportunities for the values of individuals to be respected.

Negotiation and renegotiation of boundaries with users

Evidence suggests that health service users continue to experience care structures and processes that limit their ability to participate fully in care decisions or to influence the basis on which decisions are reached (Walker and Dewar 2001). A central theme of contemporary policy agendas is the active and systematic involvement of users in decision-making (Department of Health [England] 2001b; Scottish Executive Health Department 2001; Department of Health, Social Services and Public Safety 2001). The importance of involving the individual, which runs through these various policy documents, is not new and the challenge therefore is to make systematic involvement a reality. Existing methods of involvement include user panels, forums, outreach initiatives, partners in care and advocacy (Thornton 2000). However, there is still a need to develop significantly both the process and the methods of involvement and to increase opportunities for collaborative partnership working to make the process meaningful and effective (Department of Health [England] 2001b). The prevailing culture of health care delivery is slow to change (Kennedy 2001). This is due in part to the fact that development requires a change in attitudes – that views working with patients or service users in partnership as a mutual process of growth and development. Addressing the contextual and attitudinal issues that inhibit practitioners from involving the individual and developing person-centred approaches to care requires more than the development of service standards. Creative approaches to the active involvement of service users in the assessment process need to be found. Approaches such as structured story-telling, biography, diary-writing and client-held records are enabling the development of person-centred involvement and participation of the individuals in the assessment process. These approaches can sit alongside more traditional assessment methods and frameworks and serve to enhance rather than hinder them.

Seeking and gaining consent

Health and social care practice in Western society is preoccupied with a rational discourse of informed consent (Johnstone 1989) – the person being assessed is asked for their permission for the assessment to take place. The result of this is that large sections of populations are excluded from giving consent other than through 'proxies' (someone who makes a decision on behalf of another person). Existing evidence suggests that proxy consent is unreliable, as it assumes that an individual's values are known and understood by the other person (Buchanan and Brock 1989). Because of this dominance, groups such as people with dementia are largely excluded from the consent process. Much assessment of older people with dementia is conducted via 'reliable informers' on the basis that they are able to represent the person – an unreliable position to adopt. Elsewhere I have argued (McCormack 2002) that a story-telling approach to informed consent can provide a way to engage people with dementia in the consent process. This requires care workers to go beyond listening to the content of what people say (which may sound confused and irrational) and to focus on the feelings behind what is said. Dewing (2002) argues for 'process consent' whereby the practitioner pays attention to the whole person (eg to their feelings, behaviours and responses) as a legitimate form of consent in person-centred assessment.

Representing views authentically

How are the voices of participants in assessments represented by practitioners? For example, in the writing of a care plan, the voice of the practitioner is presented through professionalised language that rarely represents 'normal talk' (Drew and Heritage 1992). The actual words of the person being assessed are often ignored or at best reworded so that they might 'fit' with the dominant professional language, key concepts and patterns of decision-making. It could be argued that, if we are truly person-centred as practitioners, both voices should be equally represented. If we are going to be person-centred in our representation of people's views, we need to agree with them how they wish their voices to be represented and strive to involve them in constructing the care plan. Practically, this means that we should strive to record each individual's words as accurately as possible.

Disengaging

It goes without saying that, if we are adopting a person-centred approach to assessment, the process of disengaging when the assessment is complete needs careful consideration. Person-centredness is predicated on the basis of a social relationship bestowed on one human being by others. The termination of any relationship needs careful planning for it to be undertaken success-fully and satisfactorily for both parties (Ridley and Jones 2002). This is no less important than any other nurse–patient relationship. The 'hit and run' approach to assessment is not person-centred but is instead an abuse of another person's humanity, as it reduces them to the level of an object that serves to meet another's (the asses-sor's) end. The appropriate management of disengagement can be a form of celebration of the completion of successful work and the growth experienced. The inappropriate management of disengage-ment results in hurt, resentment and reduced commitment by the older person and others who are significant to them.

In previous research and development work, McCormack and Ford (2000) identified key principles/values system to underpin person-centred assessment with older people. These principles act as a useful values system to guide the process of person-centred assessment in practice:

- Assessment is a comprehensive process that identifies an individual's holistic care needs based on their potential whilst considering appropriate risk factors.
- Assessment is a person-centred activity with an emphasis on establishing areas of need to maintain or increase independence and quality of life.
- Effective, comprehensive person-centred assessment includes both subjective accounts (individual experience) and objective measurement (structured instruments).
- The individual's biography is central to all assessment.
- Decisions that are supported by objective evidence, the individual's preferences and professional opinion.
- A comprehensive assessment gives a clear indication of the type and amount of care needed and the most appropriate person to provide it.
- The language of assessment should be understandable to all who participate in the process and the person who 'owns' the assessment.
- Effective assessment requires knowledge, skills and expertise in assessment processes, including interpersonal skills, communication skills and skills in record keeping.
- Comprehensive assessment needs time to be undertaken effectively.
- Effective assessment requires teamwork built on principles of effective communication, clarity of role, mutual respect and honesty.
- Interagency assessment needs to be co-ordinated from a central point, with a single point of access and systems that support effective co-ordination (including IT systems).

Conclusion

Undertaking person-centred assessment requires a sustained commitment to the development of a context that enables this kind of practice. The values that we hold about assessment and its place in health care delivery influence greatly the way we conduct assessments with older people. Equally, we cannot deny that the cornerstone of person-centred assessment is the values of the person being assessed and their articulation through the writing of an individual biography. We cannot take for granted the importance of person-centred assessment nor can we afford to be complacent about the support needed by practitioners to undertake this work effectively. Person-centred assessment thrives in person-centred cultures of practice, so it is imperative that every effort is made to develop practice contexts that view assessment as more than the completion of paperwork, rather as the key foundation stone for 'knowing the person'.

Part 2
Older Individuals

4 Biographical and developmental approaches

Diane Wells

In this chapter the value of using biographical and developmental approaches in the assessment with older people is explored and explained.

The practitioner who takes a biographical approach seeks to understand 'what matters' to the person, their values and wishes, by getting to know something of the person's life (Gearing and Coleman 1996; Wells 1998; Clarke et al 2003). The best way for this to happen is by listening to the person.

Ideas about development across a person's lifespan are important for three reasons:

- the values that are embedded in the life story are part of that person's development;
- telling the story often allows an older person to achieve a sense of wholeness or 'integrity';
- because psychosocial development is a life-long process, the best care is that which takes account of this and promotes development (Kivnick 1991).

Much assessment and care is based on the idea that people need to be able to carry out activities of daily living and, when they cannot, family, friends and professionals are called in to make good the deficits in self-care (Kivnick 1991; Broadbent 1999). For example: 'Mr Jones is no longer able to walk to the shops and so his son does the shopping for him'.

Clearly, this approach is useful but assessment and care based only on a deficit model run the risk of disregarding the person's abilities, their past and the possibility of development in the future. The aim of this chapter is to add the individual's perspective by exploring the value of both biographical and developmental approaches.

Reasons for assessment

Assessment by professionals usually takes place when there has been a change in a person's condition or situation, and a new intervention is required. For example:

- Mr James Kemp is no longer managing at home.
- Miss Renee Salt is going home after in-patient care following a fall at home.
- Mrs Ann Kalik has arrived in a care home.

Here we see three of the most frequent reasons for assessment:

- no longer managing at home;
- discharge from hospital;
- admission to a care home.

Stages of assessment

In each of these situations staff need to find out more about:

- the person, and
- the situation.

Then it is possible to consider, together with the individual, what help would be appropriate. It is important to separate the assessment of the person and the situation from the consideration of the kinds of help required.

We cannot assume what would be helpful. Also, 'person-centred care' involves working together with individuals or, if that is not possible, working with their family or friends about what would be helpful rather than trying to fit the person into the services available. (See also Chapter 3, 'Underpinning values'.)

A problem-solving approach may lead to service user passivity

Often staff define problems and move on quickly to finding solutions. For example:

Problem: Mr Kemp cannot manage to prepare his food.
Solution: He can receive meals on wheels.

Problem: Miss Salt is lonely.
Solution: She can go to a day centre.

Problem: Mrs Kalik has difficulty with mobility, eating and washing.
Solution: She will need help with all of these.

In these examples we know little about the people except for their names and their difficulties. It could be argued that 'problems have been defined' but this is not an assessment. We need to know more about the person who needs the help before we can attempt to find an appropriate response.

When practitioners focus only on defining problems and finding solutions, the person may get left out. Because it is the person who has to make use of the 'solutions', the whole plan is liable to fail. Also, when staff find solutions, the individuals may be left in a passive position. They have not been involved either in showing what matters to them or in deciding what help or care they would like. Furthermore, there is little idea of future in these solutions. Even when conversations are impossible, for example with speech impairment following a stroke, careful observation may allow for assessment of intentions and understanding the significance of actions. (See the story of Miss Naplert, later.)

The service users and carers in one study complained they felt they were treated as 'problems to be solved' not as people to be known about or understood (Baker et al 1997). It is kinder to treat the service users as people who have lived long and interesting lives. Also it is usually more efficient. The story about Mrs Peters, from the Care for Elderly People at Home Project (Gearing and Coleman 1996: 277–278), illustrates these points.

Community care for Mrs Peters

Mrs Peters was referred to the Care Coordinator by her GP, who felt Mrs Peters was lonely and isolated. The immediate community did not offer any social amenities and Mrs Peters' mobility was restricted.

Mrs Peters' family was very important to her. In her 87 years she had experienced many tragedies and upheavals, including the death of her father and her two husbands who both died of cancer. A recent move from another part of England to Gloucestershire to be near her daughter had left her feeling isolated. Her limited mobility prevented her from getting the bus into town. Nevertheless, she had an extrovert and lively outlook on life, responding to the situation she found herself in as positively as she could. Her daughter lived near enough to visit her every morning and evening to help her with housework and shopping but her own work prevented her from taking Mrs Peters outdoors.

Following the biographical assessment the Care Coordinator perceived her main task as trying to find some kind of stimulating outlet for Mrs Peters. The local authority social services department could only offer her a privately run day home, which she rejected as a place where older people with disabilities sat in their chairs all day with nothing to do. Social services was critical of her refusal of this service, regarding her as 'difficult' because she did not know what she wanted. Knowing Mrs Peters and her history, the Care Coordinator felt that, on the contrary, she was a person who very much knew what she wanted. She certainly knew what she did *not* want! The Care Coordinator felt it was her job to persevere until she found the right place for Mrs Peters.

During the next few months the Care Coordinator arranged for Mrs Peters to attend the Saturday Club at the local hospital's Elderly Care Unit, where she enjoyed the company of the younger volunteers as well as the activities and organised talks. She became physically more active, going on short walks round the corridors surrounding the unit and attending keep-fit sessions – which the Care Coordinator had instigated, knowing how important it was to Mrs Peters, a former dance teacher, that she kept as physically active as her mobility would allow.

The Care Coordinator also arranged a voluntary visitor through the local Age Concern, which partly mitigated the isolation she felt at not being able to walk outside her home. Also, as transport was available, the Care Coordinator switched Mrs Peters' chiropody from domiciliary home visits to outpatient attendance at the local clinic. The Care Coordinator also suggested and then arranged membership of a recently formed University of the Third Age branch in the city.

This story illustrates the need to 'get it right', which was made possible by getting to know what mattered to Mrs Peters. The first assessment clarified 'loneliness' as a problem and offered a 'solution' – attend a day centre. Reading the story now we can see that the solution was not accepted by Mrs Peters because it was an 'off the shelf' solution. It had no relation to the person who required the help. This sort of response to a defined problem cannot be called 'person-centred', as, although a 'problem' has been defined, the practitioner has not got to know the person. Going to the Saturday Club allowed Mrs Peters to continue activities that she had enjoyed throughout her life and also allowed for new developments as she got to know new people.

Building up a picture of the service user

Getting to know a person's life story may seem a complicated way of finding out what they want. However, questions such as 'What's important to you?' and 'What care do you need?' are not easily answered, especially with older people. It is important, therefore, to have some questions in your mind as you work with people, not necessarily to use directly but rather to inform your interactions. Then you are more likely to build up a picture over time of who the person is and what is important to them. There are many opportunities to develop conversations about the lives of your service users, especially if working in a person's home where there are often pictures of friends and family on the wall, visitors and telephone calls. In residential environments there are usually some clues in pictures and memorabilia. In acute/short-term care settings there may be more visitors and interactions with family and friends but fewer pictures as cues to conversation about the person's life.

When you are with a service user it may seem that you are chatting to them as you would with a friend but there are some important differences. Two important considerations are 'keeping the conversation person-centred' and 'attending to boundaries'.

Keeping the conversation person-centred

Here is an example:

> Practitioner knocks and, hearing 'Come in', enters the person's room/home:
>
> *Person*: Oh hello – I've just put the phone down – it was my friend.
>
> *Practitioner: (thinks)* I must return that call to my friend. *(also thinks)* That's good that she has had a call, because the other day she said how lonely she gets.
>
> If you talk about your own friend and the need to call them later, the chance to discover more about your client's friendship may be lost.
>
> Having decided on a person-centred response, there are many options; for example: 'Does your friend phone you often?' or 'Is this someone you've known for a long time?' or 'Is that the one you were telling me about the other day?'

In this kind of conversation you may discover important things not only about this friendship but also about the value placed on the friendship and how it has been sustained over the years. Such insights can help in gaining a picture of the person and their needs.

Boundaries

Two of the most important boundaries are 'time' and 'closeness/distance'. These are often closely associated, as limiting the time often helps to put a limit on involvement. Even someone who seems to want to talk for ever, may find themselves disclosing more than they meant to. It is a valuable principle to say at the beginning how long you have planned to talk with the person that day and also indicate when you plan to continue the discussion(s).

If a service user does not wish to discuss, for example, the phone call or the photos on the wall, it would be inappropriate to challenge their reticence. It is important to find the right boundaries both for them and for yourself. For example, whilst one person may like talking about their experiences of poverty in childhood, another would rather forget it. Practitioners also vary: some feel comfortable hearing about the sadness surrounding a sibling's death, another may find this too difficult, or too difficult on a certain day. Feelings about self-disclosure also change over time and in different relationships (Nichols 2003).

It is worth considering how comfortable you feel when hearing about a person's life, whether it is a happy or a sad story (Nichols 2003). Most will be a mix but it is important for a service user to have the opportunity to express a variety of feelings without being told to 'cheer up'. If someone wishes to tell you about sad times in their life, it suggests that they feel comfortable telling you. However, there are times when their story and distress feel too great for you to handle, either because the distress or the complexity of the situation is beyond your skill or because you are feeling too vulnerable to manage to listen. In either of these situations it is important to know how and where to refer the person. More often, someone's account of past and present experiences are valuable aspects of assessment and care. Service users themselves may find that talking about sad times and being heard by their practitioner helps them to come to terms with difficult situations and gain a sense of wholeness or 'integrity'. A person who feels listened to may then become more cheerful, but that is very different from being told to 'cheer up' or to 'forget it'.

To recap: getting to know who a service user is and what matters to them can be accomplished by encouraging them to tell about their life. Current needs can be viewed within their life-long achievements and development. Telling the story often gives a sense of power and supports a more equal partnership between service user and practitioner. Observations are also very valuable, especially when there is cognitive impairment such as with Alzheimer's or when speech is impaired, for example following a stroke (see the story of Miss Naplert, below).

Guidelines

The questions one can have in mind to inform conversation, observation and your reflection on these include the suggestions in Box 4.1.

Box 4.1 *Questions that acknowledge biographical and developmental influences*

The person	Who is this person?
	What has been important to them in their life? (see also Chapter 3, 'Underpinning values')
Values	What values can be distinguished from their life story? (see also Chapter 5, 'Cultural and religious needs', and Chapter 6, 'Lifestyle and health promotion')
Strengths	What are the strengths they have developed throughout their life? (see also Chapter 7, 'Coping strategies and sources of support')
Response to current situation	What is their response to the current situation (eg living with Parkinson's disease)?
	What changes have they made to manage the current situation?
	How have they managed at times of loss and change? (see Parkes and Markus 1998)
Network	What is their family and social network – who are they in contact with, how often? (see also Chapter 7)

continued

Box 4.1 (continued)

Support	What support is there in their family and social network? (see also Chapter 7)
Emotional response to changes in relationships	How does the person feel about the changes in relationships following disability; eg no longer able to give in relationships as much as they used to? (see also Chapter 9, 'Sexuality, intimacy and sexual health')
Perceptions of the future	How do they see the future?
Hopes	What would they like to achieve?
Working in partnership	Can they express the kind of help they would like? (see also Chapter 8, 'Cognitive capacity and consent')

As you work with these approaches you will realise that these ten issues are present in your conversation, observation and understanding of the service users you work with. It is not usually appropriate to try to follow these guidelines as if they are necessary questions to be answered, as each practitioner has their own way of working and it is important for you to develop that.

Miss Naplert

Miss Naplert, who had Alzheimer's disease, was being cared for in an assessment ward, where she frequently went to the door that led out onto a fire escape. Each time, the nurses led her back into the main part of the ward where they felt she would be safer. Then one nurse decided to spend a few minutes with Miss Naplert while she stood by the door. She discovered it was not the door that Miss Naplert was interested in but the plants on the window sill at the side of the door. They spent a few minutes together appreciating the plants. Then it was time to lead Miss Naplert back to be with the other patients but this time she seemed calmer than usual. Someone had appreciated what mattered to her.

. The nurse set about finding ways in which Miss Naplert could continue her interest in plants. A niece, who visited regularly, brought a trough, compost and plants. Niece and aunt together planted up the trough. Staff found a place for the trough where Miss Naplert could look after her plants.

Is it true?

Sometimes staff get worried because there are different versions of a story – perhaps from different members of the family – or staff feel they have each received a different version. Most of us when telling about our own lives are conscious of the 'audience' and are liable to 'tweak' the story to suit the occasion. It has been pointed out that 'biographies need to be kept in good repair' (Johnson 1991).

Conclusion

In the stories of Mrs Peters and Miss Naplert staff got to know their interests through listening and observation. Then for each person their current lives became more interesting, there were links with the past and new experiences were being created. We all need new stories, and new developments which become part of tomorrow's biography.

5 Cultural and religious needs

Karen Rawlings-Anderson

We live in an increasingly multiracial and multicultural society. Approximately 7 per cent of the population aged 65 and over belong to a minority ethnic group (Age Concern 2003). Patterns of migration in earlier years are reflected in the make-up of the older population. For example, large numbers of men and women from the Caribbean islands were recruited to work in the UK in the 1950s and 1960s; those over 65 years of age now make up 9 per cent of the total Black Caribbean population. Migration from African countries occurred later than this, mainly in the 1970s, and at present 2 per cent of the total Black African population are over 65 years old.

Recent migration patterns suggest that there will be an increasing number of people of Eastern European origin in future cohorts of older people. Increasingly, the older population will include people from a wide range of minority ethnic groups, and health and social care professionals need to be equipped with the knowledge to assess appropriately and sensitively their cultural and religious needs.

The need to recognise individual choice in relation to cultural and religious preference and to provide culturally sensitive care is crucial in health and social care practice. Thus when ill-health or a change in social circumstances disrupts an older person's life, it is imperative that care professionals make every attempt to assess their cultural and religious needs. Using two examples of assessment frameworks, this chapter demonstrates how these can enhance care professionals' ability to assess older people's cultural and religious needs.

Culture and religion

Culture relates to an individual's inherited view of the world and how life should be lived (Helman 2000). It is a dynamic entity that changes in response to new situations and pressures (Henley and Schott 1999). Cultural beliefs, however, are passed down through generations. They influence the accepted norms and taboos within a community and are often linked to adherence to a particular religion.

Cultural and religious beliefs pervade every aspect of an individual's lifestyle and usually influence their health behaviours to a large extent (Holland and Hogg 2001). Health professionals must understand how an older person's cultural and religious beliefs and behaviours affect their lifestyle so that appropriate care can be assessed, planned, implemented and evaluated.

Assessment of older people

Any assessment of an older person should acknowledge how their life experiences might influence their health and well-being. For example, someone who has experienced civil unrest and forced migration may well have endured malnutrition, loss of close family members, religious persecution or torture. They are also likely to have faced employment problems on arrival in the UK and this in turn could have affected their current pension and financial status. A fuller discussion of patterns of migration and settlement, socio-economic status, and the health and social care needs of older people from minority ethnic groups can be found in Rawlings-Anderson (2001).

A person's cultural and religious beliefs influence the way they view the world and consequently their everyday practices and behaviours. Some people who hold very strong religious beliefs may be able to express their wishes, for example in the choice of foods that they eat and the religious days that they observe. However, for others it may be difficult to articulate how their cultural or religious identity affects the way they carry out their daily activities as, for them, it is simply part of their everyday life.

Care professionals are expected to provide support that is both sensitive and appropriate to individual needs, and tools are available to help us assess what those needs might be. We may not fully under-stand the basis of all religions and cultural variations but assessment frameworks can help assessment to be more systematic.

The Roper–Logan–Tierney model

This model, developed over several years (Roper et al 1980, 1985, 1990, 1996), is based on the premise that each person has a unique pattern of living, which they call 'individuality in living'. Despite this individuality, however, Roper and colleagues (2000) contend that everyone is influenced to varying degrees by common concepts (see Box 5.1).

Box 5.1 *Concepts affecting individuality in living*

Activities of living (ALs)

Lifespan

Dependence/independence continuum

Factors influencing ALs

Each activity (see Box 5.2) comprises many dimensions and activities of living (ALs) inextricably linked with others; for example, eating and drinking links with elimination. ALs are also influenced by other factors (see Box 5.3) and where the individual is on the lifespan continuum. The degree of dependence or independence that they experience also influences the manner in which the individual carries out ALs.

Box 5.2 *The activities of living*

Maintaining a safe environment

Communicating

Breathing

Eating and drinking

Eliminating

Personal cleansing and dressing

Controlling body temperature

Mobilising

Working and playing

Expressing sexuality

Sleeping

Dying

Box 5.3 *Factors influencing the activities of living*

Biological	Environmental
Psychological	Politico-economic
Socio-cultural	

Whilst Roper and colleagues clearly identify socio-cultural factors as being important influences on each AL, it is worth noting that culture also strongly influences the expectations of how individuals should behave at each stage of the lifespan continuum and also the health beliefs that determine levels of independence/dependence expected at various stages of the life cycle (Holland and Hogg 2001).

It is important to determine the cultural or religious factors that can influence each AL before commencing the assessment. Box 5.4 identifies some examples of influences that could be considered under each AL. When considering the ALs, however, it is also essential to ascertain how older people are perceived within their culture, as this will influence the beliefs of the individual concerned and the support they can expect from their family. For example, if older people are seen as wise family members to be cherished, the family will have a different view about appropriate care from those who view older people as being economic burdens with little value. Additionally, it is important to establish if the older individuals and their families expect older people to be dependent despite individual ability, as this will also influence participation in self-care activities.

This model is relatively straightforward to use but care must be taken to ensure that individual needs rather than stereotypical needs are identified.

Box 5.4 *Examples of cultural and religious influences on the activities of living*

Maintaining a safe environment	Has the person suffered torture or abuse in the past due to religious beliefs?
	Is the person likely to be traumatised or depressed due to life events?
Communi-cating	Dialect – does this reflect societal standing or geographical origins?
	What non-verbal communication is appropriate (eg eye contact)?
	Is language age-appropriate?
Breathing	Is breathing linked with meditation?
	Is public expectoration acceptable?
Eating and drinking	Are there religious commendations or restrictions?
	What family traditions relate to eating and drinking?
	Are specific eating implements required (eg chopsticks)?
Eliminating	Are separate facilities required for men and women?
	Will women discuss elimination problems with a male health professional?
Personal cleansing and dressing	Are ablutions required before prayer?
	Is running water required?
	Is dress influenced by religion (eg body parts to be covered)?
	Are religious amulets or jewellery required?

Box 5.4 (continued)

Controlling body temperature	Is the person used to a hot climate? How do seasons affect the individual?
Mobilising	Does impaired mobility affect activities such as personal prayer, ritual washing or attendance at worship? Is physical impairment viewed as acceptable or something to be hidden?
Working and playing	Is the person from a matriarchal or a patriarchal culture? Are older people expected to work or contribute to the household work? How many times a day is the person expected to pray?
Expressing sexuality	Who makes health care decisions in the family? Will the person feel comfortable with care professionals of the opposite sex?
Sleeping	Is the person used to a siesta? Are dreams linked to energy states?
Dying	Is death welcomed or feared? Are there any rituals that must be carried out prior to death?

Giger and Davidhizar's Transcultural Assessment model

This tool was devised as a practical means of evaluating cultural variables and their effects on health and illness behaviours. The central premise is that every person is culturally unique, yet every person is influenced to some degree by six cultural phenomena (see Box 5.5). Giger and Davidhizar (1995) contend that culturally sensitive care can be delivered across an array of settings and by a range of health and social care professionals only if an appropriate assessment has taken place.

> Box 5.5 *Cultural phenomena that influence culturally unique individuals*
>
> | | |
> |---|---|
> | Communication | Time |
> | Space | Environmental control |
> | Social organisation | Biological variations |

Although some elements of this framework are similar to those proposed by Roper and colleagues (2000), there are some distinct differences. Giger and Davidhizar (1995) explain that each person is a unique being, influenced by culture, ethnicity and religion, and that these three elements interact to form a unique heritage. It is this heritage that then influences the individual's lifestyle in the expression of the six cultural phenomena. Giger and Davidhizar argue that any assessment must include the identification of the person's place of birth and, if they are immigrants, the reasons for their migration and the amount of time they have spent in the UK. This, they suggest, will give the care professional an idea of the person's unique heritage and its influence on both their health and their health care practices. They emphasise the importance of assessing whether individuals have become culturally assimilated into the dominant culture, have adapted their cultural beliefs, or continue to observe their own cultural practices. Box 5.6 outlines some of the issues that can be assessed using the six cultural phenomena.

Box 5.6 Examples of assessment of the six cultural phenomena

Communi-cation	What is the language spoken?
	What dialect do they have?
	Do they require an interpreter?
	How is silence used (is silence used for thoughtful contemplation of the questions asked or as an indication of not understanding)?
	What tone of voice/volume is used during everyday conversation (eg loud or soft)?
	What type of non-verbal communication is appropriate (eg touch, hand gestures, eye contact)?
	What naming system does the person use (ie which is their given name and which is the family name)?
	Is there a difference between greeting a friend and a stranger?
Space	What degree of comfort is observed when people move near?
	Is physical contact appropriate?
	Are movements slow or fast?
	How is personal space decorated?
	Is the person used to living in confined spaces?

continued

Box 5.6 (continued)

Social organisation	What type of family unit does the person belong to?
	Is the family of matriarchal or patriarchal structure?
	Who makes health care decisions within the family?
	What is the older person's role within the family unit?
	How is leisure time spent?
	Are friendship ties important and what are the expectations of families?
Time	What calendar does the older person adhere to?
	Is social time linked to family practices?
	Are work time and social time separated?
	What time orientation do they have (eg present, past or future orientated)?
	Is time measured by the clock or social time such as prayer time?
Environmental control	What is viewed as health and as illness?
	Are lay healers used?
	Are any traditional healing practices used?
	Is the older person's locus of control deemed to be internal or external?
	Are any particular illnesses seen as natural or unnatural (eg caused by the evil eye or outside influence)?

Box 5.6 (continued)

Biological variations	Are there any genetic susceptibilities?
	Are there any epidemiological trends that should be noted in relation to this person's ethnic group?
	Does the older person have any nutritional preferences or deficiencies?

This framework can help care professionals to discover what aspects of an older person's cultural heritage might affect the care they plan. For example, if older people are very past-orientated and believe that their ill-health is related to something that happened in their past or to the influence of some supernatural force, health promotion activities will be of limited worth as they will not 'fit' with their belief system. Additionally, an in-depth assessment can help to explain an older person's health care practices, which might not otherwise be understood.

Conclusion

Frameworks are not prescriptive checklists but tools to aid assessment. It is the skill of the care professional using the tool that is the key to appropriate and sensitive assessment. Any care professional working with older people must have the requisite knowledge to undertake a thorough assessment, but must also possess the relevant communication and interpersonal skills to do so. The use of sensitive questioning and an empathetic approach are required to convey the message that the professional is interested not just in physical aspects of care but also in the older person's beliefs about how they should live their lives.

6 Lifestyle and health promotion

Kate Davidson

It was a genuine, if somewhat misplaced, assumption at the inception of the National Health Service (NHS) in 1948 that demand for health care would diminish as medical treatment was offered 'from the cradle to the grave'. With the concentration on curative procedures, little attention was paid to, and even less investment made in, health education for the promotion and maintenance of good health in later life. In subsequent decades, the imperative to measure health 'outcomes' has relied on cost–benefit analysis and only comparatively recently has there been serious discussion on what costs may be saved by pursuing a more robust preventative model of health delivery.

Health promotion strategies for older people have been championed by some local health authorities since the 1970s, but these have been patchy at best and are often the first to be abandoned during periods of financial constraint (Cattan 2001). Therefore, although issues of lifestyle choices have long been on the health agenda, they have not received quite such notice as in the current political and fiscal climate. Media alarm has been fuelled by reports of obesity and its association with type 2 diabetes, high morbidity and mortality rates related to cardiovascular disease and increasing unsafe alcohol consumption at all ages in the UK. The clarion call of policy movers and shakers is the potential cost to the public purse for treatment of conditions over which, it can be viewed, people have (self) control.

This chapter, however, chimes a note of caution: it is very easy to subscribe to the 'blame' culture. Inasmuch as we have inherited the

Victorian moral notions of 'deserving' and 'feckless' poor, we must resist labelling people as 'deserving' and 'undeserving' sick. Health enhancing and health risk behaviours take place within a variety of contexts: spatially (from one culture to another), temporally (within any one culture over historical time) and longitudinally (through any individual's life course). Furthermore, the quality and quantity of health enhancement/risk activities may be defined differently according to sub-cultural definitions such as gender, ethnicity, age, class and regional variation.

When considering external influences and persuasions, the power of corporate interest and advertising cannot be underestimated. In the developed world, and increasingly in the developing world, major cartels dominate cigarette, alcohol, fast food and confectionery promotion. Many sports and sporting events are sponsored by them and some political parties are supported through donations. We need to seek an understanding of people's motivation, history and current experience in order to establish appropriate strategies for promoting a healthy nation.

However, recent UK policy initiatives have been a response to growing awareness of the importance of health maintenance in later life on individual, institutional and societal levels. The National Service Framework for Older People (NSFOP) set eight 'Standards' for the care of older people across health and social services. Standard 8 is the promotion of health and active life in older age (Department of Health 2001: 107). The rationale states:

'There is a growing body of evidence to suggest that the modification of risk factors for disease even late in life can have health benefits for the individual; longer life, increased or maintained levels of functional ability, disease prevention and an improved sense of well-being. Integrated strategies for older people aimed at promoting good health and quality of life, and to prevent or delay frailty and disability, can have significant benefits for the individual and society.'

It is important to recognise that the customary approach to health improvement has been to target individuals, but less attention has been paid to addressing the broad determinants of older people's health behaviours. These include biological, social, cultural and economic factors in influencing choices of health-protective strategies.

Gender, marital status and health promotion

A more holistic approach to health promotion would recognise not just the biological differences between men and women but also the socially constructed roles that shape masculinity and femininity throughout the life course. It is well documented that men are far more reluctant to seek medical consultation than are women. For men who (unlike women) have had little or no 'ongoing contact' with health professionals in their life course, it seems unlikely that they will turn to health professionals when they reach later life. Whilst women have routinely visited the doctor, for example for cancer screening, family planning, pregnancy or to take their children for clinics and immunisation programmes as well as when they are sick, men seem to consider going to the doctor as a sign of weakness (Davidson and Arber 2003). However, 'doctor avoidance' becomes a vicious circle. Most men will admit to postponing making an appointment until they are very sick. They then have negative associations with the doctor, whom they see when they are in pain or feel very unwell and, importantly, who may give them bad news about their health. It is increasingly important, then, to educate men about health behaviours in young and mid-life as well as in later life.

Marital status is an important factor, too. Over two-thirds of older men live with a spouse or partner but demographic trends reveal that an increasing number of older men live alone: in 2001, 29 per cent of men over the age of 65 lived alone compared with 16 per cent in 1971; among men currently aged 65 and over, 17 per cent are widowed, whilst only 7 per cent are never-married and 5 per cent are divorced or separated (StatBase 2002). By 2021, however, it is projected that, although the proportion of men aged 65 or over who are widowed will fall to 13 per cent, mainly because of improvements in mortality, 8 per cent will be never-married and 13 per cent will be divorced (Government Actuary's Department 2001). Older lone men in particular are less likely to have a 'caretaker' to monitor their health behaviours or a 'gatekeeper' to encourage health consultation. We know that older divorced men who live alone have higher levels of health risk behaviours, particularly smoking and drinking, and the needs of this growing segment of the population must be addressed for the twenty-first century.

Health promoting activities

When assessing older people's lifestyles there are five key areas of behaviour adaptation that can contribute to well-being and increased quality of life and can be summed up in 'CAN DO':

- **C**onsultation
- **A**ctivity
- **N**utrition
- **D**etermination
- **O**ptimism

Consultation

One of the most important aspects of growing older is the maintenance of independence and autonomy. There is an abundance of help for older people from agencies such as Age Concern, Help the Aged and the Citizens Advice Bureau, who advise on state benefit entitlement, safety in the home, keeping warm, legal matters and so on – the list is exhaustive. Consultation with these experts can empower even very frail older people and their carers to make informed choices about their lives.

Implicit and explicit in health delivery is that with advancing years comes almost inevitable sickness and disability: 'It's just your/my age' and you have to put up with it. However, most conditions in later life can be treated, or at the least ameliorated, by medical intervention. We are reminded of the story of the older woman who went to her GP complaining of a very painful right knee. He told her nothing could be done about it as the joint was wearing out because of her age. She replied that her left knee was just as old but it did not give her any problems! As discussed above, men are far more reluctant than women to go to their GP, and one strategy would be to encourage earlier consultation both when they feel unwell and, importantly, for screening for common conditions such as high cholesterol and blood pressure, and prostate cancer. Regular hearing and eyesight tests can detect and reduce sensory deprivation, which can lead to social isolation in a crowded place.

Activity

Older people who keep physically, socially and mentally active report high levels of well-being and self-esteem. A moderate amount of exercise taken daily helps all the body systems – muscular, skeletal and cardiovascular in particular. Sleep patterns, often forgotten in health promotion advice, can be stabilised, leading to greater contentment after a 'good night's sleep'.

Even if the older person has restricted physical ability, social activity from a variety of informal and formal sources – family, friends, neighbours, clubs and organisations – adds to a person's sense of worth. Mental activity stimulates intellectual acuity and has been shown to delay the onset of dementia (Kitwood 1997).

Nutrition

One of the most difficult adaptations older people have to make is in what they eat. For example, widowhood in late life is an important aspect for nutrition. With no spouse to cook for any longer, or having to cook for oneself often for the first time, meal patterns can alter dramatically. Health promotion for people who have been bereaved should take account of the physical as well as emotional disruptions attendant on solo living.

It is a truism that we are more likely to put on weight after the age of 40, and less likely to be able to shed the extra pounds with the ease we did when we were younger and more physically active. In the extreme, obesity can lead to ill-health at all ages but it is particularly evident in later life. An older person's nutritional state is frequently determined by class, and the unhealthiest diets in which high levels of fat and sugar are consumed are more commonly found in lower socio-economic groups. People who have had physically demanding jobs may be used to large volumes of high-calorific foods and find it difficult to adjust to smaller, healthier meals. Reduced physical activity should be accompanied by reduced calorie intake, increased vegetable portions and drinking more water. These last two are essential for an active digestive system but research has shown that many older people tend to eschew these and consequently suffer from chronic constipation (Hunter et al 2002). Over-the-counter laxatives are bought principally by people over the age of 65 and, as Hunter and colleagues found, may cause more digestive problems by suppressing normal peristaltic action. Roughage, fruit, vegetables and good hydration are the main stimulants for regular bowel movements.

Determination

Determination and motivation are key elements for moderating long-held habits, such as smoking, unsafe alcohol consumption or eating an unhealthy diet and minimal physical activity. A misgiving frequently expressed by older people is that a change in health behaviours in late life will not make a significant change to their health status. There is a perception that 'you can't teach an old dog new tricks' and it is 'all too late': the damage has been done and cannot be reversed. There is substantial evidence that altered lifestyle even in advanced years can lead to improved health status (Nutbeam 1999).

It is interesting that, when asked about diet, physical activity, smoking and alcohol consumption, most older people are aware of what is 'good' for them, and of the likelihood of ill-health resulting from risk behaviours. We could surmise that they are aware of health-promotion information but, like other groups in society, they do not always follow advice. However, for the population of older men in particular, the results of ignoring such advice can have more serious consequences than for younger generations, given that men continue to be at higher risk of catastrophic ill-health earlier than women (Office of National Statistics 2003).

Optimism

Last but not least on the list of 'CAN DO' is optimism. There is no doubt that a positive outlook is the cornerstone of successful ageing. Research has shown that, even with moderate to severe disability and mobility problems, the majority of older people rate their lives as satisfactory or very satisfactory.

> '*Despite the losses and difficulties that often accompany old age, it appears that people can maintain or even increase their level of self-esteem as they age.*' (Schaie and Willis 2002: 282)

Conclusion

Health and social care professionals need to be aware of the disparate influences in older people's health behaviours and choices and that health promotion is the process of enabling people to increase control over the determinants of health and thereby improve their quality of life.

7 Coping strategies and sources of support

Jill Manthorpe

Most older people have well-developed coping strategies and robust sources of support. For some, disability and illness may affect their ability to cope well, and, for some, sources of support may lessen as the years pass, either gradually or as a result of sudden changes. In both health and social care services, practitioners will need to have some understanding of individuals' coping abilities and the sources of support currently available.

The Single Assessment Process is building on practitioners' knowledge of support and coping among older people. It follows on systems developed in the 1990s to make services 'needs-led' through systematic assessment of individuals' preferences and circumstances. This was underlined in the NHS and Community Care Act 1990 and extended by the Carers (Recognition and Services) Act 1995. To some extent, assessment under mental health legislation (eg the Mental Health Act 1983) has similar purposes, especially in the focus on social circumstances undertaken by an approved social worker, but this element is not covered specifically in this chapter.

Social networks

There are several ways to collect and record information about an individual's social networks. One common, easy method is the construction of a genogram or family tree. This is generally simple and can be enjoyable for both practitioner and older person, although for some people it can raise difficult or distressing memories. Information

Figure 7.1 Mrs Lord's family tree or genogram

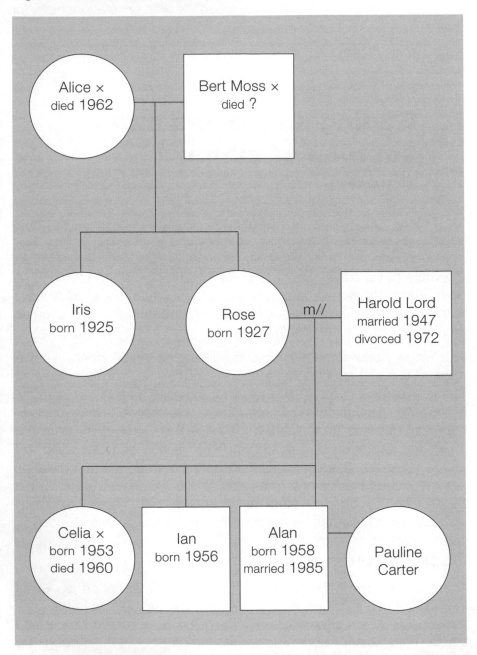

is easily recorded and can be understood by colleagues, especially if common symbols are used to represent people or relationships; for example:

- a triangle is a person (gender unknown);
- a circle is female;
- a square is male;
- a cross (x) or plus (+) means deceased;
- a double slash (//) across a line indicates it is broken (eg by divorce), a single slash (/) by separation.

Figure 7.1 is a simple example – a genogram in retrospect of 'Mrs Lord', an older woman who worked in a busy butcher's shop and was a skilled seamstress, but now is facing the challenges of a diagnosis of early dementia and the onset of severe arthritis.

The advantages of this family tree or genogram are that it sums up at a glance some of the important people in Mrs Lord's life – some of the key details such as when her husband and her daughter died – and avoids asking Mrs Lord for the same details (eg who is Mrs Moss?). But unless it is very detailed it does not set out of the type and extent of family contact, and of course it does not include the wider social network such as friends or family. Nevertheless, some practitioners working in dementia services may find this information very helpful; for example, it can help if a person is 'searching' for someone to know who that person is/was, and in any event it provides a biographical insight. Asking a relative may be one way of acquiring such information if the person with dementia is not able to provide it. Such a way of finding out about a person's life may also be used in therapeutic work; Parker and Bradley (2003) describe how this assessment can be used for such purposes as well as for part of health and social care assessment and care planning.

Such an assessment may be best if done by a practitioner who is known and trusted by the individual and has the time to explain its purpose, perhaps as part of a key worker relationship in day care or in a care home. Other assessments of this type can be around time lines; Box 7.1 gives an example of this approach, which can help set out what a person has experienced, what they are used to (eg frequent moves) and what they like or dislike.

Box 7.1 A section from Mrs Lord's timeline

1960   Death of her first child Celia from heart problems (?)

1962   Death of Mrs Lord's mother (Alice Moss) from 'old age' in hospital

1963? Mrs Lord learns to drive (she loves this)

1964   Family moves (5th time in 10 years), gets indoor bathroom

To assess wider social networks, some practitioners find an 'ecomap' a quick and helpful way of setting out the type of contacts. For Mrs Lord, Figure 7.2 illustrates this potential: the solid line indicates strength of the relationship, a broken line that the relationship is not strong, and a wavy or crossed line means that it is difficult or stressful.

Figure 7.2 Mrs Lord's ecomap

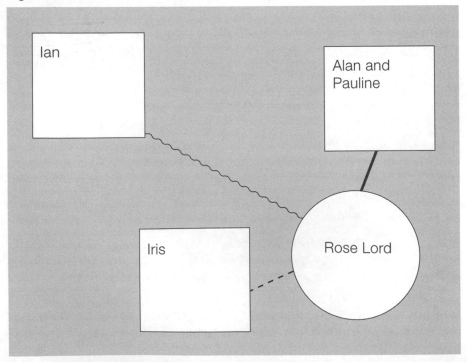

This diagram suggests that, although Mrs Lord's relationship with her sister Iris is important to her, Iris's own ill-health means that contact is infrequent (broken line). Her son Alan and Pauline (his wife) are now key people in Mrs Lord's social network (solid line), while the relationship with her son Ian is described as distant (wavy line).

The assessment of social networks is important. Wenger (1992) devised a typology that sets out the ways in which a person's social network influences both the type of help they may need if illness and disability arise and, just as important, the type of help a person is likely to accept and to find helpful in such circumstances. Box 7.2 sets out this model briefly. Wenger found that, over time, the most common shifts are to family-dependent and private-restricted networks. In the case of Mrs Lord, we can see that she has frequent support from Pauline and Alan. She might then be described as having a network that is family-dependent; she has close relationships with local family but not strong contacts with friends or neighbours.

*Box 7.2 **The network typology***

Local family-dependent – a small social network; reliant on kin, often female relative(s).

Locally integrated – close relationships with family, friends and neighbours.

Local self-contained – relationships with family exist but may be at a distance; there is contact with neighbours but this is not extensive; the person prizes independence.

Wider community-focused – active contacts with a wide social circle but less intensive involvement with them all.

Private restricted – limited social contact, perhaps the person has lived alone for some time or the couple may rely on each other and have limited relationships with other people.

Developed by Wenger (1992); see Wenger and Tucker (2002)

For practitioners this would suggest that Mrs Lord's daughter-in-law Pauline and son Alan may take on a great deal of practical support but may be at risk of isolation and depression. They may be aware that help is available but may not want to take it up, or find that it is not flexible or does not fit their routines. With Mrs Lord or, separately, the family may find someone who is able to talk to them about current arrangements and the future, and about sources of support. Benefits advice and financial planning may be crucial parts of this person-centred planning, including rights to Direct Payments, home adaptations, assistive technology and short breaks.

Promoting social support

Loneliness and social isolation can be identified through assessments of social support or may be evident at first contact. It is estimated that 10 per cent of older people in the UK are socially isolated and, although this may not be experienced as a problem, for many people this leads to loneliness. Those at most risk are people who are very old, those who are in poor health, those who are depressed and those who are poor (Cattan 2002). But loneliness can also affect those who do not live alone, such as carers and people in care homes. It can be sudden or slow to develop, and may follow bereavement or a move or retirement or occur as a result of other losses. This set of risk factors suggests that practitioners working with people in such circumstances should be alert to loneliness and its negative impact on a person's well-being.

Can practitioners do anything following such an assessment and on finding out that a person's social network is non-existent, weak or inactive? Cattan's (2002) study of services providing support to isolated older people suggests that practitioners should link their assessments to:

- Help maintain, not replace, existing contacts.
- Recognise that people may be aware that loneliness is stigmatising and may not wish to disclose their loneliness.
- Find ways in which help can be made acceptable (eg by building confidence and avoiding contacts that may be overwhelming).

- Avoid putting people on a 'waiting list' for help but trying to get something, however small, immediately.
- Think about individual support such as befriending or volunteering schemes.
- Think about practicalities such as transport and costs.

The voluntary sector may be the first port of call for information about such resources at local level. The local Council for Voluntary Service or Age Concern is likely to be a useful contact. Specific groups or services may be particularly relevant for some people, such as carers' groups, groups for people with specific conditions (eg stroke) or with similar cultural, religious or ethnic backgrounds. Local champions for older people may have local knowledge that is helpful.

Developing coping strategies

Information and social contact may help to develop or reinforce individuals' coping strategies, and assessments can help people identify the type of coping strategies they have found effective (or otherwise) in the past. In Mrs Lord's case, the early 1960s were presumably a difficult time for her, with the deaths of her mother and her daughter. How did Mrs Lord cope then? What was her source of strength? Was it Iris? Was it someone or something else?

Not all coping strategies are functional of course and some can lead to or perhaps compound difficulties. Mrs Lord, for example, took up smoking on the death of her daughter and this does not help her chest problems. She finds it comforting and cannot think of anything that would help in the same way: such information is likely to be very helpful to anyone seeking to support her if/when she goes on a smoking cessation programme.

People's coping strategies vary considerably and, whilst some may be life-long, other strategies can be learned. Older people are not 'too old' to learn; many are becoming involved in Expert Patient programmes, and form the lynchpins of self-help groups. Studies of self-help and support groups for carers reveal that, whilst they do not provide a simple resolution of carers' difficulties, they can be very supportive in providing information and social contact, providing a new social network for people who may have lost contacts or confidence.

Assessing coping strategies among people with newly diagnosed problems, such as early dementia, is also proving to be effective. Bartlett and Cheston (2003), for example, report how people can be helped to identify and develop their coping strategies. They have found that practitioners can acknowledge the coping strategies people are already using and also give them 'permission' to continue to use them. But they can also suggest other coping strategies that might not have occurred to the person but may be effective. In working with the relatives of those with an early diagnosis of dementia, practitioners can use the background they provide to help everyone understand what is significant to the person and what they might be experiencing. Later on, coping-skills training might be helpful to carers, drawing on the strengths as well as the needs a carer might have (see Marriott 2003: 198–199). Use of the Dementia Caregiver Checklist, for example, may uncover that some specific things are very difficult for a carer but may also discover sources of support or effective life skills. For example, in the case of Mrs Lord, Pauline and Alan may find that her frequent telephone calls to them are annoying but they have a strong marriage and a shared sense of humour. A practitioner may be able to suggest ways in which Mrs Lord's anxiety can be reduced or to set up a system whereby a befriender can call her for a chat.

Conclusion

Assessment of social networks remains a key task for health and social care practitioners, as there is great scope for linking people to support and sustaining networks that play such an important part in well-being. The Single Assessment Process provides a systematic basis for collecting information but, as this chapter suggests, some people may find it difficult to expose problems within their social networks. People with memory problems may need extra time and perhaps several conversations to help establish what their social network is and what they value. With the individual's permission, providing information to colleagues can be a very helpful element of an assessment of networks and coping strategies.

This chapter has mentioned briefly the importance of thinking about coping strategies. Most older people have considerable experience of managing change and coping in adversity. Whilst such strategies may not be currently available, they provide practitioners with valuable information about a person's preferences, priorities and capacity for adaptation and resilience.

8 Cognitive capacity and consent

Jan Dewing

The overarching principle with consent in health and social care is that consent – of whatever kind – is a process, not an event to sign a form. Thus it is ongoing and must be revisited at intervals to ensure that it is still freely given. How often it is revisited will vary according to the person and the situation. For example, in relation to participating in an assessment, taking medications, bathing or undergoing a medical or surgical procedure, the time intervals may range from months or weeks to several times on the same day. Consent is something that belongs to an older person to give and withdraw as they feel, and once given can be withdrawn at any time. It is best practice to assume that consent has not been given rather than to proceed with the expectation that it exists by default. The more vulnerable the older person, the greater the need there is to include the person in decision-making and to establish that consent is genuine and freely given.

For many older people, informed consent protects their best interests. With informed consent, consent is given after information has been shared, questions asked to aid clarification and reflection about risks and possible consequences, time taken to think about the issue and a decision is given voluntarily without pressure from other interested parties. Consequently, informed consent stresses reasoned decision-making. For some older people informed consent does not always serve their best interests. This is most often where the person's mental capacity and ability to go through all the steps needed to make reasoned decisions is very poor. For example, a significant number of older people have extreme changes in their memory and other cognitive functions (such as problem-solving, processing ideas, making choices, appreciating consequences, articulating thoughts). Because of the reliance on informed consent, they can be unnecessarily excluded.

Informed consent

It is a well-established part of law that no treatment can be given without the informed consent of the person (Caulfield 1996). Because the process is just as important as the outcome, a signed consent form does not mean that the consent is valid or that the intervention (such as an assessment) should go ahead. Consent obtained in a way that is not good is invalid. Adults who can give legal consent are described as being competent. A competent adult has the right of refusal even where the practitioner's experience or own beliefs differ. The 12 key points on consent and the law in England (Department of Health 2001a) and guidelines on consent for examination and treatment (Department of Health 2001b) are helpful, clarifying issues about informed consent in health care. Professional organisations for health and social care workers such as the Nursing and Midwifery Council and the Royal College of Nursing offer guidance for practitioners to work with. All practitioners should note that acting in the 'best interests' of patients/service users is said to go beyond just medical interests, to include factors such as the person's last-known wishes and beliefs as well as their current wishes.

In order for informed consent to take place, three key attributes must be present:

- the capacity for decision-making;
- informed decision-making;
- voluntary decision-making.

Capacity

Broadly speaking, 'capacity' refers to a person's ability to decide something or do something. An older person may have capacity for something but, for any of various reasons, may not achieve their capacity (Mezey et al 1997). The notion of the older person having a capacity reserve is useful to hold onto. Legally, there has been a growing interest in describing capacity. In 1995 the Law Commission issued guidelines on assessing mental capacity, which state that a person should be able to make a decision if, in broad terms, and through simple language, they understand an explanation and related information they need to make that decision. The guidelines also say that information should be retained long enough to make a decision. Whilst this does not mean that the person must be able to recall information after the event, it does still place an older person with a significant cognitive impairment at a disadvantage. The Adults with Incapacity Act (Scotland) 2000 has been in force for several years (Jones 2001) and a similar Act will shortly be enacted in England and Wales (Department for Constitutional Affairs 2004).

Clinically, capacity stems from the notion of functional capability. The way in which capacity is assessed often sets out to show what an older person is not capable of rather than what they are capable of. The use of formal assessment tools (such as Mini Mental State Examination, Geriatric Depression Scale) is common (Dewing 2001; Wills and Dewing 2001) but should not be used in isolation when making decisions about capacity. The whole team should be involved and ensure that capacity is appropriately assessed in conditions that help rather than hinder performance.

Traditionally, emphasis with informed consent has been on cognitive competence such that a person was deemed either competent or incompetent to give consent. It is now recognised that capacity is core, and capacity and consent are tied in with other factors such as well-being and personhood. In turn, well-being and personhood are influenced by a wide range of factors, including physical and mental health, environment, biographical and personality factors, lifestyle, sense of agency (being able to act for oneself and make things happen) and autonomy. When an older person is no longer competent to give their consent, it has been accepted practice that health and social care professionals, alongside families, can and should act in the best interests of the person. This position assumes that, when the legal lowest acceptable level of cognitive capacity has been crossed, the person is not capable of making any decisions. Clearly this is not so, as capacity is variable and can exist in some areas although it is reduced or absent in others and is specific to the decision in question (Meisel 1989: 180). Thus a person may no longer be able to control their own finances but could make decisions about their daily routine and indicate preferences for health and social care. Similarly, a person may have little or no capacity to decide social activities but be able to decide when or if they want to get washed or take medication. Thus the situation with capacity is constantly changing and must therefore be constantly under review. This means that health and social care practitioners and family members must adopt a flexible but organised, open and transparent approach to working out when capacity is present and when it is not.

Capacity can decline in older age for a range of reasons. For example, the person may find it hard to make decisions because of a decrease in self-esteem or because of perceived pressure within the family. Reduced social inclusion as a result of changes in sight and hearing may affect the person's ability to understand information and ask questions. Changes in memory and cognitive skills (such as take place with some strokes or dementias) may significantly decrease a person's ability. Capacity can change over time (from one year to the next but also from one day to the next) and in different environments. Thus an older person in a day centre they have been attending for a while may well have an increased capacity for decision-making in that setting but not on the same day when admitted to an A&E department following a fall.

Inherent in Western cultural history and beliefs is the idea of old age as a return to dependency and a second childhood associated with 'senility'. It is assumed that the greater the dependency, the less capacity exists. Older people with dementia are often regarded as being totally dependent and completely lacking in capacity and therefore unable to engage in consent. It must not, however, be assumed that a confusional state or mental illness in an older person means they are unable to give consent or lack capacity for consenting to everything.

Issues of capacity and consent are not just of relevance in the application of the Mental Health Act but are integral to the everyday practice of everyone working with older people. Questioning whether consent is genuine is generally not an issue when the older person's choice coincides with the family's desires and the professionals' views. An older person who co-operates is deemed to have sufficient capacity for informed choice. However, if an older person declines, families and professionals may question the degree to which that person is capable of making a decision and they demand a higher level of capacity for the decision to be validated. It is then possible to make the older person incapable of making a decision by repeatedly raising the capacity threshold.

Dewing (2002a) suggests that capacity is highly complex and must be considered in the context of:

- Who the person was and is (especially where the sense of self alters or diminishes, as in dementia).
- How a balance between an older person's last-known wishes and current wishes (as expressed through their words and behaviour) is achieved.
- Previously communicated directives or instructions.
- The person's unique responses to their physical and mental health, and how the person sees their future.
- How capacity is being supported or hindered by others on a day-to-day basis.
- Full and open discussion of multiple perspectives and not simply clinical interests of one or other professional group or an individual family member acting unilaterally.
- How capacity has been formally assessed and in what situations it does and does not exist.

Once it is established that informed consent is not achievable, health and social care practitioners can feel out on a limb. The day-to-day practicalities of establishing whether capacity exists to a sufficient degree in different situations is an experiential process for both the older person and the practitioners. Dewing (2002b) has discussed the use of 'process consent' in the research context and suggests that the method could be adapted to practice. Process consent relies on establishing how the older person with diminished capacity communicates decisions or choices and the degree to which they are content or comfortable with something. This can be communicated verbally but more often through behaviours. Over time it is possible to build up a picture of how the person gives or withholds consent. Validation by those who know the person can be helpful, especially if there is not much time to build up a picture. Often the person may need to begin the experience to know whether it is something they like the feel of and then make a choice to continue with or withdraw from. Choices are communicated through behaviours and can be seen as decisions-in-action.

Informed decision-making

Traditionally, the professionals have decided what level of information is needed in order for consent to be informed. There is now a move towards what the 'patient' considers is needed in order to make an informed decision. This requires a more individualistic approach to assessing what the older person's previous experiences have been and what they need to know. An adult incapable of giving consent because of mental illness can receive treatment under provisions set out in the Mental Health Act but there are still boundaries on this (Mukherjee and Shah 2001). For example, an older person who makes what is seen as unwise or eccentric decisions (Mental Capacity Act 2005) or decisions that others deem not in their best interest or a person with challenging behaviour cannot be compulsorily treated. The Department of Health guidance on consent and the Mental Capacity Act (Department for Constitutional Affairs 2005) highlight that there should be a presumption that capacity exists unless proved otherwise. The Act stresses that every effort must be made to enable a person to decide for themselves; substituted decision-making should not be a first option.

Voluntary decision-making

The more vulnerable or at risk the older person, the more attention should be given to the process of how consent is gained and to ensuring that decisions are voluntary. Teams working with older people need to have principles and protocols in place for how consent is sought, especially where capacity is reduced and informed consent is not possible.

There is a growing movement for establishing advance directives and similar means of self-governance that practitioners working with older people will need to work with. However, advance directives, made prior to the current real-life experience, may need to be questioned (Widdershoven and Berghmans 2001). Some people can make advance directives or instructions without fully appreciating what future experiences of illness and disability would be like.

An older person with dementia, just like anyone else, will have a range of beliefs and reasons underpinning decision-making. Decisions should not be automatically seen as unreasonable. Not all decisions (that the practitioner believes are wrong) can be allocated to cognitive impairment, altered belief or altered thought processes (Conn et al 1994). But sometimes dementia will result in the older person always saying 'No' or 'Yes' when this is not what they really mean. So the older person may need support to make their own decisions (Department for Constitutional Affairs 2004).

Consent and assessment

Most practitioners understand that everyone has certain rights and entitlements under law (Common Law, the Mental Health Act and Human Rights legislation) and usually cannot have personal information taken from them or given treatment or care without their consent. Nevertheless, it is not uncommon for older people to be deceived by activities being carried out around them but not with them. Assessment is one of those activities that can be carried out without real involvement of the older person concerned. The way in which any assessment in health and social care is carried out can in itself enhance or detract from capacity (Mezey et al 1997). The principles of the Single Assessment Process do stress gaining consent for assessment but, nevertheless, consent can become a secondary concern and it is possible to carry out an assessment without ever seeing the older person.

Bearing in mind legislation, professional codes and guidance and policy as well as the principles of person-centred practice, there are principles that apply to the process of assessment with an older person. The older person has a right to:

- Be approached with the presumption that capacity exists but that consent does not.
- Have information in advance about assessment: what it is, why it is being done and what the information collected will be used for and by whom, in both verbal and written forms.
- Have time to consider the issues.
- Have support to make their decisions (for informed consent) or indicate their degree of comfort.
- Sign a consent form for informed consent.
- Have odd or unusual decisions respected.
- Have practitioners act in their best interests but in a way that is the least restrictive of their rights and freedoms (this may mean a partial assessment).
- Be able to see/hear and read through what the practitioner has recorded.
- Have consent sought in advance of referrals made for specialist assessment.
- Have teams working with shared principles about consent (informed and process consent).

Summary

Health and social care practitioners need to keep consent central to their work with older people. Excluding an older person from consent takes away a fundamental human choice and should be avoided. Practitioners need to appreciate issues around capacity and consent in relation to assessment, as assessment is part of everyday practice, and in relation to the well-being, dignity and privacy of the older person. Any decision to assess an older person covertly should be made only in exceptional circumstances, after full consultation with the multidisciplinary team and where capacity has been formally assessed as being insufficient or lacking and there is insufficient information for process or experiential consent to be used. However, the assessment should be as limited as possible until consent can be established. Finally, open and transparent systems for establishing capacity and consent for the purposes of assessment must be established by multidisciplinary teams working with older people.

9 Sexuality, intimacy and sexual health

Isabel White and Hazel Heath

Sexuality is a complex and multifaceted concept (see Box 9.1) and remains a challenging aspect of health and social care practice. Professionals may be four generations younger than the patient/ service user and can feel uncomfortable discussing intimate aspects of life with someone who has both greater life experience and different generational perspectives. In addition, some professionals associate older people with their parents or grandparents and this can compromise constructive professional discussion.

Everyday health and social care practice intrinsically involves contact with people's bodies, emotions, relationships and lives in general. This creates a delicate interface between the professional aspects of practitioners' lives and the personal aspects that bring a range of individual and deeply held beliefs, values, desires and difficulties.

This chapter acknowledges some of the challenges in addressing sexuality and some common assumptions about older people. It offers two frameworks within which assessment can be considered. Assessment precedes intervention of course but, because it is essential that practitioners acknowledge their individual roles and levels of expertise before approaching assessment, the intervention model is discussed first.

Box 9.1 *The concept of sexuality*

Sexuality is:

- an essential integral element of the whole person;
- a creative force in human experience;
- a fundamental aspect of how individuals relate to one another;
- expressed by human beings in health, illness and disability;
- expressed throughout the lifespan.

It embraces personal choice and tolerance of difference.

Sexuality encompasses:

- self-concept, sexual identity and sexual orientation;
- psychological, social, cultural, spiritual, biological and interpersonal elements.

Sexuality is expressed:

- through personal thoughts, feelings, behaviour and presentation;
- through sensuality, intimacy and roles in life;
- negatively through power dynamics as in rape, sexual abuse and sexual harassment.

(White and Heath 2002)

Assumptions about sexuality and older people

Prevailing stereotypes suggest that older people are not interested in sexuality expression or relationships. Although this is untrue, such attitudes permeate the thinking of professionals (d'Ardenne and Morrod 2003).

Assumptions are also made that, in order to be sexually healthy and express oneself in human sexuality terms, one has to have intact hormonal, vascular and neurological systems, a reasonably good self-image and a supportive relationship (Skrine 1997). This is, of course, rarely true for anyone all of the time. Fluctuations in physical functioning, confidence, relationship dynamics and in how sexuality is expressed are part of normal life.

Such assumptions are particularly applied on the basis of older people's dependence on others for help, concurrent illness or disability, or social circumstances; for example, that a widowed man with mobility and speech difficulties following a stroke would not want to seek a sexual relationship. In reality, the effects of functional changes are highly individual and many older people adapt remarkably well. Rather than assuming that someone could not operate sexually in a healthy and fulfilling way owing to illness or disability, we should celebrate older people's resilience and resourcefulness, aided by life experience and supportive relationships, and support their individual adaptation strategies.

Assumptions can also be made about relationships; for example, that a partner is the same age, from the same culture or of a different gender, that long-lasting partnerships are happy, or that resumption of sexual activity is desired equally by both partners. There may be gender-based assumptions, for example that older women will be less interested in sex than are older men.

Assumptions might be made by health professionals that sex is not a priority – at times of illness, in making treatment choices or when a couple are faced with a life-limiting condition or end-of-life issues.

Unless practitioners acknowledge such assumptions and have the courage to explore the meaning of life events to individuals and couples, we may fail to acknowledge and support the importance and significance of intimate relationships at this time (Bancroft 1989; Clifford 2000; Rutter 2000; Searle 2001).

An intervention model

The 'P-LI-SS-IT' model (Annon 1976) identifies distinct but interconnected levels of psychosexual support and is helpful in considering the contribution that professionals can make, depending on their specific role and level of expertise (see Box 9.2). The level at which professionals are working will determine the scope of the assessment and the elements explored within this.

> *Box 9.2 The P-LI-SS-IT Intervention Model*
>
> **P**ermission
>
> **L**imited **I**nformation
>
> **S**pecific **S**uggestions
>
> **I**ntensive **T**herapy
>
> (Annon 1976)

At basic level, assessment could merely comprise a collection of facts that are noted. In contrast, in the hands of highly competent and sensitive professionals, assessment can, in itself, become a therapeutic intervention, giving voice to an area of concern that, without help, could remain unresolved or disruptive in a person's life. For example, while a district nurse was discussing options for the management of urinary incontinence, a woman remarked that she had lost all interest in sex. Practitioners operating at 'permission' level may not feel able to offer advice but a door has been opened and you could ask if she would like some information or to talk with someone who could help. A higher level practitioner could offer 'limited information' or 'specific suggestions' that enable exploration of how the incontinence may have affected her self-esteem, sexual confidence and relationship with her partner.

Appreciating distinct levels of intervention also helps to identify when practitioners should refer, and to whom. Referral is usually within one's own service first, particularly at 'permission' and 'limited information' levels, and then outside your own organisation.

For further discussion of levels of intervention, see White (2002: 243–263).

Permission

The professional relationship you create precedes the assessment itself, with 'permission' communicated through care contexts and environments, organisational cultures and systems of care delivery. It is also communicated in the practice of all health and social care professionals. The fundamental question is: how do you make it clear that it is permissible to discuss issues of sexuality?

Care contexts can communicate permission and inclusiveness by adopting, for example, images on posters and information booklets of couples who are older, from different races or in a same-sex relationship.

Permission is also created by the circumstances in which assessment takes place – how you facilitate discussion of a sensitive aspect of living by creating private space without risk of being overheard, preventing interruptions and creating the time for intimate discovery.

Your own approaches, attitudes, behaviours, knowledge and practices will communicate what is permissible to discuss and what is not. Being non-judgemental and 'normalising' sex as an aspect that makes us human, alongside other issues in life, can help facilitate disclosure. Showing tolerance of diversity and inclusivity of cultures, sexual orientations, types of relationships, sexual expression choices and individual behaviours can also help.

The timing of communication is important, ideally when the person seems ready to disclose concerns related to sexuality. Discussion can be enabled by starting with general questions and progressing to more sensitive issues; for example, asking about physical before emotional health. Two routes into discussing sexual issues may be worth exploring:

- The direct impact of illness or its treatment on sexuality expression or on intimate relationship.
- The relationship context through such questions as 'Who is around for you?', 'Who are you close to?' or 'Who is important in your life?'

In asking such questions, it is essential that we are respectful of the response. This could be something like 'It's not an issue', 'It's none of your business' or, with humour, such as 'What, at my age?' Although it may seem that further disclosure is unlikely at this time, such responses can indicate a willingness to discuss the subject.

Limited information

This level of intervention is within the scope of practice of most health and social care professionals and is characterised by the giving of factual information about sexuality as relates to the person's principal reason for accessing services, and noting referral points. It entails offering non-specialist knowledge as part of the assessment; for example, linking the side effects of medications with current concerns (eg low sexual desire as a side effect of some antidepressants). Written information (such as a booklet on sex after a stroke) and indicators for further guidance can be given but, at this level of intervention, the information is not discussed in any depth. Appropriate referral may be offered to the GP, an erectile dysfunction service or a psychosexual therapist.

Specific suggestions

Normally associated with advanced practitioners or specialists (eg in older people's care, continence, Parkinson's disease), this level of intervention can explore problems within a therapeutic relationship and offer specific and/or specialist support and information (eg alternative sexual positions for people with severe breathlessness or arthritis or following pelvic surgery; intercourse with an indwelling urinary catheter). At this level, specialists may well work in tandem; for example, a cardiac rehabilitation team and an erectile dysfunction specialist.

Intensive therapy

Generally, intensive therapy is offered by teams of people with additional specialist training in either psychosexual medicine or psychosexual therapy, working in a variety of services, who can give counselling and support over a protracted period of time in order to relieve more complex sexual or relationship problems.

An assessment framework

Hawton's (1985) framework identifies three categories of 'temporal' factors and three domains within which psychosexual difficulties can be considered (see Box 9.3).

Box 9.3 *Hawton's assessment framework*

Temporal factors:

- Predisposing factors: contextual considerations that create vulnerability in a person or couple towards the development of a sexual concern.

- Precipitating factors: key events or circumstances to which the person attributes the current sexual concern – ie what caused this, brought it to the fore or made it a reality for the person/couple so that it became an issue.

- Maintaining factors: circumstances that prevent the sexual concern from being resolved by the individual/couple so that it needs professional recognition and/or intervention.

Domains:

- Biomedical: organic and physiological system functioning that is influencing sexual expression; organic change affecting cognitive functioning; concurrent symptoms; treatments and medication side effects.

- Psychological: self-concept, self-confidence, self-efficacy; adjustment to physical and life circumstance changes; mental and emotional health.

- Relationship: current and/or desired relationship(s); the meaning and characteristics of these, particularly emotional and physical intimacy.

(Hawton 1985)

The elements in this framework interact (see Figure 9.1), providing a comprehensive and dynamic picture of the factors contributing to an individual's or a couple's sexual difficulties. Such an assessment is also helpful to both service user and professional in defining the problem and in agreeing upon the most appropriate intervention strategy.

Figure 9.1 Assessment model for development of sexual difficulties

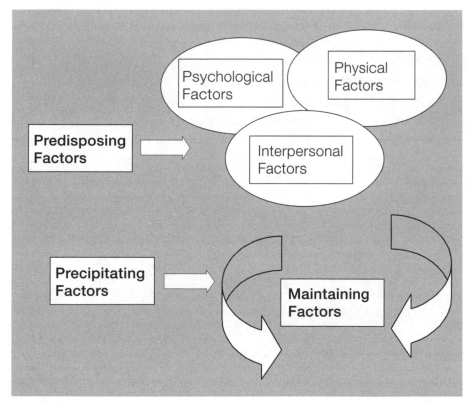

Considerations for assessing older people

The following sections illustrate issues that commonly emerge as significant in the assessment of an individual's or a couple's sexual well-being.

Predisposing factors

- *Teaching about sex*: when, what and how individuals learned about sex.

- *Religious or moral codes*: strict codes can deeply influence perceptions of sex and its meaning. For example: if sex is viewed solely as a procreative function, how does the menopause affect perceptions?; if penetrative intercourse is no longer possible, how is masturbation or oral sex viewed?

- *Cultural expectations, norms and mores*: these can strongly influence reactions to disruptions in health, particularly traditions with strong masculinities and femininities (eg the onset of diabetes affecting erectile function in a culture with strong masculine identities can strike at the core of male identity).

- *Tolerance of diversity, particularly homosexuality*: some couples will covertly go beyond religious or cultural expectations; others will not.

- *Parental and family relationships or vulnerabilities:* for example, power imbalance, manipulation, violence or abuse; family attitudes to sex; familial vulnerabilities to mental illness.

- *Unresolved losses or traumas*: experiences, such as bereavement, which affect someone's sense of security or elicit feelings of vulnerability or abandonment. Circumstances such as retirement or 'empty nest', which can affect self-esteem and sense of purpose in life. There may be previously undisclosed sexual traumas such as childhood sexual abuse or rape.

Precipitating factors

These can arise from any or all of the three domains. Common precipitating factors include the onset of physical or mental problems that disrupt sexuality, medical or surgical treatment, hospitalisation, loss of partner, change in relationship (such as becoming a carer) and change in living circumstances (such as needing extensive assistance at home or moving into a care home).

It is also worth noting that the attributed cause may not always be the main contributory factor.

Maintaining factors

Common maintaining factors include chronic illness or deteriorating health, treatment effects, difficulty in accommodating functional or sexual changes into relationships, difficulty in finding a new partner and social or family disapproval of sexual interest in later life.

Biomedical domain

- *Organ and system functioning that influence sexual expression*: for example, cardiovascular, neurological or hormonal change or pelvic/genitourinary disease.
- *Organic change influencing function*: for example, acute confusion or dementia affecting cognitive functioning or perceptual changes following stroke.
- *Concurrent symptoms*: for example, breathing problems, pain, fatigue, arthritis, obesity, infections (particularly lower urinary tract), incontinence.
- *Effects of medical or surgical treatment*: particularly medication for hypertension or depression; over-the-counter, herbal or complementary remedies should also be considered; prostate, breast or bowel surgery.
- *Current health problems in partner*: for example, any of the above.

Psychological domain

- *Psychological 'personality' related to the individual as a sexual person*: for example, how do they describe this, are they confident or insecure, how are their relationships with their peers, with potential sexual partners; do they seem vulnerable?
- *Self-concept*: for example, feelings about one's own body, degree of confidence about physical appearance; physical changes, such as disfigurements, that might affect self-concept; how the individual accepts the natural changes associated with age and how this affects confidence or perceived sexual attractiveness; sexual self-confidence (is the individual

comfortable in terms of sexual identity and orientation?); mental health issues affecting self-esteem or sexual interest, such as depression or anxiety.

- *Background*: for example, emotional traumas, loss or bereavement, particularly if unresolved; have they ever received or are they receiving counselling or treatment for an emotional or mental health problem?

Relationship domain

- *Relationship meanings*: what is the meaning and importance of current relationships, how emotionally and physically intimate? Is there more than one partner? Relationship duration is less significant than its meaning.

- *Relationship characteristics*: what characterises the person's significant relationship(s), is it supportive, emotionally fulfilled; how important is sex within the relationship (central, peripheral, variable); is there conflict and are the individuals able to resolve this as a couple; do they share lives as companions or live their own lives; does the partner know that there is a sexual concern and is the concern shared; if not, what does the individual imagine the partner would say about this? Is the relationship acknowledged or secret?

- *Relationship changes*: for example, have there been changes in the relationship, such as one partner becoming bored, conflict or antagonism; has one partner experienced a life change such as retirement; has one become a carer to the other, through illness or deteriorating health, or the inability to accommodate functional or sexual changes into relationships?

- *Influences on relationships*: for example, do living circumstances influence relationships (such as living in a care home with lack of privacy, being confronted with images of own decline and mortality, bigoted staff or restrictive regimes); family perceptions such as not seeing the older person as sexual, or disapproving of an intimate relationship? What level of support is required to maintain intimate relationships – for example, the need that people with disability or chronic illness might have for practical support?

- *Aspirations*: loss of social network; relationship issues or changes, do they want to have a partner in the future, do they aspire to this?
- *Consent*: an important consideration, which could be influenced by biomedical or psychological domains; is the person able to give consent in the relationship and able to express what they do or do not want?

Conclusions

Whilst sexuality is likely to remain a challenging aspect of health and social care practice, the challenges cannot be overcome until they are recognised. Many of the assumptions identified in this chapter arise through lack of understanding but they are maintained because, for professionals, they operate as effective buffers between personal discomfort and the realities of addressing issues of sexuality in the lives of older adults with whom we work.

Working through the implications of such assumptions can help professionals become truly person-centred and open to individual circumstances and needs. This may take some practitioners beyond their personal comfort zone but can usually be overcome within a team approach to health and social care delivery.

Negotiating boundaries and creating safety for discussion requires considerable skill and judgement that offers confidentiality and considers what needs to remain private, what is written down and what is shared with others. With permission-giving comes the need to make boundaries explicit, creating safety for both professionals and service users in the conduct of an effective sexual health assessment.

Whilst it is easy to focus solely on the professional conduct of individual practitioners, the effective management of sexual concerns in later life remains the collective responsibility of service users, practitioners, teams and the health and social care agencies dedicated to improving the quality of life for older adults in society.

Part 3
Foundations for Care

Care environments

10 **Environment**

Hazel Heath and Lynne Phair

The environment within which an older person lives can profoundly affect their health, well-being, independence and quality of life, particularly when they are vulnerable. Nightingale (1946) defined the environment as 'all external conditions and influences affecting life and the development of the organism, particularly warmth, effluvia [odours], noise and light', but there are many types of environment (see Box 10.1). An external environment could include geographical boundaries as diverse as a neighbourhood or the space surrounding a person's bed. Your physical body's internal environment can influence how you cope with the demands of the day.

Box 10.1 *Types of environment*

External	Organisational	Conceptual
Geographical	Operational	Temporal
Physical	Psychosocial	Imagined
Internal	Perceptual	

Environments can have physical attributes, and can be perceptual (to which you respond with your senses) or conceptual (the meaning to which you ascribe the symbols, language, values and culture). Two other useful concepts are: personal space (the need for privacy and boundaries, defined by the limits of one's control); and life space (physical, psychosocial, temporal [time space] and imagined). Schofield (1999) highlights that, although environments are defined by geographical and perceptual boundaries, which can expand and contract throughout the lifespan, it is important to acknowledge that the older person's mental and spiritual world has no boundaries and possibly extends beyond the scope of our comprehension.

We become accustomed to our usual environments. As Schofield (1999: 299) observes: 'most of us are immersed in a range of micro-environments in which we routinely participate with little thought as to their effects ... the usual sounds, odours, shifting temperatures and vegetation patterns. It is only when these change noticeably that we become aware that environment has meaning to us.'

The impact of environments on older people

Environments can have a significant impact on older people, and adapting to new environments can be challenging, yet there is little research on the precise nature of the impact, which varies considerably from one individual to another.

One way of considering environment–person interaction is Lawton and Nahemow's 'press–competence' model (1973). This suggests that the attributes of an environment combine to produce a set of demands or expectations which may be physical (eg to walk up stairs) or interpersonal (eg to hold a conversation). The combination of these demands is known as environmental 'press'; when they exceed a person's 'competence' to manage them (in terms of psychological adjustment or physical or cognitive abilities), the person becomes increasingly influenced by the environment. For example, if mobility decreases, the distance to the lavatory becomes increasingly significant in maintaining continence. Lawton and Nahemow emphasised that consideration of environmental 'competence' should include not only functioning and maintaining social norms but also demonstrating behaviour that is creative and fulfilling to the individual.

Levels of environmental stimulation affect sensory input that can trigger emotional responses. Sensory overload may cause anxiety, reduced concentration and a tendency to emotional peaks and troughs; insufficient environmental stimulus can lead to boredom, depression and withdrawal. Although research into the range of older people's responses to sensory stimuli is limited, it is clear that sensory input is essential to continued cognitive development and that some of the cognitive 'clouding' attributed to ageing may well be due to the absence of sufficient mental stimulation. For a person with dementia, these effects may still occur, over and above the original consequences of the cognitive impairment. As Lawton and Nahemow indicated, the more ways in which an individual's adaptation to the environment is compromised, the greater the risk to their sense of security and well-being.

Adapting to environments

Many factors influence older people's ability to adapt to environments. For example:

- In later life, changes in vision, hearing, sense of touch, dexterity, mobility or cognition can affect our ability to adapt. Sensory changes are unique to each person and the effects vary greatly between individuals.
- The slowed transmission of nerve impulses impairs the ability of older people to react quickly to hazards.
- Older people may have difficulty orientating their body in space when changes in body position are made. Their balance may be unstable and they may be less able than younger people to avoid obstacles quickly (Schofield 1999).
- Falls and accidents are a significant cause of ill-health, disability and death in older people. Although intrinsic factors (such as blood pressure) play a role in falls in people aged 75 and over, environmental factors are more significant (Minns et al 2004).
- The ability to sense extremes of heat or cold, and to regulate body temperature, may be impaired, resulting in hypothermia or hyperthermia. Sense of touch in the palms and soles declines with age and the transmission of heat or cold impulses may be slowed, resulting in damage before the person is able to move away.
- The reduction in normal pain sensations can be hazardous – for example, pressure damage when seated in one position for long periods (Schofield 1999).
- Manual dexterity may be reduced.

- Cognitive impairment can reduce the ability to make sense of the environment or to recognise locations in a new environment.

Box 10.2 Characteristics of positive environments

They promote:

- Individuality and individual life journeys
- Familiarity, with items of personal significance
- Predictability, avoiding unnecessary disruption
- Personal space and privacy
- Social engagement, when desired
- Preferred lifestyle
- Safety and security
- Independence
- Orientation
- Choice (eg in activity)
- Control (eg to open windows)
- Comfort and homeliness
- Freedom of movement
- Restfulness and relaxation
- Interesting and varied activities
- Success in achievement, including everyday tasks
- Optimal physical, sensory and psychosocial functioning

Box 10.3 Considerations for assessing environments

Lighting	Must be adequate, particularly in potentially hazardous areas such as stairs
	Glare should be avoided; diffuse lighting is more desirable than very bright lights
	Avoid sudden changes in levels, such as glaring sunlight through windows, and flashing televisions, which can make people restless and agitated
	Light switches must be accessible to all (including people in wheelchairs)
Colour and colour contrast	Colour schemes influence mood or activity; eg pale blues and greens provide a relaxing environment, yellows are cheerful, touches of bright red encourage activity
	Colour contrast is important for people to be able to see stairs or food
	A coloured object on a white surface is considered preferable to the other way around because bright surfaces reflect much more of the light falling on them
Floor covering	Carpets with rubber underlay provide better protection against falls than hard flooring (Minns et al 2004)
	Highly patterned carpet can be disorientating, particularly when looking down to use a walking aid
	Carpets can be kept fresh with regular cleaning
	Shiny floors should be avoided

Box 10.3 (continued)

Furniture	Furniture should meet individual needs
	Furniture can be discreetly protected from staining; plastic covers are not necessary
	The arrangement of furniture in rooms can facilitate or inhibit movement, and encourage social activity or isolation (Phair and Good 1998)
Sensory stimuli; noise	Preferred levels of environmental stimulation are individual and should be adjusted for personal preference
	Overly loud televisions, radios or domestic appliances can cause 'acoustic pollution' (Morrison 1997)
Hazards	Awareness of potential hazards is essential. Aspects to be avoided include glass-panelled doors where the glass is not easily visible, trailing wires, rugs, and slippery surfaces, particularly in bathrooms

continued

25

Box 10.3 (continued)

Environmental cueing	Familiarity seems to be the most successful factor in helping older people remain environmentally orientated
	Cues such as clocks and notices should be accessible to people who are visually challenged
	Environmental cueing techniques include colour coding of doors, walls or floors (Netten 1993), pictures, words or familiar items (Judd et al 1998)
	Cueing should take into account the particular sense or skill that is compromised and the most successful methods of cueing will probably involve multi-sense methods. These should be culture-appropriate and not detract from creating a domestic non-institutional environment

Box 10.3 (continued)

Technology	The use of assistive technology – technological systems and devices designed to assist people in carrying out everyday activities (Marshall 2000) – and 'telecare' – systems using a combination of manual communication technology to provide remote support via a service centre such as Lifeline (Association of Social Alarm Providers 2005) is increasing and there are various forms – computing technology, communication technology and environmental techniques. Assistive technology includes 'intelligent' telephones, which enable someone with dementia to remain in a family environment, sensor pads on beds to assist in the prevention of falls without restraining the person, and computer-linked light sensors to detect when people are moving around their rooms at night (Judd 1997)
	The ASTRID guide (produced by the Stirling Dementia Services Centre) surveys assistive technology for people with dementia and how this may be developed (Marshall 2000)
	The use of technology remains controversial. Supporters believe it to be greatly advantageous; others find it dehumanising. Ultimately, technology should be considered as a tool which must fulfil a function that someone wants to have for him- or herself. It must always serve the user (Judd 1997)

Conclusion

Professionals working with older people can play a major role in creating, maintaining and adapting environments, both physical and psychosocial (see Box 10.2 and Box 10.3). McCormack (1996) promotes the idea of a total healing environment in which the surroundings and approaches to care recognise the unique journey of each older person, alongside his or her values and priorities. Such an environment promotes individual choice, control, maximum autonomy and personal fulfilment. Staff work to support, confirm and help people to make sense of their experiences, seek meaning in them, and participate as fully as possible, including taking risks. Using the environment to support older people is now recognised as an important aspect of holistic care, and even small improvements can make a significant difference.

The effects of normal ageing

11 Normal ageing

Roger Watson

How ageing evolved is unclear and the point at which ageing begins is also uncertain. To some extent, ageing begins when we are born because, chronologically, we get older. Up to and beyond our late teenage years and early 20s we are still developing in several ways – for example, sexually and emotionally. However, we do not normally associate this early phase of our lives with ageing in the sense of being old.

Classifying individuals or identifying groups of people on the basis of age – for example, describing people over the age of 65 years as 'elderly' – has limited application in understanding the process of ageing. Such classifications can be useful sociologically because they define such things as retirement and eligibility for pensions. Sometimes the comparison between groups of older people or older versus younger people is useful, but it must be borne in mind that older people are not all the same.

Older people display a much greater variation in physical ability, income and social circumstances than is often appreciated. Individuals within groups of babies, toddlers and adolescents are far more similar than within groups of older people.

The age-specific mortality rate begins to increase after the age of about 13 years (after the effect of childhood illnesses has dissipated), so ageing, as measured as the risk of death (also known as the force of mortality), begins earlier than this. After our late teenage years and early 20s we do not continue to develop in the biological sense and, except in the case of individuals such as athletes who train very hard, we have almost universally reached our physical peak in our late 20s to early 30s. Whilst there is considerable variation in the rate and extent to which people display evidence of ageing, it is indisputable that we begin to show visible signs of ageing in our late 20s to early 30s, whether it is subjective in the sense of 'slowing down' physically or objective through such signs as greying hair and wrinkled skin. Certainly, we are unable to repeat many of the physical feats of our youth based on stamina or strength.

Nevertheless, such signs of ageing do not necessarily herald a rapid decline into frailty and dependency. In fact, the decline can be very slow in some people who retain considerable physical fitness into their later years (Peris 1995). In terms of career and family life, there may be much left to achieve. The fact is that there are many variations on the theme of ageing and it is difficult, despite the title of this chapter, to define such a thing as 'normal' ageing. There are, however, some commonalties of which professionals working with older people should be aware.

How do we age?

Although it is not entirely clear how ageing occurs, there are many theories (Kirkwood and Wolff 1995). Mostly, these are beyond the scope of this chapter but they range from: the evolutionary, such as the disposable soma theory which claims that ageing is advantageous to a species by allowing replacement of weaker with stronger individuals; to 'wear and tear' theories that envisage the body simply wearing out; through to genetic theories that explain ageing by means of genes which programme the process in the body.

Psychological aspects of ageing

One myth to be dispelled is that there is severe psychological decline in terms of loss of memory, intelligence and personality change. There are minor effects on memory and a slight decline in fluid intelligence

– the mental agility needed to solve problems. However, the effects of this decline are minimal and, unless some pathological process takes place to make them severe, they have little adverse effect on the everyday life of an older person. It is also untrue that older people become more stubborn – generally speaking, whatever personality you were born with you take into old age.

Normal versus abnormal ageing

If anyone were able to catalogue the changes that take place as we age and label these 'normal', they would have solved a big problem in gerontology (the study of ageing).

It is possible to compare two older people in their 80s and find one who is fit, active and mentally alert while the other is unable to get around and not engaged much with other people. There has been a tendency to say that the person who has aged well and retained physical and mental capacity to an advanced age has aged 'successfully', while the person who has lost physical ability and mental faculties has aged 'unsuccessfully' (Rowe and Khan 1997). However, we simply do not know which person has aged normally. Clearly, there is a distinct line between the two. One will require some help in order to lead a relatively normal life while the other will be independent. Nevertheless, the line which says that one older person is ageing successfully and another unsuccessfully is impossible to draw.

Some older people are heard to remark that 'old age does not come alone' and there is some truth in this rather dim view despite the fact that we are encouraged to hold and promote a more positive image. It is relatively easy for younger, fitter people to dismiss such notions – the two extremes portrayed above of the extremely frail and the extremely fit older people are stereotypes of how we often view ageing and how we would wish to be when older. The facts speak for themselves: as people age they experience, on average, more illness, make more use of health care facilities and consume more medications, so there must be something about the ageing process that predisposes older individuals towards poorer health. So what actually happens to us as we age?

General changes

Skin and hair

There are some obvious signs of ageing such as wrinkled skin and greying hair that signify old age (Christiansen and Grzybowski 1993). Both of these changes take place due to changes in the structure of the protein and keratin making up skin and hair. Keratin also forms nails, which become more brittle with age. The effect on hair is loss of colour because it reflects more light, and the effect on the skin is that it loses its elasticity.

Loss of hair colour has no significant effect, but the loss of elasticity in the skin can be significant in older people, especially if they are immobile or ill for prolonged periods. This may become evident in the formation of pressure sores. Changes in the skin also lead to facial and other body changes such as the skin developing more folds and sagging. While men may lose body hair with age, especially on the head, some older women begin to develop facial hair and these changes are related to hormonal changes with age.

Kidneys

The kidneys are worth special mention because this is one system that can definitely be demonstrated to decline with age (Christiansen and Grzybowski 1993). In good health this is of no consequence, but in illness when drugs, which are excreted via the kidneys, have been prescribed, this may present problems for an older person that would be of no consequence in a younger person.

Other systems

There is a decline in the capacity of organs such as the heart and lung, but we are designed with such excess reserve capacity that these are generally of no consequence to an older person (Christiansen and Grzybowski 1993). Likewise, changes taking place in the digestive system and the liver are very minor. The skeletomuscular system declines with ageing in two ways. Muscles atrophy with age and bones lose calcium, leading to the skeleton shrinking. This results in postural change and an older person may seem to stoop more. The loss of calcium from bones can be very dangerous in some older people, leading to osteoporosis.

Both of these changes are exacerbated by immobility but can be slowed down by regular exercise. This is very relevant to the care of older people in whom many conditions can lead to immobility. Gentle mobilisation, to maintain muscle tone and prevent osteoporosis, is an important part of the care of an older person in hospital.

Reproductive ability ceases in women from their late 40s to early 50s, the menopause, but the reproductive capacity of men, despite declining levels of male sex hormones, is retained indefinitely. Impotence is a problem for some older men, as it is for some younger men, but it is a fact that many older couples retain sexual activity into advanced years.

The senses

It is commonly misconceived that older people lose their senses as they age, in particular that they do not feel so much pain. This is simply not true and is of particular importance to nursing practice. The decline of taste and smell does take place with age, and there is an inevitable decline in both hearing and sight (Christiansen and Grzybowski 1993). However, caution is required in interpreting the last statement – all older people are not blind and deaf, but declining taste and smell may have consequences for nutrition. When giving advice about medications to older people it is always essential to ensure that they have heard properly and understood correctly, that they can read the labels on the medication containers and have the manual dexterity to self-administer their medication at home.

Homoeostasis

The most insidious change, which is really a result of the culmination of many minor ageing changes in the body, is the decline in homoeostatic function (Bellamy 1998). Homoeostasis is the ability to maintain a constant internal environment in the body, and controls such things as body temperature, fluid and electrolyte balance, levels of oxygen and carbon dioxide in the blood and blood pressure.

As people age, whilst they are perfectly able to maintain homoeostasis under normal, everyday circumstances, they are less able to do so under physiologically stressful conditions, such as those that exist when a person is ill. Therefore, older people are more prone, for example, to dehydration and hypothermia when they are ill. Particular attention, therefore, needs to be paid by professionals caring for ill older people to ensure that they do not become dehydrated or experience extremes of body temperature.

12 Altered presentation of disease in older age

Roger Watson

Despite the fact that the majority of people in most health care settings are older, most of what we learn about the presentation of illness refers to young and middle-aged people. For example, we learn that a patient with myocardial infarction presents with acute chest pain and a patient with an infection presents with pyrexia. However, in older people these typical presentations, linked clearly to underlying pathology, are not always observed (Heath 2000).

Using the two examples above, an older person may not experience acute pain with a myocardial infarction but may notice the circulatory disturbance in some other way – for example, by becoming dizzy. Infection in older people is not always accompanied by a rise in temperature.

It was observed by Isaacs (1981) that the reasons for the majority of older people visiting their general practitioners could be grouped under four headings, originally referred to as the four giants of geriatric medicine. These are now more commonly referred to as the four 'I's (Heath 2000):

- Immobility
- Instability
- Incontinence
- Impairment of mental function.

The four 'I's have the common features of having multiple causes and no simple cure, but their non-specific nature should not mislead the clinician – doctor or nurse – into thinking that these are inevitable aspects of old age. Nor should it be assumed that it is not worth carrying out investigations to find out what has led to such manifestations.

For example, instability could indicate a circulatory disorder and incontinence could be the first sign in an older person of a urinary tract infection. In any older person who presents with mental impairment – usually referred to as confusion – it should not be assumed that this indicates a permanent decline in mental function. For example, confusion may also be an early sign of infection, dehydration or constipation (see Chapter 20, 'Acute confusional states/delirium').

Before leaving the four 'I's it should be appreciated that they are interrelated: instability can lead to immobility; immobility can lead to incontinence, as can impairment of mental function. Any manifestation of any one of the four 'I's in an older person warrants further investigation – both in its own right and also to prevent further complications.

Diagnosing illness in older people

The process of ageing was considered in Chapter 11, and the main conclusions were that:

- certain changes take place in the body as we age and these changes are normal;
- older people experience more illnesses than younger people;
- the point at which the effects of old age end and illness begins is hard to determine.

Nevertheless, there are some illnesses that are almost exclusively observed in older people, including osteoarthritis, Paget's disease, multiple myeloma, chronic lymphocytic leukaemia, prostate cancer, cerebrovascular disease, dementia, Parkinson's disease and cataracts.

The diagnosis of illness in older people presents some challenges for physicians, and there are concomitant challenges for all professionals who care for older people. However, despite the general decline in organ, and therefore system, function in older people and the decreased ability to maintain homoeostasis, it is generally the case that body parameters such as laboratory blood values either are not altered or change in clinically insignificant ways with old age (Davies and Sinclair 1995). Some examples are given in Box 12.1.

Box 12.1 *Some laboratory values that do not alter significantly with age*

Haemoglobin	HDL cholesterol
Erythrocytes	Sodium (although wider range of values)
Coagulation tests	
Thyroid function tests	Potassium
Cortisol	pH
Bilirubin	

Adapted from Somerville (1999)

Nevertheless, there are some exceptions and these are highlighted below. The diagnosis of illness includes the measurement of deviations from normal physiological parameters such as blood values, organ and system function, and the detection of pathophysiological changes such as low blood pressure and pyrexia. The tests for such measurements are valuable if they lead to an unequivocal conclusion about the presence or absence of disease. However, normal physiological parameters are usually derived from a range of members of society that does not include older people. In these terms the normal person is approximately 35 years old and the normal range includes approximately 60 per cent of the population around this age.

Many older people lie outside this age range, and there are sparse physiological data on those aged over 80 years and almost no data on centenarians. In the past, these groups of older people were few in number. Advances in medicine, surgery and public health mean that they now constitute an increasing proportion of the population and simply cannot be ignored. The increasing number of people in these advanced age groups means that more data are always being gathered on physiological parameters in older people, and there are specific longitudinal studies being undertaken internationally in order to follow changes from relatively young people through old age.

It has already been explained that there is considerable variation among older people (Watson 2000), including physiological para-meters. The process of ageing and the experience of disease affect people differently; therefore the concept of 'normal' does not apply for some parameters, and the alternative concept of reference values to help in the diagnosis of illness is gaining popularity. In some cases the comparison of measurements made in old age can be compared with measurements made in the same person when younger, but this is not always possible as it depends on previously recorded investi-gated illness. At the very least, especially when laboratory tests are being considered, these must be looked at in older patients in 'softer, more clinical light' taking into account a greater range of factors – age, disease state, lifestyle and medication – than might be the case with younger patients.

The problem for the physician trying to diagnose any illness is the sensitivity and the specificity of the diagnostic criteria that are applied. The *sensitivity* refers to the extent to which a positive result occurs in those with the disease, and the *specificity* refers to the extent to which someone without the disease is correctly identified. Both the sensitivity and the specificity and some diagnoses are altered with ageing. The ability of a test to identify whether a disease is present depends upon the chances of someone having the disease before the test. As old people have high prevalence of disease, screening programmes are more likely to identify abnormalities.

Specific changes with age

The known spectrum of changes that take place with ageing and which alter the presentation of illness is complex and, of course, con-stantly evolving. It is possible, however, to provide a few examples.

Laboratory tests

Laboratory tests of the body fluids and tissues play a key role in the diagnosis of illness, but some may have less utility in older people. Ageing is associated with changes in serum protein levels but these are not always predictable. For example, serum albumin and trans-ferrin levels decrease slightly with age but the immunoglobulin (Ig) protein IgA levels increase, IgG ranges are wider, IgM levels decrease and the range of IgE values is narrower. Antibody levels are used in the diagnosis of infection; for example, IgM levels increase soon after infection and it can be seen how decreased levels with age might interfere with the diagnosis of infection using this parameter.

The detection of autoantibodies, associated with diseases such as diabetes and rheumatoid arthritis, increases with age, and physicians have to guard against the false positive diagnosis of diseases associ-ated with these antibodies.

Glucose tolerance, a test used in the diagnosis of diabetes mellitus, may be less reliable with older people because of delayed insulin release following a glucose load.

It is not clear whether the changes in glucose tolerance observed with old age are actually a function of ageing pathology, and the World Health Organization criteria for blood glucose intolerance and diabetes mellitus are not age adjusted (Somerville 1999).

Another example of the effect of ageing relevant to the use of diag-nostic tests is the decrease in diurnal variation, which tends to be less pronounced in older people. Glomerular filtration rate, which decreases in younger people at night but increases during the day, is influenced by ageing and immobility, and tests of kidney function, which depend upon glomerular filtration rate and may take place over 12 hours, need to be interpreted in that light. Urine collection, where clean samples are normally required for accurate measurements and detection of pathogens, can be made difficult by the presence of bladder diverticula, which make urine collection inaccurate.

The state of hydration of a patient is important when interpreting blood values. Dehydration tends to raise blood values, and dehydration is not uncommon in institutionalised older people, as the kidneys are less able to concentrate urine and the sensation of thirst decreases in older people.

Blood serum levels of sodium, urea and the haemoglobin may all be artificially raised by dehydration. Older people tend to take more medications that can be bought over the counter without a doctor's prescription (Watson 1996), and these may include dietary supplements that can influence blood levels of minerals such as calcium, phosphate and magnesium.

The erythrocyte sedimentation rate (ESR) – changes in which are commonly used non-specifically to detect illness – is influenced by many factors, including medication, existing illness, renal function, sex and age. Generally speaking, these increase with age (Somerville 1999) but the interpretation of ESR values in older people requires many factors to be taken into consideration, and it can be seen that many of the relevant factors listed above are likely to be present in an older person. A summary of laboratory values that alter with age is given in Box 12.2.

Box 12.2 **Some laboratory values that alter with age**

Decrease	*Increase*
Leucocytes	ESR
Serum iron	Alkaline phosphatase
Testosterone (men)	Serum urea
Albumin	Serum creatinine

Adapted from Somerville (1999)

Infectious diseases

Infections are more common in older people, who are more susceptible to the complications of an infection. This is, therefore, an important area for consideration under altered presentation. Whilst most older people with an infection present normally, there is a significant proportion who do not. Older people with pneumonia are less likely to complain of pain, and the usual symptoms of cystitis, pain and frequency are not common in older people. The cardinal sign of infection is pyrexia or an abnormally high core body temperature above 38.3°C. However, in some older people, pyrexia is often not present; this may be a result of a lower than average core temperature and pyrexia is taken to be present if body temperature is persistently 2°C above baseline.

Nevertheless, some older people with infections do not display pyrexia at all. Related to the above is the phenomenon of fever of unknown origin, which is particularly challenging in older people and is defined as a persistent pyrexia for over three weeks. There are several causes, including intra-abdominal abscess, tuberculosis and arteritis. Diagnosis is made difficult, for example, in the case of intra-abdominal abscess owing to the absence of the usual symptoms.

Conclusion

This chapter has provided an overview of some aspects of altered presentation of illness in old age. Future chapters consider specific areas in greater depth.

13 Neurological functioning

Roger Watson

The importance of the nervous system to the functioning of a healthy mind and body hardly needs to be mentioned. The nervous system controls such things as:

- posture and movement;
- the visceral functions (eg the digestive system) of the body;
- thought process;
- personality;
- sensations.

On the whole we take these aspects of our life for granted unless something goes wrong. However, as we age, changes are evident in the nervous system and, as with all aspects of ageing, there are problems in differentiating normal from abnormal changes. Professionals working with older people need to be aware of the parameters that may change, so that they can be alert to abnormalities, as distinct from the normal aspects of ageing. Some specific aspects of care are discussed at the end of this chapter.

The ageing nervous system

It is worth beginning by dispelling a major myth about the ageing nervous system. It is commonly misconceived that, as we age, we lose vast amounts of brain cells, our brain shrinks and we lose our mental faculties such as memory and understanding. The truth is that, as we age, the loss of brain cells is minimal and we remain, largely, cognitively intact with good memories – unless there is a specific disease process such as dementia at work. In fact, measurements of brain weight and volume 'do not differ significantly in adult or old individuals who are without neurologic and mental disorders' (Timiras 1998). The brain has considerable excess capacity or 'redundancy' among its cells, and comparison of brain size between adults and older people has been described as 'meaningless' (Timiras 1998).

The point for professional practice is that severe loss of memory and cognitive function resulting from brain abnormalities is not a normal part of the ageing process – they indicate that something is wrong and, when observed, they should be reported. Chronic changes associated with memory and cognition are normally irreversible but acute changes and delirium, for example caused by infection, are usually easily treated. Acute changes improve when the predisposing disorder, for example an infection, is treated.

Assessing the nervous system

Conventionally, assessment of the nervous system in older people – neurological assessment – will normally be carried out by a geriatrician, and a psychogeriatrician will assess personality, behaviour, cognition and mood. In practice, both specialists should examine all these aspects of the nervous system. The purpose of such assessment will be to detect how well the nervous system of the older person is functioning and to diagnose or eliminate any adverse changes that may be causing that person to require medical and nursing care.

There is a wide range of conditions affecting the nervous system but, in older people, dementia and Parkinson's disease are more common and these may be detected by neurological examination. The nervous system cannot be observed directly and must be assessed indirectly through, for example:

- the functioning of the skeletomuscular system;
- tests for cognitive function;
- memory;
- assessment of mood;
- balance;
- reflexes.

A complete neurological assessment may not be possible at one meeting with an older person, as the person may tire easily, which will have an adverse effect or may limit the assessment. Occasionally, more than one visit may be required and imaginative ways of assessing neurological function – such as observing the person undressing and dressing again – will probe several aspects of the function of the nervous system such as memory, posture, stiffness and fine movement co-ordination.

Ultimately, the challenge for the geriatrician is to distinguish between changes in the nervous system that have occurred as result of ageing and those that may be the result of disease.

Nervous system changes with ageing

There are a few gross changes to the nervous system that can be identified. However, there are some ageing changes that can be observed after death, such as:

- demyelination of nerves;
- swelling of the axons of nerve cells;
- the accumulation of abnormal areas in the brain called neurofibrillary plaques and tangles.

Cell survival in the nervous system also decreases with age. Nevertheless, the nervous system displays 'plasticity' whereby 'long-term compensatory and adaptive changes' (Timiras 1998) are displayed, which mean that the loss of function in one area is often compensated for by another area. This phenomenon, whilst slowed down with ageing, is not lost. However, when illness is present the balance can be tipped away from normal function of the nervous system. For instance, older people admitted to hospital might become confused for no apparent reason other than that they are in an unfamiliar environment – something that will pass quickly as they become used to the new surroundings and their underlying condition improves.

There are circulatory changes in the brain that correlate with common arterial ageing changes such as atherosclerosis (Timiras 1998), and this may lead to bleeding and infarcts in the brain (strokes). These can have a range of effects on an older person, from the very minor to the devastating. The levels of neurotransmitters (eg acetylcholine and noradrenaline) do not change significantly in the nervous system but the balance between these neurotransmitters changes subtly with age. In health this is usually of no consequence but in illness the balance may be tipped in favour of mental health impairment.

Sleep disturbance increases with age and the incidence of abnormalities that would be described as pathological in younger people increases with age. However, this is a difficult area of neurological assessment because individual sleep patterns vary. Whilst older people may seem to sleep for adequate lengths of time, they often undergo sleep patterns that are less restful than those of younger people (Timiras 1998).

Sensory deprivation

Many of the remaining changes in the nervous system that occur with ageing may be grouped under the heading of sensory deprivation. Such changes include alterations to:

- hearing
- vision
- smell
- taste
- physical sensation.

There is an inevitable decline in hearing with age although the extent to which this is adverse varies (Le May 1999). The reasons for hearing loss with ageing include impaction of earwax or cerumen, presbyacusis resulting from ageing of the components of the hearing system, and tinnitus which results in a constant ringing in the ears.

For some older people it is just a matter of losing higher pitched sounds, but for some it can turn others' conversation into meaningless strings of vowels as consonants are confused or lost (Surman 1998).

Vision declines with age and this happens through a combination of mechanisms, including opacity of the lens (cataracts), increased pressure within the eyes (glaucoma), weakening of the eye muscles and the muscles of the iris, drooping of the eyelids (blepharoptosis) and degeneration of the nerve supply to the eye. The combined effect with ageing is a reduction in visual field and also in visual acuity. It is harder to see colours and, therefore, contrasts between objects. It is also harder for the older person to adapt when moving quickly between light and dark environments.

The ability to taste declines with age (Pathy 1998) and the declining sense of taste affects all dimensions of taste (sweet, sour, salty and bitter). Taste is also influenced by the sense of smell and this, too, declines with age. Some older people may be observed to add large amounts of salt and pepper to their food in an effort to make it taste better (Surman 1998).

Despite the fact that older people may complain of sensory ailments such as aches and pains and may complain of feeling cold or hot when others feel comfortable, the fact is that our tactile senses do decline with age, as does our ability to detect heat and cold (Pathy 1998). However, these changes may not be very large or significant, and too much should not be made of them – they are mostly laboratory observations and contradictory evidence abounds.

What does seem clear, though, is that there is an age-associated decline in the ability of the skin to detect temperature changes through increases in the 'threshold' levels of stimuli required to evince a response. It is unclear if older people really experience less acute pain for a given stimulus than their younger counterparts (Goff 1999). There is, on the other hand, plenty of evidence that older people suffer from chronic pain from, for example, arthritis and back problems.

Reflexes

The tendon reflexes, such as the knee and ankle jerk reflexes, may be difficult to elicit in some older people. These are used to investigate the nervous system in adults but may not be applicable to all older people. On the other hand, a range of primitive reflexes usually observed only in children may reappear in some older people (Pathy 1998). There would seem to be no clinical relevance to many of these observations.

However, some of these reflexes may be more common or more pronounced in older people with dementia or Parkinson's disease. For instance, the grasp reflex, elicited by stroking the hand, is rare in healthy old age but substantially correlated with cognitive impairment (Pathy 1998). Tremor is often thought to be associated with old age but this is not supported by research. People with tremors in old age usually developed this when they were younger.

Posture

According to Pathy (1998) normal erect posture is 'relatively uncommon in old age'. Typically, an older person may stand with their hips and knees slightly flexed. Some of this is caused by changes in the skeletomuscular system, but there are aspects of the nervous system concerned with balance (vestibular) functions and the ability to sense where the body is in space (proprioception) which later alter with age.

Everyday aspects of daily life, such as rising from a chair or transferring from a bed to a chair, are dependent upon vestibular and proprioceptive function. An adverse consequence of ageing is that these complex actions may lead to falls, which are more common in older people.

Implications for care

Implications for care include aspects of neurological change in:

- hearing (see Chapter 17);
- vision (see Chapter 18);
- comfort and safety (see Chapter 22);
- taste and smell (see Chapters 33–35);
- balance (see Chapter 24).

An older person, especially one who is ill and either admitted to hospital or receiving care at home, may be unable to understand what is happening and what the consequences of illness are likely to be, not because of confusion but because of poor hearing.

However, an older person may be reluctant to admit to poor hearing and equally reluctant to wear a hearing aid. Therefore, it should not be assumed that an older person has heard and understood advice about, for example, taking medications (see Chapter 25). The professional should ensure that such advice has been heard and understood.

An older person at home may have considerable autonomy in the choice and preparation of food. However, hospital diets are notoriously bland, and nurses can help older people to select foods that are more tasty, or can liaise with catering staff to provide food to which an older person does not have to add copious amounts of seasoning.

Restricted vision can make adaptation to a new environment hard for an older person, especially if the decor and furnishing are such that there are few contrasts (Surman 1998) (see Chapter 10). For these reasons all staff should be aware of safety and orientation in an older person, particularly in hospital. Related to safety is the decreased ability in some older people to sense changes in heat and cold or to act upon these changes. Professionals must be aware of the possibilities of both hypo- and hyperthermia.

Finally, on safety, the possibility of falls in older people should always be considered – and the risk is greater in unfamiliar environments. If an older person falls, this is not normal and each incident should be reported and investigated.

14 Endocrine system function

Roger Watson

The endocrine system comprises glands that secrete chemicals, called hormones, which regulate the activity of other target tissues. Along with the nervous system, the endocrine system is responsible for maintaining homoeostasis in the body. This is enabled by a negative feedback system (Gould 1999) whereby, once the action of the hormone is complete, the response of the target tissue will ensure that the release of the hormone is decreased, and vice versa. An example of a homoeostatic system regulated by a hormone is the regulation of blood glucose levels by insulin. In response to raised blood glucose the pancreas releases insulin, which acts to lower blood glucose by increasing absorption into tissues such as the liver that use and store glucose. As blood glucose levels decline in response to the action of insulin, the secretion of insulin by the pancreas declines. The endocrine system – which comprises several glands, including the pancreas, the thyroid glands, the adrenal glands and the gonads – is under the control of the pituitary gland, which resides in the base of the brain attached to the hypothalamus with which it works closely. The pituitary is the master gland (Christiansen and Grzybowski 1993), which controls the actions of the remaining endocrine glands through its own secretions which are, in turn, controlled by negative feedback.

Ageing and the endocrine system

As with all systems of the body, there is some effect on the endocrine system as a result of ageing. The general changes are summarised in Table 14.1. It is not clear if the observed changes in the endocrine system are a prelude to ageing or whether they are a result of ageing. Whatever the primary effect, there are some clear changes in endocrine function, described below (Schofield 1999).

Table 14.1 *Age-related changes in endocrine function*

Body tissue	Changes
Most glands	Some glandular atrophy and fibrosis; decreased secretion rate; decreased metabolic destruction and renal excretion of hormones, leading to elevated blood levels
Most target tissues	Changes in sensitivity
Hypothalamus and pituitary	Decreased sensitivity to negative feedback

Adapted from Christiansen and Grzybowski (1993)

- *Antidiuretic hormone*: the ability to concentrate urine declines with age, and this may be due to decreased sensitivity of the renal tubules.
- *Growth hormone*: by the age of 65 years the levels of growth hormone fall to about 50 per cent of adult levels, which may have an influence on bone density, skin thickness and lean body mass.
- *Insulin*: glucose tolerance declines with age and this may be due to insufficient release of insulin in response to raised blood glucose levels and reduced sensitivity of cells to insulin.
- *Glucagon*: also released by the pancreas, glucagon is responsible for raising blood glucose levels; the liver cells, which are its target, show increased sensitivity with age.
- *Thyroid hormones*: despite atrophy of the thyroid gland there is little change in the activity of thyroid hormones with age. Nevertheless, older people are more susceptible to hypothy-

roidism, a condition where there is decreased thyroid hormone secretion – considered below.

- *Cortisol*: corticosteroids (glucocorticoids and mineralocorticoids) are secreted by the adrenal gland. Cortisol, which is secreted by the adrenal cortex and plays a role in glucose metabolism, is produced in a diurnal pattern under the control of adrenocorticotrophic hormone, and the amplitude of this pattern decreases with age.
- *Adrenaline and noradrenaline*: the levels of these hormones increase with age but the sensitivity of target tissues declines. One consequence may be orthostatic (or postural) hypotension (Reeve 2000).
- *Sex hormones*: in women the production of oestrogen and progesterone declines with age. Following the menopause the ovaries lose their responsiveness to circulating sex hormones and there is some evidence that testosterone levels decline with age in females. In males, the production of testosterone declines with age but the renal clearance is reduced and circulating levels remain sufficient for reproductive capacity well into later years.

Consequences of changes with age in the endocrine system

In common with many other changes that accompany ageing, the changes observed in the endocrine system have no serious consequences in healthy older people but will become more evident in illness. Older people are less able to maintain homoeostasis than their younger counterparts, especially in illness, and this may be a consequence of changes in the endocrine system. However, two major endocrine disorders are associated with old age: diabetes mellitus and thyroid disease. They are considered below (Christiansen and Grzybowski 1993).

Diabetes mellitus

Diabetes mellitus is the most common endocrine disorder in old age, and adult-onset (type 2, or non-insulin-dependent) diabetes is more common in older people. This may be the result of autoimmune disease whereby the body begins to attack and destroy its own tissues. Older people do have impaired glucose tolerance as described above and there may be some overlap between the changes observed as a result of ageing and type 2 diabetes, making diagnosis quite difficult. Moreover, the widely accepted criteria for diagnosing diabetes mellitus and those for impaired glucose tolerance published by the World Health Organization are not age-adjusted (Sommerville 1999). There are some signs and symptoms that may indicate diabetes mellitus in older people and these are given in Box 14.1.

Box 14.1 Signs and symptoms suggesting diabetes mellitus in older people

General: increased eating and drinking, increased urine production and weight loss

Recurrent infections

Neurological disorder: loss of sensation and weakness

Arterial disease

Small vessel disease: kidneys and eyes

Skin lesions

Adapted from Goldberg, Andres and Bierman (1984)

Thyroid disease

Disorders of the thyroid are relatively common in older people, and hypothyroidism (reduced thyroid secretions) is more common than hyperthyroidism (increased thyroid secretions). Hypothyroidism, in common with diabetes mellitus, may be another autoimmune disorder, and will lead to lethargy, cold intolerance and immobility. Hyperthyroidism, or thyrotoxicosis, in older people will lead to heat intolerance, weakness, muscle wasting and weight loss (Christiansen and Grzybowski 1993). The classic signs of this disorder in younger people – goitre and protruding eyes – are rarely observed in older people.

Assessing endocrine function in older people

Assessing endocrine function in older people is focused on detecting diabetes mellitus and thyroid disorders.

Table 14.2 *Essential components of endocrine system assessment in older people*

History	Component
Family	History of diabetes or thyroid disease

Symptoms	Component
Diabetes mellitus	Fatigue; weakness; excessive appetite; thirst; rapid weight loss; obesity
Hypo-thyroidism	Decreased cold tolerance; lethargy; constipation; muscle weakness; pain; stiffness; loss of sense of smell; slow/inappropriate answers to questions
Hyper-thyroidism	Angina; confusion; emotional lability; weakness; fatigue; weight loss; increased cold tolerance; decreased heat tolerance

Physical	Component
Diabetes	Thinning of skin; skin infections; decreased temperature sensation; cataracts; diminished reflexes
Hypo-thyroidism	Lifeless, dry hair; coarse, dry and thickened skin; prominent lips and nostrils; sparse eyebrows; enlarged heart; husky, weak voice
Hyper-thyroidism	Skin warm, damp, fine and smooth; staring eyes; tremor; tachycardia

Adapted from Linton, Lee and Matteson (1988)

Endocrine system assessment can be considered under history and physical assessment. Table 14.2 lists the aspects of history that should be taken into consideration and the relevant features of physical assessment. Many of the signs of hypothyroidism are commonly overlooked. If diabetes mellitus is diagnosed, the assessment is not complete until the older person's ability to cope with the condition is assessed. Box 14.2 lists some factors that should be taken into account.

> **Box 14.2 *Factors interfering with control of diabetes in the older person***
>
> Alterations in the senses: diminished vision and smell, altered taste perception
>
> Difficulty preparing and eating food: tremor, arthritis, poor dentition, altered gastrointestinal function
>
> Altered renal and hepatic function
>
> Diminished exercise and mobility
>
> Presence of other diseases: other chronic diseases, cancer, infection, neuropsychiatric impairment, depression, dementia
>
> Social factors: poor education, poor diet, living alone, poverty
>
> Drugs: other medications, alcoholism
>
> Adapted from Lipson (1985)

Conclusion

The changes that take place with ageing in the endocrine system are subtle and generally, with the possible exception of the changes in the reproductive system in middle-aged women and older men, of little consequence in health. However, diabetes mellitus and thyroid disorders (hypo- and hyperthyroidism) are sufficiently common for special attention to be paid to these conditions in the assessment of older people.

15 **Skin**

Mary Woolliams

As the largest organ in the body, the skin can offer valuable information about the general health of an older person. The importance of the skin as an organ of the human body for people of all ages is often underestimated, but it has several vital functions.

This chapter aims to inform the reader of the basic tools needed in order to carry out a comprehensive assessment of an older person's skin. The functions of the skin and the ways in which the ageing process and specific medical problems can affect the skin are discussed in a holistic approach to skin assessment. The chapter focuses on assessment of skin for general health, rather than on the diagnosis and treatment of specific dermatological conditions. For further information on common skin disorders in older people, see Smoker (1999), Penzer and Finch (2001) and Hill (2002).

Functions of the skin

The skin has several vital functions:

- acting as a barrier to the external environment, protecting the body from pathogens, irritants, trauma and ultraviolet light, and preventing dehydration;
- holding internal organs together, keeping the body in the correct shape;
- providing immunological protection;
- sensory – the skin has an important role in the body's perception of external physical stimuli;
- temperature regulation;

- synthesis of vitamin D;
- enhancement of body image and comfort – healthy skin contributes to a greater self-esteem and can make a great difference to a person's comfort.

Each of these functions is important in maintaining good general health and illustrates the importance of the skin as an organ of the body. Care of the skin is therefore essential in the prevention of illness and the promotion of good health for older people.

Changes to the skin in ageing

The ageing process can adversely affect skin functioning. Physiological changes, along with medical problems, can have a significant impact on the health of the skin of an older person:

- dermal cells are replaced more slowly, slowing the healing process;
- blood vessels become more fragile, reducing the supply of blood to skin;
- elastin and collagen fibres become linked more loosely; skin is less elastic and therefore more vulnerable to trauma and shearing forces;
- sensory receptors transmit sensation less rapidly, resulting in a slower response to pain and other stimuli, which can in turn result in damage to skin;
- reduced activity of skin cells that produce natural oils means that the skin dries more quickly;
- the subcutaneous fat layer becomes thinner (Christiansen and Grzybowski 1993).

Other common problems that older people may experience can also threaten a person's skin integrity. These include:

- Decreased peripheral sensation: reduced response to pain; increased risk of trauma and pressure ulcers.
- Decreased mobility: increased risk of pressure ulcers; slowing of circulation, especially venous return; increased risk of limb oedema and leg ulceration.

- Incontinence: increased risk of skin maceration and breakdown (Lyder et al 1992).
- Depression/dementia: increased risk of self-neglect/self-harm, which could potentially lead to poor skin integrity.
- Polypharmacy: increased risk of drug reactions such as rashes of varying severity; long-term use of some drugs – steroids, for example – can affect skin integrity.
- Diabetes: can affect wound healing, sensation, circulation.
- Vascular changes: peripheral vascular disease, for example, can cause poor circulation to skin and extremities, and this will result in slower healing, ulcers, and so on.
- Poor nutritional status: can lead to poor healing and to greater vulnerability to pressure sores and skin breakdown.
- Heart failure: can lead to oedema, causing the skin to be more vulnerable to damage.
- Pruritus (itching): this affects at least 50 per cent of people aged 60 and over (Hill 2002). The main cause of pruritus is dry skin. If itching is persistent and does not respond to emollients, underlying causes should be looked for. Common causes include renal failure (uraemia), liver disease, iron-deficiency anaemia, diabetes and hypothyroidism.

Many of these problems are treatable; if treated, the condition of the skin can be greatly improved and the risk of skin breakdown reduced significantly. There are therefore many factors to take into account when assessing the skin of an older person, and an informed assessment can be extremely important in assisting an older person's recovery from illness.

The process of assessing skin

Assessment of skin should not be a single event when a practitioner first meets an older person; rather, it should be an ongoing process. In assessing a person's skin, the goals will be to treat any existing problems, in partnership with other members of the multidisciplinary team, and to prevent potential problems through education and intervention. Empowerment – encouraging involvement of the older person in planning care for his or her condition – is also important to consider.

Both acute and chronic skin problems may be identified. Acute problems will require an immediate response, whereas chronic problems will require more long-term planning.

A holistic and systematic approach to the assessment of the skin of an older person makes use of the following four senses.

Listening

Ask the person and/or carers sensitively about any previous skin problems. Have there been any recent changes to the skin? Refer also to the person's medical notes and nursing history for any details relating to skin. Ask about:

- *Past medical history* Any skin problems past or present noted? Any other medical problems that might affect skin quality or healing – for example, diabetes or peripheral vascular disease?

- *Drug history and current medications* Any treatment for skin conditions in the past? Any current drugs or treatments for the skin? Is the person taking any other drugs that might affect skin condition – steroids, for example? Any history of drug allergies? Is the person taking any drugs that might cause allergic reactions – for example, antibiotics?

- *Skin care routine* What is the person's current skin care routine? What products, such as soap and creams, are currently used? Have any products been changed recently?

- *Psychological well-being* Is the older person under any particular stresses at present?

- *Body image* How does the person feel about his or her body image?

Looking

When observing the person for skin problems, photos, drawings, accurate measurements and detailed descriptions can be used to make ongoing assessment as simple and as accurate as possible. They can be particularly useful when the specific cause of a change in the skin is not easily identified. They can also be used in conjunction with assessment and planning tools such as wound charts.

Assess general skin quality of the whole body. Look for specific problems such as dry skin, oedema, variations in skin colour, bruising, inflammation, jaundice (eyes and skin), swelling (shiny skin), breaks, sores, lesions, warts, and so on. Look for and describe any specific problems such as rashes, infestations such as head lice or scabies, broken areas (damaged barrier function), ulcers, and infections such as ringworm or athlete's foot.

Assess pressure areas for signs of potential or actual breakdown. If there are any breaks, take a photo if possible or draw a picture, giving accurate measurements and showing exact shapes. Again, try to describe what you see as clearly as possible. A useful and widely used tool to assess for the risk of developing pressure sores is the one developed by Waterlow (1988). It is reasonably quick and simple to use. Such a tool enables the nursing team to plan interventions needed to prevent breakdown of the skin and to assist the healing of existing sores.

Assess for any continence problems that may affect the condition of the skin, and consider how management of the incontinence might be improved. Examine the flexures (skin folds) – parts of the body where two layers of skin rub together, such as breasts, groins, axillae and between the toes. These are vulnerable to problems such as infection and breakdown. Warm, relatively damp conditions in these areas are ideal conditions for developing fungal infections, so they need to be washed and dried carefully, and the use of unperfumed talc is recommended.

Touch

Use your hands to assess the following:

- *Texture and moisture* Is the skin smooth or coarse? Is it dry?
- *Turgor* Is the skin layer firm and resistant to being pinched – on the forearm or chest, for example? Or does the skin 'tent' or stay in condition when pinched? Tenting can be a result of normal changes in ageing skin but can also be an indicator of dehydration or malnutrition.
- *Temperature* Is the skin hot or cold? Are there variations around the body? A hot area could indicate inflammation (eg cellulitis); a cold area could indicate decreased arterial blood supply and vascular changes.

Smell

Although we might not use this sense consciously, our sense of smell can tell us a lot about a person's skin condition. Has the older person been able to wash adequately? Is there a related odour? What is the condition of the flexures – between the toes, for example, or under the breasts? Are there indications of incontinence? Are there any areas of the body that seem to smell more, or differently, than others? This might not necessarily be related only to hygiene; for example, in some malignant diseases the skin can emit specific odours (McGovern and Kuhn 1992; Pedley 1999).

Conclusion

A thorough assessment of the condition of an older person's skin is extremely important. Effective partnership and communication between practitioners, the older person, the person's carers, the multidisciplinary team and dermatology specialists is vital to ensure that both acute and chronic problems are attended to effectively and that ongoing solutions to these problems are planned appropriately. Such interventions can help improve significantly the quality of life for older people.

16 **Laboratory tests**

Philip Woodrow

Blood is the transport mechanism of the body, and measuring the blood content of a range of substances provides information about what is happening in the body. With nurses undertaking advanced practice roles in health care, interpreting and acting on blood results will be more common. Therefore, knowing normal ranges of blood values and likely causes of abnormalities from more commonly encountered diseases enables earlier intervention.

There are many tests that can be performed on blood. This chapter describes briefly some of the more important tests for:

- haematology
- liver function tests (LFTs)
- cardiac enzymes
- biochemistry.

Abnormally low levels of anything in blood are caused by one or more of:

- dilution
- loss
- failure

of supply or production.

High levels are caused by one or more of:

- dehydration (haemoconcentration)
- excessive intake/production

- failure to clear (usually kidney and/or liver failure).

Older people may experience any of these due to illness (acute or chronic), treatment (eg diuretics) or declining function (including mobility).

This chapter focuses on diseases that may cause abnormal blood results in older people, but the possibility of underlying water imbalance, which will affect most results, should also be considered. The possibility of two or more different problems affecting results, in either similar or dissimilar ways, should be considered as well.

Normal ranges are cited in brackets after each subheading and in tables, but 'normal' varies between different laboratories and texts, so readers may find slightly different ranges given in their workplace. Results should be interpreted for each individual, considering their own normal function, the trend from any previous tests and their response to any treatments.

Ageing

Healthy ageing should not significantly affect most blood results, although functional and hormone-related changes can occur. Many substances carried in the bloodstream are metabolised by the liver and excreted by the kidneys. Age-related decline in renal and/or hepatic function may therefore cause higher than 'normal' levels of some blood results. With mild liver or kidney dysfunction, abnormal blood results may be the only sign of problems, enabling earlier and often easier treatment. However, blood levels are usually tested when there is some concern, so reduced function and disease often cause abnormal levels. Many diseases, such as type 2 diabetes, are more likely to occur in older people.

Haematology

There are three types of blood cells:

- erythrocytes (red)
- leucocytes (white)
- thrombocytes (platelets).

So a full blood count measures:

- haemoglobin (oxygen carriage)
- white cell count (WCC – immunity)
- platelets (clotting).

Normal levels are listed in Table 16.1 and clotting studies are covered later, in the section on liver function tests.

Table 16.1 **Full blood count (FBC) – normal range**

Test	Normal range
Haemoglobin (Hb)	Female 12–14 grams/decilitre (g/dl) Male 14–18 grams/decilitre (g/dl)
White cell count (WCC)	5–10 × 10^9/litre
Platelets	150–400 × 10^9/litre

All blood cells are produced in bone marrow, so disease (eg cancer) or suppression (eg chemotherapy) of bone marrow causes low counts. Underlying diseases should be treated either actively or palliatively. Palliative treatment or complications from active treatment may necessitate supplements of factors that are low.

Haemoglobin (Hb)

[female 12–14, male 14–18 grams/decilitre (g/dl)]

Although gender differences are widely cited, in younger people these are caused mainly by menstrual blood loss and, to a lesser extent, by testosterone-mediated production. Somerville (1999) suggests that for both genders haemoglobin levels are not significantly affected by ageing.

Haemoglobin may be increased to compensate for chronic hypoxia. In very high altitudes (eg in the Andes), this occurs because of low oxygen pressure in air. Older people with lung disease, such as chronic obstructive pulmonary disease, often develop compensatory polycythaemia. As this response is a symptom, not a cause, of the problem, compensatory high haemoglobin levels should not be treated.

More often, low haemoglobin levels are seen. Low levels may be caused by:

- blood loss
- bone marrow suppression
- anaemias.

Haemoglobin carries oxygen, so low haemoglobin may necessitate blood transfusion (packed cells) to increase oxygen carriage. Causes of anaemia should be treated. Iron deficiency is the most common cause of anaemia in older people (Somerville 1999). People with iron-deficient diets should be offered advice about dietary sources of iron, such as liver, but may need iron supplement tablets or injections. Pernicious anaemia is caused by lack of the intrinsic factor produced in the stomach, from partial or total gastrectomy, or from prolonged gastritis, so vitamin B_{12} supplements may be needed, often for the remainder of the person's life.

Oxygen delivery to tissues, rather than oxygen carriage in blood, should be the goal of treating abnormal haemoglobin levels. Oxygen delivery relies on capillary perfusion, which is improved with a slight anaemia.

White cell count (leucocytes)

[total WCC 5–10 × 10^9/litre]

White blood cells (leucocytes) are part of the immune system, so deficiency places people at greater risk of infection. Older people tend to produce fewer white cells (Somerville 1999), contributing to impaired immunity in many. Numbers of white cells are measured in units of 10^9/litre (Table 16.2).

Table 16.2 *Types of white cells (× 10^9/litre)*

Type of white cell	Normal range
Neutrophils (polymorphs)	2.5–7.5
Basophils	< 0.2
Eosinophils	0.04–0.44
Monocytes	0.2–0.8
Lymphocytes	1.5–4.0

White cell counts are usually raised by the body mobilising and producing more cells because of infection or immune responses, and are a sign of underlying problems usually requiring treatment. Temperature, traditionally considered a sign of (or absence of) infection, may not be raised despite infection, especially in older people, or may be raised from non-infective causes. Where infection is suspected, or the person is unaccountably drowsy or confused, a white cell count can help indicate or exclude problems. However, immunodeficiency may inhibit white cell production, so infection cannot be excluded in people who do not have raised white cell counts, especially older people. If counts are raised from inappropriately excessive immune responses, production can be reduced with steroids.

Severe infection, such as severe sepsis, can cause abnormally low counts, as white cells are destroyed more quickly than they can be produced. More often, counts are low owing to impaired production (bone marrow suppression from disease or treatments). The white cell count can be increased by giving granulocyte colony-stimulating factor (G-CSF), but this is relatively expensive and takes about one week to become effective, so tends to be used only in specialities such as oncology. A low white cell count (leucopenia) exposes people to greater risk from infection, so infection control becomes especially important. Protective isolation (reverse barrier nursing) may be necessary with very low counts. Granulocyte counts below $0.5 × 10^9$ often necessitate isolation, although decisions to isolate protectively should be individualised, weighing benefits of preventing infection against psychological and other problems caused by isolation. Asepsis with careful hand-washing, plastic aprons and gloves often provides sufficient protection, although current practice tends to favour isolation and hand hygiene.

In addition to measuring the total white cell count, identifying different types of white cells can indicate specific problems. Viewing under a microscope enables division into two main groups – granulocytes and agranulocytes, depending on whether granules are seen in the cell membranes. There are further subgroups, described below and identified in Table 16.2.

Granulocytes

Granulocytes circulate to destroy invading organisms. Laboratory staining can identify three types:

- neutrophils
- basophils
- eosinophils.

Most white cells (50–70 per cent) are neutrophils; neutrophil levels increase with acute inflammation. *Neutrophils* are polymorphonuclear, sometimes abbreviated to 'polymorphs'. A low neutrophil count is called neutropenia. *Basophil* counts increase during healing or prolonged inflammation. *Eosinophils* destroy parasites (Minors 2001) and remove immune complexes from blood; raised eosinophil counts can be caused by parasitic infection or allergic conditions.

Agranulocytes

Normally, there are few agranulocytes present, but levels increase with chronic conditions. Agranulocytes are either monocytes or lymphocytes (T cells, B cells, that recognise and destroy antigens).

Platelets

[150–400 × 10^9/litre]

Platelets (thrombocytes) are used to form blood clots. They are normally kept inactive by various chemicals (eg prostacyclin) produced by the endothelium lining blood vessels. Following a cut, endothelium of damaged blood vessels fails to produce inhibitory chemicals and platelets are activated.

Platelet counts may be low if production fails (bone marrow suppression) or large numbers are used or lost – for example, during haemorrhage. Underlying causes of low platelet counts may require treatment. Each person should be assessed individually for risk factors; for example, people prone to falls or undergoing highly invasive procedures, such as surgery, may need platelet transfusion to restore near-normal levels ('platelet cover'). Bone marrow suppression may be an unfortunate but unavoidable side effect of therapies such as chemotherapy, so, if the problem cannot be treated, people should at least be warned that they are at risk of prolonged bleeding and should therefore minimise risks. For example, electric razors may be preferable to wet shaving.

Spontaneous bleeding is rare provided that counts remain above 40–50, so platelet transfusions are not routinely given until levels fall to 10×10^9/litre. However, if invasive procedures (such as the removal of epidural catheters), investigations or treatments (eg surgery) are planned, platelet cover may be given to prevent excessive bleeding.

Liver function tests

Except for the brain, the liver is probably the most complex of all vital organs. It has very many functions, so liver dysfunction can be measured by raised blood levels of various enzymes and metabolites normally cleared by the liver. The main tests are listed in Table 16.3.

The liver metabolises bilirubin (a waste product from the breakdown of old red blood cells), so with cirrhosis, and other diseases that obstruct flow through the liver, bilirubin levels are raised, and the person often appears jaundiced.

The liver produces albumin (the main plasma protein) and clotting factors. With liver failure, serum albumin is low and clotting times are prolonged.

Table 16.3 *Main liver function tests (LFTs) – normal range*

Test	Normal range
Bilirubin	1–20 µmol/litre
Alkaline phosphatase (Alk Phos)	< 100 iu/litre
Aspartate aminotransferase (AST)	< 40 iu/litre
Alanine aminotransferase (ALT)	< 40 iu/litre
Albumin	35–50 g/litre
Total protein	60–80 g/litre
Gamma glutamyl transpeptidase	10–48 iu/litre
(Activated) Partial thromboplastin time (PTT/APTT)	28–34 seconds
Prothrombin time (PT)	10–12 seconds
International normalised ratio (INR)	0.9–1.1

Albumin

[35–50 g/litre or 3.5–5.0 g/decilitre]

Albumin is produced, but not stored, in the liver. It has a half-life of about 20 days and levels start to decline significantly after ten or more days of liver dysfunction. Albumin is the main plasma protein, so low serum albumin causes excessive extravasation of plasma, hypovolaemia and hypotension.

Clotting

[PTT 28–34 seconds; PT 10–12 seconds; INR 0.9–1.1; D-dimer < 250 nanograms/ml or micrograms (µg) litre (or 'negative')]

Clotting factors are produced in the liver, so liver damage or anything that interferes with coagulation causes prolonged clotting. With anti-coagulant treatment (such as warfarin), the INR should be maintained at 2–4 (Minors 2001).

The main clotting tests are:

- (activated) partial thromboplastin time (PTT or APTT)
- prothrombin time (PT)
- international normalised ratio (INR)
- D-dimers.

PTT, PT and INR all measure clotting ability. Normal prothrombin time can vary between different batches of thromboplastin, so PTT and PT are usually given against a control (Minors 2001).

When fibrinolysis dissolves clots, fibrin degradation products (FDPs) are released. FDPs are therefore useful indicators of thrombus formation (eg pulmonary emboli, deep vein thromboses). D-Dimers are the most frequently measured FDP: they have a half-life of eight hours, and are cleared through urine. Normal levels are sometimes reported as 'negative'. Higher levels are often found in older people, especially if renal function is impaired.

Cardiac enzymes

When cells are damaged or destroyed, enzymes from inside the cell are released. Measuring enzymes produced only by heart cells therefore enables assessment of whether myocardial infarction has occurred. Creatine kinase (CK), and its cardiac-specific isoenzyme CK-MB, used to be the main enzyme employed to detect myocardial infarction, but the Joint European Society of Cardiology/American College of Cardiology Committee (2000) recommend troponin testing instead, because troponin tests are more reliable.

There are two types of cardiac-specific troponin – T and I. Both are released within three hours of cardiac injury and remain raised for up to two weeks (Jowett and Thompson 2003). In health, troponin levels are normally undetectable, although this may reflect relatively poor sensitivity of current tests. Damage to the cells of other organs may also release small amounts of troponin, but levels above 1 microgram/litre usually indicate myocardial infarction; results may be given as 'positive' or 'negative'.

Enzyme tests can also be used to identify other tissue damage, depending on the type of enzyme tested. For example, cerebral vascular accidents (CVAs, strokes) can be detected by creatine kinase (CK) and its brain-specific isoenzyme CK-BB.

Biochemistry

Biochemistry results are too extensive to include here in full. The most important tests are usually:

- sodium
- potassium

and, to a slightly lesser extent,

- glucose
- phosphate
- magnesium
- calcium
- urea
- creatinine.

Most of these are included in urea and electrolyte (U+E) tests, although blood glucose generally requires a separate sample. Normal ranges are shown in Table 16.4.

Sodium (Na$^+$)

[135–145 mmol/litre]

Sodium is the main plasma and interstitial cation (positively charged ion). Hyponatraemia is most often caused by sodium loss, and is the most common electrolyte disorder in older people (Somerville 1999). Reabsorption of sodium in the kidney is controlled by the adrenal hormone aldosterone, so lack of aldosterone causes excessive loss of renal sodium and hyponatraemia. Severe hyponatraemia (< 120 mmol/litre) can cause encephalopathy. Other possible causes of sodium loss include vomiting, diarrhoea and excessive sweating.

Table 16.4 **Main biochemistry results – normal range**

Test	Normal range
Sodium (Na^+)	135–145 mmol/litre
Potassium (K^+)	3.5–4.5 mmol/litre
Glucose, fasting	3.3–6 mmol/litre
Phosphate (PO_4^{3-})	0.85–1.45 mmol/litre
Magnesium (Mg^{2+})	0.70–1.05 mmol/litre
(total) Calcium (Ca^{2+})	2.25–2.75 mmol/litre
Urea	3–9 mmol/litre
Creatinine	60–120 micromole (µmol)/litre

Sodium can be replaced in the diet or by intravenous infusion. With intravenous replacement, normal saline (0.9%) will usually be given, as healthy kidneys reabsorb most (99 per cent) sodium, but will excrete excess water.

Hypernatraemia is usually caused by dehydration (water loss), both from the body (eg polyuria) and into tissue spaces and cells (oedema). This causes the total amount of sodium in the blood to remain the same but concentrated into a smaller volume. With dehydration, most other results will similarly be raised. The treatment for dehydration is to rehydrate the person using oral fluids if possible, but with intravenous fluids (eg 5% glucose) if oral replacement is impractical.

Management of salt (and water) balance will be influenced by individual conditions. For example, patients with congestive cardiac failure and/or renal disease may be managed with fluid or salt restrictions.

Potassium (K+)

[3.5–4.5 mmol/litre]

Nearly all potassium loss from the body is in urine – 90 per cent – so abnormal potassium levels usually reflect abnormal urine output. Although excessive potassium loss is usually caused by polyuria, it can also be caused through poor diet or large gastrointestinal loss (eg vomiting). Potassium is used for cardiac conduction, so hypokalaemia can cause failure of cardiac conduction, whilst hyperkalaemia can cause over-excitable cardiac conduction and, potentially, cardiac arrest. Slightly high levels are better for cardiac conduction than slightly low levels, so therapeutic levels are often maintained at 4–5 mmol/litre.

Hypokalaemia should be treated with potassium supplements (diet, tablets or intravenous). Intravenous potassium can cause thrombophlebitis, and is often painful, so should be very dilute (eg 20 or 40 mmol/litre). Whenever giving intravenous potassium, nurses should observe for thrombophlebitis or other signs of discomfort/irritation, stopping infusions if these occur. Long-term diuretic therapy should use potassium-sparing diuretics.

Hyperkalaemia is usually caused by:

- renal failure (failure to excrete potassium);
- severe injury (release of intracellular potassium into serum).

Severe hyperkalaemia (serum levels of 7–8 mmol/litre) may be treated with:

- glucose and insulin (IV).

Less severe hyperkalaemia may be treated with:

- calcium resonium (oral, rectal).

Intravenous glucose and insulin lowers serum potassium by transferring potassium from extracellular into intracellular fluid. This quickly averts life-threatening hyperkalaemia but means that the potassium remains in the body, so may re-transfer later back into the plasma. Intravenous calcium counteracts the effects of hyperkalaemia on the heart (Jowett and Thompson 2003). Calcium resonium in the gut acts less quickly, but excretes potassium from the body, provided that resonium is evacuated from the gut.

Glucose ($C_6H_{12}O_6$)

[fasting 3.3–6 mmol/litre]

Blood glucose provides the main source for mitochondria (part of the cell) to produce adenosine triphosphate (ATP), which is used to provide energy for the cell. In health, blood glucose levels are controlled by hormones, of which insulin is the most important. Insulin transports glucose across cell membranes, so insufficient pancreatic production of insulin (diabetes mellitus type 2) or resistance to the effect of insulin (eg from stress, some drugs, diabetes mellitus type 1) cause hyperglycaemia. One in 20 people over 65 have diabetes, rising to one in five over the age of 85 (Department of Health 2003). Most (90 per cent) of people with diabetes have diabetes mellitus type 2, which becomes especially prevalent with increasing age. Insulin overdose causes hypoglycaemia, as excessive amounts of blood sugar are transferred into cells.

Normal blood sugar in people without diabetes was traditionally cited as 4–8 mmol/litre, but Van Den Berghe and colleagues (2001) found that critically ill patients were more likely to survive with blood sugar maintained between 4.4 and 6.1 mmol/litre. Increasing recognition of risks from even slightly elevated blood sugars, together with the National Service Framework for Diabetes, is likely to lead to increasingly active control of hyperglycaemia. With greater prevalence of diabetes, including undiagnosed diabetes, among older people, aiming to maintain blood sugars between 4.4 and 6.1 mmol/litre is likely to reduce risk factors from complications.

Phosphate (PO_4^{3-})

[0.85–1.45 mmol/litre]

Normally, gut intake of phosphate matches renal loss, and is regulated by parathyroid hormones. Excessive intake, reduced loss, hypoparathyroidism or major trauma may cause high levels; reduced intake, excessive loss or hyperthyroidism may cause low plasma

levels. Alcoholics are especially at risk of having phosphate deficiency. Hyperphosphataemia rarely causes significant problems, and
although hypophosphataemia is usually asymptomatic, it can cause
muscle weakness, increasing the risks of chest infection, reducing
mobility and increasing mortality.

Magnesium (Mg⁺⁺; Mg^{2+})

[0.70–1.05 mmol/litre]

Magnesium is used for energy storage and production, cardiac conduction and vasodilatation. Low levels cause:

- general weakness
- dysrhythmias
- hypertension.

Magnesium is found in many foods, including green vegetables,
cereals and meat. Likely causes of low magnesium are:

- Malnutrition (eg prolonged 'nil by mouth' regimens, difficulty
  swallowing, or other physiological or psychological or social
  causes, including alcoholism).
- Excessive urinary loss (eg poorly controlled diabetes, excessive
  diuretics).
- Excessive gut loss (profuse vomiting, nasogastric drainage,
  diarrhoea).
- Impaired renal conservation.

Muscle weakness from low magnesium (and/or phosphate) means
that attempts to mobilise and rehabilitate people after major illness or
surgery are unlikely to succeed.

Calcium (Ca⁺⁺; Ca^{2+})

[total 2.25–2.75 mmol/litre; ionised 1.13–1.32 mmol/litre]

Most (99 per cent) calcium in the body is in bone. The one per cent
in blood has many important functions, including:

- cardiac conduction;
- cell division and repair;
- hormone and neurotransmitter production;
- enzyme activity;
- cell membrane structure;
- blood coagulation.

About half of total blood calcium is normally bound to plasma proteins, of which the main one is albumin. Laboratories usually measure total serum levels, but blood gas and other analysers usually measure ionised calcium. Only the free (ionised, or unbound) calcium is physiologically active, so, with abnormally high or low albumin levels, calcium may be 'corrected' to reflect more accurately its physiological effect.

Blood calcium levels are regulated by various hormones (especially parathyroid). Age-related decline in hormone production can cause leaching of bone calcium into the blood, resulting in brittle bones and hypercalcaemia. Hormone replacement therapy (HRT) may prevent this leaching, so resolving both osteoporosis and hypercalcaemia (Wood 2000).

The main cause of hypocalcaemia is hyperparathyroidism, malignancy being the second most common cause. Other causes include:

- renal loss exceeding gut and bone absorption;
- heparin therapy;
- sepsis;
- pancreatitis.

Hypocalcaemia may necessitate calcium supplements (dietary, tablets or intravenous).

Urea and creatinine

[urea 3–9 mmol/litre; creatinine 60–120 micromole (µmol)/litre)

These are two easily measured waste products of metabolism. High levels normally indicate renal failure.

Urea is produced by protein metabolism, so may also be elevated with (Mahon and Hattersley 2002):

- high-protein diet;
- chronic malnutrition (increased protein metabolism);
- gastrointestinal bleeds (increased protein absorption);
- dehydration (increased urea absorption).

Uraemia is neurotoxic, so may cause acute confusion.

Creatinine usually rises steadily by 50–100 micromole/day, so creatinine levels provide a useful way of assessing how long kidney function has been failing.

Conclusion

The results of blood tests assist medical diagnosis and management. Although diagnosis remains a medical role, nurses often receive blood results first, and so are best placed to recognise complications and initiate interventions (Gibson 1997). Nurses have long been used to monitoring blood sugars to determine insulin therapy. Understanding problems and treatments helps make nursing more interesting and rewarding. But, more important, understanding normal and abnormal levels of other blood results, and likely causes of any abnormalities, enables nurses to initiate earlier interventions or changes of treatment, or contact other professionals. The sooner patients receive any treatment, or changes in treatment, they need, the fewer complications they are likely to suffer.

Sensory functioning and communication

17 **Hearing**

Irene Schofield

The identification and support of older people with hearing disability remains a neglected area, especially among nurses (Tolson 1997; Heron and Wharrad 2000). Auditory assessment must be a fundamental aspect of professional health assessment, considering that poor communication can lead to confusion concerning care, treatment and prognosis, and unnecessary anxiety (Hines 1997; Royal National Institute for Deaf People 2004a). Hearing loss has been reported to cut people off from the world and so they become isolated and at risk of loneliness and depression (Mulrow et al 1990; Strawbridge et al 2000; Tomita et al 2001). A person may have tried a hearing aid for a short time and discarded it because it did not provide the expected improvement in hearing. Care professionals have an important part to play in encouraging older people to have a hearing assessment, and to provide ongoing support to hearing-aid users (Tolson 1997). Support with hearing impairment is an aspect of care where there is enormous potential for care professionals to make a difference to the quality of older people's day-to-day lives (Mulrow et al 1990).

Poor hearing can exacerbate cognitive impairment in older people with dementia (Allen et al 2003), and people with learning disabilities often have some concurrent hearing loss (Lavis 1997). It is important, therefore, to attempt assessment with the help of family or carers and to make a referral to specialist services if hearing disability is detected. This chapter highlights the extent of hearing disability in the older population and provides suggestions on how care professionals can sharpen their assessment skills.

Prevalence of hearing disability

Hearing disability is a common but not inevitable accompaniment to ageing. About 9 million people in the UK have some kind of hearing impairment; some 2 million people have hearing aids but only 1.4 million use them regularly. It is estimated that another 3 million who do not have a hearing aid experience hearing difficulties and would benefit from an aid (Royal National Institute for Deaf People 2004b). Studies carried out by nurses in continuing care wards and nursing homes found that up to 90 per cent of people experienced a degree of hearing disability (Mahoney 1992; Tolson et al 1992; Heron and Wharrad 2000). Hearing loss can be classified in different ways (see Box 17.1).

Box 17.1 Classification of hearing loss

Severity – mild, moderate, severe, profound

Type – sensorineural or conductive

The age at onset of the deafness – pre-lingual or post-lingual

(Slaven 2003)

The majority of hearing-impaired older people will have developed hearing loss after the acquisition of spoken language (post-lingual). A small minority, however, will have been born with or have developed hearing loss prior to this (pre-lingual). Age of onset has implications for the communication approaches required to complete a comprehensive assessment of a person's needs.

Age-related hearing disability

Presbyacusis is the term used to describe hearing impairment brought about by age-related sensorineural changes. Impairment is thought to be caused by loss of hair cells and nerve fibres within the organ of Corti near the oval window of the ear, where high-pitched sound is converted to nerve impulses. The process is bilateral and starts from around the age of 40 years. Presbyacusis is characterised by hearing loss for high-frequency sounds, resulting in poor speech discrimination for consonants. Reduced hearing acuity is exacerbated by high levels of background noise. Normal or slightly louder than normal speech may be perceived as unpleasant or even painful. This hypersensitivity is known as loudness recruitment, and may affect a person's ability to tolerate a hearing aid. Impaired sound localisation makes it difficult to detect where sound is coming from. Sometimes older people are unfairly accused of hearing selectively: it is not uncommon for family and professional carers to say of a person: 'She can hear when she wants to'. According to Gilhome Herbst (1999), patchy auditory performance is characteristic of presbyacusis. This is explained in part by enabling and disabling factors within the listening environment, with the result that on occasions a person will hear conversations, words and names quite clearly, especially if the name mentioned is their own.

Tinnitus can present as an additional problem. This is a constant or recurring high-pitched whistling, buzzing, hissing, ringing or other sounds in the ear, which may be on just one side or on both sides (unilateral or bilateral) and becomes most acute at night and in quiet surroundings. Tinnitus may also be caused by medications, infection and cerumen (wax) accumulation. There is now help available to people who develop tinnitus. Knowledgeable staff can provide information to help people manage the condition (Clinical Guidelines Working Group of the British Tinnitus Association 2001).

Atrophic changes in the sebaceous and apocrine glands in the auditory canal lead to drier cerumen. This, coupled with a narrowed auditory canal and stiff, coarse hairs lining the canal (especially in men), can lead to cerumen becoming impacted. Excessive cerumen causing complete obstruction in the ear canal will dull the hearing and temporarily exacerbate hearing loss caused by presbyacusis.

Otosclerosis or arthritic conditions that affect the joints between the malleus and stapes in the middle ear, causing joint fixation or reduced vibration of these bones, lead to conductive hearing loss.

Older people with impaired hearing may therefore have a combination of problems resulting from sensorineural and conductive causes. Asymmetrical or sudden hearing loss is not characteristic of presbyacusis and needs referral to ear, nose and throat (ENT) specialist medical services. Although presbyacusis is likely to be a major cause of hearing disability in later life, Lim and Stephens (1991) have cautioned that this is not always the case, and that hearing loss might signal an underlying medical condition or be caused by ototoxic medications (eg gentamicin and furosemide).

Hearing loss tends to happen gradually and people with mild to moderate disability may be unaware of any difficulty unless it affects their daily life. An older person might first realise that they have some hearing disability on admission to hospital, especially if they have to strain to hear what is being said against the background noise of a busy ward. Gilhome Herbst (1999) suggests that older people might not want to reveal that they are hard of hearing because of the stigma attached to hearing loss and its association in people's minds with 'senility'. Those who have severe hearing loss are often the butt of jokes. Wearing a hearing aid is a visible sign of hearing disability and a person may decide to postpone acquiring an aid until it seems absolutely necessary. For some people this stage is never reached.

Assessing hearing disability

Someone who was born with or who developed pre-lingual deafness will most likely use British Sign Language (BSL), so it will be important to arrange for a BSL/English interpreter before attempting to carry out a comprehensive assessment. The Royal National Institute for Deaf People (RNID) can advise on how to access this service. A person who already has a hearing aid and uses it regularly will obviously benefit from wearing it, switched on, prior to the assessment. For people who do not use an aid and rely on a combination of lipreading and residual hearing, a range of strategies (see Box 17.2) can be employed by the assessor to promote effective communication during the assessment.

Box 17.2 Strategies for the communicator

Look directly at the person and maintain eye contact.

Don't obstruct your face or turn away when you are speaking.

Make sure the light is on your face.

If the person wears glasses, suggest that they wear them to aid lipreading.

Speak clearly, and a little more slowly than usual.

Rephrase rather than repeat, or write things down.

Use 'plain' everyday language – avoid medical jargon.

Selected from Boots Healthcare and Hearing Concern (undated)

In addition to the above, Tolson (1995 unpublished) has emphasised the importance of a conducive listening environment. In institutional settings, high levels of background noise are common but often avoidable. For example, unwanted noise produced by unregulated and spontaneous use of television and radio, staff talk that ignores the person's comfort, failure to close doors between service and patient areas, and poorly maintained equipment such as trolleys and commodes with squeaky wheels. A quiet, well-lit room with curtains and carpets to minimise echo provides an optimum environment for simple auditory assessment.

The best judge of a person's hearing capability is often the older person themselves (Wu et al 2004). Clark and colleagues (1991) found high levels of accuracy of self-reported hearing loss in older women if it interfered with their day-to-day lives. A few simple questions and observations can reveal a great deal about hearing ability. Reuben and colleagues (1998), in a community study, found that asking only three questions could successfully identify older people with hearing impairment (see Boxes 17.3 and 17.4). Some authors, however, caution against using self-report owing to its lack of sensitivity (Nondahl et al 1998).

> **Box 17.3** *Three key questions for hearing assessment*
>
> Do you have any difficulty hearing and understanding words (even with an aid) in normal conversation?
>
> Do you hear words clearly over the telephone?
>
> Do you hear well enough to carry on a conversation in a crowded room?
>
> (Reuben et al 1998)

A formal screening tool such as the Hearing Handicap Inventory for the Elderly–Short Version (HHIE–S), which consists of 10 items and takes five minutes to administer, might be selected (Ventry and Weinstein 1982). This tool measures emotional and social problems as a result of hearing impairment. It was developed in the USA, however, and cultural differences may preclude its use in the UK. It has an overall accuracy of 75 per cent (Mulrow and Lichenstein 1991). A combination of simple questions about day-to-day living and observations of the person's behaviour during questioning, as suggested in Box 17.4, may provide sufficient clues.

> **Box 17.4** *Questions and observations*
>
> *Questions to ask the patient or service user*
>
> Do you have to turn up the television or radio more than you used to, or does your family complain that the sound is too loud?
>
> Do you sometimes wish people would speak clearly, and stop mumbling?
>
> Do you ever miss your name being called, for example at the doctor's surgery?
>
> Do you sometimes miss what people say to you?
>
> Do you find yourself asking people to repeat things?
>
> Do you find it difficult to hear at social gatherings, in places of worship, or when there is some background noise?

continued

Box 17.4 (continued)

Do you ever have difficulty hearing the door bell or telephone?

Observations

Consider if the person:

- is inattentive to others;
- fails to respond to sounds in the environment;
- asks for things to be repeated;
- cups an ear towards the speaker;
- has difficulty following clear directions;
- seems to be withdrawn or alone much of the time.

Examine the ears with an auroscope for cerumen, signs of infection, and inflammation (following relevant training by, for example, an ENT specialist nurse).

Adapted from Le May (1999) and Help the Aged (1996)

The six-inch whispered voice test (Swan and Browning 1985) (see Box 17.5) is a commonly used simple screening tool but in a recent study it achieved only moderate repeatability (Philp et al 2002). A quiet environment is crucial to reliable use of this test, and training is required to use it. If the person is unable to repeat the message, in the first instance an appropriately trained nurse can examine the ear for signs of cerumen impaction and infection. Cerumen impaction affects up to 34 per cent of people over 60 years (Lewis-Cullinan and Janken 1990), and 90 per cent of temporary hearing loss is caused by occlusion of the ear by impacted cerumen. If the ear canal is blocked by cerumen, current opinion suggests the administration of two or three drops of ordinary olive oil or almond oil (if nut allergy is excluded) over a three-week period in order to soften and dissolve the wax prior to ear irrigation (formerly known as ear syringing). Another suggestion is the weekly administration of olive oil drops, as prophylaxis so as to prevent the need for ear irrigation completely. Practical Support for Clinical Governance (2004) recommends tap water, 0.9%

sodium chloride or sodium bicarbonate ear drops to soften and dissolve cerumen. If ear irrigation needs to be carried out, use of the metal ear syringe is now contraindicated and the pulsed water-jet system is the recommended method (Royal National Institute for Deaf People 2004c).

Box 17.5 *The six-inch whispered voice test*

The assessor stands behind the person at a distance of six inches, takes a deep breath in and, in breathing right out, whispers 'Three-A-Two'.

The person is then asked to repeat this.

If the person failed to hear, the assessor repeats the test once more, this time whispering 'One-F-Three'.

(Swan and Browning 1985)

Use of communication aids

Considering the number of people who experience hearing loss and who are not currently using an aid, it is useful to have an amplification device for communal use, known as a conversation aid, until a personal hearing aid can be dispensed. Amplification devices vary in sophistication and price but generally consist of a battery unit, a microphone and earphones. Almost as effective is a simple ear-trumpet consisting of a tube with an earpiece and a bell shape to concentrate sound. ENT or audiology departments are often willing to lend amplification equipment or to advise on a 'best buy' for your area. The Royal National Institute for Deaf People will also advise on communication aids.

Availability of hearing aids

If the client is willing to be referred for further hearing assessment, perhaps with a view to obtaining a hearing aid through the NHS, it is necessary to be referred by a doctor to an ENT consultant for further specialised assessment. In some areas, people are referred direct to an audiologist for technical assessment and fitting of a hearing aid.

Aids that are purchased privately do not require referral by a GP and are fitted by hearing-aid dispensers.

Purchasing a private hearing aid can be very expensive, and they are not always any more satisfactory than those provided by the NHS. If someone is keen to purchase their own aid, the factsheet published by the Royal National Institute for Deaf People, entitled *Buying a Hearing Aid,* provides helpful guidance. Digital hearing aids that are programmed more accurately than the traditional analogue aid to correct the individual's pattern of hearing loss are now available on the NHS.

NHS audiology services have been criticised in official reports throughout the UK. The reports have also highlighted that sometimes hearing aids are of poor quality and that people have to wait an unacceptable length of time from referral to obtaining a hearing aid. Modernisation programmes are now in progress.

18 **Vision**

Julie Tillotson

In the UK today there are about 2 million people registered blind or partially sighted; 90 per cent of these are aged over 60 (Royal National Institute of the Blind 2002). Many have had visual impairment from an early age and have adjusted to their disability; others have developed eye conditions leading to reduced eyesight at an older age and may cope less well. This chapter identifies the leading causes of visual impairment, suggests ways of assessing visual function and gives practical guidance on actions that can be taken when eyesight is reduced.

Causes of visual loss

Kane (1999) identifies four major causes of sight loss: glaucoma, diabetic retinopathy, cataract and macular degeneration.

Glaucoma

Glaucoma is the term used for a group of eye conditions usually associated with raised pressure within the eye, resulting in damage to the optic nerve. If detected in the early stages, it can be controlled with medication, usually eye drops, surgery or laser treatment. However, if left untreated, it can lead to significant visual field loss with resultant 'tunnel vision'.

The onset of chronic simple or open-angle glaucoma is insidious and the person often has no symptoms. By the time it has affected their vision and they have noticed that they have a 'visual field defect', the optic nerve has already been irreversibly damaged and visual loss cannot be regained. Regular checks at the optometrist's are therefore essential after the age of 40 and, most important, if there is a family history of glaucoma (International Glaucoma Association 2000).

Diabetic retinopathy

This is a condition in which the blood vessels in the retina become leaky; new blood vessels grow, which can leak, resulting in bleeding at the back of the eye (Halle 2002). In the early stages, any effect on the vision generally goes unnoticed. Regular screening can detect retinopathy in the early stages, and laser treatment has proved effective in preventing the progression of retinopathy.

Cataract

A cataract is opacity (clouding) of the lens, the eye's focusing mechanism; causes include trauma, metabolic disease such as diabetes, and age-related changes (Kanski 1997). Cataracts are largely treatable by removing the opaque lens, but patients may have to wait some time for this operation. In the meantime they are visually impaired and can experience problems similar to those of other people with a visual impairment that cannot be treated.

Macular degeneration

Usually referred to as age-related macular degeneration (ARMD), this condition affects about 500,000 of the UK population (Macular Disease Society 2002). Kanski (1997) defines macular degeneration as a degree of visual loss associated with atrophy of the retinal pigment epithelium at the macula in individuals over 50 years old. The macula is a small area of the retina that is responsible for central and detailed vision; damage to this area results in a reduction or loss of central vision and abnormal colour vision.

There are two types of ARMD:

* *Dry (atrophic) ARMD* accounts for about 85 per cent of cases. It is slowly progressive, usually resulting in mild to moderate sight loss, although after 10 years the effects may be more severe

(Macular Disease Society 2002). There is currently no medical treatment for dry macular degeneration but ophthalmologists specialising in this area advise patients who have developed the disease to stop smoking and to take multivitamins in an attempt to prevent the disease from progressing. Research suggests that smoking more than 20 cigarettes a day doubles the risk of ARMD by reducing protective antioxidants in the eye.

- *Wet (neovascular) ARMD* is caused by the growth of abnormal vessels in the macula. These vessels leak into the macula, resulting in blurred and distorted central vision. Although 'wet' ARMD accounts for only 10–15 per cent of all ARMD cases, the visual loss is more severe and occurs within months. Photocoagulation, or more recently photodynamic therapy (PDT), may halt the progression of 'wet' ARMD. However, the treatment is expensive and available only for patients on the NHS who meet the eligibility criteria as laid down by the National Institute for Health and Clinical Excellence (NICE).

See Box 18.1 for a summary of age-related changes within the eye and orbit.

Assessing visual function

Formal assessment of visual function can include (Kelly 1996):

- testing distance vision with a Snellen chart;
- assessing the ability to read with a near test type;
- visual field assessment to detect any gaps in the peripheral vision.

This assessment is carried out in the GP surgery, optometrist's or local eye department. Most people do not have the facility to carry out formal visual assessment but it is possible to assess visual function informally, as outlined below.

Observations of a relative, friend or client

The following are indications that a person may have a problem with their vision:

- Regularly bumping into objects, signs of bruising.
- Often tripping or falling for no apparent reason. As many as 40 per cent of older people who present in A&E departments after a fall have a visual impairment (RNIB 1999).
- Generally unkempt appearance of someone who previously paid attention to hygiene and clothes.
- House or garden neglected, not due to physical or mental disability.
- Physically and mentally fit but reluctant to go out or use public transport.
- The person has stopped reading, sewing, cooking or pursuing their hobby.

Halle (2002) recognises that some older adults may not want to admit that their vision is getting worse, so they continue to drive – which puts them and others at risk. Others isolate themselves because communicating becomes more difficult if you cannot see well.

Questioning

By asking some simple, non-threatening questions it is possible to determine the extent of the sight impairment (Halle 2002):

- Can the person recognise faces of friends and relatives?
- Can they see the number on buses?
- Can they still use the telephone or watch television?
- Are straight lines such as the door post distorted?
- Do they have problems matching the colour of clothes?

Action needed

If someone complains, or you suspect, that their vision is not good, it is important to find out how long this has been going on. If it is recent, swift action is needed, as treatment may be available to restore the vision or prevent further loss (wet ARMD, vitreous haemorrhage, retinal detachment, and circulatory problems). Where visual loss is gradual or long-standing, treatment may be available to restore vision (cataract) or prevent further visual loss (chronic simple glaucoma) (Halle 2002).

Referral to the local eye department is still important so that a full assessment can be made and any further medical help offered if available. At this stage, even if medical treatment is not available, other agencies can help by offering support and practical solutions.

The first person to contact is the GP or optometrist, who will assess the problem and refer on to the local eye department as appropriate. If visual loss is sudden or associated with pain or discomfort, contact your local eye department or NHS Direct for advice straight away.

Practical help

In the person's own home setting, the social services rehabilitation or sensory loss team is generally the first point of contact for help, advice and support. Many offer meetings for the visually impaired person (VIP) and can include:

- Question-and-answer sessions about their condition.
- Practical help such as the use of 'eccentric vision' (gazing past an object to maximise use of peripheral vision when central vision is hazy).
- Psychological support in the form of counselling or peer support.
- Details of voluntary support and resource centres.

Most important is that they allow visually impaired people to get out and meet other people who have the same problems and have often come up with solutions. Social services also visit individuals in their home and offer advice about practical problems and information about benefits available.

Sperazza (2001) believes that everyone with a visual impairment should have a low-vision assessment. No matter how poor the vision is, the correct low-vision aid can enhance the use of any remaining sight. Many eye departments or opticians offer this service and can lend high-powered spectacles, magnifying glasses and telescopes. Local voluntary organisations or resource centres for visually impaired people offer a large number of devices such as talking clocks, watches, weighing scales and measuring jugs. Devices for signatures can help individuals maintain financial independence. Telephones with large numbers mean that visually impaired people can contact friends and relatives without assistance. Advice about colour-coding clothes is available, with devices to ensure that matching items are worn. Resource centres or voluntary organisations are usually staffed by people who have visual impairment themselves. This means that they fully understand the problems and can help, advise and support others with similar problems.

Conclusion

This chapter has highlighted the main causes of visual loss, how visual function can be assessed and what action should be taken if vision is reduced. Many older people have a visual impairment and can suffer physically and emotionally as a result. Some visual impairment can be prevented if detected early and professional help is sought. Where vision has already been lost there are many ways that the visually impaired person can be helped practically to make the most of the small amount of vision they have so that they can remain active and continue in their chosen lifestyle.

Box 18.1 *Summary of age-related changes*

Age-related changes	Outcomes	Health prevention, promotion and main-tenance
Lid elasticity diminishes	Pouches under the eyes	
Loss of orbital fat		
Decreased tears	Excessive dryness of eyes	Use artificial tear eye drops as needed
Arcus senilis (white line round cornea) becomes visible		
Sclera yellows and becomes less elastic		
Yellowing and increased opacity of cornea	Lack of corneal lustre	
Increased sclerosis and rigidity of the iris		
Decrease in convergence ability	Presbyopia	Have eyes examined at least once a year

continued

Box 18.1 (continued)

Age-related changes	Outcomes	Health prevention, promotion and maintenance
Decline in light accommodation response	Lessened acuity	Use magnifying glass and high-intensity light to read
Diminished pupil size	Decline in depth perception	Increase light to prevent falls
Atrophy of ciliary muscle	Diminished recovery from glare	Clip-on sunglasses, visors, sunhat, non-glare coating on prescription glasses/ sunglasses
Night vision diminishes	Night blindness	Don't drive at night Keep nightlight in bathroom and hallway

Box 18.1 (continued)

Age-related changes	Outcomes	Health prevention, promotion and main-tenance
Yellowing of lens	Diminished colour perceptions (blues and greens)	
Lens opacity	Cataracts	Surgical removal of lens
Risk of increased intraocular pressure	Rainbows around lights Altered peripheral vision	Yearly eye examination, including eye pressure testing
Shrinkage of gelatinous substance in the vitreous	Vitreous 'floaters' in vision	Eye examination to exclude retinal tear or retinal detachment
Thinning and sclerosis of retinal blood vessels		
Atrophy of photoreceptor cells		
Degeneration of neurones in visual cortex		

Adapted from Le May (1999)

19 Memory and cognition

Nicky Hayes and Henry Minardi

What are memory and cognition? Most days we do not need to concentrate on normal or routine activities. We can hold a conversation, make breakfast or return home without having to think consciously about it. Yet all the time we are carrying out complex underlying cognitive tasks. Our cognition ensures that we make sense of what is going on around us, remember routes and routines, and make quick judgements and choices. Memory plays a significant part in this.

Stereotypes of old age tend to portray memory as failing conspicuously. Yet the truth is that, although there is some normal decline in aspects of memory with increasing age, it is not normal for people to fail to cope with routine activities when they get older. In later life, people often compensate for normal memory changes by drawing on their store of expertise or by an increase in effort, concentration, attention and motivation. This illustrates the complex and interrelated nature of the processes that make up cognition and the adaptability that helps people to cope with normal change in later life. It is only when abnormal changes occur, such as a dementing illness, that problems may result.

Although cognition, over all, is very complex, the processes involved can be described as:

- Memory – a complex process in itself, which involves both the storage and the retrieval of information.
- The speed with which we process information – which includes our ability to attend to this information.

- Perception – which is the way our brain makes sense of the information our senses bring in from the outside world.
- The ability to learn new information.
- The ability to solve problems, in real or hypothetical situations.
- Language – not just the physical uttering of words but also the way we translate our thoughts into speech and comprehend the speech of others.

A reduction in cognitive processing is often described as *cognitive impairment*. Although some global changes occur in many aspects of cognitive function with age, normal ageing does not result in significant cognitive impairment. This is why it is important that assessment attempts to distinguish between normal and abnormal ageing.

Cognition is just one aspect of our psychological well-being, which is summarised in Figure 19.1. This Figure shows us that all of these factors are interrelated. Because of this, there are some important points to remember when assessing an older person. These and some other fundamental practice points are identified in Box 19.1.

Box 19.1 Practice points

Older people's previous physical condition, experiences, cultural development and knowledge may have an effect on their current presentation.

Older people may need more time to process and respond to different situations, especially if they are complex.

Health and social care professionals need to be alert to negative stereotypes and also to be aware of their own expectations of cognitive ageing.

Labelling of people as 'impaired' or 'demented' should be resisted and challenged.

Figure 19.1 *Factors influencing psychological development in later life*

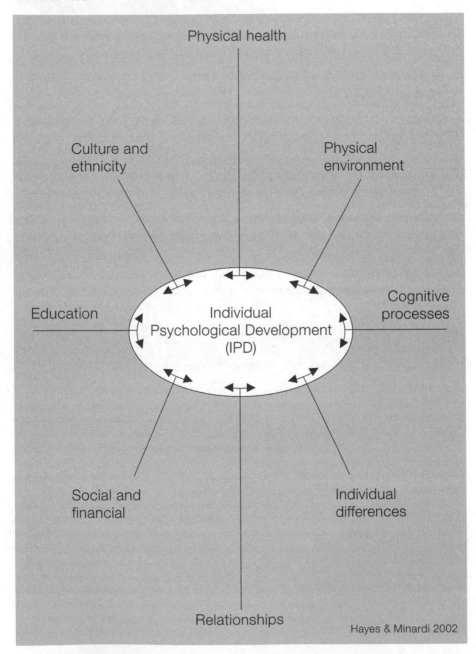

Approaches to assessment of cognition

Basic cognitive assessment is an important part of an overall assessment of physical and psychological well-being; for example, a Single Assessment Process overview assessment in a community setting, a hospital admission assessment or continuing care assessment. Assessment should follow the principles of a person-centred approach, in order to:

- understand the person's strengths and ability to function rather than just focusing on their impairments;
- distinguish between normal and abnormal ageing;
- screen for possible depression and take appropriate action;
- identify any potentially reversible causes of confusion so that appropriate action may be taken;
- trigger a plan of care, including risk management and appropriate onward referral if required for treatment or investigations.

Dementia and depression are problems that commonly affect cognition in old age (see Table 19.1). Although depression is a mood rather than a cognitive disorder, detection is important because it can sometimes seem to manifest as cognitive impairment and often also coexists with dementia. Other problems that assessors should be alert for include suicide risk and anxiety. Delirium, though affecting cognitive processing, fluctuates in its presentation and is considered a medical emergency (see Chapter 20). Although these problems cannot be fully diagnosed through a basic cognitive assessment, this process should equip health and social care professionals to recognise risks and the need to refer on for a specialist assessment if any of these problems is suspected.

Table 19.1 **Prevalence of mental ill-health in older people living in the community**

	Prevalence
Depression	4.8–13.1%
Dementia	4.1–5.5%
Anxiety	0.6–1.1%
Phobia	0.2–0.8%
Hypochondria	0.8%
Schizophrenia	0.2%
Obsessional	0.1%

(Minardi and Hayes 2003)

Components of basic assessment

Taking a history from the person and/or from a carer

Taking the history (Box 19.2) should be carried out with tact and sensitivity, as many people may be embarrassed about admitting that they have not been coping well or are depressed. It is important to avoid cultural bias when taking a history, as people from different backgrounds may not recognise problems in the same way as the assessor, or may attach stigma to mental health problems. If the person is confused or has difficulty answering questions, a history should also be taken from a carer who knows the person well.

Box 19.2 *Taking a history*

The person's usual level of function – ability to manage their daily tasks

Any recent changes that have been noticed, including memory, behaviour, sleep pattern, self-care

Social support

Social isolation

Alcohol use

Prescription medicines

Any significant life events

Bereavement

Any other current difficulties

To prepare for basic assessment and history taking, the assessor should ensure that the interview will be private. The person's verbal permission for the assessment should be requested and the purpose explained. This might be broached through the use of statements such as 'May we have a chat about how you have been feeling in yourself lately?' The mention of formal assessment should be used with caution, as it might be intimidating or provoke anxiety. The assessor should ensure that the environment is quiet and comfortable, ascertain the person's first language, and check that they can hear and see well enough for the interview to be carried out.

Carrying out screening tests of cognitive function and for depression

Screening tests are used to give an overall indication of 'mental status', and have been developed for brief routine use by a variety of practitioners. It must be remembered that they only screen for possible problems, which may need specialist referral, and are not diagnostic tests. Two well-known, valid, screening tests of cognitive function are the Mini-Mental State Examination (MMSE; Folstein et al 1985) (Box 19.3) and the Abbreviated Mental Test (AMT; Hodkinson et al 1972) (Box 19.4). These tests include a general test of orientation plus simple tests of memory and other processes. A score is calculated; for example, the MMSE gives a score out of a maximum of 30. Short tests such as the AMT might be used as part of an overview type of assessment within the Single Assessment Process.

Box 19.3 Mini-Mental State Examination   Score [__ /30]

Orientation

1. What is   the year?   [__ /1]
                the season?   [__ /1]

     What is   the date?:   [__ /1]
                the day?   [__ /1]
     What is   the month?   [__ /1]

2. Where are we:
        country?   [__ /1]
        county?   [__ /1]
        town?   [__ /1]
        hospital?   [__ /1]
        floor?   [__ /1]

3. Registration
     Name three objects, taking one second to say each.
     Then ask the person to name all three. Give one point
     for each correct answer. Repeat the answers until
     the person learns all three.   [__ /3]

4. Attention and calculation
     Serial sevens: ask the person to count backwards
     from 100, by subtracting 7s (93, 86, etc) Give one point
     for each correct answer. Stop after five answers.
     (Alternative: spell 'world' backwards.)   [__ /5]

5. Recall
     Ask for the names of the three objects learned in
     question 3 (above). Give one point for each correct
     answer.   [__ /3]

Box 19.3 (continued)

Language

6. Point to a pencil and a watch: ask the person to name them as you point. [___/2]

7. Ask the person to repeat 'No ifs, ands or buts'. [___/1]

8. Ask the person to follow the three-stage command: 'Take the paper in your right hand. Fold the paper in half. Put the paper on the floor.' [___/3]

9. Ask the person to read and obey the following: 'Close your eyes.' [___/1]

10. Ask the person to write a sentence of his or her own choice. (The sentence should contain a subject and an object, and make sense, but ignore spelling.) [___/1]

11. Show the design printed below, and ask the person to copy it. [___/1]

Give one point if all sides and angles are preserved and if the intersecting sides form a quadrangle.

(Folstein et al 1985)

A screening test for depression supplements information that may have been obtained through taking a history. A test that has been widely used with older people is the Geriatric Depression Scale (GDS; Yesavage et al 1983) (Box 19.5). This may be administered by a health or social care professional, taking care to ask the questions if possible as part of a conversation or discussion rather than reading from a checklist. This will ensure that the person who is being assessed feels as comfortable as possible with the assessment process. If the person is unable to answer questions directly, an alternative test that can be used is the Cornell Scale (Alexopoulos et al 1988) (Box 19.6).

This asks questions of the carer about the way in which the older person's mood is manifested.

Box 19.4 *Abbreviated Mental Test*

1 'How old are you?' (exact age only)

2 'What is the time?' (to the nearest hour)

3 Give the person the following address to recall at the end of the test: 42 West Street. (It should be repeated by the person to ensure it has been heard correctly.)

4 'What year is it?'

5 'What is this place?' (the name of the hospital or care home or the person's exact home address, according to where you are)

6 'What jobs do these people do?' (show the person two pictures – eg a postman and a cook – or point to, say, a doctor and a nurse)

7 'What is your date of birth?'

8 'What was the year of the First World War?' (year of start or finish)

9 'What is the name of the present monarch?'

10 'Please count backwards from 20 to 1.' (no errors, no clues, but the person can correct themselves)

Then ask the person to repeat the address from question 3.

Score 1 for each correct answer (there are no half marks): 0–3 indicates severe impairment; 4–6 moderate impairment; 7 and above is normal. (It is important, however, to take account of the person's educational level when interpreting the test.)

Adapted from Hodkinson (1972)

Box 19.5 *The Geriatric Depression Scale*

Answer all the following questions by ringing either 'Yes' or 'No'

1 Are you basically satisfied with your life?   Yes / *No*

2 Have you dropped many of your activities
   and interests?   *Yes* / No

3 Do you feel that your life is empty?   *Yes* / No

4 Do you often get bored?   *Yes* / No

5 Are you in good spirits most of the time?   Yes / *No*

6 Are you afraid that something bad is going
   to happen to you?   *Yes* / No

7 Do you feel happy most of the time?   Yes / *No*

8 Do you often feel helpless?   *Yes* / No

9 Do you prefer to stay at home, rather than
   going out and doing new things?   *Yes* / No

10 Do you feel you have more problems with
   memory than most?   *Yes* / No

11 Do you think it is wonderful to be alive now?   Yes / *No*

12 Do you feel pretty worthless the way you are now?   *Yes* / No

13 Do you feel full of energy?   Yes / *No*

14 Do you feel that your situation is hopeless?   *Yes* / No

15 Do you think that most people are better off
   than you are?   *Yes* / No

TOTAL SCORE   _____

Score 1 point for each *italicised* answer. A total score of 6–15
suggests depression.

(Yesavage et al 1983)

Box 19.6 Cornell Scale for Depression

A. Mood-related signs
1 Anxiety – anxious expression, ruminations, worrying
2 Sadness – sad expression, sad voice, tearfulness
3 Lack of reactivity to pleasant events
4 Irritability – easily annoyed, short tempered

B. Behavioural disturbances
1 Agitation – restlessness, hand wringing, hair pulling
2 Retardation – slow movements, slow speech, slow reactions
3 Multiple physical complaints (score 0 if gastrointestinal symptoms only)
4 Loss of interest – less involved in usual activities (score only if change occurred acutely – ie less than 1 month)

C. Physical signs
1 Appetite loss (eating less than usual)
2 Weight loss (score 2 if loss greater than 12.5kg/5lb in 1 month)
3 Lack of energy – fatigues easily, unable to sustain activities (score only if change occurred acutely – ie less than 1 month)

D. Cyclic functions
1 Diurnal variation of mood, symptoms worse in morning
2 Difficulty falling asleep
3 Multiple awakening during sleep
4 Early morning awakening (earlier than usual)

E. Ideational disturbance
1 Suicide – feels like life is not worth living, has suicidal wishes, has made suicidal attempts
2 Poor self-esteem – self-blame, self-deprecation, feelings of failure
3 Pessimism (anticipation of the worst)
4 Mood-congruent delusions – delusions of poverty, illness or loss

Rating: a = unable to evaluate   1 = mild or intermittent
               0 = absent   2 = severe

(Alexopoulos et al 1988)

Box 19.7 *Factors that may affect test performance*

Education – people with a low level of education can perform less well on the MMSE (Wiederholt 1993)

Hearing

Cultural background

Language

Depression – may adversely affect cognitive tests and should therefore be screened for separately

Perception of relevance of the test to everyday life – older people may resent 'silly questions'

Test setting – people may score higher on the MMSE at home than they do in a clinic setting

(Ward et al 1990)

As with taking a history, care should be taken to ensure a suitable environment for testing. A number of factors can specifically affect performance in a cognitive screening test and these are summarised in Box 19.7. The overall advantages and disadvantages of using screening tests are summarised in Table 19.2.

Table 19.2 **Advantages and disadvantages of screening tests**

Advantages	Disadvantages
Objective – use standardised questions	May be negatively perceived by the person being assessed
Can be used by a range of health and social care professionals	Do not give a picture of the whole person
Can be used to evaluate progress, through use of repeat scoring	Risk of scores being wrongly interpreted and leading to labelling of the person
Readily available, accessible and familiar	May not be culturally sensitive

Carrying out investigations

It is important that appropriate investigations are made to exclude reversible causes of cognitive impairment. Physiological changes such as high blood pressure, heart failure and lung disease can all affect cognition because of their effects on blood supply to the brain. Infection, vitamin deficiencies and abnormal organ function can also have a profound effect on cognition, but many conditions are treatable and for this reason these causes must be detected (Box 19.8).

Box 19.8 Commonly encountered reversible causes of cognitive impairment

Infection

Vitamin B_{12} or folate deficiency

Abnormal liver, kidney or thyroid function

Abnormal urea and electrolytes

Abnormal blood glucose

Abnormal calcium levels

Syphilis

(Taylor and Shah 2001)

Physiological causes of depression, such as abnormal thyroid function, may also be identified this way. For older people living in the community, referral should be made to their GP or practice nurse, who will decide whether these investigations are required. In hospital, people presenting with confusion should have these investigations ordered as routine. A CT scan of the head may also be ordered.

Conclusion

All health and social care professionals should be able to carry out basic cognitive assessment, using a holistic person-centred approach. Basic history taking and the use of routine brief screening tests may be useful, together with access to investigations for reversible causes of cognitive impairment. Screening tests such as the MMSE should be used only in the context of a model of psychological assessment that includes background information, behaviour and, where necessary, more formal or detailed cognitive testing. With this approach, the screening test is seen as a part of assessing the whole person in the context of the factors identified in Figure 19.1.

Assessment is pointless unless the results are acted upon, and it is essential that health and social care professionals use cognitive assessment in the context of the Single Assessment Process. This means that action plans are agreed with the older person and/or their carer, including onward referral for specialist or in-depth assessments where appropriate.

20 Acute confusional states/ delirium

Irene Schofield

'Delirium' is the term widely used in the literature to describe the phenomenon of acute confusion, or acute confusional states. Practitioners themselves, however, are most likely to use the term 'acute confusional state' in the course of their daily work. Practitioners tend to understand 'delirium' in the context of 'delirium tremens', the term used to describe the withdrawal symptoms that accompany alcohol abuse. Delirium tremens is a form of delirium and requires a specific type of management. It is important to be clear at the outset that 'delirium' used in the context of this chapter does not relate specifically to alcohol use but refers to a complex phenomenon that commonly affects older people when they become ill.

Consequences of delirium

Although delirium can affect people at any time in life, it is most likely to occur at the extremes of the lifespan. In older age, people who already have cognitive impairment such as dementia are especially at risk of developing delirium (American Psychiatric Association 1999). Delirium can result in a number of undesirable consequences. For example, a slower rate of recovery prolongs the time spent in hospital. Older people who develop delirium are more likely to be admitted to a care home, more likely to develop dementia, and are more likely to die. It is important, therefore, that practitioners are able to recognise delirium and the underlying cause during initial and ongoing assessment. There are now recognised risk factors for developing delirium, and identification of these risk factors followed by specific interventions in the hospital setting decreases the likelihood of a person developing delirium (Inouye et al 1999).

Predisposing and precipitating factors for delirium

Delirium in older people occurs because of a disturbance of physiology in the ageing brain. The decrease in reserve capacity as a result of age changes makes the brain less able to adapt to the stress of acute illness, chronic co-morbidity and multiple medications. The experience of being in an unfamiliar environment, such as occurs on admission to hospital, can aggravate delirium. Major features of delirium are changes in level of alertness and an abrupt change in mental state. These features develop over a short period (a matter of hours) and have a tendency to fluctuate during the course of the day. In addition, there is evidence from the person's history, the examination or investigations that the delirium is a direct consequence of a general medical condition (American Psychiatric Association 1994). Definitions of delirium and diagnostic criteria are given in Box 20.1.

Delirium can be described as a multifactorial syndrome, in that there is a complex interrelationship between factors that predispose a person to developing delirium and factors external to that individual. For example, a person with severe dementia might develop delirium after receiving a single dose of a benzodiazepine hypnotic. Conversely, it could take major surgery such as a heart bypass operation and a stay in an intensive care unit to cause a fit 80-year-old with no obvious cognitive impairment to develop delirium.

Delirium is commonly the only sign of 'hidden' and serious life-threatening illnesses such as pneumonia and myocardial infarction in older people. Delirium is potentially a medical emergency, so it is important to be able to recognise it and take appropriate action. Prompt medical referral is needed to diagnose and treat the underlying condition, if the person is to be likely to regain their usual level of function. Care of someone with delirium consists of treatment of the underlying cause and at the same time providing physical, psychological and environmental support until the episode of delirium has resolved (Inouye et al 1999).

Delirium occurs in about 15–20 per cent of all general admissions to hospital, and most of the literature deals with delirium in the context of acute hospital care. Now, more attention is being given to the occurrence of delirium among nursing home residents, and in older people living in their own homes. In one study, 35 per cent of older people living at home were identified as having delirium. Although it can signal urgent need for medical attention, delirium is not always recognised in clinical practice, and non-detection rates of 33–66 per cent have been reported (Johnson 1999). Front-line care professionals have a key role to play, therefore, in the recognition and support of older people who develop delirium. For example, in general, care homes do not have medical cover on site, so health care professionals who work regularly in care homes need to be skilled in the speedy recognition of delirium and to follow this up with urgent referral to a GP.

Box 20.1 *Diagnosing delirium*

In order to make a diagnosis of delirium, a person must show each of the features below:

- Disturbance of consciousness (ie reduced clarity of awareness of the environment) with reduced ability to focus, sustain or shift attention.

- A change in cognition (such as memory deficit, disorientation, language disturbance) or the development of a perceptual disturbance that is not better accounted for by a pre-existing or evolving dementia.

- The disturbance develops over a short period of time (usually hours to days) and tends to fluctuate during the course of the day.

- There is evidence from the history, physical examination or laboratory findings that the disturbance is caused by the direct physiological consequences of a general medical condition.

(American Psychiatric Association 1994)

Identifying people with delirium

The single word 'confusion' is widely used by care teams to describe a person who shows signs of cognitive impairment. It is crucial, however, that they try to avoid using 'confusion' as a diagnosis but ask themselves 'What's causing the confusion?' An important first step is that professionals can differentiate between confusion caused by altered cognition as in delirium, which is temporary and reversible, and cognitive changes caused by dementia, which is chronic and progressive. Diagnosis is complicated by the fact that people who have dementia are at greatest risk of developing delirium.

The cardinal features of delirium are its rapid onset and inattention (difficulty focusing, maintaining and shifting attention). A person with delirium seems easily distracted by stimuli in the surrounding environment and has difficulty maintaining a conversation and following commands. Other key features are disorganised thinking and altered level of consciousness. Less common are the easily recognisable signs that are most frequently associated with delirium, such as disorientation, memory impairment, psychomotor agitation, perceptual disturbances (illusions and hallucinations), paranoid delusions and reversal of the sleep–wake cycle. Nurses who observe these features and older people who experience delirium are most likely to recall these unusual and sometimes disturbing features.

To add to its complexity, delirium can present in a hypoactive or hyperactive form or a combination of the two. The hypoactive form of delirium is characterised by lethargy and reduced psychomotor activity and is easily missed. Fluctuation between the hypoactive and hyperactive forms is the most common presentation of delirium.

In assessing a person who shows signs of confusion it is necessary first to determine whether this is a new and sudden development and whether the person has been confused for some time or, in fact, has already been diagnosed with dementia. It is important to involve and listen to family members or anyone who knows the person well, at the time of the assessment if possible. Family and close contacts will be familiar with the person's usual level of cognitive functioning and will recognise when that person is behaving in ways that are unusual (Royal College of Nursing and Help the Aged 2000). Fick and

Foreman (2000) reported that none of the individuals with delirium superimposed on dementia in their study was recognised by hospital staff as having delirium, although relatives had identified a change in their behaviour. The hospital staff insisted that the patients' behaviour was attributable solely to the dementia.

Bear in mind that, as people with dementia are most at risk of developing delirium, care professionals may be confronted with someone who has delirium superimposed on dementia. A person with dementia may become more confused than usual or unusually drowsy. People with dementia who suddenly decrease their food intake and become less active may be developing delirium (Johnson 1999), and this is most likely to be the hypoactive subtype. There is a risk that the hypoactive form might be mistaken for depression, and it is important to consider whether the person has a past history of depression or has experienced critical life changes that may be affecting their mood. More unusually, they may be developing psychosis. Use of assessment tools will help to identify such people so that they can be referred quickly for specialist psychiatric support. In seeking to identify the reasons for the onset of confusion, it is crucial that care professionals are able to differentiate between dementia, delirium and depression and less common conditions such as psychosis, to provide the most appropriate support and treatment. Table 20.1 contains some of the chief predisposing and precipitating factors for delirium that need to be considered when making an assessment.

In addition to carrying out cognitive screening, the search for the underlying cause needs to be commenced. A comprehensive history that includes medication and alcohol use will provide clues. For example, intoxication with alcohol or a range of drugs such as benzodiazepines followed by abrupt cessation of alcohol and drugs can precipitate withdrawal delirium. Infection is one of the most common causes, so taking vital signs, a physical examination and collecting specimens for laboratory testing in order to identify a source of infection should follow. It is appropriate for nurses with extended clinical skills to take on this role.

Table 20.1 Predisposing and precipitating factors for delirium

Predisposing factors	Precipitating factors
Dementia	Medications
Severe underlying illness	Immobilisation
Functional impairment	Use of indwelling catheters
Advanced age	Malnutrition
Chronic renal failure	Iatrogenic (eg transfusion)
Dehydration	Infections
Sensory deficits	Metabolic disturbance Environmental and psychosocial influences

Using a screening tool

There are recognised cognitive screening and assessment tools that require only a small amount of training to use them. The Abbreviated Mental Test cognitive screening tool (Hodkinson 1972) is commonly used in the UK to identify cognitive impairment in older people (see Chapter 19: Box 19.4). The tool on its own does not provide a definitive diagnosis of delirium or dementia but it does indicate that cognitive impairment is present; it can also be used to monitor changes in cognition. Attention/inattention can be assessed using simple tests such as asking the individual to recite the months of the year backwards or count backwards from 20 to 1, something that a person with delirium will be very unlikely to achieve.

A quick and simple method of screening patients for delirium is the Confusion Assessment Method (CAM; Inouye et al 1990), outlined in Box 20.2. The CAM is in the form of an algorithm and is a useful guide for all care professionals. It provides a sound basis for clinical decision-making and articulation of the presenting problems to a medical colleague. The CAM takes the form of nine reflective questions which require some interpretation, followed by an algorithm based on the cardinal features of delirium. It fits well into routine care, with little

Box 20.2 *The Confusion Assessment Method (CAM)*

Feature 1 Acute onset and fluctuating course

This feature is obtained from a family member or nurse and is shown by positive responses to the following questions:

- Is there evidence of an acute change in mental status from the person's baseline?
- Did the (abnormal) behaviour fluctuate during the day – that is, did it tend to come and go or increase and decrease in severity?

Feature 2 Inattention

This feature is shown by a positive response to the following question:

- Did the person have difficulty focusing attention – for example, being easily distractible, or having difficulty keeping track of what was being said?

Feature 3 Disorganised thinking

This feature is shown by a positive response to the following question:

- Was the person's thinking disorganised or incoherent, such as rambling or irrelevant conversation, unclear or illogical flow of ideas, or unpredictable switching from subject to subject?

Feature 4 Altered level of consciousness

This feature is shown if any answer other than 'alert' is given to the following question:

- Over all, how would you rate this person's level of consciousness? Alert [normal], vigilant [hyper-alert], lethargic [drowsy, easily aroused], stuporous [difficult to arouse], or comatose [unrousable].

The diagnosis of delirium by CAM requires the presence of features 1 and 2 and either 3 or 4.

Source: Inouye, VanDyck, Alesse et al (1990)

burden on patients and staff, and has been used as the sole method of identifying delirium in a number of large studies. The CAM is easy to use, completion taking less than five minutes, and the method seems to have better sensitivity and specificity than other cognitive screening instruments.

The NEECHAM Confusion Scale was developed by nurses in response to dissatisfaction with the questionnaire approach to cognitive assessment. The nurses argued that some patients might be disadvantaged by lack of formal education, fatigue and an unfamiliar environment. Besides, nurses preferred to assess patients based on observation, in the course of their usual practice. The scale consists of nine components of information processing, performance and vital function items. It combines nursing assessment and brief interactions with patients in a hospital setting, and completion of the scale takes 10 minutes; it has good validity and reliability (Neelon et al 1996).

Preventing delirium

It is now recognised that, in many instances, delirium can be prevented by identifying modifiable risk factors during the assessment process and responding with the appropriate intervention (Inouye et al 1999; Inouye 2000). Risk factors might consist of predisposing factors that are present on admission to hospital, such as dementia and dehydration.

Precipitating factors develop or unfold during the period of hospitalisation; for example, following insertion of a urinary catheter. Admission to hospital itself is a predisposing factor and many people develop delirium during a stay in hospital, which is often due to acquired infection. Prompt identification and treatment of common conditions such as chest and urinary tract infection, and the use and review of medications that commonly predispose to delirium, in the home or care home setting, have the potential to avoid the need for hospital admission. Inouye and colleagues (Inouye et al 1999; Inouye 2000) have shown that, by taking the following steps to prevent delirium, it is possible to minimise or avoid its undesirable consequences:

- Orientation to time and place (this may not be appropriate for people with severe memory loss).

- Keeping the person stimulated and abreast of daily events.
- Ensuring uninterrupted sleep at night by minimising noise.
- Welcoming and supporting close family members to be with the older person to provide support and continuity with life outside the hospital/care home.
- Ensuring that the person has and is using hearing aid and/or spectacles as needed.
- Encouraging and ensuring adequate fluid intake.
- Minimising the use of procedures, such as catheterisation, that restrict early mobilisation.

The ability to understand the significance of abrupt-onset confusion and to react appropriately and quickly when it occurs is one of the central tenets of working effectively with older people.

21 Communication

Henry Minardi and Nicky Hayes

Communication is complex. It is transmitted and received by many routes, serves a multitude of purposes and is undertaken by all living creatures. Box 21.1 suggests some purposes of human communication, each of which has a number of subdivisions. Communication is a two-way process with internal and external influences on each of the participants (Figure 21.1). The form that communication takes (Box 21.2) depends on the individuals involved and the context in which it takes place, such as personal, professional, parental, sibling, marital, child, gender, racial and/or ethnic. When communicating in social or health care settings with older adults, all of these factors must be considered.

Box 21.1 **Some purposes of human communication**

Be understood

Develop, maintain and/or end a relationship

Give and receive information

Exchange ideas

Solve problems

Express distress

Display an emotional state

Make intentions clear

Hide true intentions or feelings

Distract or deceive

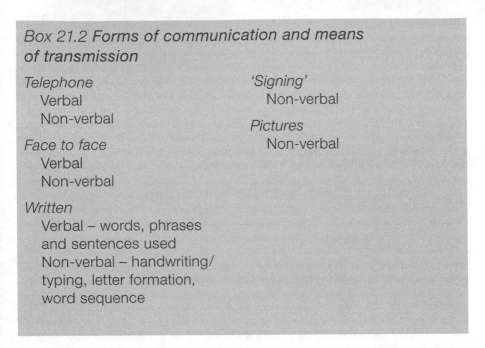

Box 21.2 Forms of communication and means of transmission

Telephone
  Verbal
  Non-verbal

Face to face
  Verbal
  Non-verbal

Written
  Verbal – words, phrases
  and sentences used
  Non-verbal – handwriting/
  typing, letter formation,
  word sequence

'Signing'
  Non-verbal

Pictures
  Non-verbal

Figure 21.1 Message transmission and reception

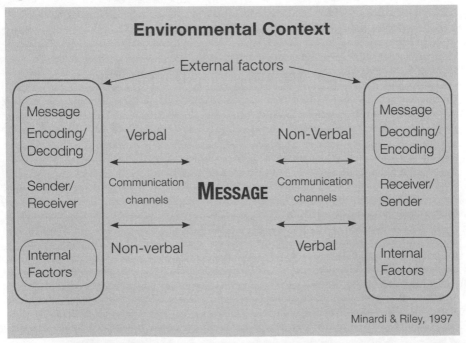

Environmental Context

External factors

Message
Encoding/
Decoding

Sender/
Receiver

Internal
Factors

Verbal

Communication
channels

MESSAGE

Non-verbal

Non-Verbal

Communication
channels

Verbal

Message
Decoding/
Encoding

Receiver/
Sender

Internal
Factors

Minardi & Riley, 1997

This chapter explores three components of effective communication: communication skills, a therapeutic relationship and knowledge of oneself and others. These three components of effective communication must work as an integrated whole, although they are described separately for convenience.

Skills in effective communication

All communication is received through our sensory channels of skin, vision, hearing, smell, taste and proprioception (see Chapters 15, 17 and 18). That we communicate is an unalterable fact. However, to communicate for a specific purpose is not inevitable but a skill that needs to be learned. For example, a sports commentator needs to learn how and when to get the appropriate information transmitted. Similarly, for the purposes of effective social and health care communication with older adults, this also needs to be learned.

Conventionally, the basic skills are divided into verbal techniques and non-verbal messages. However, added to this must be the skill of active and attentive listening, which is a combination of using and being aware of verbal and non-verbal communication – yours and that of the person you are assessing.

Listening is one of the most important skills social and health care workers need for effective communication (Scrutton 1997). It is through listening attentively and taking an active part in the discussion at appropriate times that a more accurate assessment of needs will be obtained. By listening to the words, phrases and sentences used there will be a better understanding of the individual and their personality (Groom and Pennebaker 2002). It is necessary to recognise that 'listening' is done not only with your ears but also with your eyes. In the latter sense, it is about observing the non-verbal messages transmitted by the individual and trying to make sense of them in relation to any verbal messages heard, your knowledge of the older person's present situation and the understanding you have of their personal history. Attentive listening also uses the skill of 'silence'. It is very simple yet extremely difficult for people to use silence. This is because there is often a temptation to interrupt the flow of a person's speech for clarification or to offer advice, when such interventions could easily wait until later in the interaction. Active listening involves

Box 21.3 *Verbal communication techniques*

Skilled questioning techniques

Open questions An open question has no specific focus and invites the person to respond from their own frame of reference. Open questions usually begin with words such as 'What?', 'How?', 'Who?', 'Where?', 'When?'

Clarifying questions Clarifying questions aim to make clear the meaning of a person's statement. The questioner becomes increasingly focused on the subject matter and begins to explore issues in depth.

Probing questions Probing questions enable the practitioner to explore more specific issues in the relationship. They are differentiated from open questions in that the subject tends to be of the practitioner's choosing.

Closed questions Closed questions are useful only in obtaining specific details, such as age, name, address, contacts, etc. They often elicit only a one- or two-word response (eg yes or no) and, as such, they should be used sparingly to avoid overwhelming the person. Often such questions begin with 'doing' words such as 'Have?', 'Did?', 'Is?', 'Can?', 'Are?', 'Would?', 'Could?'

Skilled responding techniques

Echoing Echoing is the repeating of the last word or phrase of the person's statement in a questioning tone of voice. It is used to encourage the person to explore further the issues raised.

Reflecting feelings This offers the person your perceptions of the feelings that seem to be entwined in their verbal communication. Sometimes there may be a range of feelings and the practitioner will need to clarify what is uppermost for the person.

Box 21.3 (continued)

Paraphrasing This is the rephrasing of the person's previous statement as you understand it, with a view to clarifying what is being said, encouraging further exploration of the issue and demonstrating to the person that you are listening to them.

Summarising This is the rephrasing of important aspects of the person's overall communication. Summarising may include the person's statements from previous sessions and it can be used to clarify and review.

Facilitative statements These clarify what the person has said either verbally or non-verbally by the use of statements beginning with phrases such as 'I wonder ...' or 'I imagine that ...'. They enable the person to perceive that they are being listened to and that the practitioner is aware of the feelings behind what the person is saying. Such a statement does not imply or require a response.

Validation Validation is communicating to the person a genuine appreciation of their personal worth and value, without any quali- fication. It may be in relation to something the person has done or said but may also simply be a means of valuing the person as a individual.

Self-disclosure Self-disclosure is the *limited* sharing with the person of positive or negative thoughts, feelings and experiences from your own life in order to demonstrate a level of empathy and understanding of the person's situation. Such a response must be used judiciously, as it can be overpowering for both partici- pants. It should be noted that even the physical presence of the practitioner is a source of self-disclosure.

(Minardi and Riley 1997)

participating verbally in the assessment/discussion with the person but at an appropriate time, with statements and questions being led by what has been said by the person, sometimes even using their own words.

Verbal communication techniques can be divided into questioning and responding (Box 21.3; see Minardi and Riley (1997) for more details).The skill in using questioning effectively is knowing which type of question to use at a specific time in the interview and for a particular purpose. For example, at the beginning phase in the interview (see 'Communication and the therapeutic relationship', later), it might be useful to ask a mixture of open and closed questions to obtain the person's own view of what their needs are. In the middle phase of the relationship it may be appropriate to ask more clarifying and probing questions to explore how they see these needs being met or what makes them believe they cannot be helped. It is important to recognise that, contrary to what is sometimes suggested, closed questions can be used skilfully (eg to obtain an age or address) and open questions can be used in a way that is not skilled (eg when you just need to know how many siblings a person has rather than how they feel about them at the moment).

Similarly, skilled responding relates not only to the actual technique used but to timing as well. For example, using supportive and clarifying interventions is appropriate at the beginning of the relationship. Using challenging responses in the working phase, once the relationship has begun to solidify, is also appropriate. However, using statements that encourage more exploration at the end of the interaction is not appropriate, unless it is to encourage the person to do some work independently after you break contact.

Often, when discussing the skilled use of communication, it is verbal techniques that are the focus. This is despite common knowledge that the majority of our communication is non-verbal (Geerts et al 1997), being transmitted through a variety of means (see Box 21.4). It is by observing, 'listening to', an individual's non-verbal messages that information, factual and emotional, can be obtained to enhance any assessment that is being undertaken. In a study comparing depressed and non-depressed men and women, Troisi and Moles (1999) found that depressed participants were more restricted in their non-verbal expressiveness, with a tendency to social with-drawal, as compared with non-depressed participants. However, in a later study by Troisi and colleagues (2000) it was found that, although the depressed and anxious participants were unable to express their emotional distress non-verbally in usual ways such as facial expression, they displayed an increase in displacement activities such as hair twirling, hand–mouth movement or scratching to express their emotional distress. This result demonstrates the importance of being aware of the nuances of non-verbal communication, such as a brief movement of an eyelid, eyebrow, hand or leg.

Box 21.4 ***Examples of non-verbal communications***

Silence	Speed of speech
Body movements	Voice pitch
Facial expression	Pallor/Flushed
Gaze/eye contact	Odour
Limb movement	Clothes
Body posture	Sweating
Body space	Neck blotching
Tone of voice	Hair style

It is also important for social and health care workers to monitor their own non-verbal messages. Just as Troisi and colleagues (2000) suggest that displacement activities are 'leakages' of people's emotional states, care staff may also non-verbally communicate how they feel about particular situations. For example, a facial expression of disgust may be displayed when helping someone get clean after being incontinent of faeces while verbally telling the person not to be concerned about what has happened.

Sometimes during an interaction it is appropriate to use complex communications to combine a number of skills for a particular purpose. For example, basic counselling skills may support the individual, get more complex information and help the individual explore how to manage their presenting problems. In this instance it is appropriate to use some of the counselling skills listed in Box 21.5. As with all of the skills presented in this chapter, they need to be practised regularly with appropriate clinical supervision to ensure that they are used most effectively.

Box 21.5 **Basic counselling skills**

Supporting Acknowledging, unconditionally, the strength and value that you perceive in the person.

Concreteness Inviting the person to describe specifically what they are perceiving, feeling and thinking.

Informing Offering the person information that seems relevant to their expressed needs and concerns.

Acknowledging conflict Recognising the person's simultaneous expression of opposite thoughts, feelings and experiences.

Interpreting Offering the person the helper's way of understanding the situation that they present.

Challenging Inviting the person to examine the strengths or discrepancies they present, which you have perceived in their thoughts, feelings and behaviours.

Immediacy Offering information to the person about how you experience them so that they may be encouraged to consider how they are presenting within the therapeutic relationship.

Examining polarities Asking the person to consider the possible results for them of doing, feeling and thinking the opposite of what they are presenting.

Table 21.1 **Examples of barriers to effective communication**

Physical	Psychological	Social
Service user		
Dysphasia Oral cavity disfigurement Lack of dentures Cerebral trauma Auditory/Visual deficit Cognitive processing deficit Breathing difficulties Pain Drug intoxication Alcohol intoxication Delirium	Withdrawn Delusional thinking High levels of anxiety Confabulation Inattention Preoccupations Hallucinations Misidentification Fear Misinterpretation	Language difference Accent Cultural differences Prejudice Beliefs Social history
Social/Health care worker		
Audio/Visual deficit Speech impediments	Misinterpretation Misunderstanding Fear Stereotyping Inattention	Language difference Accent Cultural differences Prejudice Beliefs Social history

However, there are times when it may be difficult to begin or maintain effective communication with the person being assessed. Barriers to communication could have physical, psychological, social or mixed origins and could originate from either the person or the social/health care worker. Examples can be found in Table 21.1; although these are not exhaustive, they will alert social and health care workers to be aware that barriers can be multifactorial. Awareness of these barriers will help them realise that they might need to communicate differently during the assessment – for example, reducing the complexity of questions without being patronising.

Knowing why you are communicating with this individual at this particular time is an important part of being a skilled communicator. It is also important to know whether you want to address factual or emotional material, and the purpose(s) of the interaction with the person. It can be useful to ask, and answer, a number of questions to yourself before the discussions begin and periodically while the interview is taking place. Some of these questions can be found in Box 21.6. Although these are not definitive, they can help avoid focusing on irrelevant information or prompt you to examine relevant material that you might have missed.

Communication and the therapeutic relationship

Relationship development is an important factor when considering effective communication with anyone involved in social and health care. Tschudin (1999) has suggested that it is the 'third element' when two people meet and communicate. However, this 'third element' can be either positive or negative, depending upon a number of circumstances. Dryden and Feltham (1994) have noted that, no matter how skilled a communicator the social/health care worker is when developing and sustaining a good working alliance, other factors such as age, gender, race, personality differences, etc, can cause difficulties. It is important that these problem areas are recognised and borne in mind to try to overcome, at least partially, their impact on developing a 'good enough' relationship.

Box 21.6 *Questions to ask yourself before and during the interviews*

What is the purpose of this interview?

What might be the best strategy for me to use so that I can develop a mutually beneficial therapeutic relationship?

How much time do I have to undertake this assessment?

What is the person's background?

How might both of our backgrounds affect the interview?

How much information do I need in this first encounter to ensure the service user's and personal safety?

How am I going to gather this information?

How much is therapeutically useful to disclose of myself in order to develop and maintain a good working relationship?

What non-verbal messages am I presenting, and are these likely to help or hinder the interviews?

How might I deal with giving/receiving potentially awkward information?

How might I respond if the person becomes emotionally upset, angry, silent, challenging, or responds tangentially?

The development of a therapeutic relationship is usually described as being in three stages: beginning, middle and end (Dryden and Feltham 1992; Tschudin 1999). Another way of conceptualising relationship development is that it happens in phases (Box 21.7 and Figure 21.2): pre-interaction, interaction and post-interaction. This implies that each part has some level of impact on the other. Thus, in the model presented in Box 21.7 and Figure 21.2, influences on the total encounter start before any 'face to face' (or 'voice to voice' in telephone interactions) meeting ever takes place.

Box 21.7 *Phases of therapeutic relationship development*

1 Pre-interaction phase
   a   Anticipation of the contact and interactions
   b   Assumptions about the person
   c   Purpose of the interaction

2 Interaction phase
   a   Beginning
      i the relationship fluctuates between distant and close
      ii types of statements/questions help determine
         relationship development
      iii balance between general and specific discussion

   b   Middle (working)
      i Therapeutic work

   c   Ending
      i Ending the contact/relationship

3 Post-interaction phase
   a   Maintenance of future relationship
   b   Development of future relationships

It is important to acknowledge that the phases are relevant to all individuals involved in the interactions.

The first phase can be identified as the *pre-interaction* phase where there is an anticipation of the encounter that will take place. A sequence of anticipating questions, or just one statement, could be formulated for the start of the interview – for example, 'Tell me about yourself'. The flow of the person's discourse can then determine how the *interaction* phase will begin to develop.

The *interaction* phase is divided into three sections: beginning, middle or working, and end. In the beginning section of this phase, participants in the encounter assess each other in terms of trust, what to disclose and whether they want to continue with the interaction.

Figure 21.2 **Phases of therapeutic relationship development**

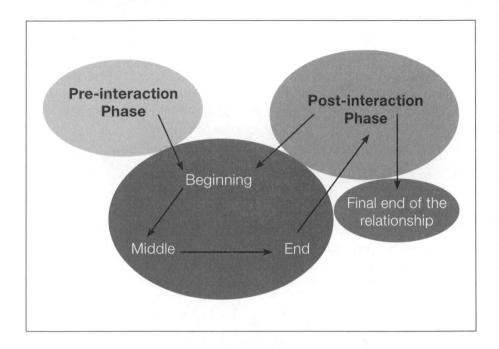

By being exploratory, supportive but not collusive, asking open and appropriate closed questions, listening with focused attention and using clarifying interventions, the social/health care worker is more likely to move the relationship into a working one. In a study of factors that might influence interactions to move from the orientation (beginning) to the working section of the relationship, Forchuk and colleagues (1998) elicited from service users comments that listening and consistency were important for the relationship to move to a working one. It is then, in the middle or working section, that more in-depth information is shared and an understanding of the individual develops. It is here that interventions to explore the person's situation in more detail are used. Interventions also challenge any distortions in thinking or behaviour the person may hold. The last part of the interaction phase entails ending the encounter and/or the relationship, depending on the purpose of the encounter.

The third phase of the relationship development is that of *post-interaction*, after both parties have parted, regardless of whether there will be a further meeting or it is only a 'one-off' assessment. At this point what Schön (1983) described as 'reflection on practice' takes place to examine the interaction that has just occurred and to see what communication techniques can be altered or added for subsequent or new encounters. It is only if the relationship is ending completely that its termination is addressed in the end stage of the *interaction* phase, and the *post-interaction* reflections are usually about the whole of the encounter and future meetings with others.

It is important to recognise that, although there are a number of phases in the development of a therapeutic relationship, these can all take place within the confines of one encounter, such as when assessing the mental health of an older adult in a general hospital ward (see the Case study, below). It is also necessary to recognise that a trusting relationship develops within the 'envelope' of a psychologically safe atmosphere (Minardi and Hayes 2003). Such an environment contains the core conditions of genuineness, acceptance and accurate empathy to increase the likelihood that a trusting relationship will develop (Figure 21.3). It is through a psychologically safe environment that service users will feel they are being listened to and understood.

Case study

I was asked to see Mrs C, who was admitted to an elderly care ward in an acute hospital because this was her third fall at home for unknown reasons in the last two months. Her medical notes also stated that she had 'acopia'. The ward nursing staff asked me to see her because she was not eating or drinking much, refusing to participate in physiotherapy, staying on her bed for most of the day and not speaking very much, which nursing staff were told by her visitors was unusual. The nursing staff also said she was confused at times in the evening in that she didn't seem to remember where her bed was when returning from the toilet. Some staff thought she was depressed whilst others thought she was confused.

Having talked with the nursing staff, I began to think about how I might gather information to make as accurate an assessment as possible while also helping Mrs C feel secure enough to talk with me. I first read through her notes and spoke to nursing, physiotherapy and medical staff to get different perspectives of what she has been like on the ward. I would have spoken to any visitors if they had been present. This is the *pre-interactive phase* of relationship development. I decided that, after introductions and telling her the purpose of my visit with her, I would ask her to tell me how she is, keeping the interview as open as possible. I also thought that I would monitor her non-verbal messages to see if I could detect distress at this approach so it could be changed.

Upon approaching Mrs C, I was aware of my non-verbal presentation – ie keeping my facial expression as relaxed as possible and my approach calm and respectful of her personal space. My initial introduction was kept uncomplicated but not patronising – an adult-to-adult interaction – and my tone of voice was warm. I interwove questions (open, probing, clarifying, etc) and responses (supportive, challenging, paraphrasing, etc), some of which related to the purpose of my interview – ie assessment – and others to getting to know her, and disclosing a little of myself to help build a relationship. I also listened attentively to what she had to tell me so that I could incorporate this into the discussion, occasionally using her words. By this time in the working part of the relationship, she seemed to feel safe enough for me to undertake formal cognitive testing and a test to assess her for depression. We also talked a little while about her personal history. During the ending section of the *interaction phase,* we recapped what had been discussed and shared thoughts about what this might mean for her. I then sought her permission to discuss salient parts of our talk with some members of the staff. We also discussed whether or not she was satisfied with the outcome.

Finally, I reflected on what had just taken place – the *post-interaction phase* – and finally formulated my opinion. This was discussed with the ward staff and recorded in the patient's file.

*Figure 21.3 **Psychological safety***

GENUINENESS
The helper becomes aware of her/his own feelings and attitudes and is willing to express these in words and behaviours.

The RELATIONSHIP will feel real

Psychologically Safe Atmosphere

The person may come to be more real within her/himself

The person may come to be more caring and accepting of her/himself

The person may come to be more attentive to her/his own feelings and perceptions

Psychologically Safe Atmosphere

The RELATIONSHIP will feel caring

The RELATIONSHIP will feel supportive

ACCEPTANCE

The helper feels a spontaneous valuing of the person as an individual and a willingness for the person to possess her/his own feelings in her/his own way.

EMPATHY

The helper senses the feelings and perceptions of the person in the way that the person experiences them.

Knowledge associated with skilled communication

The knowledge associated with good communication requires both technique and a good understanding of yourself – self-awareness – and of others with whom you are communicating.

The importance of self-knowledge is that it will help you keep 'in touch' with how you present to others – verbally and non-verbally. Awareness of messages you transmit, especially the non-verbal ones through body posture, gestures, tone of voice or facial expression, can reduce the risk of cross-communication, which may have a deleterious effect on the therapeutic relationship. For example, in a study by Kemper and colleagues (1998), young participants unconsciously used a type of speech they termed 'elderspeak' (characterised by speaking slowly, using uncomplicated grammatical structure, repetition and shorter sentences – ie an assumption of cognitive impairment when there is none) with older partners when giving them road map directions. By being more aware of how you communicate, you are more likely to do so appropriately with those who do or do not have cognitive problems.

It is also important to have knowledge of the needs and history of the older person with whom you are communicating. This information can help you know how to address that individual and what communication techniques might be helpful. For example, someone with a hearing deficit may need the help of a specially amplified communicator; do not automatically assume that their lack of understanding relates to a cognitive deficit.

Conclusion

Health and social care professionals who come into contact with older adults must have appropriate communication skills to undertake accurate and realistic assessments. They must be able to take a holistic view of the person with whom they are working, and know how to build a therapeutic relationship. This chapter has explored three essential components of communication, which must be used together in order to make an assessment of an older person:

- Skills in effective communication.
- Communication and the therapeutic relationship.
- Knowledge associated with skilled communication.

By integrating these components, the assessor may achieve an assessment process that is both person-centred and effective.

Risk assessment: an introduction

22 **Rights and risks**

Jill Manthorpe

Risk assessment is a key task for professionals (although it is also an important part of ordinary life). This chapter looks at some of the approaches to risk assessment in the context of individual rights. Risks and rights are not opposites and it can help to consider them together. Both present challenges to professionals, such as dilemmas over the balance between promoting individual autonomy and safety and fears that professionals can get either very wrong.

All interventions require an assessment of the profit and hazards of treatment compared with inaction: in other words, a risk assessment. Many NHS Trusts and local authorities have developed risk policies and have trained staff to use certain risk assessment procedures or guidelines (see Box 22.1). Some of these concentrate on harm and danger, rather than seeing risk as something that may enhance a person's quality of life. Within clinical governance systems of the NHS, managers address risk to patients and to the Trust; in some organisations such risks are put on a Risk Register to enable them to be addressed and monitored. In the light of public anxiety about major risks – for example, in public health such as 'mad cow disease' – the Government has been keen not only to improve professionals' management of risk but also to persuade the public that a 'risk society' requires a sophisticated understanding that not all risks can be eliminated (Cabinet Office 2002). Box 22.1 provides some examples of the frequency of risk policies in one area of practice.

> Box 22.1 *Risk policies in practice – examples from a survey of dementia services*
>
> Most practitioners (80%) use a risk assessment policy.
>
> Most policies are under review.
>
> Some policies/risk assessment tools are devised for people with dementia; others are more general.
>
> Two-thirds of practitioners had received training on risk assessment.
>
> (Clarke et al 2004)

Risk assessment

Much of ordinary life is a matter of assessing risk and making choices about likelihood and outcomes. Risk assessment is a collection of information leading to a decision that may involve the management of risk. Because risk is a calculation of likelihood (probability) and outcome, it is not a matter of certainty. Risk assessment is a process that aims to collect relevant information. Such information can include general vulnerability factors, people's values and preferences, the views of significant others and people's strengths. At times, information may be incomplete or conflicting. It is important to note that this may be so; decisions sometimes have to be made in the light of partial information.

In all risk assessments, management and decision-making, subjective perceptions or judgements are involved: we cannot eliminate these but it does help to acknowledge their influence. Many professionals, for example, may view relatives as likely to be 'risk averse' or extra cautious about safety issues, but some research suggests that relatives, like older people themselves, may often be 'risk experts'. Their expertise lies not in knowing a lot (although sometimes they do) about a particular disability or illness but in knowing a great deal about the individual and his or her past behaviour, and the context in which they live. Clarke (2000) sees this intimate knowledge as very useful to understanding what will be acceptable to and work for an older person. She suggests that practitioners should seek to understand how carers and older people view risk, and that relatives should also be helped to see that the professionals' wider knowledge may be important and relevant. Better mutual understanding of each other's expertise can result in better support for a vulnerable older person.

Things that have gone wrong for us in the past or for the organisation where we work may also influence us. For example, if we have been working with a person who has harmed him- or herself, such as by suicide, while in our care, we may be very anxious about this. It can be helpful to be aware of our own likely reactions and to seek other people's views when making calculations of likelihood or probability. This can include other people in a team but also people from a wider circle who may have other valuable insights or perspectives. Older people, who have generally been very capable of managing risk, may be involved in risk assessments, either as part of their own self-assessment or in other settings, such as planning for discharge from hospital. We do not have very much evidence about such involvement but we do have some evidence that people are not always included in discussions about their risks (Box 22.2).

Box 22. 2 Assessing rights and risks: what do service users think?

We do not know very much about what people think who have been subject to a detailed risk assessment and have been assessed as presenting serious risks to themselves or other people. One study of mental health service users who had been assessed as presenting high levels of risk found:

- Many did not know they had been assessed for risk.
- No one had told them about the implications of being assessed as presenting major risks.
- Professionals' information gave cause for concern, as it could be inaccurate and conflicting.
- Professionals felt that a good relationship with the service user made for better assessment of risk.

(Langan and Lindow 2004)

Box 22.3 *Some guidance on recording risk in reports*

Specify the purpose of the report (who it is for, why it is being done).

Think about data protection issues (will the report be shared; should anything be confidential; why?).

Quote the sources of information (and reference).

Be clear about the use of research and theory, and acknowledge sources.

Estimate probability or likelihood.

State the limitations of your evidence or opinion (eg 'I was only able to talk with Mrs Smith's daughter once on the phone').

Let the evidence drive the conclusion.

Drawn from Moore (1996)

Box 22.4 *The Human Rights Act 1998*

The Articles of the European Convention on Human Rights have been incorporated into the law of England and Scotland in relation to public bodies. The key articles include:

- Freedom of thought, conscience, religion.
- Freedom of expression.
- Freedom of assembly and association.
- The right to respect for privacy and family life.
- The right to marry.

Many practitioners working with older people seem to accept (Alaszewski and Manthorpe 2000) that risk is a matter of balance: balancing possible danger (such as falling) with the harm or distress that might occur if a person has to lead a more restricted and, to him or her, lower quality of life. The National Service Framework for Older

People (Department of Health 2001) recognises that /
take risks is a sign of independence. For older peop
seen as something that they face from others (eg risk ̆
is associated with mental or physical problems (eg leaving the gas
on, for people with dementia) and the needless harm that may result
from their vulnerability or disability.

Risk assessment is a process that is carried on as a matter of practice, through observation and general awareness. Only rarely do we
formalise this continual process by completing a risk assessment –
we could do nothing if we risk assessed everything in sight! A formal
risk assessment may be done by completing a written document, at
its most limited a tick box approach, or it may be an extensive piece
of work with input from many professionals, carers or family members
and the older person him- or herself, supported by an advocate if one
is needed and available. Box 22.3 lists some good practice points for
presenting a written report in a risk assessment process, such as a
case conference, a clinical governance review or a tribunal.

Such good practice needs also to consider the rights of the older
person. At its most basic element: will the older person you are writing the report about see the report? Will they be able to comment on
the facts you present and challenge them if necessary? Will they be
able to present alternative views or opinions? As Box 22.4 suggests,
the Human Rights Act 1998 provides a framework for the protection
of freedom of expression, privacy and so on.

However, such rights are very general and may seem hard to relate
to everyday practice. It has been proposed that a Human Rights
Commission might help make human rights more relevant to older
people and other excluded groups. Research from the British
Institute of Human Rights (BIHR) (Watson 2002) suggests that such a
Commission could provide good-quality advice, guidance and training, and increase awareness of the Human Rights Act. The British
Institute of Human Rights found that lay people and professionals
in public services often had limited understanding of the potential of
the Human Rights Act. Moreover, individual staff had little awareness
of their responsibilities under the Act. Few people knew how the Act
could help resolve dilemmas, help in assessing risk or help resolve
competing interests.

nclusion

rawing this together, thinking points on undertaking a risk assessment include:

- Sources of information – are these broad? How long has the informant known the older person and how well?
- Is there a way of getting views from people who may not write reports or turn up to meetings? Who should do this?
- How can the older person's views be fed into the risk assessment process in a meaningful way?
- Who is responsible for telling the older person what is happening? Is there an advocate or can someone take on this role?
- Be specific and do not use jargon; this will help other professionals, non-professionals, families and the older person. It will also make reports clearer.
- If the older person is at a meeting where risk is being considered (eg hospital discharge planning meeting, case conference), who is responsible for ensuring that they know what is going on and that their communication needs are addressed (eg considering hearing loss or the need for interpreters)?
- In written reports and verbal comments, be specific; avoid the term 'at risk' (of what?).
- Attempt some estimate of probability, and in a way that other people will understand what you mean (eg use a numerical or numbering scoring system instead of a vague phrase; for example, 'I think there is a 10 per cent chance that Mrs Jones will leave the gas on', rather than 'I think there is a real risk that Mrs Jones will leave the gas on').

These practice points can help with a variety of dilemmas relating to rights and risk. The issue of restraint, for example, is one where rights may be in conflict (Harding and Gould 2003). New legislation in England, the Mental Capacity Act 2005, may help practitioners in health and care settings by providing greater clarity about when it is lawful to restrict a person's liberty. In such circumstances, formal risk assessments are likely to be necessary, perhaps with the older person having some very limited access to an 'independent consultee' if they have no one else, such as a family member, who can speak on their behalf.

In summary, safety and risk are not opposites; safety and danger are at either end of a spectrum. Risk is a matter of calculation; if something was certain it would not be a risk. As Reed and her colleagues (2004) observe, 'there is a tension between living a life and maintaining safety'.

23 Musculoskeletal function

Roger Watson

The musculoskeletal system comprises two body systems – the skeleton and the skeletal muscular system – which work together to provide the body with posture and movement. The skeleton is made up of over 200 bones and is mainly composed of calcium phosphate. It is a living system of the body, each bone having its own blood supply and nervous system. In the early stages of life the skeleton develops by a process whereby soft cartilage is replaced by hard bone. After birth, the skeleton grows and becomes more solid until about the late teenage years when it stops growing. However, the skeletal material is constantly being deposited and reabsorbed throughout life. If a bone is broken, it is able to heal. The process of skeletal development depends on such factors as a good diet and exercise, and the skeleton is especially susceptible to deficiency of vitamin D.

The bones provide protection and support. For example, the vertebrae house the spinal cord and together provide the support for the upper part of the body and the attachment for the ribs, which are used in respiration. The bones of the head protect the brain. The skeleton also permits movement at articulations commonly known as joints. Some articulations – for example, those between the vertebrae – allow for a relatively limited range of movement, whilst others – such as the shoulder joint – allow for the greatest possible range of movement. Bones that articulate are held together by ligaments composed of collagen. The ligaments permit the range of movement for the joint but prevent the bones from becoming separated: they are flexible but not elastic.

The movement of the skeleton is enabled by the musculoskeletal system, and the skeletal muscles are attached to the skeleton by tendons. At each joint there are pairs of muscles where the muscles that comprise the pair are antagonistic to one another: that is, one muscle will contract, to move the joint in one direction, while the other relaxes to permit this movement; when the other muscle contracts, the original muscle relaxes and the joint is moved in the opposite direction. An excellent example of an antagonistic pair of muscles is the biceps and triceps of the arm, which move the lower arm.

The effect of ageing

The general effect of ageing on the musculoskeletal system is less strength and less flexibility. Generally speaking, however, in the absence of other disease processes these should not adversely affect the life of an older person. Nevertheless, many older people do have complaints that emanate from deterioration of the musculoskeletal system. The tendons become stiffer with old age because they are composed of collagen, a protein that changes in structure with age and becomes less flexible.

The skeleton undergoes profound changes with age. The balance between the deposition of calcium phosphate and its reabsorption changes with age such that there is a net loss of bone material. Whilst bones of an older person may seem to be of normal size, they tend to be more hollow than the bones of younger people (Christiansen and Grzybowski 1993). In older people Paget's disease, in which the bone that is deposited is immature and therefore soft, is more common. Often this condition is not noticed until X-rays are taken, but there can be symptoms such as pain, swelling of bones and deformation of the spine.

Another common condition with age is osteoporosis, especially in older post-menopausal women. There is an overall loss of bone material and a tendency for the bones to fracture and the spine to compress. This condition can be very debilitating.

Because of many of the normal changes with age and the disease conditions described above, fractures are more common in older people. Some of these fractures are normal – breaks as a result of trauma such as a fall, for example. However, older people also suffer from pathological fractures that occur spontaneously as a result of lower bone density, and these, in turn, can lead to falls and further injury (Simpson and New 1999). The rate at which bone heals slows with age, so a fracture may be a more serious proposition in an older person than in a younger person owing to the possibility of extended immobility, which has many serious consequences for older people.

In addition to changes in the bones with age, the articular hyaline cartilage at joints becomes thinner. The combined effect of the loss of bone material and cartilage is that, with age, posture changes and height is lost. It is estimated that, after the age of 40, 1.5cm is lost every 20 years (Christiansen and Grzybowski 1993). The forward curvature of the spine becomes exaggerated (kyphosed), and this contributes to the loss of posture. The shape of the bones at joints changes with age and, together with changes in hyaline cartilage and less flexible tendons, the range of movement at joints becomes restricted. In addition to this normal aspect of ageing, there are two major diseases affecting the joints of older people (Christiansen and Grzybowski 1993): osteoarthritis and rheumatoid arthritis.

Osteoarthritis occurs at weight-bearing joints, especially the hips but also at the knees. Osteoarthritic changes are normal with age and lead to the smooth articular surfaces at joints becoming roughened, less mobile and painful. In some older people this can become extremely debilitating at the joints of the hip and knee, leading to severe immobility in addition to pain. Severe osteoarthritis is commonly resolved these days by the replacement of knee and hip joints by artificial joints, resulting in a very significant improvement in quality of life for the recipient.

Rheumatoid arthritis increases with age and is possibly an autoimmune condition in which the body mistakenly regards the synovial membrane and synovial fluid as foreign material and attacks them. The condition leads to inflammation, swelling and deformity of joints; in addition to being painful, it leads to an inability to carry out activities of daily living, as it tends to affect joints such as the finger joints (Ryan 1999). It also affects the toes and can lead to immobility.

The skeletal muscular system undergoes a general loss of muscle mass with age. This is not normally a problem but many older people complain of weakness. It is hard to distinguish in such cases between the effects of ageing and the effects of disuse. Another feature of the ageing skeletal muscular system is cramp, which is very painful. Cramp can lead to insomnia, depression and even suicide.

Problems arising from ageing

Whilst it must be re-emphasised that the effect of old age on its own will not lead to significant problems for older people provided that they remain free of disease and keep active, it is also the case that the consequences of deterioration in the musculoskeletal system of older people, whether through ageing or through disease, can have very serious results. One of the major problems is immobility and the effects of immobility are very wide, including further deterioration in the musculoskeletal system. These effects include loss of bone density and atrophy of the muscles. It can be hard to distinguish the effects of deterioration in the nervous system of older people from deterioration of the musculoskeletal system but the combined effects of deterioration in either or both of these systems can lead to falls: muscle weakness, pain and pathological fractures can lead to falls; falls may lead to further immobility; and a vicious cycle is established.

Deterioration due to rheumatoid arthritis, in addition to causing immobility, can lead to an inability to prepare food and to maintain hygiene. Therefore, because of the potentially serious consequences of deterioration in the musculoskeletal system, a thorough assessment is essential. This may reveal the extent to which an older person is able to cope, and identify what help is required with mobility and activities of daily living. The results of an assessment may also point to ways in which problems can be relieved: for example, through physiotherapy or medication. The everyday complaints of aches and pains so common in older people, and often ascribed to a vague condition or 'rheumatics', should not be treated as a trivial matter.

Conclusion

In common with other assessments involving older people, assessing the musculoskeletal system combines a thorough history and a physical examination from which a great deal can be learned about the older person's past abilities and how these might have changed over the years (Matteson 1997). Much can be learned from the physical appearance of the person: are they erect or bent over, and is this normal for them? In addition, a handshake can reveal the ability of the person to carry out a simple manual task and reveal the strength with which they can grip. Box 23.1 outlines the components of an assessment of musculoskeletal function in an older person. In common with other assessments – for example, of cardiovascular or respiratory function – it is the effect that any deterioration is having on the quality of life of the older person that is important. In other words, in the process of an assessment the older person should be asked how they think they are managing and what, if anything, could be better for them.

Box 23.1 *Assessment of the musculoskeletal system*

History

Mature height and weight
Pattern of activity and rest
Diet
Medications
Functional status (eg activities
of daily living)
Aids or barriers to normal
function
History of falls and/or injuries

Symptoms

Pain
Stiffness
Weakness
Lack of feeling
Cramps
Tender joints
Fatigue
Problems with balance

Physical assessment

Height, weight and posture
Alignment of body
Movement: voluntary and
involuntary
Strength and endurance
Reflexes
Joints:
- swelling
- redness
- deformity
- contractures
- crepitation
- atrophy of muscles
  around joints
- nodules and skin changes

Use of aids to mobility
Evidence of injuries
Activities of daily living

Adapted from Matteson (1997)

24 Risk of falling and hip fracture

Jan Beynon

Standard 6 of the National Service Framework for Older People aims both to reduce the number of falls that result in serious injury and to ensure effective treatment and rehabilitation for those who have fallen (Department of Health 2001). In the UK, falls and their consequences are a major public health and economic issue. Falls by older people are often a sensitive signal of unidentified and unmet health risk and health care need. Over 400,000 older people in England attend casualty (A&E) departments following an accident (Department of Trade and Industry 1997), and up to 14,000 people a year die in the UK as a result of a hip fracture caused by their fall (Melton 1988). However, evidence exists that falls can be prevented, and skilled and well-organised clinical management after falls and fractures both improves services and benefits patients.

The interrelationship between falls and hip fracture

Older people who have osteoporosis are at particularly high risk of fracture when they fall. Around 5 per cent of falls in older people result in a fracture; 1 per cent result in hip fracture, which is the most serious osteoporotic fracture (Tinetti et al 1988). More than 95 per cent of all hip fractures in older people occur as a result of a fall, spontaneous fractures being very rare (Grisso et al 1991). Over 90 per cent of all hip fractures in people 75 and over occur as a result of osteoporosis. Preventing falls is an important aspect of hip fracture reduction (National Osteoporosis Society 1999).

Osteoporosis is defined as a skeletal disorder characterised by compromised bone strength, predisposing a person to an increased risk of fracture (National Institutes of Health Consensus Development Panel 2001). Bone strength primarily reflects the integration of bone density and bone quality, bone density accounting for 66–74 per cent of bone strength. The relationship between bone density and fracture risk is not simple, as is borne out by the differences in bone density and fracture risk over time. At the age of 75, bone density is only about 4 per cent lower than at the age of 65, yet the incidence of hip fracture is about four times as great at 75 as at 65 years and 12 times as great at 85 years (Arden and Spector 1997). This increase is not due primarily to further loss of bone but rather to a large increase in the risk of falling at more advanced age. Hence, falls and fracture risk are closely interlinked. To prevent future fractures, it is important to identify those individuals who have osteoporosis and are at high risk of falling.

Assessing an individual's risk of falling

One definition of a fall is:

> 'a sudden, unintentional change in position causing an individual to land on a lower level, on an object, the floor, or the ground, other than as a consequence of sudden onset of paralysis, epileptic seizure, or overwhelming external force.'
> (Tinetti et al 1997)

If a person has fallen, it is important to identify the reason for the fall, review their risk factors for falls and aim to prevent further falls and injury. In a review by Rubenstein and colleagues (1994), an underlying cause for a fall could be identified in all but 8 per cent of cases, so it is important to review patients to identify the cause of the fall (Table 24.1). Falls in older people are a dynamic interaction between 'intrinsic' factors such as underlying medical conditions, poor mobility and poor vision and 'extrinsic' factors such as medication and environmental hazards (see Box 24.1). Many older people who fall do not seek medical help but they may be identified as being at risk by the presence of risk factors. Several studies have shown that the risk of falling increases as the number of risk factors increases (American Geriatrics Society et al 2001). Interventions aimed at identifying both multiple risk factors for individuals and environmental hazards are most successful (National Service Framework for Older People, Standard 6).

Table 24.1 **Circumstances of a fall**

	Incidence
Accidental or environmental factors	37%
Drop attacks	12%
Postural hypotension	5%
Dizziness, vertigo	8%
Disturbance of gait or balance	12%
Other causes: acute illness, sedative drugs, poor eyesight	18%
Unknown	8%

Box 24.1 **Risk factors for falling**

Intrinsic risk factors

Balance, gait or mobility problems, including those due to degenerative joint disease and motor disorders such as stroke and Parkinson's disease

Visual impairment

Impaired cognition or depression

Postural hypotension

Extrinsic risk factors

Taking four or more medications daily, in particular centrally sedating or blood-pressure-lowering medications

Environmental hazards in the home, including poor lighting, steep stairs, loose carpets or rugs, slippery floors, badly fitting footwear or clothing, lack of safety equipment such as grab rails, inaccessible windows

Box 24.2 Falls Risk Assessment Tool (FRAT)*

Is there a history of any fall in the previous year ?	Y / N
How assessed? Ask the person	

Is the person on four or more medications per day?	Y / N
How assessed? Identify number of prescribed medications	

Does the person have a diagnosis of stroke or Parkinson's disease?	Y / N
How assessed? Ask the person	

Does the person report any problems with their balance?	Y / N
How assessed? Ask the person	

Is the person unable to rise from a chair of knee height without using their arms?	Y / N
How assessed? Ask the person to stand up from a chair	

Scoring FRAT: if the answer to the question is 'Yes', score 1; if 'No', score 0. A score of 3 or above indicates high risk.

*Reproduced with kind permission of Professor G Feder, Department of General Practice and Primary Care, Queen Mary School of Medicine and Dentistry, University of London

A Falls Risk Assessment Tool (FRAT) for identifying older people in primary care and care homes who are at high risk of falling has been developed as part of the Department of Health funded guidelines for the prevention of falls by older people (Nandy et al 2004). The tool has been derived from sound, randomised controlled trials that have shown a reduction in the risk of falling or falls injury. The FRAT consists of five questions (see Box 24.2) and guidelines on further management for high-risk groups (scoring 3 or above). It is simple to use and can, with appropriate training, be used by the primary health care team, hospital staff and social care workers.

People at risk of falling should be assessed to modify their risk factors. A recent systematic review and meta-analysis by Chang and colleagues (2004), of interventions for the prevention of falls in older adults, indicated that the most effective intervention is a multifactorial falls risk assessment and management programme (see Box 24.2). Data from a study on the prevention of falls in older people showed that, if people who attend an accident and emergency department with a falls-related injury are referred on for a comprehensive medical and occupational therapy assessment, the incidence of future falls can be reduced by 50 per cent (Close et al 1999). If falls are prevented, hip fractures are prevented. The National Service Framework for Older People suggests that the following groups of older people should be referred to a specialist falls service for such an assessment:

- Have had a previous 'fragility' fracture.
- Attended A&E, having fallen.
- Called an emergency ambulance, having fallen.
- Have two or more risk factors in the context of a fall.
- Have frequent unexplained falls.
- Fall in hospital, nursing home or care home.
- Live in unsafe housing conditions.
- Are very afraid of falling.

Assessing the risk of hip fracture

As indicated above, over 95 per cent of hip fractures are falls related. Hip fractures occur not only because of reduced bone density (osteoporosis) but also as a result of independent risk factors (see Table 24.2) by factors associated with increased frailty and an increased propensity to fall.

When assessing an individual's risk for hip fracture, all these factors need to be addressed. Moreover, once someone has sustained a hip fracture, they undergo a rapid loss of bone and have an increased risk of recurrence, and thus should undergo a fall and osteoporosis assessment.

Identifying those at high risk of osteoporosis

The Royal College of Physicians guidelines on the prevention and treatment of osteoporosis (1999) have identified a number of risk factors for osteoporosis. They include:

- Previous 'fragility' fracture.
- Women with an early surgical or natural menopause (45 or younger), pre-menopausal amenorrhoea for more than six months not due to pregnancy.
- Predisposing factors such as liver disease, alcoholism, thyroid disease, malabsorption, rheumatoid arthritis, and hypogonadism in men.
- Current or prolonged oral corticosteroid use (for three months or more).
- Family history of osteoporosis, especially a maternal history of hip fracture.

The management of people at high risk of osteoporosis is determined by their level of activity. In people who are active, mobile and independent, investigations such as measurements of bone mineral density using a DEXA scan (dual-energy X-ray absorptiometry) should be considered. The results of this scan will indicate whether further investigations and treatment with bisphosphonates, selective oestro-

Figure 24.1 **Medical management of patients 45 and over who have or who are at risk of osteoporosis (Royal College of Physicians 2000)**

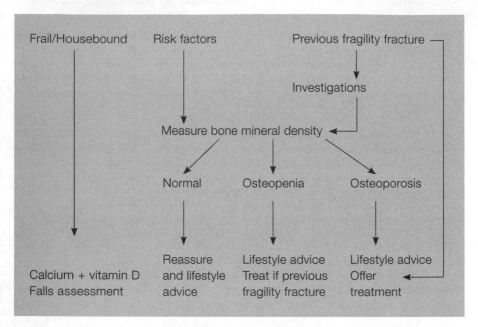

gen receptor modulators or hormone replacement therapy should be offered.

All individuals, however, should be given lifestyle advice, which includes:

- Eating a balanced diet rich in calcium.
- Maintaining regular physical activity and exposure to sunlight.
- Moderating alcohol intake.
- Stopping smoking.

For people who are frailer, who are often older and who are more immobile and housebound, bone density measurements and extensive investigations to exclude secondary causes for osteoporosis are inappropriate. They may benefit more from supplements of high-strength calcium and vitamin D, a comprehensive assessment of their risk of falling and the use of hip protectors for those in care homes.

It has been shown that older people develop a vitamin D deficiency and secondary hyperparathyroidism, which results in weakening of bones. Daily treatment with 1200mg of calcium and 800iu of vitamin D_3 reverses this biochemical abnormality and reduces the incidence of hip fracture (Chapuy et al 1992) (Figure 24.1).

Identifying independent risk factors for hip fractures

In 1995 Cummings and colleagues identified a number of independent risk factors for hip fracture. Each factor alone increases a person's risk of fracture; multiple factors significantly increase their risk of fracture. Not all of these risk factors are modifiable – Table 24.2 lists them in two groups: those that are modifiable and those that are not modifiable.

Table 24.2 **Risk factors for hip fractures in older white women**

Non-modifiable risk factor	Modifiable risk factor
Previous history of fracture after the age of 50	Inability to rise from a chair unaided
Maternal history of hip fracture	Physical inactivity
Tall at the age of 25	Poor contrast sensitivity and depth perception
Tachycardia at rest	Rated own health as poor
History of hyperthyroidism	Smoking and alcohol use
	Low body weight
	Use of benzodiazepines, neuroleptics and anticonvulsants

Summary

A comprehensive assessment of falls and hip fracture risk will not only benefit a person's physical and psychological well-being but will also in the long term have a positive impact on the health economy.

25 Older people using medication

Roger Watson

As people grow older they experience more illness, and frequently they experience more than one illness. It is also often the case that an older person may be taking several medications at the same time (Swift 1998). Special care and attention are required with medications for older people because of some of the normal physiological changes that accompany ageing. The key to benefiting older people through medication lies in the proper diagnosis of illness, correct prescription of drugs and vigilant monitoring of intended and unintended drug actions.

Multipathology

Commonly, an older person admitted to a care home with nursing may have four or five conditions, including, for example, arthritis, cardiovascular disease, diabetes and bronchitis. Each of these conditions will require treatment, which may lead to an older person taking a selection of drugs, each drug having its own effects, side effects and possible interactions with other drugs, and this leads directly to the phenomenon of *polypharmacy*.

Polypharmacy

The features of polypharmacy are shown in Box 25.1. Other factors that contribute towards polypharmacy (Watson 1996) are:

- self-administration of over-the-counter medications that are not prescribed;

- self-administration of old drugs, prescribed for previous illnesses, which are no longer required;
- poor adherence to prescribed drug regimens;
- effects of old age.

Box 25.1 **Features of polypharmacy**

Use of medications for which there is no apparent indication

Use of duplicate medications

Concurrent use of interacting medications

Use of contraindicated medications

Use of inappropriate dosage

Use of drug therapy to treat adverse reactions

Improvement following discontinuation of medications

As people become older, some physiological changes in the body may have an impact on medication. These effects of old age may account for the phenomenon of polypharmacy and also for some aspects of poor adherence to prescribed medication regimens.

Possibly the most marked effect of ageing that has implications for medication is the reduction of blood flow to the kidneys, which has an effect on drug kinetics (pharmacokinetics): the levels of drug(s) in the blood and the distribution between body compartments. The kidneys are responsible for filtering the blood and excreting toxic waste products such as the breakdown products of drug metabolism, which takes place in the liver. A slight reduction in liver size with age may reduce the metabolism of some drugs but this is not considered to be significant. The filtering of blood in the kidney takes place in the glomerulus, and the amount of blood filtered at the glomerulus is expressed as the glomerular filtration rate. It has been estimated that the reduction in blood flow to the kidney between a group of people aged 30 and a group of people aged 80 is 50 per cent, and that after the age of 40 glomerular filtration rate reduces by 10 per cent per decade.

In normal circumstances this reduction in filtration at the kidney with age has no adverse consequences. However, the kidney is the prime site for the excretion of medications from the body, often as break-down products, and the reduction in filtration becomes significant for many medications. The effect on the older person is that the levels of a drug in the body remain higher than in a younger person, owing to the decreased excretion. This means that, for a given quantity of a medicine, the dose of the drug is effectively higher in an older than in a younger person.

The dynamics of drugs, the effects that they exert on target tissues through binding at specific cell receptors, are also adversely affected by ageing but the picture is quite complicated. Generally, however, it is possible to say that the receptors at which drugs work in the body become less sensitive with age – they become 'down regulated'. To achieve a given effect, therefore, the temptation of the prescriber is to increase the dose of the drug. However, given what has been described above in terms of drug kinetics, a vicious circle may be established whereby increasing the dose will lead to an even greater increase in blood levels and to an increase in any side effects of the drug.

One effect of the process of ageing is that homoeostatic mechanisms become less effective, and this can have an adverse effect where drugs work on such homoeostatic systems as the regulation of blood pressure, temperature or heart rate. In the presence of disease the homoeostatic mechanisms will be affected more adversely than nor-mal and, of course, the presence of disease may be one reason for the prescription of drugs. Another vicious circle may be established.

In terms of the changes with ageing described above, the general principle to be applied by those prescribing drugs for older people is to lower the dosage and lengthen the period between doses.

Drug interactions and adverse reactions

The adverse effects that drugs can have in older people are a combi-nation of the facts that older people take more drugs than their younger counterparts and that there are age-related physiological changes that reduce the capacity of older people to handle some of the adverse consequences. The adverse consequences of polypharmacy include interactions between drugs and adverse reactions of drugs.

There are many ways in which drugs can interact and these are usually, although not exclusively, concerned with the pharmacokinetics of the drugs. Some drugs may inhibit absorption by slowing the emptying of the stomach (anticholinergics, for example) or increase absorption by speeding up the emptying of the stomach (for example, metoclopramide; O'Mahoney and Martin 1999). Antacids, commonly bought over the counter and used by older people, can bind to digoxin in the stomach. Digoxin is commonly prescribed for heart failure in older people and the binding to an antacid will effectively reduce its level in the stomach, thereby limiting its availability to the body (bioavailability). Some drugs, such as warfarin, used to reduce blood-clotting time, bind to the plasma proteins in the blood and are transported in the blood in this way. The drug phenytoin, used in epilepsy, also binds to plasma proteins; if the phenytoin displaces the warfarin from the plasma proteins (Watson 1996), thereby increasing the free and therefore active levels in the blood, this can have very serious consequences for the patient in terms of excessive bleeding as a result of reduced clotting time. However, it has been said recently that drug interactions, through their effect on binding to plasma proteins, may be minimal and that such interactions take place through effects on the metabolism of drugs in the liver.

Drugs that are largely eliminated from the body by first-pass metabolism (that is, their levels are reduced significantly through metabolism by liver enzymes the first time they pass from the gastrointestinal tract to the liver via the hepatic portal system) will have their levels increased by other drugs that use the same liver enzymes for metabolism – a phenomenon known as *competition*. For example, the drug cimetidine, taken to resolve peptic ulcers, reduces the liver metabolism of a range of drugs such as the benzodiazepines, the beta-blockers and warfarin (O'Mahoney and Martin 1999). Increased levels of these drugs will lead to increased toxic side effects. On the other hand, drugs such as carbamazepine, which induces liver enzyme activity – the production of enzymes involved in the metabolism of drugs – will reduce the activity of drugs that are metabolised by the same enzymes such as warfarin, thereby reducing the efficacy of these drugs. Drugs interact in other ways such as diuretics increasing digoxin toxicity by lowering blood potassium levels, and when beta-blockers and verapamil are taken together hypotension and heart block may occur (O'Mahoney and Martin 1999).

Adverse drug reactions are more common in older people, and it has been reported that one person in ten aged over 60 is admitted to hospital because of an adverse drug reaction (O'Mahoney and Martin 1999). Some adverse reactions are idiosyncratic (type B), possibly genetic in origin and unrelated to the dose of the drug being taken – the mechanism for these adverse reactions is not known. Other adverse reactions are predictable (type A), given the known effect of the drug, and result from an enhanced effect (and side effect) of the drug and, therefore, are related to the dose of the drug.

Some drugs are particularly prone to having adverse reactions. For example, the benzodiazepines, to which older people are particularly sensitive, and nifedipine, which may cause prolonged hypotension in older people (Swift 1998).

Conclusion

The effects of polypharmacy are insidious and may not prompt the nurse or physician immediately to consider that what is being observed in a patient is the result of the drug therapy. Any of the signs listed in Box 25.2 may be observed in older people (McConnel et al 1997). If any of them is observed in an older person, it is worthy of investigation, and a factor that should always be taken into account is the medication the person is taking. The correct course of action, if an adverse effect of a drug is suspected, is for the prescribing doctor to be informed as soon as possible.

Box 25.2 Factors for assessment in older people using medications

Restlessness	Depression
Falls	Constipation
Confusion	Incontinence
Drowsiness	Parkinsonism

---

26 **Restraint**

Roger Watson

Restraint may be considered either for the protection of an individual or for the protection of others. Restraint may possibly arise in any care setting, but care of older people and those with mental health problems (Evans and Strumpf 1989) are two areas where restraint is sufficiently common for there to be specific guidance. It should be noted that, unless an individual is being held under the relevant section of the Mental Health Act, no one has the right to restrain them. This is the situation that prevails in most settings where older people receive care, with the possible exception of some psychogeriatric settings. Restraint is a moral, ethical, legal and human rights issue, and all of the methods listed in Box 26.1 can be considered as restraint.

---

*Box 26.1 **Methods of restraint***

Bedrails
Harnesses
Sedative drugs
'Baffle' locks
Locked doors
Arranging furniture to impede movement
Inappropriate use of nightclothes during waking hours
Chairs constructed to immobilise older people
Isolation from others
Mattresses on floors
Controlling language, body language and non-verbal behaviour

Adapted from Royal College of Nursing (1999)

It is not the intention of this chapter to suggest that, in the absence of legal grounds, there are absolutely no circumstances in which restraint of an older person is justified. Without meaning to infantilise older people, just as a restraining hand may save the life of a child who would otherwise cross a busy road without looking, it may be justified, to save an older person from harm or death, to restrain summarily. However, care professionals should be aware of the limits to which they may restrain another individual and that, when someone is restrained, it should be justified and not prolonged.

What is restraint?

Any definition of restraint must take into account the involuntary nature of the action with respect to the person being restrained. The most obvious form of restraint is the prevention of movement in one person by the use of physical force by another or others. This may include holding back, redirecting by force or even immobilisation by confinement to a chair or by being pinned to the ground. At another level it may mean the prevention of movement of a person from a relatively limited environment – for example, a room, ward or hospital premises – whether by force, by locking in or by using a system of access that prevents that person from using it while those doing the restraining can move freely. In tandem with physical restraint is chemical restraint by the use of tranquillising medications. This shares all the cardinal features of physical restraint in that it is often, although not always, involuntary on the part of the person being restrained.

In situations where restraint is applied to someone, it is most likely that the carer considers that the older person is likely to come to harm through their own actions. In other words, carers may believe that they are acting in the best interests of the older person. The harm may be physical, as in injury, or spatial, as in being lost. Whilst the following do not constitute a justification for applying restraint, reasons for its use may include:

- wandering by a confused older person;
- an unsteady gait, which means that the person may fall;

- confusion, where an older person may wander at mealtimes and take food from other people, or may use the wrong bed or interfere with the belongings of others.

Indeed, a confused person may come to harm by wandering into areas where hot food, water and heavy equipment are located and may, ultimately, leave the area and become lost, after which they may be exposed to further harm from, for example, traffic, cold and injury. In such situations the carer might feel justified in applying some kind of restraint, which may be relatively mild. Nevertheless, in many cases carers may be acting in their own best interests – protection from accusations of negligence – rather than in the best interests of the older person (Hantikainen and Käppeli 2000).

Restraint versus abuse

While not minimising the problems faced by staff with older people who are mentally confused or who constantly wander, even in situations where they feel that restraint is justified staff may actually be abusing the person whether or not they are solving the problem.

Although there are ways of handling difficult situations with older people who wander, it should be obvious that restricting someone's movements against their wishes is entirely wrong in almost all circumstances, whereas engaging them in some activity whereby they voluntarily choose not to wander is a different matter.

Harmful effects of restraint

The imposition of restraint also has physical and psychological consequences, and these are particularly severe in older people. In physical terms, the list of deleterious effects includes muscle atrophy, loss of bone density, pressure sores and incontinence but, as indicated in Box 26.2, there are many more consequences.

Box 26.2 *Harmful effects of restraint*

Depression	Injury
Cognitive decline	Strangulation
Emotional isolation	Functional decline
Confusion	Reduced appetite
Agitation	Cardiac stress
Increased morbidity and	Muscle wastage
mortality	Incontinence

The information in this Box, which is not comprehensive, is compiled from Burton et al (1992), Castle et al (1997), Evans and Strumpf (1989), Morse and McHutchion (1991), Werner et al (1989).

Avoiding the use of restraint

Avoiding the use of restraint usually involves an element of risk assessment by care professionals and, in fact, the willingness to take risks to preserve the freedom and dignity of older people. Carers are often too quick to implement restraint, usually in response to the fall of an older person, when proper assessment would obviate the need for it. There is, in fact, ample evidence that restraint can be reduced in the care of older people (Evans et al 1997); measures include policy change, in-service education and individualised care.

An early study in the UK by Watson and Brunton (1990) demonstrated that the elimination of bedrails, one form of restraint, was possible in a small hospital unit caring for older people. This study, although very small, found all the features of restraint-reduction outlined above. Additional strategies for avoiding restraint are listed in Box 26.3.

> **Box 26.3** *Strategies for avoiding the need for restraint*
>
> Treatment of underlying physical disease
> Treatment of depression
> Alleviation of pain and discomfort
> Modifying the environment
> Changing to another environment
> Providing space and security
> Reviewing medication

Conclusion

In the UK the Royal College of Nursing (RCN) has been proactive in heightening awareness of restraint use in the care of older people and has published guidelines (Royal College of Nursing 1999). Within these guidelines the key question for assessment is: 'What is the meaning behind this behaviour?' A whole range of factors can contribute to behaviours that may trigger consideration of restraint. Those identified by Strumpf and colleagues (1998) are given in Box 26.4.

> **Box 26.4** *Causes of challenging behaviour in older people*
>
> Dementia
> Delirium
> Depression
> Pain
> Environment
> Invasion of personal space
> Loneliness
> Medication side effects
>
> (Strumpf et al 1998)

Figure 26.1 **A scheme for the implementation of restraint**

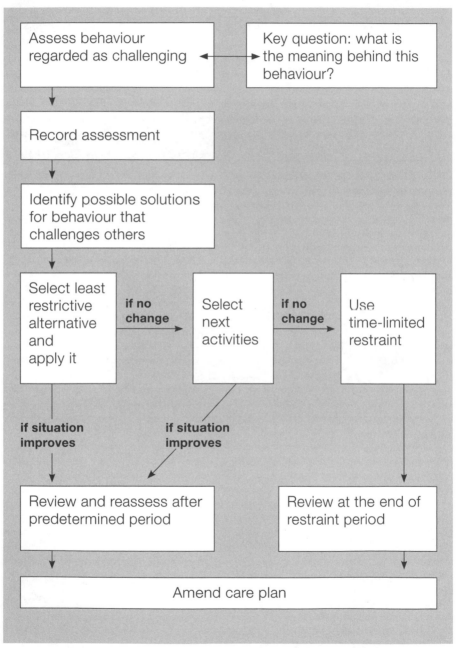

Source: Royal College of Nursing (1999)

According to the Royal College of Nursing, restraint:

'... should only be used when all other methods of managing the identified problem are not considered suitable or have failed. To use restraint appropriately, it should be reviewed regularly as an integral part of the nursing care programme.'

The RCN does not altogether eschew the use of restraint with older people but does provide a framework for its implementation, as shown in Figure 26.1. More recently, Counsel and Care (2001) has addressed the issue of restraint in nursing and care homes and their recommendations are based on the Royal College of Nursing guidelines (Figure 26.1).

27 **Preventing and responding to elder abuse**

Jill Manthorpe

The abuse or mistreatment of older people achieved particular prominence during the 1990s in the UK. The Department of Health guidance *No Secrets*, and similar guidance in Wales and Scotland, defines abuse as '... a violation of an individual's human and civil rights by any other person or persons' (Department of Health 2000: 9). This chapter focuses on assessment, but practitioners need to be able to respond to abused older people and must be able to provide them with support or refer them to such services. In the UK, the work of Pritchard (2000) provides practitioners with ideas about the organisation and running of support groups and sets out the value of helping relationships for people who have been abused.

Assessment

No Secrets identifies different types of abuse, though these may occur singly or in combination (see Box 27.1), and makes it clear that all staff have a responsibility to protect vulnerable adults (not just vulnerable older people). There has been some debate about whether systems of adult protection should cover all adults or just those who are vulnerable (Health Select Committee 2004) but currently *No Secrets* defines a vulnerable person as someone

> '... who is or may be in need of community care services by reason of mental or other disability, age or illness; and who is or may be unable to take care of him- or herself, or unable to protect him- or herself against significant harm or exploitation.' (Department of Health 2000: 8–9)

Practitioners therefore need to consider their roles and responsibilities in any contact with older people who fall in this category, avoiding an ageist tendency of 'let's rescue older people' (Homer and Gilleard 1990). This means they must work to local procedures, must report suspicions of abuse and must work collaboratively across agencies or organisations, above all asking older people what help they might want. *No Secrets* includes expectations that each area will produce locally agreed multiagency policies and procedures, will ensure that staff are trained, will consider setting up a local Adult Protection Committee and will establish local authorities as lead agencies. This does not mean that responsibility for investigation lies with the local authority alone; responsibility is shared.

---

*Box 27.1 **Summary of forms of adult abuse***

Physical

Emotional or psychological

Sexual

Financial or material

Neglect and acts of omission

Discriminatory

Each area therefore has its own set of policies and procedures (these will be available from managers or the key policy lead). For frontline practitioners these policies set out responsibilities for all those supporting vulnerable older people. They include:

- Being aware of responsibilities to inform managers of any suspicions.
- Being prepared to raise concerns – for example, by going beyond managers and whistle-blowing if nothing is done.
- Setting out responsibilities to preserve evidence, to keep adequate records and to communicate with other professionals.
- A responsibility or duty of care to make sure that the person is protected from harm but that their rights are not neglected or overridden without proper and full consideration (eg by using the Mental Health Act 1983).

Assessment processes

Such responsibilities can seem very general. It may be helpful to take two examples (see Case studies, below) to illustrate instances where concerns about abuse have emerged. The precise steps that should be followed are outlined in local multiagency policy and procedures documents: these range in style and content, often including general principles and local contacts, and sometimes, but not always, including detailed guidance for practitioners (Mathew et al 2004). An assessment of elder abuse should be done with reference to these policies. Like most policies, however, they do not get rid of the dilemmas for practitioners, such as striking the right balance between risk and rights, or maintaining trust and passing on information. If there is a local source of support of advice, such as an adult protection co-ordinator, this may be helpful in thinking through the issues. Policy and procedures also help by setting out time scales for response and the way to record suspicions. Research by Mathew and colleagues (2004) found that a named contact in the police is also likely to be a helpful source of advice at early stages. Such contacts are easier when there is joint training with the police.

Case study 1

Mrs Green complains to the community nurse that her home help is stealing money from her handbag. The community nurse makes a note of what is said, tells Mrs Green that she will have to report this and offers Mrs Green reassurance because she is very distressed. The community nurse passes this information to her team manager, together with a copy of her written record. The team manager contacts the police on the advice of the social services adult protection co-ordinator. The police and a social worker visit Mrs Green together and the home help is later interviewed. In this case, Mrs Green turns out to be in dispute with the care agency and there is no evidence that any money has been taken. The home care service is started again with home care workers under instruction to be very careful about issuing receipts and making sure that Mrs Green has her handbag with her at most times.

In this case the community nurse followed procedures and left investigation to those responsible. Good practice means that the community nurse was informed about the outcome of the investigation.

Case study 2

Mrs Brown turned up repeatedly at the health centre; many staff there thought she enjoyed the company and liked the young doctor. Over recent months, however, she had started to appear very anxious and seemed to want more help with various stomach complaints and her nerves. In conversation with the practice nurse, she revealed that her son had recently moved in with her and that this was causing some anxiety. Eventually Mrs Brown broke down and revealed that her son had a major problem with alcohol and was taking most of her pension. Bills were accumulating and she was frightened of his unpredictable 'binge' drinking. Again the practice nurse listened calmly and made some notes. She assured Mrs Brown that she would tell someone but that this would be kept confidential (on a need-to-know basis) and that Mrs Brown could get some immediate advice about her financial position and safety at the health centre if she did not wish anyone to call at her home. After speaking to the GP, the practice nurse made a referral to the local authority and, following a case conference, a joint plan of support was set up. Mrs Brown said she did not want to attend this meeting, so the social worker met with her at the health centre to find out her views. In the event Mrs Brown was able to arrange for the household bills to be paid through her bank. Her son still lives with her but the practice nurse is in regular contact (on behalf of the other agencies) and has talked to Mrs Brown about possible ways to support her son. Mrs Brown feels that she has a choice, she knows whom to call if things get worse, feels that she has been listened to and that she can cope again.

In both these cases, assessment was a matter of listening and supporting the individual. Staff were careful in writing down what they were told and did not offer to do anything they could not guarantee. After the investigation, the staff were available to provide further support.

Research on adult protection case conferences has found that 'victims' choose virtually always to remain in the allegedly abusive situation (Jeary 2004); another study showed that GPs report that the most common risk situation in their experience is where an older person is being looked after by a relative with problems of their own, such as alcohol misuse or mental health problems (McCreadie et al 2000). A separate assessment of this person may therefore be helpful. The second most common situation was where older people with dementia were living alone. They may be vulnerable to neglect, or to those who prey on their assets. Gaining their confidence and trust may be an important first step in assessing what is going on.

Other key assessment roles for staff include:

- Being alert to changes in behaviour or appearance, habits or morale, and keeping 'eyes and ears open' to any hints of abuse or neglect.
- Sharing concerns with other practitioners.
- Asking the older person if anything is troubling them, if they are feeling frightened or if they would like to talk to somebody.
- Using body maps to indicate the size, colour and location of any injury.

In Mrs Brown's case, a case conference was called. This is itself a process of assessment, based on the idea that pulling together the views of several practitioners and those of Mrs Brown herself, if possible, may help practitioners to understand what is going on and construct a protection plan. Such a conference may ask individual workers to attend, and to share their notes or records. The conference will assess risk and may seek a legal view about what can be done to protect the vulnerable adult. In some areas these can be quite formal meetings: senior staff will attend, the meeting will have a chairperson, and minutes will be taken about the decisions reached and why. Preparation for such a meeting is important and it may be helpful to ask about the procedure being followed and who else will be present. Someone will need to support the older person, and in some cases may need to advocate on his or her behalf.

Disclosing abuse

It is hard for anyone to reveal that they have been abused or mistreated; feelings of stigma and shame may interfere, and for other people there may be risks in complaining. It can also be hard for staff to hear about abuse: it can be shocking, or it can involve people who are colleagues or friends, and it can be difficult to think how we might have missed clues that are 'obvious'. Many of the inquiries into care settings, for example, seem to blame all staff for not spotting what was going wrong and not taking action.

Assessment of the possibility of abuse is not a separate activity from any other assessment; all practitioners need to be alert to the possibility of abuse. We have few reliable risk factors that can serve as guidance for identifying people most at risk. There is some evidence that those who are very reliant on an older person may be at risk of abusing them, less evidence that carer stress contributes to abuse. Some work concentrates on 'human' factors and tries to reduce the likelihood of abuse occurring by checking that a care worker does not have a criminal record. Other system changes are seen as more or equally potentially relevant, such as ensuring that care homes are subject to inspection and keep to minimum standards at least. Barriers to disclosure among practitioners seem to be reluctance to report suspicions unless people feel confident that abuse *has* occurred, and a desire for concrete evidence. Some practitioners also feel reluctant to break confidentiality. Training seems to have a positive effect in raising the likelihood that a practitioner will report possible abuse (Taylor and Lamb 2004). This makes the role of qualified workers very important when working with colleagues who may have had very little training, such as those in residential or home care services. There is some evidence that the risk of abuse is greater in care settings if staff:

- receive little support;
- lack training;
- receive inadequate guidance;
- have low self-esteem;

- have poor personal standards;
- work in isolation (Juklestad 2001).

Whatever the setting, the monitoring of care by qualified staff can provide important evidence that a person is – or is not – being neglected or abused. In a recent survey of community nurses, 88 per cent reported that they encounter abuse during the course of their work (Community and District Nursing Association 2004).

Summary

Good practice in assessment requires the exercise of all the senses: assessment of abuse similarly requires practitioners to look and listen, and to establish a trusting relationship with older people and with colleagues. A thorough assessment may uncover issues that merit investigation: an assessment that has been carefully recorded, has gained the consent of the older person to take matters forward (unless the person is unable to do this) and leaves the older person safely is an assessment that will equip colleagues to take action if need be.

Dealing with a disclosure and then assessing what has to be done is something that can be personally troubling. Support and supervision for staff are important here.

In conclusion, some guidance for practitioners undertaking assessments, which may lead to indications of possible abuse or neglect, is:

- Don't look surprised or shocked at what you see or hear.
- Don't promise that the conversation or information will be kept confidential.
- Don't ask leading questions.
- Keep any relevant material (eg clothing).
- Make sure that the person is as safe as possible.
- Write up what you have seen and heard.

- Keep up to date with good practice, local resources and policies.
- Tell your manager.
- Seek support for yourself through supervision, your professional association, or human resources department or a group such as Action on Elder Abuse.

Part 4
Life Functioning and Enjoyment

Functioning for everyday life

28 Cardiovascular functioning

Roger Watson

The cardiovascular system comprises the heart and blood vessels. The heart circulates the blood through the vascular system to supply oxygen and nutrients to the body's tissues and to remove carbon dioxide and other waste products. The blood has other functions, such as distributing heat around the body and fighting infection. With the cardiovascular system it is difficult to separate the effects of normal ageing from disease processes. However, the process of atherosclerosis ('hardening of the arteries') is almost universal in older people and is largely responsible for the higher prevalence of cardiovascular problems in older people.

Atherosclerosis

Atherosclerosis is a combination of atheroma – the deposition of fatty plaques within the cardiovascular system – with sclerosis or thickening and fibrosis of the blood vessels. With age the process of atherosclerosis increases, possibly starting before birth, and every part of the cardiovascular system is affected. For example, these changes decrease the contractility of the heart and its compliance (responsiveness) to the volume changes that accompany exercise. The loss of compliance in the large arteries leads to increased blood pressure which, in turn, means that the heart has to work harder to circulate the blood and this may, eventually, lead to heart failure. Among other things, these age-related changes in the cardiovascular system lead to decreases in maximal heart rate, stroke volume and cardiac output.

The maximal heart rate (beats per minute) in an older person may be estimated from the formula 220 minus age in years, which indicates a decreasing ability to respond to exercise. The stroke volume – the amount of blood ejected from the heart at each contraction – is a factor in the cardiac output, which is the volume of blood (in litres) ejected from the heart in one minute.

Heart failure

Failure of the heart to carry out its normal circulatory function is common in old age. However, this is another aspect of cardiovascular function where it is difficult to distinguish between illness or disease and ageing because there are 'similarities between the structural and functional changes associated with age, independent of heart failure' (O'Keeffe and Lye 1999). Heart failure has several features, including loss of function of heart cells and loss of contractility. The physiological mechanisms that compensate for this lead, initially, to hypertrophy of the ventricles, but eventually the ventricles become thinner and dilated. As the heart continues to fail, the venous return (blood returning to the heart through the veins) is reduced and there is back-pressure in the venous system and retention of fluid which is apparent as peripheral oedema (fluid retention in the ankles). The capacity for physical work declines in the ageing heart but the failing heart is much less able to adapt to changes in demand such as those required in exercise (O'Keeffe and Lye 1999).

Vascular system

In the vascular system atherosclerotic changes may lead to angina pectoris if the coronary arteries are affected, and even to myocardial infarction (heart attack) or chronic heart failure. There are a number of risk factors for atherosclerosis, such as smoking and obesity, and there is evidence that reducing risk factors can reduce the atherosclerosis in older people. Another consequence of atherosclerosis is an increase, with age, in blood pressure – there is an association between increasing blood pressure and morbidity and mortality up to about the age of 80 years. Hypertension (high blood pressure) is present, according to the World Health Organization definition, if someone's blood pressure is 160/90 mmHg or higher. There is some controversy over which older people should be treated for hypertension but, generally speaking, those aged up to 75 benefit best from treatment (Fairweather 1998). There is less of an association between hypertension and morbidity and mortality over 80, and the side effects of the drugs used to treat hypertension may increase. Table 28.1 lists some of the main changes associated with the ageing cardiovascular system and the major consequences.

Table 28.1 **Age-related cardiovascular changes and consequences**

Change	Consequence
Decreased cardiac output	Dyspnoea
Decreased stroke volume	Fatigue
Fibrosis and sclerosis of heart	Postural hypotension
Stiffening of vasculature	Hypertension
Increased peripheral resistance	Systolic hypertension

Adapted from Rush and Schofield (1999)

Principles of assessment

Any nursing assessment of cardiovascular function in an older person is made against a background of considerable change due to the ageing process. The problem of assessment of cardiovascular function in an older person is further confounded by other factors such as multipathology (other illnesses) and mental impairment. If an older person has a degree of memory loss, their reporting of signs and symptoms of cardiovascular disease may become unreliable. If the person has other illnesses or conditions – for instance, respiratory disease – it can be hard to differentiate between the effects of the respiratory disease on exercise from decline in cardiovascular function. A classic example of where pathology of the cardiovascular system in an older person can differ from that in a younger counterpart is in their experience of myocardial infarction, which is often less painful for older people. However, the extent to which myocardial infarction is 'silent' or completely painless in older people is often exaggerated (Fairweather 1998).

Ultimately, diagnosing cardiovascular disorder in an older person rests with the physician. On the other hand, nurses can make a significant contribution towards this by accurate assessment of cardiovascular function in older people.

History and physical assessment

The two key aspects to the cardiovascular assessment of an older person are history and physical assessment (Harrell 1997). The history should include any existing cardiovascular problems the person may have such as hypertension, previous myocardial infarction, angina and heart failure and any medications that may be prescribed. Any history of family cardiovascular disease should also be elicited. The extent to which the older person manages normal daily activities should be established: this can be done by asking about their normal daily routine, any changes in ability, and signs and symptoms such as shortness of breath, chest pain, dizziness or fatigue (this list is by no means comprehensive).

Questions about lifestyle should be included and details about such things as diet, alcohol intake and smoking should be established. Box 28.1 lists the essential components of a physical assessment for cardiovascular function in an older person. Particular attention should be paid to the measurement of blood pressure; there are published guidelines by the British Hypertension Society (1997) to which reference can be made. The guidelines are summarised in Box 28.2.

Box 28.1 *Essential components of physical assessment of an older person for cardiovascular function*

Blood pressure
Pulse – rate, rhythm and strength
Cough or wheeze
Haemoptysis
Distension of neck veins
Shortness of breath after exercise
Waking with sudden breathlessness at night
Peripheral oedema
Apex/radial pulse check
Chest pains

Adapted from Rush and Schofield (1999)

Box 28.2 *Measurement of blood pressure (BP)*

The patient should be seated

Use a conventional mercury manometer with an appropriate bladder size

Diastolic reading is taken at the disappearance of sound (phase V)

Record to the nearest 2mmHg

At least two BP measurements should be taken at each visit

Four separate visits should be made to determine the BP thresholds

In mild hypertensives and older people with isolated systlic hypertension, but no target organ damage, measure over a period of 3–6 months

In severe hypertensives, measure more often (eg weekly for 1 month)

Standing BP measurements are important for older people and diabetic hypertensives in whom orthostatic hypotension is common.

See also Chapter 29

Adapted from Rush and Schofield (1999) based on guidelines of the
British Hypertensive Society (1997)

The data gathered by the assessment outlined above may contribute to the diagnosis of cardiovascular disorder in an older person. However, the primary purpose of conducting assessment is to obtain information that will be useful in the planning and delivery of nursing care. In addition to the details of assessment directly related to the function of the cardiovascular system, therefore, the assessor should be probing, sensitively, about the likely impact that cardiovascular disorder is having on the life of the older person. The extent to which an older person can cope with activities of daily living (eg washing, dressing, feeding) and the instrumental activities of daily living (eg shopping, socialising and looking after the home) should also be assessed. In older men and women there may a degree of sexual dysfunction due to exercise intolerance and, specifically in men, erectile dysfunction due to cardiovascular disorder and/or the side effects of medication. If it is considered that an older person's diet is poor, the assessment is not complete until a dietitian has carried out an assessment, usually at the behest of the physician. Other members of the multidisciplinary team, such as the occupational therapist, should also be involved in order to assess activities of daily living and instrumental activities of daily living.

Conclusion

Care professionals have an important role in the cardiovascular assessment of older people. Whilst both the normal ageing process and disease play a role in the decline of cardiovascular function with age, there are some clear diagnoses such as heart failure, angina and hypertension in older people. Assessment should include history and a physical assessment, with particular attention being paid to the measurement of blood pressure. The assessment is not complete until the impact of cardiovascular disease on the individual older person has been ascertained and the appropriate members of the multidisciplinary team have been involved in the assessment.

29 **Blood pressure**

Philip Woodrow

Blood pressure is a vital sign. Like all physiological measurements, there is a range of healthy blood pressures. Normal blood pressure ranges from 100/60 to 140/90. Blood pressure below 100/60 is usually considered to be hypotensive (low), whilst blood pressure above 140/90 is usually considered to be hypertensive (high). However, measurements should be considered in the context of each person's 'normal' pressure; a difference of more than 10 per cent is usually regarded as being significant. Like any observation, trends over a few measurements are more reliable and significant than single measurements.

Blood pressure is the pressure exerted on the blood vessel wall. Arterial blood pressure is created by three factors:

- heart rate;
- stroke volume (the amount of blood ejected by the heart with each contraction);
- systemic vascular resistance (also called peripheral vascular resistance – the resistance to blood flow created by blood vessels, especially arterioles).

If the blood pressure is too high or too low, one or more of these factors is abnormal. For example, people with peripheral vascular disease have significantly increased systemic vascular resistance, so, unless other factors compensate for this, blood pressure will be raised.

Complications from many diseases (cardiac, vascular, stroke, diabetes) are less likely to occur as rapidly or as seriously if blood pressure is maintained within normal range. Staff measuring blood pressure may be the first to detect problems that have not yet caused symptoms but which, if untreated, may progress. Sustained blood pressures above 140mmHg systolic and 90mmHg diastolic should be actively treated.

Ageing

Hypertension is often considered to be an age-related disease: 30 per cent of people over 50 years of age are hypertensive and 50 per cent of people over 70 have peripheral vascular disease.

Vascular resistance increases by about 1 per cent each year from the age of 40 (Herbert 1999) but diastolic blood pressure often falls after the age of 50–60 (Franklin et al 1997) and healthy hearts often beat slower in older age. In health, blood pressure is similar in young and old people. Therefore, any difference from normal blood pressure should be considered pathological, potentially requiring treatment. The once widely used formula for normal systolic blood pressure of 100 plus the person's age can result in dangerous complacency.

Factors affecting blood pressure

Stress, anxiety and pain increase blood pressure. Therefore, measurements should be taken when relaxed. Significant differences (greater than 20mmHg) in systolic pressure may also be caused by (Beevers et al 2001):

- breathing deeply
- emotion
- exercise
- meals
- tobacco
- alcohol
- temperature
- bladder distension
- circadian (daily) rhythm.

As with other observations, blood pressure should be interpreted in the context of the person in whom it is measured. For example, consider also any medical conditions or treatments that may affect the reading, such as heart failure or diuretic therapy.

Accuracy

Blood pressure is now usually measured with automated blood pressure devices, such as Dynamaps®. Provided that the equipment is serviced regularly (usually annually), blood pressure devices used in health care settings are accurate (Jones et al 2003). However, many people own sphygmomanometers or measure their blood pressure with devices in shopping areas, and the accuracy of these machines is variable (O'Brien et al 2001). Wrong-sized cuffs give inaccurate measurements: if too small, readings are falsely high; if too large, readings are falsely low (Beevers et al 2001). Cuff bladder width should be at least 80 per cent of the arm's circumference (Beevers et al 2001) (Table 29.1). Large cuffs may be needed for people who are obese, whilst small cuffs may be needed for very thin, emaciated people or people with exceptionally small builds.

Table 29.1 **Blood pressure cuff size**

Cuff size	Cuff length (cm)
Normal adult*	23
Small adult	Less than 23
Large adult	35

*Arm circumference 26–33 cm

Measurement is reduced ('dampened') by anything between the blood vessel and the cuff, so clothing should be removed from the measurement site. Cuffs should be wrapped firmly round the limb, without any slack. Blood pressure is usually measured on an arm, with the cuff placed 2–3 centimetres above the elbow and the centre of the bladder (where the tubes are) on the inside of the arm, over the brachial artery (Nicol et al 2000).

Pressure can vary between different sites. Beevers and colleagues (2001) recommend initially measuring both right and left arm blood pressure. If differences exceed 20mmHg systolic or 10mmHg diastolic, the person should be referred to a cardiologist. Because blood pressure measurement is used to assess heart function, it should ideally be measured on the left arm, although this is not always possible. The person should be sitting or lying, with their arm comfortably supported on the same level as their heart (Beevers et al 2001). Conditions such as muscle contractures from strokes, or stiff joints, may limit the ability to place the cuff effectively, thereby affecting the accuracy of readings. Leaving the arm unsupported may increase diastolic blood pressure by up to 10 per cent (Beevers et al 2001).

Systolic blood pressure

Systolic pressure is maximum (peak) pressure created when pulses surge through blood vessels, stretching the vessel wall. With vascular disease, the blood vessels become 'hardened' (atherosclerosis), losing much of their ability to stretch and thus increasing systolic pressure. Excessive peak pressure may cause bleeding; Lip (2003) suggests that 40 per cent of strokes occur when systolic pressure exceeds 140mmHg.

There are many drugs that can be used to reduce blood pressure, but beta-blockers, such as atenolol and propranolol (and other drugs ending in '-olol'), remain the most widely used and useful antihypertensives. As with any other drugs, excessive doses can cause the opposite problem to the one they are prescribed to solve. With many people needing to remain on long-term beta-blocker therapy, inadequate medical review of prescriptions can lead to beta-blocker overdosage, causing hypotension. Low systolic pressure may indicate poor perfusion (see below) but mean arterial pressure (see below) is a better way to assess perfusion.

Diastolic blood pressure

Diastolic pressure is pressure in the blood vessel between pulses. It changes less than systolic blood pressure. Significant falls (greater than 10 per cent) in diastolic pressure may indicate excessive vasodilatation (widening of the blood vessels) or hypovolaemia (lack of blood volume), and should be reported.

Mean arterial pressure

Mean arterial pressure (MAP) averages blood pressure across the whole pulse cycle. Most automated blood-pressure monitors measure MAP. Perfusion, which delivers oxygen and nutrients to and removes waste from the tissues, occurs throughout the whole pulse cycle. Maximum perfusion occurs during systole; minimum perfusion occurs during diastole. But systole is very brief. Therefore, averaging pressure across the whole pulse cycle provides a better indication of perfusion than either systolic or diastolic blood pressure alone (Darovic 2002). When blood pressure is low, mean pressure provides a better indication than either systolic or diastolic pressure of whether the person's brain and other vital organs are receiving sufficient oxygen. Although transient falls in blood pressure may be insignificant, sustained hypotension, usually defined as lasting more than one hour, can cause diseases such as acute renal failure.

Stereotypical blood pressure of 120/80 would make MAP about 93mmHg. Like any other assessment, MAP should be individualised to the patient, and significant changes reported. Significant falls (greater than 10 per cent) in blood pressure are usually caused either by acute blood loss or by vasodilatation. Either can cause shock, resulting in inadequate perfusion. Therefore, significant hypotension should be reported, and monitored by measuring mean arterial pressure. MAP below 65mmHg indicates poor perfusion (Treacher 2003), which will probably damage all major organs. Mean arterial pressure above 110mmHg indicates hypertension.

Pulse pressure

The difference between systolic and diastolic pressure is the 'pulse pressure'. This is affected by the blood vessel's ability to stretch (Mitchell et al 1997), thus indicating a condition/disease of the artery. Stereotypical blood pressure of 120/80 creates a pulse pressure of 40mmHg. Higher (wider) pulse pressures in older people usually indicate 'hardened' arteries (Asmar et al 2001); pulse pressure greater than 50mmHg may be an early sign of diseases such as chronic heart failure (Haider et al 2003), dementia and Alzheimer's disease

(Qui et al 2003). Narrow pulse pressure (less than 30mmHg) often indicates lack of blood volume (hypovolaemia).

Lying/Standing blood pressure

Two centres (cardiac, vasomotor) in the brainstem receive information about arterial blood pressure via specialised nerve endings called baroreceptors. If pressure falls suddenly, such as when getting up from bed in the morning, baroreceptors stimulate the vasomotor centre to constrict the blood vessels, thereby restoring blood pressure and maintaining perfusion to the brain.

Baroreceptor responses can be assessed by measuring the person's blood pressure when lying down and when standing. Measurements between these lying and standing measurements should not be significantly delayed – ideally within one minute (Baguet et al 2001), as diseased baroreceptors will still respond, albeit more slowly. In health, differences between lying and standing blood pressure should be about 5mmHg (Baguet et al 2001).

Older people are more likely to have postural hypotension because of slower baroreceptor responses. When getting up, people with postural hypotension initially feel dizzy and sometimes faint, so usually get up slowly, allowing time for their baroreceptors to respond. Diseases that often cause delayed baroreceptor response include chronic hypertension, diabetes and Parkinson's disease (Baguet et al 2001), all of which are more prevalent in older people.

Conclusion

Healthy ageing does not significantly affect blood pressure. However, many older people develop cardiovascular disease. Measuring blood pressure provides an easy and effective way to assess and monitor cardiovascular health. Ways to achieve accurate assessment have been identified in this chapter. Sustained blood pressure above 140/90mmHg should usually be actively treated. In addition to systolic and diastolic measurements, mean arterial pressure (MAP), pulse pressure and lying/standing blood pressure provide further information for assessment.

30 **Pulse**

Philip Woodrow

The pulse is created by blood ejected from the left ventricle of the heart travelling though the blood vessels. In health, a normal-sized left ventricle can hold about 130ml of blood (Ganong 2001). Some, but not all, of this blood is ejected when the ventricle contracts. The amount ejected (stroke volume) depends on the strength of myocardial contraction, which in health varies to meet the body's demands. In the average person, normal stroke volume is 70–90ml (Ganong 2001). Differences between total ventricular volume and stroke volume can be measured in specialist areas, such as cardiac function laboratories, and is called the *ejection fraction*. A normal ejection fraction is 0.60–0.75 (Jowett and Thompson 2002), although this is more often expressed as a percentage (60–75 per cent).

In health, the heart rate normally ranges between 60 and 100 beats per minute (bpm). Heart rate is affected by both the sympathetic nervous system, which increases heart rate, and the parasympathetic nervous system, which slows it down. Therefore, in health, the heart rate varies between individuals, during different activities and because of other factors that stimulate the nervous system such as pain or anxiety. Whenever possible, pulse should be measured when the person seems relaxed and comfortable.

Ageing

With age, the atrioventricular node thickens, slowing down heart rate. Therefore, healthy older people usually have slower heart rates than during their younger adult years. Rates may be mildly bradycardic (50–60 beats per minute), but this rarely causes problems. Provided that normal sinus rhythm remains, the rate should stay regular and the strength of the pulse at rest should not feel especially strong or weak.

In contrast with healthy ageing, diseases and physiological problems that occur more frequently in later life may affect heart rate. Although incidence is usually higher in older than younger people, these diseases are not age-specific and are not part of normal ageing.

Diseases that affect the heart (such as atrial fibrillation) or blood vessels (such as atherosclerosis or peripheral vascular disease) may make the pulse more difficult to feel in older people. Other problems, such as tremors from Parkinson's disease, may also make pulses difficult to detect. In contrast, loss of subcutaneous fat and tissue may make the pulse easier to feel. But with healthy ageing, taking the pulse should not be significantly different than in younger adults. If in doubt, automated blood pressure monitors and pulse oximeters will confirm heart rate, whilst heart rate could be counted by listening to the heart beats over a full minute through a stethoscope.

Tachycardia (rate more than 100 bpm)

Fast heart rates are usually the heart's attempt to compensate for increased oxygen demand. However, both filling of the heart's ventricles and delivery of oxygen to the heart's own muscle occur during diastole and, as diastole is the gap between systoles, an increased number of systoles reduces both ventricular filling (stroke volume) and myocardial oxygen supply. Tachycardia also increases myocardial oxygen demand and may cause angina or myocardial infarction (heart attack).

Healthy hearts can usually cope easily with the mild and brief compensatory tachycardias that may occur during vigorous exercise or heavy work such as gardening, and people will usually stop and rest. But with faster and prolonged tachycardias (eg 150 bpm), other conditions that affect breathing or cardiac disease are likely to put people at greater and earlier risk. Chronic respiratory disease may cause chronic increases in heart rate. This attempted compensation for hypoxia (low oxygen) with chronic respiratory disease often fails to provide normal (healthy) tissue oxygenation, resulting in the heart muscle consuming more oxygen while receiving less. Chronic respiratory failure, therefore, often eventually causes enlargement of the heart (cardiomegaly) and heart failure.

As a 'first aid' measure, very fast and immediately life-threatening tachycardias (eg 180 bpm) may be slowed by carotid massage, which stimulates the parasympathetic vagus nerve. Parasympathetic nervous stimulation reduces the rate of the sinoatrial node (the normal pacemaker of the heart) and slows atrioventricular node conduction, so carotid massage may stimulate the vagus nerve sufficiently to reduce tachycardia. However, tachycardias originating from abnormal pacemaker cells are unlikely to be affected by carotid massage. Any resulting reduction in rate is usually only temporary, the tachycardia often resuming once carotid massage is stopped. Carotid massage should be used *only* by someone who knows how to perform it.

Whether or not carotid massage is attempted, if there is any sudden and significant sustained increase in heart rate (eg 30–40 bpm above the person's normal rate), help should be summoned urgently, oxygen given, other vital signs assessed and, if possible, a 12-lead ECG performed and cardiac monitoring initiated. In an immediately life-threatening emergency, maintaining an adequate oxygen supply to tissues is vital. Provided that medical help is likely to arrive quickly, this often requires 100% oxygen, whether or not the person has chronic respiratory disease. Any other tachycardias giving cause for concern should also be referred for medical review, but are less likely to need urgent intervention.

Bradycardia (less than 60 bpm)

Blood pressure is the sum of heart rate multiplied by stroke (pulse) volume multiplied by systemic vascular resistance (BP = HR × SV × SVR). Therefore, unless other compensatory mechanisms occur, bradycardia may reduce the blood pressure.

Bradycardia may have various causes, such as:

- reduced oxygen demand (such as while sleeping overnight);
- increased parasympathetic (vagal) nerve stimulation;

- drugs that slow heart rate (such as digoxin, beta-blockers, metoclopramide);
- blocks in cardiac conduction (often causing rates below 40 bpm);
- other diseases/problems (such as hypothermia or hypo-thyroidism).

If bradycardia causes insufficient perfusion of the brain, the person is likely to feel giddy and, if perfusion is not improved, may faint (syncope). If bradycardia is a problem, underlying causes should, if possible, be removed or resolved. For example, drug-induced bradycardia indicates toxic doses, which may need to be reversed actively, and the prescription should be reviewed in any case. Unless the person's normal rate is significantly faster, mild bradycardias (50–60 bpm) do not usually cause significant problems, but slower rates are more likely to cause insufficient perfusion and tissue hypoxia. As the main problem is likely to be tissue hypoxia, oxygen should usually be given. Drugs, such as atropine, can be used to increase heart rate.

Regularity

A healthy heart in sinus rhythm (usually 60–100 bpm, the rhythm originating from the sino-atrial node) produces a regular pulse. However, regular pulses are not always healthy. For example, ventricular tachycardia produces a regular weak pulse but is immediately life-threatening, necessitating cardiopulmonary resuscitation (CPR). Provided that the person's pulse is regular, automated blood pressure monitors should accurately measure heart rate, but regularity of the pulse can be assessed only by feeling the pulse or viewing a cardiac monitor. If the pulse feels irregular, note whether there is any pattern to the irregularity, such as coupled beats. Any new irregularity should be reported to medical colleagues and recorded in nursing notes.

Diseased hearts may develop many different (abnormal) rhythms, but atrial fibrillation (see below) causes an irregular pulse. Irregular pulse may affect the accuracy of other measurements from machines such as automated blood pressure monitors and pulse oximeters.

Strength

The pulse may feel:

- strong/bounding
- normal
- weak/thready.

The strength of the pulse indicates stroke volume and blood pressure. Significant changes in strength of the pulse should be recorded and reported.

An abnormally strong pulse may be an early indication of problems. Strong, bounding pulses are often caused by excessive myocardial work, attempting to compensate for other problems such as hypervolaemia (excessive blood volume). The person may maintain normal or have high blood pressure, and appear well perfused (warm, normal-colour skin), but experience palpitations and breathlessness. High resistance in the blood vessels from vascular disease can also create a bounding pulse. Prolonged excessive myocardial work may cause myocardial ischaemia (inadequate blood flow to the heart muscle), angina and infarction.

A weak, thready pulse usually results in poor perfusion or poor stroke volume, so the person may have cold and pale or clammy hands and feet and have low blood pressure. The weak pulse therefore indicates either that the heart is unable to meet the body's needs (heart failure) or that the person is hypovolaemic – or both.

Atrial fibrillation

Atrial fibrillation (AF) is the most common dysrhythmia, and is more likely to occur as people age. Around 5 per cent of people over the age of 65, and 10 per cent over 75, have atrial fibrillation (Royal College of Physicians 1999).

Atrial fibrillation is caused by lack of co-ordination and conduction in atrial muscle. Erratic impulses of differing strength reach the atrioventricular (AV) node very rapidly and irregularly, often at 300–500 bpm (Ganong 2001). Fortunately, the atrioventricular node is incapable of transmitting such fast rates, so most atrial impulses are blocked, only the strongest being conducted into ventricular muscle. Ventricular conduction is normal (unless the person has some other conduction disease) but the pulse is irregular, with no pattern, and the volume (strength) of each pulse varies. Some pulses may not be strong enough to reach the peripheral blood vessels, causing lower pulse rates in arteries further away from the heart (*apex-radial deficit*). For example, ventricular rates of 100 bpm might produce rates of only 50 in the brachial arteries (where the automated blood pressure cuff is usually placed) and even lower rates in the radial artery (where the pulse is usually felt for manual assessment).

Atrial fibrillation may be an acute complication of other disease. Acute atrial fibrillation is often treated initially with the drug amiodarone or by cardioversion – pre-planned defibrillation. More often, atrial fibrillation is a chronic condition that the person will have for the remainder of his or her life. Provided that atrial fibrillation is 'controlled', people can live healthily despite the chronic condition. It is usually controlled with drugs, which require regular medical review.

Although many drugs may be prescribed to treat or control atrial fibrillation, the most widely used drug is digoxin, which slows and strengthens the heart rate. Slowing the heart rate reduces myocardial workload, while strengthening the pulse enables more pulses to reach peripheries, thereby improving perfusion. Digoxin has a narrow therapeutic range: overdose can cause bradycardia, often with coupled beats, while underdoses are ineffective. Digoxin levels should therefore be checked periodically by sending blood samples to the laboratory.

Because digoxin slows the heart rate, it should not be given if the heart rate is below 60 bpm. However, as apex-radial deficits cause fewer pulses to reach the peripheries, if the radial or the brachial pulse rate is below 60 bpm, the apex rate should be counted (using a stethoscope placed over or near the sternum – the best position varies slightly between individuals) for a full minute; digoxin should then be omitted *only* if the apex rate is below 60. If a colleague is available, the radial pulse should also be counted over the same minute, so that the apex-radial deficit can be measured. Observations should be recorded and, if significantly different from previous observations, reported. If the radial or brachial rate is above 60, the apex rate must be at least as high, so digoxin can be given safely.

Loss of co-ordinated atrial contraction in atrial fibrillation results in blood within the atria remaining fairly static. This increases the risk of thrombus formation, which may cause emboli. Emboli entering the left ventricle are especially likely to flow into cerebral blood vessels, causing a cerebrovascular accident (stroke). Strokes are six times more likely in people who have atrial fibrillation than in the rest of the population (Hart et al 2003), so people with atrial fibrillation are usually given anticoagulants (Walraven et al 2002), usually warfarin. Warfarin also requires careful titrating and monitoring.

Digoxin and warfarin, or other drugs prescribed to control chronic atrial fibrillation, will usually be needed for the remainder of the person's life, but should be monitored by regular medical review because requirements may change or complications may occur.

Sick sinus syndrome

Various diseases of the heart can affect conduction. Although disease is not a normal part of ageing, heart disease is usually more likely to occur with advancing years. The sinoatrial (SA) node, which is the normal 'pacemaker' of the heart, may fail intermittently, resulting in periods of normal sinus rhythm alternating with one or more of various abnormal rhythms. The person often feels dizzy or faints during bouts of abnormal rhythms.

Sick sinus syndrome may be caused by cardiac disease (such as ischaemic heart disease or cardiomyopathy), cardio-active drugs (such as digoxin, quinidine or beta-blockers) or toxicity from other chemicals that can affect cardiac function (such as nicotine from smoking and caffeine from coffee or other drinks).

Sick sinus syndrome is usually confirmed by recording a 24-hour ECG (Houghton and Gray 2003). If possible, causes of sick sinus syndrome should be removed. If this is not possible or bouts of non-sinus rhythm are prolonged and/or immediately life-threatening, medical intervention is necessary, which may include drugs and temporary or permanent pacing.

Conclusion

The pulse is a vital sign and can provide useful information about cardiovascular function. But it may be affected by various factors and should be interpreted in the contexts of both other vital signs and the individual. Most nurses are used to recording heart rate but, in addition to using information from automated blood-pressure monitors, pulse oximeters or cardiac monitors, nurses should feel the pulse for regularity and strength. The pulse can usually be felt most easily at the radial artery. With irregular pulses, nurses should assess whether they can detect any pattern to the irregularity.

In health, heart rate slows slightly over a normal lifetime but continues to meet the body's needs. But heart disease is more likely to occur with increasing age. Abnormal pulse rate, regularity or strength may provide an early sign of acute or chronic problems. Any significant changes in pulse rate, regularity or strength should therefore be reported and recorded.

31 Respiratory functioning

Philip Woodrow and Roger Watson

Breathing is essential to life, but respiratory assessment remains the most neglected vital sign in most areas of health care. Respiratory rate and oxygen saturation provide major early warning signs of critical illness (Intensive Care Society 2001) but half of patients whose medical/nursing notes identify respiratory problems do not have their respiratory observations recorded (Kenward et al 2001).

Assessment is necessary to give effective care. Much useful information can be gained by simply looking at the person, which is an assessment tool available to care professionals in hospitals, care homes and the community. Additional information may be obtained with equipment such as peak flow meters and pulse oximeters, which are not discussed in this chapter.

Normal physiology

In health, the respiratory system maintains blood levels of oxygen and carbon dioxide within narrow limits (Hall et al 1993). Oxygen is needed by all body tissues, and all tissues produce carbon dioxide as a waste product of metabolism. Exchange of these gases in the lungs is therefore sometimes called 'external respiration', and exchange at tissue level is 'internal respiration' (Watson 1999). Transporting gases relies on perfusion by the cardiovascular system, both of the lungs and of the tissues. If the cardiovascular system fails to perfuse the lungs adequately, inadequate exchange of oxygen and carbon dioxide occurs in the alveoli.

Air is approximately 21% oxygen and 79% nitrogen, with very little else (only 0.04% is carbon dioxide). Nitrogen is not exchanged, so exhaled air also contains 79% nitrogen; the other 21% is made up of both oxygen and carbon dioxide. Movement of air in and out of the lungs is called *ventilation*. Carbon dioxide clearance depends on the amount (volume) of ventilation, so *hyper*ventilation (deep and/or rapid breathing) clears more, whilst *hypo*ventilation (shallow and/or slow breathing) clears less.

Breathing relies on negative pressure: as the diaphragm moves down and the ribcage moves out, the increased space in the thorax makes intrathoracic pressure negative to atmospheric pressure. This draws air through the nose and/or mouth into the lungs. Ventilation is therefore affected by factors such as posture and the ability of lung tissue to stretch (compliance).

Inspiration (breathing in) is an active process, controlled by two respiratory centres in the brainstem. Specialised nerve endings (called chemoreceptors) measure levels of carbon dioxide, acid and oxygen in arterial blood, sending signals to the respiratory centres, which increase rate and depth of breathing if carbon dioxide is raised or if blood is acidic (pH below 7.35) or hypoxic. Expiration (breathing out) is a passive activity, muscles recoiling back to their resting state.

Effects of ageing

At rest, only a fraction of respiratory capacity is used. Age-related changes occur in all parts of the respiratory system (Herbert 1999) but reserve capacity is usually sufficient to maintain adequate function, provided that disease is absent. The upper airway becomes obstructed due to loss of airway muscle tone, and the protection of the lung against infectious disease is reduced owing to an impaired cough mechanism, reduced ciliary action in the trachea and bronchi, and decreased activity of specific and non-specific protection mechanisms (Harrell 1997).

Whilst the total lung capacity does not change with age, the volume of air that can be breathed in after maximum expiration is reduced and residual capacity increases (Christiansen and Grzybowski 1993). This makes older people more prone to breathlessness on exertion, but normal exercise should not cause problems. Observable signs should not therefore differ significantly during healthy adult life.

However, reduced reserve capacity makes older people more susceptible to:

- acute respiratory disease, such as flu (hence immunisation programmes each autumn);
- chronic respiratory diseases.

Chronic respiratory disease often causes distinctive ribcage malformation ('barrel chest'). COPD (chronic obstructive pulmonary disease) mainly affects the bronchioles, causing fibrosis of distal airways and emphysema (Barnes et al 2003), leading to potential accumulation of secretions and bacteria in the lungs. Coughing becomes less effective (Hall et al 1993), so secretions and infection are removed less effectively, causing exacerbations of COPD from acute chest infections. Chronic respiratory limitations impair quality of life and make acute infections more likely.

Musculoskeletal changes can affect breathing. Demineralisation of bone causes the skeleton to shrink, and a stooped posture called kyphosis. This posture reduces chest volume, making ventilation more difficult. Demineralisation of the ribs, degeneration of the joints where they articulate and stiffening of intercostal cartilage from calcification reduce thoracic compliance, thereby limiting ventilation. Diaphragm and intercostal muscles also atrophy (Tolep and Kelsen 1998) but, although the strength of respiratory muscles decreases with age, it is unclear whether this affects endurance. With respiratory disease, other muscles called accessory muscles of respiration may be used for breathing – especially shoulder and abdominal muscles. However, these accessory muscles will also atrophy with age. Collagen in connective tissue loses its flexibility, making older lungs less elastic, thus reducing both their compliance on inspiration and recoil during expiration.

With age, control of breathing becomes less responsive to changes in blood levels of oxygen and carbon dioxide, because the central and peripheral chemoreceptors undergo degenerative changes (Hall et al 1993). Gas exchange becomes less efficient in the older lung, as ventilation and perfusion become mismatched if the cardiovascular system dysfunctions, as for example in heart failure. Age-related changes are summarised in Table 31.1. Various other factors, mainly connected to lifestyle and environment – for example, smoking, obesity, immobility and surgery (Harrell 1997) – also affect the respiratory health of older people.

Table 31.1 *Age-related changes in lung function*

	Change
Total lung capacity	Unchanged
Vital capacity	Decreased
Functional residual capacity	Decreased
Residual volume	Decreased
Peak flow	Decreased

Adapted from Hall et al (1993)

Smoking remains the single main cause of respiratory disease (British Thoracic Society 1997) but work-related environmental pollutants, such as in coal-mining, also cause much ill-health. Health professionals should not 'blame' people for disease, but assessing risk factors, such as whether they smoke or are exposed to other pollutants that can be removed, enables care professionals to offer health advice and plan care. For example, stopping smoking significantly reduces loss of function (Pelkonen et al 2001). Whether a person has been active, either through their occupation or by participating in sport or exercise, affects their respiratory health.

Assessment

Any assessment, but especially that in an older person, should begin with a thorough history, followed by physical assessment (Box 31.1). If shortness of breath is observed, the signs listed in Box 31.2 can identify how far it affects the person's life; quality of life is possibly more important than the observation per se of shortness of breath.

Box 31.1 *Essential components of pulmonary assessment in older people*

History

Previous and existing respiratory diseases
Smoking and exposure to pollutants
Symptoms such as cough, shortness of breath, wheezing, haemoptysis, chest pain, orthopnoea

Physical assessment

Inspection
Posture
Skin colour
Chest shape, symmetry and expansion
Sputum: colour, smell, amount
Palpation
Ribs
Skin temperature and hydration
Percussion
Bilateral lung fields for flatness and dullness of sounds
Auscultation
Audible breathing sounds

Adapted from Harrell (1997)

Box 31.2 *Grading shortness of breath*

1 Short of breath hurrying on level or walking up hills or stairs
2 Short of breath walking on level with people of same age
3 Short of breath walking on level at own pace
4 Short of breath on washing or dressing
5 Short of breath while sitting quietly

Adapted from Caird and Judge (1979)

With actual/potential breathing problems, observations should include:

- rate
- depth
- pattern
- breath sounds
- skin colour
- carbon dioxide
- cough reflex
- sputum.

Noting whether each is normal or abnormal and recording details of observations in nursing records may help the medical diagnosis, and provide 'baseline observations' if changes occur. Lung function is more difficult to interpret in older people, as age-related changes in older people resemble signs of airway obstruction in younger people (Hall et al 1993).

Rate

In health, the resting respiratory rate is 10–18 breaths per minute (bpm) (Darovic 2002). Irregular breathing may cluster most breaths over relatively few seconds, so the rate should be counted over a whole minute. However, people who are aware that their breathing is being watched may alter their rate. You should count breaths while appearing to be doing something else, such as feeling the pulse.

Fast rates (tachypnoea, breathlessness) are usually caused by a need for more oxygen or to clear more carbon dioxide. The effectiveness of treatment (eg administered oxygen) can be assessed by whether the rate and other signs improve. Breathlessness is distressing and makes activities of living such as eating, drinking and sleeping difficult, thereby exacerbating problems. Prolonged severe breathlessness may cause complete exhaustion and respiratory arrest.

Very slow rates (bradypnoea) are usually caused by depression of the respiratory centres in the brain from:

- brain damage (eg stroke);
- drugs (eg opoids; sedation).

Depth (breath size, tidal volume)

People with respiratory disease are especially likely to have smaller (shallower) breaths. In health, the main respiratory muscles are the diaphragm and intercostal muscles (between the ribs). Intercostal movement is visible but normal diaphragm movement is not easily seen.

Trying to breathe deeper and laboured breathing (dyspnoea) use accessory muscles: abdominal (to help diaphragm expansion) and clavicles (shoulder – causing distinctive lifting of the shoulder blades). Like all body tissues, respiratory muscles need oxygen. Oxygen consumption by respiratory muscles is called 'work of breathing'. At rest, respiratory muscles use only 1–3 per cent of total body oxygen, but in respiratory disease can consume 25–30 per cent (Hinds and Watson 1996), leaving less oxygen for other vital organs (such as the brain and heart).

Peak-flow monitoring measures the maximum size of expired breaths (the best of three is usually recorded) and can assess the effectiveness of bronchodilator nebulisers or inhalers (Frausing et al 2001).

Depth of breathing is reduced with nerve inhibition from diseases that paralyse or weaken muscles. For example, Parkinson's disease often causes shallow breathing (and weak coughs). Pain is usually worsened by deep breathing and anyone in pain usually tends to breathe shallowly; to compensate for lack of depth, the rate usually increases. Pain relief is therefore desirable both for humanitarian reasons and to enable deep breathing. Shallow breaths use only the upper parts of the lungs, leaving a warm, moist and static area at the bases where bacteria may breed. Care professionals can reduce the risks of people developing chest infections by encouraging them to breathe deeply.

Pattern

Normal (subconscious) control of breathing by the respiratory centres creates a reasonably regular rate and pattern. Irregular patterns can occur with brain damage and conscious alteration of breathing, so observing patterns, describing any abnormalities, may indicate neurological complications.

Breath sounds

Healthy breathing (at rest) is usually barely audible but abnormal breathing may sound:

- laboured;
- wheezy, from narrowed airways (treated with bronchodilator drugs);
- 'bubbling' or 'rattling', from excessive sputum or other fluid in the airways (usually indicates chest infection).

In a younger person basal crepitations (crackling/rustling sounds heard through a stethoscope at the lung bases) indicate disease, but in older people may be caused by their cough being too weak to clear secretions.

Skin colour

Cyanosis – giving a bluish skin colouring – usually occurs with hypoxia. It is clearest in: nail-beds, mucous membranes (eg lips, mouth), the tip of the nose and the earlobes (Darovic 2002). Cyanosis occurs at very low saturations (less than 80 per cent) but may not occur with very low haemoglobin levels (less than 5 mg/dl) (Darovic 2002). Although it is a relatively late and unreliable sign, cyanosis should be reported. If available, pulse oximeters provide far more reliable information about oxygenation. Skin colour may also indicate other problems; for example, nicotine staining of the fingertips indicates heavy smoking.

Carbon dioxide

Whilst oxygenation is fairly easily assessed by skin colour and pulse oximetry, estimating carbon dioxide is more problematic without taking an arterial blood gas sample. However, slow (less than 10 bpm) or shallow (including shallow and fast) breathing is likely to cause blood levels to be raised. A number of devices have been developed for less-invasive and non-invasive assessment of carbon dioxide. At the moment, the reliability of these devices is questionable but it is likely that within a few years simple and clinically reliable non- or minimally invasive means will be available.

Cough reflex

Coughing is a reflex action to remove foreign bodies (eg bacteria trapped by mucus, tar) from the airways. A cough is therefore a sign of problems. If it is present, note whether it is strong or weak, whether it is productive and how it sounds (dry, hoarse, barking). Absence of coughing may mean absence of any problem, or that the reflex has failed to occur. If a cough is present, it may be assessed by asking the questions listed in Box 31.3.

Box 31.3 Assessment of cough

How long has the cough persisted?

Is the cough dry or moist?

Is it producing phlegm?

If phlegm is present, are the secretions from the chest or the back of the throat?

What colour is the phlegm?

Adapted from Rush and Schofield (1999)

Coughs are distressing. If they are 'productive', benefits from removing infection may justify this distress. But unproductive coughs cause unnecessary distress and should be relieved. There is no ideal way to suppress an unproductive cough. Simple linctus is widely available and safe, although not always effective. More effective cough suppressants usually contain other drugs, such as codeine, which may cause other problems to some people. Dry or hoarse-sounding coughs may be eased by using a 2ml saline nebuliser, although some people prefer steam inhalers. People with dry coughs should be assessed to ensure that they are drinking enough fluids. Sometimes a warm drink such as tea can provide relief.

Sputum

If a cough is productive, note the characteristics of the sputum (also called phlegm), including amount, colour (eg white, black, pink, green/yellow/creamy), consistency (eg frothy, thick, watery) and purulence (foulness). The amount can be assessed by weight of the sputum pot, whilst a brief glimpse inside should quickly provide the remaining information. Sputum is normally white, with small (if any) amounts being coughed up. Black sputum may result from (old) blood, cigarette tar or coal (in former coal-miners). Pink sputum indicates fresh bleeding or, especially if frothy, pulmonary oedema. Green, yellow or cream sputum suggests infection. Different bacteria produce different colours, so recording the colour rather than 'infected' may assist the medical diagnosis.

Nursing interventions for breathlessness

Although detailed discussion of medical treatments is beyond the scope of this book, there is much that nurses and other care professionals can do. Sitting breathless people upright allows gravity to help diaphragm expansion. Sitting forward, with forearms resting on a table and pillow, also helps intercostal muscle expansion.

Inactivity increases mortality (Martinson et al 2001) and early mobilisation can literally be life-saving. When people are bed-bound, encourage them to take at least six deep breaths every hour (keep numbers and time simple to remember).

Stress can cause constriction of the airways, which further reduces breath size. A calm, controlled environment can help reduce fear, thus giving both good psychological care and improving (relaxing) breathing. Explaining the treatments and care helps to reduce distress (Hayward 1975).

Conclusion

Oxygen is essential for human life. Respiratory distress is usually the first sign of serious illness and can progress rapidly. Staff in the immediate area of the person may be the first to detect problems and should understand how to recognise and assess respiratory failure. When planning care, each person's functional ability and limits should be assessed. Many chronic respiratory problems are caused by lifestyle (eg smoking) but health care staff should help people achieve the best possible quality of life by offering them help and advice, not blaming them for their disease.

Although many technical ways exist for the detailed assessment of respiratory function, much useful information can be obtained without any specialised equipment. None of the following – shortness of breath, coughing, haemoptysis (coughing up blood) or chest pain – is normal and each may indicate an underlying pathology. However, care staff should also be concerned with the effect any respiratory limitations may have on an older person. In common with assessing the cardiovascular system (see Chapter 28), assessment of activities of daily living and instrumental activities of daily living should be carried out, including more discreet questions, if appropriate, about any sexual dysfunction. Gathering this information during the initial assessment, and subsequent treatment, enables effective care to be planned.

32 Body temperature

Philip Woodrow

Thermoregulation balances heat gain (such as muscle exercise) with heat loss (such as convection of heat from skin) to maintain 'normal' body temperature. In addition to behavioural responses to warm up or cool down, the hypothalamus initiates physiological responses: sweating and vasodilatation to increase heat loss, or vasoconstriction to conserve heat and shivering to produce more heat.

Extremes of life for human body temperature range between 24°C and 44°C, normal core temperatures being from 35.6°C to 37.8°C and averaging 36.2°C (Marieb 2004). Normal temperature varies with daily body rhythm (circadian rhythm), changing about half a degree during each day (Weller 2001), mainly from alterations in metabolic rate (Clancy and McVicar 2002). Temperature normally peaks in the early evening, so once-daily temperature should be measured at 6 pm (Samples et al 1985).

As living cells metabolise energy sources, such as sugars, into adenosine triphosphate (ATP; a chemical needed for cell function), heat is released. Because body heat is produced by metabolism, temperature varies in different parts of the body. At rest, more metabolism normally occurs in the liver than anywhere else. Therefore, at rest the liver is normally the warmest part of the body. Rhoades and Pflanzer (1996) suggest that only one-fifth of chemical energy from food is metabolised into energy for external work, leaving four-fifths available for conversion into body heat.

Skeletal muscle work can produce 30–40 times as much heat as the rest of the body (Marieb 2004), so exercising skeletal muscles, such as running or digging a garden, significantly increases heat production. Shivering is skeletal muscle work, which makes the shivering reflex an efficient way of increasing body heat. Differences in temperature between different parts of the body mean that temperature measured at one site may not fully reflect temperature elsewhere (Lattavo et al 1995).

The ideal temperature to measure is the temperature of the blood perfusing the brain (core temperature). Sites where temperature is measured in practice are approximations of core temperature. The benefits and problems of various measurement sites have been much debated, but Dowding and colleagues (2002) and many others recommend tympanic measurement (in the ear).

Ageing

Thermoregulation remains healthy in most older people (Herbert and Rowswell 1999), although Schofield (1999) suggests that responses to extremes of temperature change after the age of 70. Ageing and disease can cause loss of muscle mass, which reduces the basal metabolic rate, whilst homoeostatic responses (reduced vasoconstriction and cardiac output, impaired sweating, diminished shivering, loss of subcutaneous tissue which provides 'insulation') may be less effective (Eliopoulos 2001). Age-related decline in nerve conduction may impair the perception of feeling cold (Herbert and Rowswell 1999), whilst muscle weakness or other limitations can prevent people from trying, actively, to keep warm or to cool down. Therefore, whilst most older people maintain healthy thermoregulation, they are also more at risk. Imbalanced thermoregulation can complicate other problems. Care professionals should therefore assess the individual's abilities as part of their holistic care.

Pyrexia

Excessive body temperature (pyrexia, fever) may be caused by:

- metabolic heat production exceeding the ability to lose heat;
- infection;
- damage to the thermoregulatory centre in the hypothalamus.

Hypothalamic damage may be transitory (cerebral oedema) or permanent (cerebrovascular accident/stroke). If it is transitory, underlying causes should be treated; for example, cerebral oedema is usually removed with diuretics such as mannitol.

Although pyrexia is often viewed as a sign of infection, and infection should be considered as a possible cause, excessive metabolic heat production may occur with:

- post-operative inflammatory response;
- blood transfusion;
- tumours;
- drugs that increase metabolism.

Health care staff caring for feverish people with any of these factors present should assess whether the raised temperature is caused by increased metabolism, infection or both. Post-operative pyrexia more often results from metabolism than from infection (Perlino 2001). Metabolic heat production exceeding the ability to lose heat means that the person feels hot and wants cold drinks and other means to cool down. Metabolic pyrexia is often, although not always, lower than infective pyrexia (often below 38°C).

Infection

Pyrexia inhibits bacterial growth (Ganong 2001) and mobilises immune defences (Rowsey 1997), damaging the membranes of both the body's own and especially bacterial cells. Cell damage releases chemicals called pyrogens into the blood. Pyrogens increase prostaglandin production, which resets the body's thermostat in the hypothalamus to a higher temperature (Marieb 2004). The hypothalamus therefore attempts to maintain the body at the new higher temperature. If body temperature is below the new hypothalamic set point, the person feels cold, seeking ways to keep warm, and shivers.

Pyrexia provides a defence against infection, so failure to respond to infection by becoming pyrexial facilitates bacterial growth. But some diseases (immunocompromised) and treatments (chemotherapy) inhibit pyrexial responses. Immune function declines with age, and some older people may remain apyrexial despite infection (Watson

2000). Very high temperatures often cause confusion, although this is an unreliable sign as there are many other causes of acute confusion. Individual assessment is therefore needed to identify infection or malfunction of thermoregulation.

Benefits and burdens

Medieval science viewed pyrexia as beneficial, inducing it deliberately. More recently, pyrexia was considered a problem requiring treatment. Both extremes are over-simplistic. Pyrexia is a symptom, so, like any other symptom, should be treated only if problems outweigh benefits. Health care staff should assess people individually rather than respond to a thermometer measurement (Marik 2000).

Increased metabolism hastens tissue repair (Marieb 2004) whilst increased oxygen unloading from haemoglobin delivers more oxygen to tissue cells (Manthous et al 1995). However, increased metabolism also consumes more oxygen and nutrients while producing more metabolic waste (carbon dioxide and acids). For healthy people these may not cause problems, but for the malnourished, people with respiratory or renal impairment or the acutely ill, the costs of pyrexia may exceed benefits.

Age-related decline in all body systems reduces reserve function (the ability of the system to increase function in response to increased demand). Whilst the systems of most healthy older people usually have sufficient reserve function to cope, a significant minority do have chronic respiratory and/or renal impairment/disease and may not be able to cope with increased demand. In hospitals, the minority of older people with chronic ill-health usually form the majority of patients. Assessing the cost of pyrexia to the person therefore depends on:

* how high the temperature is;
* the person's respiratory and renal function;
* any other symptoms that cause concern.

Cooling

Having assessed whether the costs of the pyrexia exceed the benefits for that person, problem pyrexias should be reversed by cooling. Traditional ways of cooling were by reducing bedding or clothing and using fans and cool water. With metabolic pyrexia, where heat production exceeds ability to lose heat, the person may want these and they may be beneficial. But with infective pyrexia, where the hypothalamus attempts to maintain an abnormally high temperature, peripheral cooling causes skin thermoreceptors (specialised nerve endings measuring temperature) to detect temperature below the set point. This triggers heat conservation (vasoconstriction) and production (shivering) responses (Bartlett 1996). Peripheral vasoconstriction traps body heat in vital organs, increasing their temperature, while skeletal muscle shivering increases nutrient and oxygen consumption by 35–40 per cent (Marik 2000) and increases the production of metabolic waste. Because body temperature is cooled below the set point, the person feels cold and distressed.

Pyrexia is a defence mechanism against infection, so removing the pyrexia removes the defence. Many otherwise healthy people put up with minor chest infections without seeking medical help. However, people with fewer reserves, more susceptible to illness or with more extensive infection are less likely to be able to cope with the problems caused by pyrexia. This makes older people an especially vulnerable group. Antibiotics are usually a more effective way of destroying bacteria than pyrexia is. Therefore, care professionals detecting signs of bacterial infection, such as green/yellow/creamy sputum, should seek medical advice. With antibiotics prescribed, infective pyrexia can be reversed by preventing prostaglandin production with drugs such as aspirin, paracetamol and non-steroidal anti-inflammatories (such as ibuprofen), thereby restoring normal hypothalamic set point. These drugs seldom reverse pyrexia linked to non-infective causes.

Additional considerations

After profuse sweating, people often appreciate a wash and change of clothing. Sweating, vasodilatation and increased capillary permeability ('leakage') may cause hypotension and dehydration, and fluid replacement should be provided. If people are able to drink, they should be encouraged to take oral fluids, ensuring that drinks are both accessible and appetising.

Fluid shifts (see Chapter 38) may cause electrolyte imbalances, whilst increased metabolic acid production may cause acidosis. Biochemical imbalances can be assessed by blood tests. When infective pyrexia is suspected, blood cultures may identify organisms. Although there is no absolute right or wrong temperature at which to take blood cultures, above 38°C or 1°C above baseline are often suggested because these are more likely to indicate infective than metabolic pyrexia. Antipyretic drugs remove a natural defence against micro-organisms, so antibiotics should usually be prescribed. As well as promoting comfort, health care staff should monitor the effectiveness of treatments, reassessing temperature frequently (probably every hour initially).

Hyperpyrexia

With temperatures above 40°C (hyperpyrexia), cardiac function is impaired (Hinds and Watson 1996), convulsions are likely at 41°C, and death follows at about 43°C (Marieb 2004). Hyperpyrexia is life-threatening and requires urgent treatment. If caused by a brainstem cerebrovascular accident (stroke), it is a sign that death is imminent. Otherwise, it is a rare condition, especially among older people.

Hypothermia

Watson (1993) suggests that over 1,000 people in the UK die each year from hypothermia, most being over 65 years old. But Herbert and Rowswell (1999) argue that, with most older people having healthy thermoregulation, hypothermia is over-emphasised.

Although mild hypothermia may be used therapeutically during cardiac surgery or neurological injury, moderate (below 32°C) to severe (below 28°C) hypothermia causes thermoregulation failure, hypometabolism and life-threatening cardiac dysrhythmias.

Rapid rewarming can cause profound hypotension, severe electrolyte imbalance and acidosis. Hinds and Watson (1996) cite rewarming rates ranging from 1°C to 4°C each hour, although 1°C is often used.

Conclusion

Body temperature is a vital sign. Thermoregulation balances heat gain against heat loss, and is controlled by the hypothalamus. Pyrexia may be caused by hypothalamic damage, hypermetabolism or infection. Appropriate management of pyrexia therefore requires individual assessment of the causes and costs of pyrexia. Infective pyrexia should be reversed with central antipyretics (such as paracetamol) rather than peripheral cooling (such as fans). In addition to providing comfort, health care staff should assess and monitor the temperature of their patients, using evidence-based knowledge rather than traditional rituals.

Eating and drinking

33 Eating and drinking in everyday life

Chris Eberhardie

Eating and drinking involve a series of complex psychomotor skills that are, in part, instinctive and partly the result of early learning. They are physical skills that are taken for granted and rarely thought about by the time we reach adolescence, when social skills assume a greater importance. In later life, subtle physical and social changes can lead to malnutrition if they are not identified and dealt with quickly.

Several research studies have established the prevalence of under-nutrition in older people (Great Britain Working Group on the Nutrition of Elderly People 1992). The King's Fund report *Nutrition: a positive approach to treatment* (1992) expressed concern that nutrition in general was not being given enough attention in hospital, and encouraged health care professionals to regard nutrition as a therapy. McWhirter and Pennington (1994) carried out a major study into the nutritional status of people in a general hospital. Among them were 100 patients in wards caring for older people, 43 per cent of whom had been undernourished on admission to hospital. The situation had not improved much by 2000 (Kelly et al 2000). In the community, the picture of malnutrition is no better (Edington et al 1996; Hamilton et al 2002).

Most older people wish to live independent lives in the community. It is important, therefore, for health care and social work professionals to make older people aware of common factors that have a significant impact on their nutritional health and quality of life.

Most nutritional assessment tools do not include a functional holistic assessment of the whole process of eating and drinking and its associated social attitudes and actions. The assessment of eating and drinking in the older person needs to address physical, psychological, socio-economic, cultural and religious factors.

Nutritional assessment can be carried out in a health education context such as in pre-retirement programmes, which inform older people planning for the future. This could range from learning to use a microwave oven to buying food on a limited budget. Equally, health care professionals can develop multidisciplinary and interprofessional approaches to eating and drinking. Such approaches should be developed in a cohesive manner so that professional boundaries are respected but the individual is offered a seamless and comprehensive assessment between the community and other parts of the health service.

The key points in this chapter are:

- To discuss the need for a holistic assessment of eating and drinking that includes the physical, psychological, socio-economic, cultural and religious factors.
- To offer some practical suggestions for preventing or overcoming common eating and drinking problems that can arise in old age.
- To provide reference and other learning material for the reader.

Holistic assessment of eating and drinking

Biological factors

The process of ensuring a good nutritional intake in the healthy adult requires a fully functioning body and, in particular, nervous and sensorimotor function. Before eating and drinking can take place, the individual needs to be motivated to search for food, choose safe and appetising ingredients, bring them home, prepare and/or cook them, have sufficient perceptual and locomotor function to take the food from a serving receptacle to the mouth and then bite, chew, salivate and swallow (Eberhardie 2004). As can be seen in Table 33.1, the biological basis of eating and drinking is not only complex but also, at any stage, vulnerable during the normal ageing process let alone when ill-health affects it. If there is an unrecognised problem at any stage, undernutrition and other problems will ensue.

Table 33.1 **The biological effect of ageing and its effect on eating and drinking**

System/ Function	Effect of ageing	Effect on nutritional status
Nervous	Paresis or paralysis of muscles	Impaired ability or inability to shop, carry or prepare food
	Loss of co-ordination	Difficulties in swallowing Unsafe to handle hot foods
	Poor attention and concentration	Impaired ability to shop, prepare and eat food
	Sensory impairment	Clumsy handling of cutlery
	Diminished taste and smell	Altered diet, reduced enjoyment of taste of food
	Visual and hearing impairment	Fear of going shopping

Table 33.1 (continued)

System/ Function	Effect of ageing	Effect on nutritional status
Locomotor	Joint rigidity Reduction in lean muscle mass	Difficulty in shopping and preparing food
	Immobility Risk of osteoporosis	Unable to carry heavy loads Impaired manual dexterity
Immune	Reduced efficiency in the immune function	Infection more likely if food hygiene is poor
Homoeo-stasis	Reduced efficiency	Fluid and electrolyte balance easily disturbed
Reproduc-tive	*Post-menopausal women:* Stress incontinence	Altered shopping habits
	Higher risk of osteoporosis and cardiovascular disease	Reduced ability to seek and prepare food Impaired calcium and vitamin D status
	No menstrual blood loss	Requirement for iron reduced

continued

Table 33.1 (continued)

System/ Function	Effect of ageing	Effect on nutritional status
Gastro-intestinal	Poor dentition	Inability to bite and chew
	Reduced efficiency in absorption	Risk of nutrient deficiencies
	Immobility leads to constipation	Need for a bulkier diet
	Reduction in size and capacity of the liver	Monitor drug nutrient interaction Need to reduce protein intake and monitor vitamin A intake
Skin	Tendency to dry skin Loss of adipose tissue Loss of skin elasticity Vulnerable to wound breakdown	Nutrients required for wound healing
Endocrine	Insulin production less efficient	Restrict glucose intake if necessary
	Osteomalacia	Increase vitamin D

Table 33.1 (continued)

System/ Function	Effect of ageing	Effect on nutritional status
Renal	Fear of incontinence	Fluid balance needs careful monitoring
	Impaired haemostasis of water and sodium	Reduce sodium intake

(Eberhardie 2002)

Psychological factors

Psychological problems such as depression, memory loss, anxiety and fear contribute to poor nutrition. Sometimes these are organic in nature (eg endogenous depression or dementia) but equally they can be the result of bereavement, loss, isolation and loneliness. The death of long-standing friends and acquaintances make the sense of loss more acute. As age and the losses increase, loneliness and social isolation can become more of a problem, especially in winter. Loneliness and social isolation play an important role in malnutrition and increased mortality (Chen et al 2001).

Socio-economic factors

Moving from a full and adequate salary to a reduced pension without adequate planning often results in a need to reduce expenditure. Some people choose to make those cuts in the food budget. Careful planning, even to the point of moving home to a cheaper, smaller house in a less expensive area, nearer to the shops, can ensure a healthy and good-quality life despite a reduced income.

Cultural and religious factors

People who adhere to a religion that has strongly held beliefs about food and, in particular, taboo foods may find it difficult to fulfil their needs if they are infirm and progressively more isolated from shops. How will they obtain halal or kosher foods without the help of family and friends? Fear of eating taboo foods may cause them to refuse food from non-believers.

Food and drink play an important role in the cultural and religious life of the individual. There are fasting periods and festivals to manage. The ability to adhere to the religious food taboos plays a significant role in the life of a believer. For instance, a Muslim or a Jew may suffer from malnutrition if they are unable to obtain to obtain halal or kosher meat or cannot be sure that meat and dairy produce have been kept separately. Fear that it may not be pure in the religious sense may result in a more restricted diet, which may not provide all the nutrients required for a healthy diet.

Older members of the community may need help to cope with major religious festivals, which often result in large meals being served. One only has to think about the huge meals consumed at Christmas to realise how difficult it must be for an older person with loss of appetite or fatigue. Those who are already malnourished may refuse dietary supplements if there is no guarantee that taboo foods are absent.

The effect of normal ageing on eating and drinking

In normal ageing a number of physiological changes take place. The speed and severity of those changes depend on genetic, lifestyle and health factors. However, sooner or later, the older person is likely to encounter one or more of the following (McCormack 1997; McLaren 1999):

- less strength in the muscles and joints;

- altered or loss of acuity of taste, smell, sight, hearing;
- reduction in gastric secretion and motility;
- short-term memory loss;
- slower reflexes;
- reduced appetite or poor appetite control;
- loss of bone density;
- poor dentition;
- poor bladder and bowel control;
- tendency to constipation.

The assessment of those changes may not take place until the person is so frail that hospital admission is required.

Managing eating and drinking following age-related pathophysiological change

As ageing progresses there is a greater risk of pathological change. For example, less elasticity in the muscles of the cardiac sphincter, where the oesophagus enters the stomach, can result in gastro-oesophageal reflux; even minor swallowing problems can bring chest infection, poor dentition can result in poorly chewed food, a painful mouth and, in some cases, choking. Poor co-ordination and tremor can result in scalding and dehydration. Poor memory can lead to weight loss or hyperphagia (pathological overeating). These are a few examples that are considered in more depth below.

Gastro-oesophageal reflux

Gastro-oesophageal reflux is best managed by making some lifestyle changes, which include the avoidance of alcohol and large fatty meals immediately before going to bed. Eating the main meal of the day at lunch time is better than late at night, as lying flat after a meal can make these symptoms worse and, if they occur while the individual is asleep, may bring about a choking fit and a chest infection. Questions about sleep patterns (see Chapter 41) and night-time 'heartburn' or regurgitation should be asked during a first assessment.

Losing weight and stopping smoking can also reduce the severity of the symptoms. Antacids and 'proton-pump inhibitors' (eg omeprazole or lansoprazole) may be prescribed.

Swallowing difficulties

Many older people have some form of swallowing problem. For some, particular types of food trigger it: toast or biscuits or crumb-like textures such as mince. If avoiding foods that trigger the response does not resolve the problem, further assessment and referral to a doctor and speech and language therapist may be necessary.

It is essential that older individuals are screened for the possibility of dysphagia (difficulty swallowing) and those at risk referred to the speech and language therapist for more detailed assessment. In this way the person's safety is assured and scarce resources are better used. Swallowing screening techniques vary and, as Perry and Love (2001) have clearly pointed out in their review, there is a need for more interprofessional research in this area.

Dentition

Ill-fitting and painful dentures are a frequent reason for older people to change their diet. If this leads to the removal of the denture, the older person may tend to eat a soft diet and this may not be fully nutritious. It could also lead to problems in the intestines such as constipation.

In some individuals the 'trigger point' at the junction of the hard and soft palate is overlapped by the upper denture plate, thus putting them at risk of choking because the function of the trigger point is to instigate the closure of the epiglottis to protect the trachea. Cleaning the mouth properly twice a day as well as cleaning the dentures helps to prevent fungal and other infections of the mouth.

Reduced muscular strength and restricted movement in the joints

Eating and drinking suffer if a person's wrists are weak and the hands stiff, painful or unable to grip and open jars or bottles easily. Sometimes holding cutlery, pans and plates is a problem.

Specialised items of equipment are available from shops selling aids for the disabled. However, a pair of household or non-latex household gloves (for those who can wear them) will do just as well to take off bottle tops. Tins are best opened with a wall-mounted electric tin-opener. Padded handles for cutlery or, in some cases, angled cutlery can be beneficial. Two-handed beakers are also useful to minimise tremor.

Detailed information about such equipment can be obtained from the Disabled Living Foundation. More must be done to ensure that such equipment is offered to those who need them. Although they are not cheap, they are less expensive than the consequences of poor diet – infection, poor tissue healing and depression.

Managing impaired sensory acuity

With age the acuity of the taste and smell receptors is reduced. Failure to smell food that is deteriorating or burning is dangerous. However, for older people the issue is one of quality of the eating experience. A frequent complaint is that the food does not taste as good as it did when they were young. Some are dissuaded from eating as a result. Adding herbs and spices in small quantities or eating foods with strong flavours may make the experience more enjoyable.

Bowel and bladder problems

Anxieties about bladder and bowel function often preoccupy older people (see Chapter 39). Sometimes this anxiety results in restricting fluid intake for fear of incontinence, and it can lead to constipation. As part of an eating and drinking assessment, the pattern of daily fluid intake and triggers for incontinence (eg caffeine-containing drinks) in menopausal women should be taken into account. Foods that are avoided are as important to record as those they prefer.

Over-the-counter medicines and supplements

A record should be kept of all over-the-counter medicines and other supplements such as vitamin and mineral supplements, pain-killers, laxatives, herbal remedies and other preparations that could have an effect on other medicines or on nutritional status (see Chapter 25).

Summary and recommendations

In this chapter formal and informal holistic assessments of eating and drinking have been addressed, from the prevention of malnutrition to the management of some of the normal changes in ageing that affect nutritional status.

Recommendations

- A simple but holistic eating and drinking skills assessment tool should be developed for use by the multidisciplinary health care team.
- Encourage local authorities and voluntary organisations to increase awareness among middle-aged and older people of the need to look out for the biological changes outlined above and prepare for them.
- Encourage independence by ensuring that eating aids are readily available.

34 Oral health

Mary Clay

Assessment of oral health is an important, but neglected, area of health care. This chapter describes an assessment tool and accompanying good practice guidelines for establishing and maintaining good oral health. Although its benefits are well documented (Turner 1996), the assessment of oral health is not commonplace in health care settings (Adams 1996). In addition, although there is substantial literature on oral care, procedures are often based on tradition, anecdotal evidence and subjective assessment rather than research evidence that identifies best practice (Evans 2001).

Oral health has been described as the 'standard of the oral and related tissues which enables an individual to eat, speak and socialise without active disease, discomfort or embarrassment and which contributes to well-being' (Department of Health 1994). There is a direct correlation between nutritional status and oral health (Shepherd 2002), and mouth care is important in preventing infection (Xavier 2000).

Despite recommendations by the British Dental Health Foundation (2000) and the Health Education Authority (1996) that everyone, including older adults without natural teeth, should have annual dental checks, research shows that only 50 per cent of the UK population receive dental care (Todd and Lader 1991). This suggests that some people may have dental problems prior to admission to hospital, and even those with previously adequate oral health may find it compromised by certain medications and treatments. Various authors, including Heals (1993), Holmes (1996) and Xavier (2000), suggest that an examination of the mouth should be included routinely in the initial holistic physical assessment of a patient, rather than addressing problems when they occur.

A government initiative to raise standards of care (Department of Health 2001) provides a benchmarking standard on oral hygiene, with the overall outcome being that patients'/service users' 'personal and oral hygiene needs are met according to their individual and clinical needs'. Oral hygiene is defined as the 'effective removal of plaque and debris to ensure the structures and tissues of the mouth are kept in healthy condition', and a healthy mouth as one that is clean, functional, comfortable and free from infection. It suggests that care for oral hygiene is negotiated with individuals, based on assessment of their particular needs and that care is continuously evaluated, reassessed and the care plan renegotiated.

Barnett (1991) found that greater emphasis on assessment did not always generate good care. It is suggested that including nursing interventions related to the findings of assessment will prompt good practice. To facilitate assessment and appropriate intervention, a published combined oral assessment and intervention tool is suggested (Roberts 2001) (see Box 34.1). This tool was designed for use with older people in a hospital rehabilitation setting, following an extensive review of the relevant literature. It was developed with multidisciplinary input, piloted, reviewed, amended and fully implemented in the rehabilitation wards. It was subsequently introduced into continuing care, where older people had very complex needs, and was considered equally reliable. This experience indicates that it is likely to be suitable for use in the acute hospital setting where most patients are older people, many of whom have complex needs. The tool guides the assessment of the mouth and key related factors such as swallowing, nutrition, dexterity problems and cognitive function, and is easily completed by circling 'yes' or 'no' answers. Interventions are listed related to the findings of assessment.

To provide the rationale for interventions, accompanying good practice guidelines were developed by Clay and Nelson (2002) (see Box 34.2) and formatted to fit on the other side of the assessment and intervention tool, so that they are immediately accessible to staff responsible for meeting oral health needs. A recent publication by the Relatives and Residents Association (2004) includes a dental health assessment form for use on admission to care homes. This useful booklet includes information on the funding arrangements and the provision of dental services for older people in residential care. A range of free helpful leaflets are available from the British Dental Health Foundation, which may support the verbal information and advice given to older people at the time of oral assessment (they also have an advice line).

Conclusion

Care professionals, and particularly nurses, have an important role in providing effective oral care, and a health-promotion role in teaching people about the importance of oral assessment and oral care (Holmes 1996). Standard oral care regimens cannot meet the needs of all patients. Whilst most people with dental caries or abscesses will report their discomfort, staff need to observe carefully those who cannot communicate for possible indications of oral health problems. These may include refusal to eat, changes in food preferences, facial grimaces during chewing or persistent touching, pushing or pulling at a certain area of the mouth or face (Fahs 1981). People's oral status is a good indication of the care they have received (Heals 1993). Having appropriate documentation and easily accessible information to provide evidence-based care can make meeting the oral health needs of older people a reality.

Box 34.1 The oral assessment and intervention tool

Name   Hospital number   Ward

What is your normal mouth care routine at home?

When did you last see a dentist?

Assessment: Use tongue compressor and pen torch to examine oral cavity		Circle which is appropriate		Suggested nursing care
Lips	Dry/cracked?	Y	N	Apply petroleum gel
Tongue	Dry/coated?	Y	N	Clean with a soft toothbrush and toothpaste Offer frequent fluids and fruit juices
	Evidence of ulceration/soreness?	Y	N	Refer to doctor

		Y	N	
Saliva?	Dry mouth (xerostomia)	Y	N	Offer frequent fluids and/or iced water Offer mouthwash If symptoms persist, refer to doctor for saliva substitute
Teeth	Own teeth?	Y	N	Encourage independence with cleaning teeth, night and morning, using soft toothbrush and toothpaste
	Evidence of plaque/ debris?	Y	N	Supervise with oral care Use soft toothbrush and toothpaste
Dentures	Top denture? Lower denture?	Y Y	N N	Encourage independence with cleaning dentures night and morning with soap and water; rinse dentures after meals
	Dentures and own teeth?	Y	N	Clean teeth as above Remove dentures at night and leave to soak
Pain	When eating/drinking: caused by teeth/ dentures?	Y	N	Refer to dentist
Gums/soft tissue	Evidence of soreness/ ulceration?	Y	N	Refer to doctor

continued

Box 34.1 (continued)

Assessment: Use tongue compressor and pen torch to examine oral cavity		Circle which is appropriate		Suggested nursing care
Swallowing	Difficulty with swallowing?	Y	N	Clean teeth and/or dentures and mouth after each meal Refer to speech therapist
Nutrition	Fluid/dietary intake poor?	Y	N	Offer hourly fluids – may require hourly mouth care
	Dehydrated?	Y	N	Offer hourly fluids – may require hourly mouth care
Speech difficulties	Due to dry mouth?	Y	N	Offer frequent fluids (see above)
	Due to dentures slipping when speaking?	Y	N	Refer to dentist
Dexterity problems	Having difficulty holding toothbrush?	Y	N	Refer to occupational therapist for toothbrush adaptations May need supervision with night care
Cognitive function	Evidence of short-term memory loss and/or confusion?	Y	N	May need supervision with mouth care

NB 'At risk' factors in oral health: diabetes, antidepressants, anticonvulsants, large-dose antibiotics, mouth breathing, low haemoglobin.

The aim is to promote health and independence.

Signed

Role

Date

Re-assessment dates

Date	Signed	Date

Box 34.2 *Oral health – best practice guidelines*

Why assess?

Identify person's usual routine – unless contraindicated, include in the care plan

Establish the baseline on admission

Identify actual or potential problems and treat to prevent them from getting worse

Reassess regularly to evaluate the effectiveness of mouth care interventions

Key factors influencing oral status

Effects of the ageing process

Tooth structure changes due to wear and tear, and gum recession predisposing to periodontal disease

A reduction in thirst reflex and in saliva production, and multipathology requiring polypharmacy, means that 75% of older people have a dry mouth

Physical disability, poor vision and reduced cognitive function can make it difficult for some people adequately to meet their oral health needs independently

Dry mouth (xerostomia)

In addition to age-related changes, mouth breathing, oxygen therapy, suction, inadequate nutrition and hydration or parenteral nutrition, a wide range of medications (400+), diabetes, anxiety and depression, smoking and using over-the-counter mouthwashes can cause mouth dryness. This predisposes people to oral infections, thrush, mouth ulcers, dental caries and loss of appetite.

Cytotoxic therapy, radiotherapy, HIV therapy

Care of dentures

Consider the privacy and dignity of the individual

Dentures should be brushed using cold, running water, a small amount of liquid soap or toothpaste and a soft toothbrush

Box 34.2 (continued)

Ideally, dentures should be soaked overnight in a named denture container, in cold water, as allowing them to dry out may cause them to warp

After soaking, discard the water and rinse the dentures in cold water (hot water must not be used to clean or soak dentures, as it may cause them to warp)

Equipment
A soft-to-medium toothbrush is the most effective tool to remove plaque and prevent decay

A small amount of fluoride toothpaste will help resist decay and periodontal disease

Tap water is the ideal rinsing agent – the pH is similar to that of saliva

Foam sticks are useful for moistening and cleaning the inside of the mouth, but are ineffective at removing debris or cleaning teeth and should be used only when a toothbrush cannot be tolerated

Chlorhexidine mouthwash, spray or gel is recommended if maintaining oral hygiene is difficult, as it inhibits bacterial growth – it tastes unpleasant and prolonged usage stains teeth

Petroleum gel is recommended to keep the lips moist and to prevent cracking

Varied cultural approaches to oral care include using medicinal sticks and tongue scrapers

Technique
While promoting independence, best practice includes people having access to the level of assistance they require to meet their individual oral hygiene needs (Department of Health 2001)

Gloves should be worn to reduce the risk of infection to both the person and the professional

Partial dentures should be removed at the outset and cleaned separately

continued

Box 34.2 (continued)

The toothbrush should be held at a 45-degree angle to the teeth and all surfaces should be cleaned

Gums and tongue should be brushed to remove debris and encourage tissue perfusion

The mouth should be thoroughly rinsed with water, as fluoride toothpaste dries the mouth

Brushing someone's teeth is easiest done standing behind, keeping the head supported

Frequency of oral care

Depends on the assessment of the individual's needs, and may be required hourly

Teeth should ideally be cleaned twice daily, especially at night

Dentures should be cleaned at least daily, but ideally after meals

(Clay 2000)

35 Gastrointestinal tract functioning

Roger Watson

The upper gastrointestinal tract

The gastrointestinal (GI) tract runs from the mouth to the rectum and includes the oesophagus, the stomach, the small intestine and the large intestine. The upper GI tract comprises the mouth, the oesophagus and the stomach. The mouth contains the teeth, the tongue and the salivary glands and is responsible for chewing food, which is carried out by the combined action of the jaws and the teeth and the tongue, and breaking it down into smaller particles. In addition to chewing, the food is also lubricated by the release of saliva into the mouth. Saliva contains an enzyme, salivary amylase, which is responsible for beginning the chemical breakdown (digestion) of starch in food. The tongue contains taste buds which, along with olfactory bulbs in the nose, are responsible for the sensation of taste.

When chewing is complete, the food in the mouth is formed, by the action of the tongue, into a bolus that is swallowed and passed into the oesophagus where it is propelled towards the stomach by the action called peristalsis. The bolus of food enters the stomach at the cardiac sphincter, formed by the fold between the top of the stomach and the oesophagus, and remains in the stomach for further digestion of protein by the action of the enzyme pepsin. The stomach also secretes hydrochloric acid, which has the dual action of killing any bacteria in the food and of activating pepsin from an inactive form. Once digestion in the stomach is complete, the food is passed, via the pyloric sphincter, into the first part of the small intestine – the duodenum – for further digestion.

Changes in the upper GI tract with ageing

Ageing affects all aspects of the upper GI tract to some extent. However, as with most aspects of ageing (Watson 2000a), the function of the GI tract normally remains intact. Nevertheless, there are some problems, associated with ageing, that are more common in older people. In the mouth, ageing affects the teeth, the tongue and the production of saliva (Schofield 1999). With age, the teeth become worn and discoloured and it is common for the gums to recede, a phenomenon that has led to the expression 'long in the tooth'. Whilst a great many people have lost all of their teeth (ie they are edentulous), this may be as much a social factor as an aspect of ageing. Clearly, old age will lead to an increase in the problems, primarily tooth decay, which results in tooth extraction. Moreover, the teeth become brittle with age, making them more likely to break. However, as diet and dental care improve with greater awareness of the effect of a diet high in unrefined sugar and more emphasis on preservative dentistry rather than extraction of teeth and provision with dentures, more older people will retain some or all of their own teeth into old age. Nevertheless, it is currently estimated that approximately 50 per cent of older people are edentulous (Molyneux 1998).

The production of saliva decreases by about 25 per cent with age (Schofield 1999) and the tongue, in common with all skeletal muscles, becomes atrophied and the sense of taste becomes less acute (McLaren 1999). The condition of the tongue, which should normally be pink and moist, is a good indicator of oral health and of general health. In older people the tongue may become swollen and sore, especially in an edentulous person where the tongue is used to compensate in chewing (Linton 1997). The production of salivary amylase decreases, leading to decreased digestion of starch in the mouth, but this is unlikely to be significant because starch digestion is completed in the small intestine. The temporomandibular joint – the articulation between the upper and lower jaw – may become damaged in old age. This joint is capable of movement in three planes – up and down, front to back and from side to side – and is used in a circular motion when chewing. The net effect of the changes with ageing is that older people may find it harder to chew food because of the reduced action of the temporomandibular joint and the blunting of teeth or the use of dentures.

Reduced salivation and sense of taste may lead to an older person not enjoying eating as much as in their younger days, which may have consequences for nutrition (see Chapter 36). Reduced salivation may lead to dryness of the mouth (xerostomia, a condition that can be present in many older people, especially in older women), and dryness of the mouth may lead to soreness and lesions in the mouth, which can further reduce the pleasure of eating.

The effect of ageing on the oesophagus is the result of the effect of ageing on all the muscles of the body: atrophy. In the oesophagus, in common with other areas of the GI tract, this leads to reduced peristalsis, resulting in food being propelled less efficiently into the stomach. In the older person, this may lead to difficulty with swallowing (dysphagia) and to a feeling of fullness as the food collects and distends the lower part of the oesophagus, above the cardiac sphincter. This may also lead to reflux of gastric contents, which are acidic, causing 'heartburn' (Hall et al 1993).

In common with the rest of the GI tract, the stomach atrophies and there is a loss of the parietal cells which produce hydrochloric acid. This, in turn, will lead to less activation of pepsin and a reduced digestion of protein. As a result of these changes an older person may complain of discomfort in the stomach or 'indigestion'. Another effect of the atrophy of the stomach may be a reduced production of the intrinsic factor that is essential for the absorption of vitamin B_{12}, leading to a deficiency of this vitamin (Hall et al 1993) which can result in pernicious anaemia, the risk of which will be increased in an older person with a poor diet. Some of the changes in the upper GI tract outlined above and some of the effects are summarised in Table 35.1.

Table 35.1 Age-related gastrointestinal changes and outcomes

Change	Outcome
Decreased taste acuity	Diminished taste and reduced food intake
Decreased saliva production	Dry mouth and choking
Brittle teeth	Decay and loss of teeth, difficulty chewing
Decreased oesophageal peristalsis	Dysphagia, feeling of fullness and heartburn
Decreased gastric secretions	Indigestion

Adapted from Rush and Schofield (1999)

Abnormal changes with ageing

Whilst the changes and effects mentioned above may be considered to be within the normal range of events for the ageing upper GI tract, there are a number of changes that are more serious, and even life-threatening, which are more common with age. They include:

- Reflux oesophagitis – where the contents of the stomach are forced back up into the oesophagus, leading to 'heartburn' and regurgitation of stomach contents. This causes inflammation of the lower oesophagus and, whilst it is normally treatable with antacid drugs and raising the head of the bed, surgery is occasionally required to repair the cardiac sphincter or to repair damage to the lower oesophagus.
- Hiatus hernia – where the upper part of the stomach herniates through the respiratory diaphragm. Sometimes this does not cause a problem but can lead to reflux oesophagitis, heartburn and regurgitation. The condition is present in 69 per cent of adults over the age of 70 years but is less common in younger people.

Box 35.1 *Assessment of the upper gastrointestinal tract*

History

Mouth, pharynx and larynx

Sense of taste

Soreness or bleeding of tongue, lips and gums

Changes in salivation

Dental problems

Presence and comfort of dentures and chewing ability

Last visit to dentist

Difficulty with swallowing

Sore throat

Hoarse voice

Lump in throat

Upper GI tract

Diet

Fluid intake

Appetite

Weight loss or weight gain

Food intolerance

Nausea (time, place, circumstances)

Vomiting (time, quantity, colour, circumstances)

Heartburn

Pain

Physical assessment

Face (abnormal shape, front and side view)

Lips (shape, colour, masses)

Teeth (decay, broken or missing)

Mucosa of mouth (colour, moisture)

Tongue (colour, moisture, top, sides and underside)

Palate (lesions, deviation of uvula)

Throat (colour)

Adapted from Linton (1997)

- Gastritis – due to atrophy of the stomach, this leads to irritation of the stomach, vomiting and regurgitation of stomach and intestinal contents. The condition may be the result of auto-immunity (an abnormality of the immune system that leads it to attack the cells of the body) – something that increases with age.
- Peptic ulcers – which may occur in the stomach (gastric ulcers) and in the duodenum (duodenal ulcers). Peptic ulcers are painful and life-threatening, as they may lead to haemorrhage. Gastric ulcers may also become malignant.
- Oesophageal cancer – which is more common in older men than in older women – leading to difficulty with swallowing and a very poor prognosis in those affected.
- Adenocarcinoma of the stomach – is particularly considered to be a disease of old age and is associated with gastritis and pernicious anaemia.

Assessment of the upper GI tract in older people

Any nursing assessment of the upper GI tract should include, as well as diet and oral hygiene, visual inspection of the mouth and the face and head; any abnormalities should be recorded and reported to the physician (Linton 1997). Otherwise, the assessor should be trying to ascertain from the patient any clues regarding upper GI function such as pain, discomfort, vomiting or bleeding, which may provide evidence of underlying changes. A suitable scheme for the assessment of upper GI function is outlined in Box 35.1.

The lower GI tract from the duodenum to the rectum

The mouth and the stomach are responsible for initiating the physical and chemical breakdown of food, and the remainder of the GI tract completes the process of digestion, absorbs nutrients into the bloodstream and excretes waste products. Specifically, the small intestine is responsible for completing the digestion of carbohydrate and protein that was initiated, respectively, in the mouth and stomach, in addition to digesting fat, which is uniquely digested in the small intestine. In the small intestine the products of the digestion of carbohydrates, proteins and fats – monosaccharides (glucose, fructose and galactose), amino acids and triglycerides, respectively – are absorbed into the bloodstream for delivery to other organs of the body, principally the liver, where they can be further metabolised (Watson 2000b). Monosaccharides and amino acids are absorbed directly into the bloodstream, whereas triglycerides are absorbed into the lymphatic system and delivered via the lymph, which is returned to the bloodstream from the peripheral tissues.

The contents of the small intestine are mixed by segmentation and propelled by peristalsis to the large intestine. The large intestine acts to store and transport faeces and removes the majority of the water from foodstuffs. By the action of commensal bacteria, some food-stuffs that are not digested higher up in the GI tract are broken down. Modified peristaltic movement takes place in the large intestine to propel food towards the rectum which, when full, stimulates the body to undergo the process of defaecation, whereby the contents of the rectum are expelled via the anus. The anus is kept closed by two rings of muscle called sphincters: an inner smooth muscle sphincter which is involuntary and an outer sphincter which is composed of skeletal muscle and is under voluntary control. In short, while the process involves a combination of reflex and voluntary actions, the urge to defaecate can be controlled within reasonable limits.

When food leaves the stomach, it enters the duodenum, which is a very important region of the GI tract. The duodenum receives food from the stomach, neutralises it by the presence of alkaline sodium bicarbonate, completes the digestion of carbohydrate and protein, initiates the digestion of fats by the secretion of a range of digestive enzymes and produces hormones that provide feedback to the stomach both to stimulate and decrease its digestive actions. Ultimately, the stomach is emptied and digestion is brought to completion. The duodenum is also where the fats come into contact with bile, a substance that emulsifies the fats – produces smaller droplets with a larger surface area, thus rendering fats more susceptible to the action of lipases, the enzymes that digest fat. The duodenum receives from the gall bladder digestive enzymes and sodium bicarbonate (pancreatic juices) from the pancreas and bile, which is made in the liver. The pancreatic juices and the bile enter the duodenum at the same point, the ampulla of Vater, which is kept closed by the sphincter of Oddi until the stimulus to open is provided by hormones released by the duodenum. Assessment of the lower GI tract in the older person therefore requires consideration of the small intestine, the liver and gall bladder, the pancreas and the large intestine.

Ageing and the lower GI tract

The effects of ageing on the lower GI tract may be summarised as atrophy resulting in decreased motility and decreased absorption. In addition, the liver, which is closely associated with the lower GI tract, reduces in size. In common with many other systems of the body reviewed in this book, this has no significance in health; there is ample capacity in the GI tract to allow normal digestion, absorption and defaecation and, despite the higher incidence of certain problems in the lower GI tract, it is rarely possible to ascribe these solely to the process of ageing.

A common feature of the colon of older people are diverticuli: pockets that form in the intestine – possibly due to reduced motility but also, perhaps, due to a low-fibre diet – where intestinal faeces may be stored instead of passing along the GI tract. Diverticuli are not normally a problem but their contents can become infected, which can lead to bleeding that is noticed because of blood being passed in the faeces. The incidence of gallstones – crystals of cholesterol and bile salts – being formed in the gall bladder increases with age (Morris 1998) but this is only a problem if the person experiences pain, the outlet to the gall bladder becomes blocked leading to jaundice or the gall bladder becomes infected (cholecystitis).

The incidence of appendicitis does not increase with age but two of the cardinal symptoms – pain and temperature – may be masked in many older people, making diagnosis more difficult (Hall et al 1993). The incidence of pancreatic cancer increases with age.

Constipation

It is a widely held view – by health professionals and the general public, including older people (Ebersole and Hess 1990) – that constipation is more common in old age. Constipation has many causes (Box 35.2) but, as mentioned above, there is no particular aspect of the process of ageing that leads to constipation (Clinch and Hilton 1998). Nevertheless, older people report this more frequently than their younger counterparts and the problem has to be taken seriously. It is certainly the case, for reasons that are not fully understood, that many older people become 'obsessed' by their bowel habits and become unduly worried if they do not have a bowel movement every day. It is demonstrable, possibly as a result of this, that older people are major consumers of laxative medications (Harari et al 1993). There is, in fact, no figure that can be produced for normal bowel habits. The range of frequency that individuals consider normal for themselves ranges from three times daily to three times weekly (Koch 1998).

Box 35.2 **Some causes of constipation related to ageing**

Delay in transit through colon	*Difficulty with evacuation*
Low dietary fibre	Hard faeces
Immobility	Secondary (eg to haemorrhoids)
Parkinson's disease	
Drug-induced (eg opoid, anticholinergic)	General debility
	Confusion and dementia

Adapted from Norton (1999)

Cancer of the colon

Colorectal cancer is more common in people over 60 years of age (Dew 1999). Those presenting with this condition typically complain of a change in bowel habit, often accompanied by rectal bleeding; it is often the case that, by the time symptoms have been noticed and reported, the disease has spread elsewhere in the abdomen.

Conclusion

The lower GI tract cannot really be assessed separately from the upper GI tract and, in taking a history from an older person, aspects of both the upper and the lower GI tract should be considered together. Some of the domains of assessment that were raised elsewhere (Watson 2000c), such as the presence of nausea and vomiting, are also relevant to the lower GI tract. Box 35.3 outlines the main areas of assessment of the lower GI tract. Jaundice, which may indicate problems with the liver or the head of the pancreas, will definitely require further medical and possibly surgical investigation. Urinalysis would normally be carried out as part of any assessment procedure and the nurse should be careful to observe and report accurately on the presence of bile products in the urine. Otherwise, a great deal of information can be gained from an older person and this will provide a picture of the function of the colon. Change in bowel habit, pain, masses, bleeding and discomfort from flatulence can be indicators of a wide range of conditions from the relatively innocuous, such as diverticulitis, to the more serious cancer of the colon. The baseline upon which any assessment of the lower GI tract and, especially, bowel habit should be built is that change in bowel habit and, in particular, bleeding are not a normal part of the ageing process. These things are always worth reporting and investigating.

Box 35.3 *Assessment of the lower gastrointestinal tract*

History

Pain (type, location, duration, intensity)

Jaundice

Bowel habits (frequency, regularity)

Use of laxatives

Flatulence (wind)

Stools (colour and consistency: eg presence of blood or black stools)

Physical assessment

Inspection for lesions, masses, tautness of abdomen

Presence of bowel sounds

Palpation for tenderness of enlarged internal organs

Adapted from Linton (1997)

36 Nutritional status

Sue Green and Tina McDougall

Nutritional status can be defined as 'the state of health produced by the balance between requirement and intake of nutrients' (Barker 2002: 4). Nutritional status is considered when assessing or screening for malnutrition. A person with a poor nutritional status can be considered to be malnourished and may be referred to as over- or undernourished though, generally, the term 'malnutrition' is applied to undernutrition. Estimates of the proportion of older adults in hospital who are malnourished ranges from 20 to 50 per cent (Baxter 1999). In older patients with mixed diagnoses, studies indicate that up to 85 per cent may be considered at risk of malnutrition or frankly malnourished on admission to hospital (Stratton et al 2003). Older adults living in the community may also be malnourished. A national dietary and nutritional survey of people aged over 64, living in their own homes or in institutions (Finch et al 1998), highlighted that, whilst many were adequately nourished, some were not. Those without natural teeth, living in institutions, of a low socio-economic group and the very old were more likely to be malnourished.

Poor nutritional status is caused by a wide variety of factors ranging from disease process to socio-economic status. An understanding of the causes of malnutrition can facilitate the screening process and enable an appropriate plan of care to be formulated. An understanding of the nutritional requirements of older people also helps to facilitate nutritional screening and planning of care. Optimum nutritional intake for older people is difficult to define because there is a lack of data on particular nutrient requirements (Department of Health 1991). In addition, the term 'older person' covers a wide age range and the nutritional requirements of people in their eighth decade of life are likely to be different from those who are approaching 100 years of age. Differences in requirements between older and younger people reflect the effect of ageing on gut function and metabolism. Energy expenditure, and therefore requirement, tends to decrease gradually with age, increasing the risk of nutrient deficiency as less food is consumed. Clinical deficiencies of some micronutrients can be seen in older people – for example, low plasma levels of vitamin D (Department of Health 1991). Energy expenditure may be increased by surgery or illness in older age, and this is often accompanied by a reduction in food intake.

Poor nutritional status

Poor nutritional status is associated with increased susceptibility to conditions such as chest infection, depression and poor wound healing, which can reduce quality of life and prolong a stay in hospital (Bond 1997). Good nutritional intake can prevent nutrition-related problems such as constipation, anaemia and osteomalacia (McLaren and Crawley 2000). A number of recent national publications have highlighted the need for nutritional screening and assessment.

Therefore, screening and assessment of nutritional status need to be considered an integral part of assessment for older adults in all care sectors. An appropriate plan of care can then be developed, implemented and evaluated.

Nutritional screening and assessment

In the health care setting, nutritional screening and assessment aim to identify individuals who are malnourished or at risk of becoming so, and to evaluate the effectiveness of any nutritional support. Nutritional screening and assessment often take place on admission to care but it is important to remember that ongoing assessment is essential. The terms 'screening' and 'assessment' are often used interchangeably in the context of nutrition. *Screening* can be considered to be a process that identifies people with, or at risk of, malnutrition who may require comprehensive nutritional assessment and referral. *Assessment* can be considered as a more detailed process using a range of methods to identify and quantify impairment of nutritional status (Barrocas et al 1995). No single method can give a full picture of a person's nutritional status; rather, a combination of methods can be used or a screening tool that incorporates a number of measures.

Basic methods of nutritional screening and assessment

Assessment of nutritional intake

Basic consideration of nutritional intake examines recent and current food intake (including nutritious fluids) and influential factors. At a primary level, care professionals can identify whether a person is eating, if an interest in eating is shown and whether a range of foods is eaten (Copeman 1999). A more detailed evaluation can consider quantity and types of food eaten, nutrient intake and reasons why food intake may be poor. Examination of dietary intake cannot give a measure of nutritional status but it can highlight particular areas of concern that relate to nutritional status.

Food intake may be assessed either by direct observation or by examining dietary history. The choice of method really depends on what is considered most appropriate for the situation. If poor intake is identified, further assessment can examine the cause. If several individuals within the care setting have a poor dietary intake, it is useful to consider a review of the food provision system (Nutrition Advisory Group for Elderly People 1994). It is essential that measurements of dietary intake are as precise as possible in order for nutrient intake to be accurately assessed and for documentation to be valid.

Direct observation and recording of food intake (food chart)

One of the simplest methods of assessing dietary intake is by the use of a food chart. With this method the person or their carer or nurse completes a chart indicating the amount and type of food and fluids presented and the amount eaten. The information obtained can be used to give an indication of the quantity and nutritional value of food eaten and how much is being offered.

Food charts should show the date and time; an accurate description of food and fluid before and after a meal; and an accurate description of the portion. To assess whether intake is likely to be nutrient deficient the following can be considered:

- Types of food eaten – consumption of a limited variety of foods can lead to poor nutrient intake.
- Time foods are eaten – for example, if the evening meal is refused each evening, this will lead to poor nutrient intake unless a substantial amount is eaten in the earlier part of the day.
- Amount eaten. This should be related to the weight, activity level, mental state and presence of disease and nutritional requirements. Consumption of less than 50 per cent of a standard hospital meal should cause great concern.

If food intake is poor, referral to the dietitian or other health care professional such as the speech therapist or occupational therapist may be necessary, depending on the cause of the poor intake. The dietitian may request continued completion of the food chart to monitor progress and to accurately assess dietary intake in terms of nutrients consumed.

Serving and removing uneaten food is a role often designated to care assistants, but the registered nurse is responsible for ensuring that the nutritional needs of patients are met (UKCC 1997) and that any record keeping is undertaken to a reasonable standard. The value of recording a food chart should be carefully considered because it is time consuming. Filling it in half the time is not particularly useful.

Food intake can be overestimated in written reports of intake; photographing a meal before and after it is eaten may be a useful method of recording intake (Simmons and Reuben 2000). Photography is quick, allows visual estimation of food intake after the eating episode and gives good documentation provided that it is labelled appropriately, although cost implications need to be considered.

Dietary intake record (food diary) If a person is able to record in a diary what they eat over a few days, eating patterns can be highlighted and nutritional intake estimated. For example, a practice nurse advising a person with obesity on how they might reduce the fat content of their diet may ask them to complete a record of what they eat over several days. This process can then highlight types and amounts of foods that can be moderated to reduce the fat content. In addition, the process of recording intake can make the person more aware of their eating habits. Asking a person to weigh and describe all the food and drink they consume for seven days is considered to be one of the most accurate methods by which nutritional intake can be assessed. This type of record can be inaccurate, though, as people tend to underestimate the amount they are eating, modify what they eat and not record some things they have eaten! Training concerning the completion of the record needs to be undertaken to try to prevent this.

Food frequency questionnaire A food frequency checklist asks a person to record how often they eat particular types of foods. Screening tools for malnutrition may incorporate an element that uses a food frequency approach. For example, the Mini Nutritional Assessment tool for use with older adults questions whether the person consumes two or more servings of fruit or vegetables a day (Vellas et al 1999).

Recall Asking a person to recall what they have eaten and drunk in the recent past can give some indication as to whether they are managing to consume a normal diet. Usually a person is asked what they have consumed in the past 24 hours, termed '24-hour recall'. However, this method can be very inaccurate when the person is confused or disorientated or has a limited concentration span. In addition, intake in the previous 24 hours may not be representative of normal intake. The care team should try to obtain as complete a record as possible, as foods such as snacks are often forgotten (Webb and Copeman 1996).

Webb and Copeman (1996) highlight several ways in which the accuracy of the reported food intake can be improved:

- Ask about the times of day rather than using terms such as 'tea', the meaning of which can vary.
- Ask who was with the person at the time, as this may help to recall items.
- Do not make assumptions or comments about the type of foods that people eat.

- Ask about the brand or recipe of foods eaten, as this leads to greater accuracy.

Some items can be cross-checked at the end; for example, asking how many slices of bread are eaten a day generally and checking whether this is consistent with the record. It is also useful to ask if the plate was cleared at each meal.

Dietary history

On admission to care, a basic dietary history can provide much information concerning normal habits and food intake, and highlight areas of concern. Perhaps the simplest question to ask concerning dietary intake is 'Have you been eating less than usual?' (Lennard-Jones et al 1995). A more thorough assessment can include questions such as those in Box 36.1. It is particularly important to obtain this information in situations where individuals are not able to express their dietary preferences or are in a continuing care setting. The information can form the basis of the nutritional care plan. For example, in care homes a record of the type of drink a person prefers is often absent, which can result in a disliked beverage being given by carers who do not know the individual.

Clinical examination

A clinical examination is usually part of the admission process undertaken by the nurse. Factors considered in the assessment, such as presence of disease, period of ill-health and social, family, environmental and therapeutic factors, can all influence nutritional status. The following factors should be considered in the physical or clinical assessment, as they can relate directly to nutritional status:

- physical stature (eg thin appearance, skin condition);
- oral health/dental health;
- recent history of weight loss or gain (eg self-reports, fit of clothes);
- recent poor appetite and intake;
- functional assessment of feeding ability;
- mental factors, such as depression or dementia;

Box 36.1 *Questions to ask concerning dietary intake*

Usual intake

Number of meals consumed a day

Type of diet followed (eg therapeutic diet, cultural diet)

Disliked and liked food and drink

Prescribed medication

Nutritional supplement(s) taken

Presence of any difficulties with eating (eg dysphagia)

Oral condition

Mobility

Ability to shop, prepare food and cook

Help received from carers or health care agencies

- medical history, diagnosis and treatment;
- drug therapy;
- symptoms such as diarrhoea or vomiting;
- reading and writing difficulties (eg inability to complete a hospital menu).

If particular issues are identified, referral to a dietitian, doctor or other professional should be considered and an appropriate plan of care written.

Anthropometric measures

Anthropometry refers to physical measurements of body size and dimensions (Webb and Copeman 1996). Some measures of anthropometry, such as weight, are used routinely by nurses. Weighing a person is a simple procedure that can give a good indication of nutritional status, but accurate weighing scales of an appropriate type, such as a weighing chair, are required. This may seem obvious but research has suggested that weighing scales can be inaccurate or missing (Micklewright and Todorovic 1997; Chu et al 1999). Calibration of the scales needs to be carried out regularly according to the manufacturer's instructions. An isolated weight measurement is less useful than sequential measuring, which enables assessment of weight loss or gain. To ensure accuracy, the person should, if possible, be weighed on the same scales, at the same time each day, in the same or similar clothes, and after emptying bladder and bowels.

The proportion of weight lost can give a good indication of nutritional status and risk of malnutrition – more than 10 per cent lost over three months is suggestive of malnutrition:

$$\% \text{ weight gain/loss} = \frac{\text{usual weight} - \text{current weight (kg)}}{\text{usual weight (kg)}} \times 100$$

Weight alone is less useful than a consideration of weight and height. A tall person who weighs the same as a short person will have less body reserves in the form of fat. Body mass index (BMI) can be used to consider weight in relation to height. In older people height can be difficult to determine because of spine curvature or inability to stand. If height cannot be measured, an estimation can be made using demi-span (distance from web between middle and ring finger along the outstretched arm to the sternal notch (Webb and Copeman 1996) or ulna length (Elia 2003). A dietitian should be able to provide information on these measures. The International Obesity Task Force (2000) has outlined that a BMI of less that 18.5 suggests a person is underweight, although commonly used cut-off points range from 18.5 to 20 (Stratton et al 2003). A person with a BMI of 25.0 to 29.9 is considered overweight and a person with a BMI of 30 or more is considered obese. The relationship between BMI and body composition can be influenced by age, gender and race as well as nutritional status (Stratton et al 2003). The usefulness of BMI as a predictor of risk of morbidity and mortality (illness and death) in the very old has been questioned (British Dietetic Association 2003). Therefore, BMI should be used with caution with older adults. In some areas nurses may use anthropometric measures such as body composition and mid-arm muscle circumference, although in the health care setting these are usually used by the dietitian. Whilst weight is a simple measure, in some situations it may not give a good indication of nutritional status, as conditions such as oedema, dehydration and tumour growth can affect body weight.

Waist circumference is increasingly being used to screen for cardio-vascular risk in primary care, as it can give a quick indication of the amount of abdominal fat a person carries. A waist circumference greater than 102 cm in men and 88 cm in women indicates that advice on how weight can be reduced may be beneficial. However, as with BMI, this measure may not be appropriate for use with older adults, particularly the very old.

Biochemical measures

Biochemical analysis of plasma, urine and other parts of the body may be used to assess nutritional status, although the relationship between the test result and nutritional state needs to be considered carefully.

Routine tests, such as determination of haemoglobin, can give an indication of nutritional status but they do also reflect disease proc-esses. Other tests, such as serum protein values (eg pre-albumin and retinol-binding protein) may be used as markers of nutritional status, although they are influenced by factors such as liver disease, treatment with blood products and over-hydration and so should not be used in isolation. Circulating lipoprotein levels give an indication of cardiovascular risk that may be related to dietary intake, and nitro-gen balance studies can give an index of protein status. In addition, specific vitamin (eg vitamin C) or mineral (eg selenium) levels can be evaluated. The interpretation of biochemical measures with respect to nutritional status needs to be considered by the dietitian, doctor and biochemist as well as by the nurse.

Functional tests

Functional tests measure an aspect of the body's capacity, and include tests such as hand-grip strength. These tests are not gener-ally used by nurses to assess nutritional status, although dietitians or doctors may use them.

Tools and protocols

A number of national protocols exist that highlight what should be considered in the assessment or screening of nutritional status (British Association of Parenteral and Enteral Nutrition 2003). Local protocols concerning nutritional assessment and screening, based on national protocols, often exist within Trusts.

Nutritional screening and assessment tools or instruments typically use a questionnaire format that examines factors known to lead to, or be associated with, malnutrition. This approach to screening is similar to that used by pressure-ulcer risk-assessment tools. An appropriate course of action may be detailed, and the tools can serve as a useful aid to memory and prompt to record information. There are many nutritional screening or assessment tools and some have been designed specifically for use with older adults. Tools should be quick, easy to complete and understand, and acceptable to the person being assessed. Choosing one should involve the consideration of issues of validity and reliability – that is, the tool has been shown to measure what it purports to measure and the score obtained is consistent. The British Association of Parenteral and Enteral Nutrition has designed a screening tool, 'the MUST tool', for use by nurses in all areas of clinical practice. It is considered to be a valid and reliable tool with which to screen for malnutrition (Elia 2003). Other tools that have been validated include the Subjective Global Assessment (Detsky et al 1987) and the Mini Nutritional Assessment (Vellas et al 1999). If a tool is introduced into a clinical area, appropriate training is necessary. It is important to remember that a tool is an aid to decision-making and not a substitute for clinical judgement.

Conclusion

The nutritional status of older people should be screened or assessed on admission to care and periodically thereafter. There are a variety of methods that can be used to screen or assess nutritional status. Once screening or assessment has taken place, an appropriate plan of care must be made. The National Service Framework for Older People (Department of Health 2001) highlights that good diets can help older people to enjoy many years of active life. The Framework also proposes emphasis on promoting healthy lifestyles with easier access to advice and support. Identifying people with or at risk of malnutrition is an essential part of this process.

Elimination

37 Renal function

Mark Bevan

This chapter outlines the key issues related to assessing renal function in the older adult. It focuses on the initial meeting between the patient and the non-specialist health care professional. The assessment of the older person may relate to both acute and chronic renal failure but the main thrust is towards chronic failure. It does not include the important area of the older dialysis patient, because of its specialist nature.

The older person is susceptible to the same range of diseases as that of the younger person (Baylis 1997). However, the incidence of disease is different. For example, the older person is more likely to present with arterionephrosclerosis ('hardening' of the microscopic blood vessels in the kidney) as a result of the ageing process. The kinds of disease that affect people over 65 years old are predominantly vascular disorders and diabetes mellitus. In fact, diabetes mellitus, both type 1 and type 2, is seen as the major cause of all end-stage renal disease (ESRD) world wide, and it is getting worse (De Zeeuw et al 2004). Older people are at risk of other disorders such as multiple myeloma, acute renal failure and the vasculitides (inflammatory immune diseases of the blood vessels). Therefore, when assessing older people, an open mind must be maintained until sufficient information is collected.

The kidney and ageing

Assessment must be based on an understanding of the physiological changes that can occur in the kidney.

Changes in renal function due to normal ageing processes begin from about the third decade of life, resulting from arteriosclerosis (Baylis 1997). The sclerosing ('hardening') of arteries – arteriosclerosis – includes the renal arteries and increases with age, leading to reduced renal plasma flow, though this does not explain it completely. Renal blood flow would appear to be reduced from about 1150ml/minute to between 650 and 300ml/minute, or about 10 per cent per decade. The reason for the arteriosclerosis is not clear but it has been thought that a protein-rich diet may play an important role. It seems that the aged kidney has altered ability to vasoconstrict or vasodilate (contract or stretch). For example, there is an exaggerated vasodilatory response to inhibition of angiotensin II (a potent vasoconstrictor), but the use of non-steroidal anti-inflammatory drugs inhibits prostaglandin production, thus precipitating vasoconstriction and leading to an increased risk of acute renal failure.

The kidney reduces in size by about 0.5cm per decade after the age of 50, and this leads to a potential for a reduction in its ability to filter blood effectively, thus causing a reduced glomerular filtration rate (GFR) and a susceptibility to drug toxicity (Baylis 1997). The reduction in GFR begins from about 30 years of age. This decline in GFR is about 10 per cent per decade. The aged kidney does not have the capacity to cope with major demand but the following important issue should be noted. Older people can easily have a normal blood creatinine level even when they are in advanced renal failure. Therefore, renal function in older people needs to be carefully assessed using body weight, age, plasma creatinine and gender to assess GFR and to avoid missing renal failure.

There are alterations in renal tubular function involving electrolyte balance that will affect the older person and how they present with illness (Baylis 1997). Older people can be at risk of becoming depleted in sodium, and if they are taking diuretics they are at even more risk of hyponatraemia. Conversely, there is also a problem in excreting sodium: sodium takes almost twice as long to be excreted in the older person as in someone less than 30 years old. The implications for this are that older people are at risk of sodium overload, oedema and 'salt-sensitive' hypertension (Baylis 1997).

Problems with tubule function also affect potassium balance. The aged kidney has a reduced potassium-conserving ability (Baylis 1997). Whilst plasma potassium levels remain the same in older people as in younger people, in older people there is an increase in the potassium content of the urine. This means that the older person is also at risk of potassium depletion, especially when taking diuretics. There is also a problem with water balance in the older person. The thirst mechanism is blunted, which means that it requires a higher level of dehydration to occur before the thirst response will have an effect which will result in a decreased fluid intake. All these alterations in the older person lead to an impaired capacity to concentrate urine. An additional problem is caused by a defect in the renal medulla where there is an increase in medullary blood flow, thus reducing the osmotic gradient (where there are high levels of urea and sodium in the tissues surrounding the renal tubules required to cause a gradient to allow water to move out of the tubules and be retained by the body) necessary for concentrating urine. To add to this there is an impairment of the antidiuretic mechanism, causing an increased loss in water that can be seen in the need of older people to pass urine at least once during the night (nocturia).

Assessment of renal function in the older person

One of the problems associated with renal failure is that the manifestation of symptoms does not occur until there is significant damage to the kidney. Therefore, it is not unusual for someone to have some degree of renal impairment without knowing anything about it. This makes the identification of affected individuals very difficult. Hence, many people are asymptomatic and their condition is picked up by chance, such as finding a raised blood pressure. Alternatively, others present with vague symptoms that are investigated for another disease, such as urinary tract problems in the older male. A family history may indicate the potential for renal disease; alternatively, the person may have a systemic disease that is also a risk factor for kidney disease. People who are at high risk for renal failure need to be identified and assessed regularly; they include those with high blood pressure (hypertension), diabetes mellitus, ischaemic heart disease, peripheral vascular disease, rheumatoid arthritis and prostatic disease, and Asian and Afro-Caribbean groups. An important history finding is that of haematuria, the source of which may be renal or urinary tract, and will require urgent investigation. The older person is also at increased risk of acute renal failure for all the reasons cited both above and below.

Health history

Presenting complaint

- Assessment begins with a history of the presenting complaint or symptom. Quite often the older adult may simply complain of tiredness or being short of breath but puts this down simply to getting old.
- Identify: when the symptom first started, whether it has been present before, how long it has been present, and whether anything makes it worse or better (Epstein et al 2003).

Past medical history

- Past medical history is important in order to identify any relevant issue such as abnormality of micturition in childhood or unexplained feverish episodes in childhood. A history of hypertension is of particular importance because of its association with renal failure.
- A history of diabetes mellitus is important, as this is a known cause of renal dysfunction. Included for consideration should be tuberculosis and thyroid and parathyroid disease, as they too can affect renal function.
- Other illnesses that may affect the kidney include systemic lupus erythematosus (SLE), amyloid disease, rheumatoid arthritis and hyperparathyroidism. Many renal diseases in older people do not present in the usual manner such as vasculitic disorders where the usual systemic symptoms may be absent.
- A history of pregnancy and childbirth in women may uncover hypertensive problems; a history of urinary outflow (difficulty

passing urine and emptying the bladder adequately) in the older male may indicate prostatic disease.

Medication history

- A history of medications currently being taken and those that have been taken is essential. One must also include drugs bought in supermarkets and health shops, herbal remedies and illicit drug use. The trend towards herbal remedies – in particular Chinese herbal remedies – has seen people develop acute renal failure and permanent renal failure as a consequence (Baker 2002). Examples of some common drugs that cause hypertension are listed in Box 37.1. Of particular concern are the non-steroidal anti-inflammatory drugs, as they have a vasoconstrictive effect on the kidneys, which may worsen renal function, especially in older people. Examples of some common drugs that cause renal dysfunction are listed in Table 37.1.

Box 37.1 **Drugs that cause high blood pressure (hypertension)**

Sympathomimetics: MAO inhibitors, phenylpropranolamine (eye or nasal drops), metoclopramide, imipramine, haloperidol

Steroid-induced: glucococorticoids, mineralocorticoids, anabolic steroids, liquorice, contraceptive pills, oestrogens

Non-steroidal anti-inflammatory drugs (NSAIDs): ibuprofen, indometacin, naproxen, aspirin, piroxicam

Cocaine

Erythropoietin

Vasopressin (ADH)

Ciclosporin

Mitomycin

Methylmethacrylate

(Davison and Grunfeld 1998; Robertson and Ball 1994)

Table 37.1 **Examples of common drugs and their potential renal toxicity**

Drug	Effect on the kidneys
Angiotensin-converting enzyme inhibitors (ACEIs) Non-steroidal anti-inflammatory drugs (NSAIDs) Ciclosporin Radiocontrast agents	Altered renal blood flow dynamics
Radiocontrast agents Gentamicin, vancomycin Cisplatin NSAIDs Amphotericin	Tubular cell toxicity
Penicillins (eg amoxicillin, ampicillin) Cephalosporins (eg cefazolin, cefuroxime) NSAIDs Lithium	Interstitial nephritis
Recreational drugs such as ecstasy, cocaine	Rhabdomyolysis and tubular toxicity

- Lithium used for psychiatric disorders also causes kidney dysfunction (eg nephrogenic diabetes insipidus, nephrotic syndrome and interstitial nephritis).

Dietary history

- Dietary history is important; for example, excessive intake of sodium increases the body's resistance to antihypertensive drugs, used to dilate blood vessels and lower blood pressure. Inadequate fluid intake can, in some people, cause recurrent renal stones. Alcohol intake needs to be estimated for a general understanding of consumption and, in high intake, as a contributor to high blood pressure. The amount of tea and coffee needs to be estimated in relation to their contribution to polyuria (need to pass water frequently). The fat consumption also needs to be known in order to estimate the cardiovascular risk.

- Uraemia, the syndrome attributed to the collection of signs and symptoms of renal failure, is implicated in malnutrition, anorexia, nausea and vomiting. Malnutrition in people with renal failure has been linked to a poor prognosis, and may confuse the initial diagnosis by providing low serum urea and creatinine levels despite advanced renal failure (Renal Association 2002).

Social history

- A social and family history will help in gaining an understanding of the person's social situation as well as identifying any familial conditions such as polycystic kidney disease, thyroid disease and diabetes mellitus. The ethnic aspect also remains important; for example, Asian people have an increased incidence of diabetes and coronary heart disease, placing them at high risk for renal failure (Renal Association 2002). Social deprivation is linked to higher acceptance rates for dialysis, which in part can be explained by ethnic minorities living in areas of social deprivation. People from these areas also tend to have higher co-morbidity (Renal Registry Report 2003).

- Occupation may be important, as exposure to various chemicals has been implicated in renal disease; for example, hydrocarbons may trigger Goodpasture's syndrome (a life-threatening disease in which the body attacks itself, especially the kidneys and lungs).

- Level of consumption of tobacco is important, as it is a major cardiovascular risk factor and, by narrowing renal arteries, is implicated in renovascular disease.

- Recent travel abroad and hospitalisation need to be known in case of any exposure to infections such as malaria, surgery, blood transfusions and medication.

Psychiatric history

- The person's psychiatric history is important because, as noted above, some psychiatric medications can cause renal dysfunction.

- The more uraemic a person becomes, the more likely that it will have an impact on their cognitive and emotional states. Uraemia is associated with depressive illness or depressive affect but can be improved with treatment of the renal disease/failure. Therefore an older person may present with classic signs of depression: for example, ahedonia (inability to enjoy experiences), anorexia, insomnia, irritability and lethargy but in fact they may have advanced renal failure.

Ethnic and geographical history

Ethnic and geographical history has become increasingly important, particularly with increasing migration into the UK. For example, systemic lupus erythematosus is more common in people from the Far East whereas tuberculosis may be more common in people of Asian or African origin.

Clinical examination and investigations

Once a detailed history has been taken, there should be a review of the physiological systems undertaken both by questioning and by physical examination. Symptoms of uraemia relating to each physical system can be found in Table 37.2. It is important to note that people often present with very few outward symptoms, which is why it can be difficult to identify renal problems without doing further investigations.

Blood specimens should be obtained, to include urea and electrolytes. Potassium is important for the obvious reason of detecting high and low levels, which may require urgent treatment. Bicarbonate will indicate whether there is some evidence of acidosis but blood gases will provide a more accurate reading. Sodium will reflect the hydration sodium balance. Measurement of creatinine is of significant importance, as it helps in the clinical estimation of renal function. If a 24-hour urine collection is not obtained for creatinine clearance, the glomerular filtration rate can be estimated by using the Cockroft–Gault formula (Stewart Cameron and Greger 1998) (Figure 37.1). Table 37.3 lists the common investigations required for the assessment of renal function, especially in chronic renal disease.

Table 37.2 **Systemic clinical symptoms/features of uraemia**

System	Clinical features/Symptoms
Respiratory	Oedema, pleural effusions, infection, breathlessness, respiratory failure, TB
Cardio-vascular	Hypertension, hypertrigliceridaemia, ischaemic heart disease, pericarditis, left ventricular hypertrophy, heart failure
Gastro-intestinal	Anorexia, nausea, vomiting, gastritis, ulceration, constipation, diarrhoea, pancreatitis, bleeding, hiccough, stomatitis, parotitis, uriniferous breath
Haemato-logical	Chronic anaemia, platelet dysfunction (bruising), white cell dysfunction (infection)
Musculo-skeletal	Osteomalacia, osteosclerosis, osteitis fibrosa, proximal myopathy, cramps, restless legs, bone pain
Skin	Dry, itching, excoriation, reduced sweating, reduced sebum, pigmentation (yellow or darkening), hypothermia
Eyes	Conjunctivitis, calcification of cornea and conjunctiva, glaucoma, cataracts
Genitourinary	Renal cysts, infection, blood, protein, stones, cystitis, impotence, sterility, cervical cancer, decreased libido

continued

Table 37.2 (continued)

System	Clinical features/Symptoms
Neurological	Polyneuritis, peripheral neuropathy, autonomic neuropathy, headache, irritability, tics, erratic memory, low attention span, motor weakness, insomnia, drowsiness, slurred speech, depressed affect, convulsions, stupor, tremor, coma
General	Fatigue, malaise, thirst, weight loss, chemical diabetes
Increased hormones	Prolactin: lactation; luteinising hormone: gynaecomastia; gastrin: gastritis; renin: hypertension; glucagon: glucose intolerance; parathyroid hormone: osteitis fibrosa
Decreased hormones	Vitamin D: osteitis fibrosa; erythropoietin: anaemia; testosterone: impotence; follicle-stimulating hormone: impotence

Table 37.3 **Investigations of renal function and renal disease**

Investigation	Purpose
Blood specimens	
Urea	Raised: estimate renal failure and protein intake
Creatinine	Raised: estimate glomerular filtration rate (GFR)
Sodium	Often normal; reflects sodium/water balance
Potassium	Often raised, needing careful assessment and urgent treatment

Table 37.3 (continued)

Investigation	Purpose
Bicarbonate	Lowered, reflecting acidosis
Calcium (adjusted)	Lowered, owing to low vitamin D
Phosphate	Raised, owing to retention
Albumin	Nutrition, drug-binding, urine-loss
Liver function (LFT)	Liver function
Alkaline phosphatase	Reflects bone activity in renal bone disease
Cholesterol	Raised: must be treated
Hepatitis B and C	Only if there is some indication for dialysis or recent travel abroad
Full blood count	Assess anaemia, infection
Haematinics	Assess iron, folate and vitamin B
C3, C4, CRP, electrophoresis, ANCA, ANA, anti-GBM antibody	Markers of inflammation in specific diseases such as Goodpasture's syndrome
HBA1c and blood sugar	Diabetes mellitus
	Urine tests
Dipstick	Blood, protein, pH, infection, specific gravity, dextrose, ketones
24-hour collection	To measure a range of levels such as creatinine (GFR), sodium, catecholamines, protein, volume
Microscopy	Assess sedimentation for cellular casts
Electrophoresis	Multiple myeloma

continued

Table 37.3 (continued)

Investigation	Purpose
	Other
Renal ultrasound	Renal size, shape and density
Renal isotope	Perfusion and function
Intravenous pyelogram	Perfusion and function; rarely performed because of risk of nephrotoxicity
Biopsy	Histological examination for specific disease
ECG, echo-cardiograph	Cardiac function
Rectal examination	Prostatic hypertrophy, pelvic mass

Figure 37.1 **The Cockroft–Gault formula for estimating glomerular filtration rate (Stewart Cameron and Greger 1998).**

$$\frac{(140 - \text{age}) \times \text{weight (kg)}}{\text{Serum creatinine } (\mu mol/l \div 88) \times 72 \; [\times 0.85 \text{ for females}]}$$

Collection of urine is important but volume can be misleading in renal failure. People with chronic renal failure can pass normal volumes of urine; however, if someone is taking diuretics, a high volume is to be expected. Low urine output may be indicative of dehydration, acute renal failure or urinary obstruction such as prostatic hypertrophy or pelvic mass.

Conclusion

Assessment of the person with suspected renal dysfunction begins at a very clinical and basic physical level. The basic physical level provides a wealth of information, which may lead to other forms of assessment. For example, a *renal biopsy* is undertaken only if there is uncertainty about the diagnosis and it may indicate the possibility of treatment, as in specific glomerular diseases. It is invasive and carries the risk of haemorrhage. The *renal ultrasound* is very useful, as it allows the simple differentiation relating to size: for example, in chronic renal disease the kidneys are smaller than normal (10–12cm long).

Regardless of the more complex investigations, the fact that the older person is at greater risk of renal failure because of an age-related reduction in function means that care professionals need to be vigilant in their dealings with older people. What, on the surface, may appear as bruising from suspected elder abuse may in fact be caused by uraemic platelet dysfunction. Similarly, what may be seen as age-related physical or mental 'slowing down' might be due to anaemia or uraemia. Indeed, it is likely that these nondescript symptoms are how people present, rather than in outright failure. However, what is encouraging is that, despite the reduction in renal function in older people, most of them do not need any intervention at all. Those who do have renal dysfunction should be referred to a nephrologist, and age should not be used as a barrier to effective treatment and care.

38 Fluid balance

Philip Woodrow

About 60–80 per cent of the human body is water. Normally, water in different parts of the body is kept within a fine balance. But ill-health or impaired function of body systems (especially the kidneys) can cause fluid imbalances and complications for other systems.

This chapter describes how normal ageing and ill-health can affect fluid and electrolyte balance, and ways to replace fluid. Renal failure, discussed in Chapter 37, is not covered in this chapter. Although discussion focuses on differences between intravenous fluids, when people can eat and drink they should usually be encouraged to do so.

Distribution of body fluids

In health, the volume of body water is mainly affected by the amount of body fat. Fat repels water whereas muscle contains relatively large amounts, so obese people have fewer 'stores' of water than muscular people. Observing a person's appearance, together with insights into their lifestyle, can give some indication of likely amounts of total body water.

Electrolytes and other solutes differ between fluid in body cells (intracellular) and outside body cells (extracellular). Extracellular fluid includes both fluid in the blood vessels (intravascular) and fluid between blood vessels and tissue cells (interstitial) (Figure 38.1). Intravascular and interstitial fluids are chemically virtually identical, but imbalances between volumes can complicate disease. This chapter describes three fluid compartments within the body:

- intravascular
- interstitial
- intracellular.

Although the normal fluid volumes of an average healthy person are cited, wide variations occur between individuals, especially with ill-health, so all figures cited are given only to illustrate trends.

Of the five litres average blood volume, about two litres are blood cells and three litres are plasma – and plasma is mainly (90 per cent) water. Blood volume is important, because it:

- perfuses all body tissue – delivering oxygen and nutrients, while removing waste from cells;
- is measurable (eg blood pressure, or strength of the pulse);
- forms urine – which removes waste from the body, and is easily measurable;
- is the main route for replacing fluids – including oral fluids, which are absorbed through the gut into the bloodstream.

However, plasma contains only about 7.5 per cent of total body water. To prevent excessive loss of this relatively small volume, albumin and other plasma proteins attract water to remain in the blood vessels. Normal plasma albumin is 35–50 grams/litre, but illness often lowers plasma albumin levels, causing excessive extravasation (movement from the blood stream into the extravascular compartment) of fluid. This causes both hypovolaemia (reduced blood volume, detected by hypotension) and oedema (see page 372).

Figure 38.1 Fluid compartments in the body, showing their relative values.

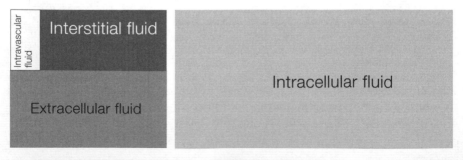

Plasma water moves relatively freely across capillary membranes, which is why intravascular concentrations of electrolytes and other solutes are similar to interstitial concentrations. However, the volume of interstitial fluid is considerably larger: about 12–14 litres (Marieb 2004), making 30 per cent of total body water.

Most body water is inside cells: 25–28 litres (Marieb 2004), making 62.5 per cent of total body water. Each cell is surrounded by a membrane, which controls movement of chemicals and substances into the cell. Relative proportions of the three fluid compartments described are shown in Figure 38.1.

Factors affecting fluid compartments

Fluid moves constantly between body compartments, delivering oxygen and nutrients to tissues while removing waste products (carbon dioxide, metabolic acids). Each day 24 litres moves from capillaries into tissues – about six times the total plasma volume. Most (85 per cent) of this is reabsorbed by the same capillaries, the remainder forming lymph, which eventually drains back into the cardiovascular system (Ganong 2001). Therefore, most fluid, whether a cup of tea or intravenous infusion, transfers into interstitial and then intracellular fluid compartments. Deroy (2000) suggests that only 85ml of each litre infused intravenously remains in the blood, although the amount and timing of movement varies between different fluids, depending on the size of solutes.

In health, most water loss is in urine, which can be easily measured. Renal function is usually adequate provided that 450ml of urine is passed daily, but most people excrete far more to remove excess body water. Increased water loss dilutes urine, lowering its specific gravity to near that of water (1.0). In health, kidneys therefore increase or decrease urine volume to maintain total body fluid balance. Renal excretion of water is regulated by hormones, especially antidiuretic hormone (ADH).

Various diseases and treatments can affect urine volume. For example, diuretics such as furosemide (frusemide) block the effect of ADH and, therefore, increase urine volume. High blood sugar levels from poorly controlled diabetes mellitus cause glycosuria, which inhibits renal reabsorption of water, causing polyuria (large volumes of urine) and hypovolaemia. Hypovolaemia causes thirst (polydipsia), the other classic symptom of diabetes.

Insensible loss

Smaller but still significant amounts of body water are lost through other means, more difficult to measure. The main sources of this 'insensible' loss are:

- perspiration;
- defaecation (faeces);
- respiration (breathing).

Normally, estimated daily insensible loss is 500ml, but other factors that may increase or decrease insensible loss include:

- pyrexia (fever; increases perspiration);
- diarrhoea/constipation;
- tachypnoea (rapid breathing);
- breathing very dry air or unhumidified oxygen.

In ill-health, insensible loss may double to one litre. Although calculating insensible loss is guesswork, increased insensible loss can explain causes of dehydration.

Effects of ageing

The body aims to maintain a balance between these compartments. Age-related changes and ill-health can alter this balance, creating potential complications. There is some age-related decline to all aspects of fluid balance, but healthy ageing is unlikely to cause problems for people. So whilst urine volume may decline, in the absence of disease it usually remains adequate to remove body waste. However, various factors identified above may affect the body's fluid balance. For example, many older people have less muscle but more fat than when they were younger, and so have fewer water 'stores', making them more prone to dehydration.

More often, people may respond to problems such as nocturia, frequency or incontinence by restricting their fluid intake and not taking prescribed diuretics, especially when going out or near to bedtime. Nocturia and polyuria are symptoms of an underlying problem, so restricting fluid intake may cause dehydration and further problems, such as hypotension and predisposing to urinary tract infection. Cystitis and pain on urinating may further discourage people from drinking. Therefore, when caring for people who are reluctant to drink, practitioners should explore the cause of the symptom.

Prevalence of acute and chronic diseases (eg type 2 diabetes, chronic obstructive pulmonary disease, chronic heart failure) in older people makes them more susceptible to fluid imbalances. Physical limitations, such as immobility or arthritis, may discourage them from getting drinks or urinating.

Assessment

There are many aspects to assessing fluid balance but all signs should be interpreted in terms of the person as a whole. Although symptoms may have other causes, key assessment questions include:

- Does the skin look or feel dry?
- Does the skin look or feel loose? (Subcutaneous fat and muscle wasting indicate fewer water reserves.)
- Does the skin look or feel oedematous? Is it pitting oedema?
- Does the skin look poorly perfused (eg discoloured white, blue or purple; ulcers)?
- Do the mouth or lips look dry?
- Does hair look or feel dry?
- Is urine output normal?
- Are there any problems passing urine (eg incontinence, pain)?
- Are there any other sources of fluid loss (eg stomas, surgical drains)?
- Does the person have any disease that affects water loss (eg diabetes mellitus, pyrexia)?
- Does the person have any disease or treatments that affect internal fluid balance (eg heart failure, steroids)?
- Do any treatments affect water loss (eg diuretics, dry oxygen)?

- Are there signs of hypovolaemia (eg hypotension, weak thready pulse)?

Like any assessment, potentially embarrassing issues (eg questions about urine) or intimate aspects, such as touch, should be handled sensitively. Other multidisciplinary assessments, such as blood tests, may provide further information, so referral to other professionals may be appropriate.

Electrolytes

Blood carries many important electrolytes, and the positively charged ions (cations), sodium (Na^+) and potassium (K^+), are particularly affected by fluid imbalances. Plasma electrolytes are discussed in Chapter 16.

Electrolyte concentrations of intracellular fluid are significantly different from extracellular concentrations. For example, normal extracellular (intravascular and interstitial) sodium concentration is 135–145 mmol/litre and potassium 3.5–4.5 mmol/litre. The sodium–potassium pump in cell membranes almost reverses intracellular concentrations of these electrolytes, to potassium of 140 mmol/litre and sodium of 14 mmol/litre.

Inflammatory response

Inflammation increases capillary permeability, enabling migration of antibodies and leucocytes into infected tissue to destroy bacteria. Extravasation of plasma causes oedema, stimulating pain receptors to cause the typical ache of inflammation. Local inflammatory responses, such as an infected wound, will not significantly alter fluid balance. But widespread (systemic) inflammation, which may occur during a critical illness or following surgery, can cause significant 'loss' of intravascular volume into the far larger interstitial compartment, resulting in hypovolaemia and hypotension.

Oedema

Oedema – excessive extravascular fluid – may be interstitial or intracellular, or both. Unlike intravenous volume, extravascular fluid cannot be measured directly in clinical practice.

Many acute and chronic diseases, such as heart failure, cause interstitial oedema. This often causes visible puffiness around the ankles and elsewhere; often indicating poor perfusion. It also impairs oxygen delivery to tissue cells. Excess water significantly increases weight, so weighing patients daily will monitor the accumulation or removal of oedema. Pitting oedema (where skin remains depressed after pressure from a finger has been removed) suggests an especially large accumulation of interstitial oedema.

Intracellular oedema is not easy to detect but causes more problems. Cell damage causes the sodium–potassium pump (see above) to fail, and so sodium moves into the cell to form concentrations similar to extracellular fluid. Sodium draws in water, increasing intracellular fluid volume. Intracellular oedema places more pressure on the already damaged cell membrane, causing further failure, and potential cell death (necrosis). Whilst the death of one cell is usually insignificant, cells are the functional part of any organ, so widespread cell death or damage results in organ failure.

Fluid replacement

Fluid imbalances can occur to any or all compartments. Assessment may identify problems such as polypharmacy (taking several drugs), reluctance to take prescribed medicines (such as diuretics), incontinence or physical limitations, which can be referred to other health care professionals. Major blood loss (whether from trauma or surgery) and widespread acute inflammatory responses need short-term intravascular filling, whereas total body dehydration often occurs with malnourishment (someone found collapsed at home, for example) and needs total body hydration.

Oral fluids

A healthy body maintains homoeostasis. Whenever possible, people should be enabled to meet their own fluid needs. Oral fluids are usually the ideal, and normal, way to replace body fluid. But many older people take insufficient fluids (Coutts 2001). Immobility, one of the 'four 'I's' of old age (Heath 2000), may prevent people at home or in hospital from reaching drinks. Drinks should therefore be placed within easy reach of anyone with limited mobility. Other limitations, such as arthritis, may prevent people from being able to turn taps or open bottles. Occupational therapists may be able to supply aids to help regain this ability.

Drinks in hospitals or other institutions often lack appeal: jugs of room-temperature water are not appetising. Tea and other hot drinks are not always offered or available between meals, and, compared with ranges available in supermarkets, the choice of flavours is often limited. Age-related reduction in taste may further reduce the appeal of drinks. Assessment should therefore acknowledge individual preferences, encourage the supply of flavours (fruit squashes, for example) and offer drinks between times of set 'rounds'.

Intravenous fluids

Intravenous fluids are often divided into two groups:

- crystalloids
- colloids.

Crystalloids (eg 0.9% 'normal' saline, 5% glucose) contain solutes with small molecules, so can move relatively freely between fluid compartments. Most body water is extravascular, and crystalloids are ideal for maintaining total body hydration. Crystalloids are cheap and relatively safe to give. Maintenance infusions of normal saline can also be given subcutaneously, into the interstitial compartment, provided that infusion is reasonably slow.

Crystalloids extravase (leave the venous system) rapidly. After 20–40 minutes only one-fifth of normal saline remains intravascularly (Haljamae and Lindgren 2000). With acute hypovolaemia, crystalloids are usually adequate, but prolonged hypotension in critical illness may necessitate fluids with longer half-lives (time taken for loss of half the effect of the substance). Extravasation of crystalloids may also cause oedema: one study found that 70 per cent of older people treated with crystalloid for shock developed pulmonary oedema, compared with 25 per cent of those given colloids (Boldt 2000). So, rapid infusion of large volumes of crystalloids is usually best avoided, especially in older people.

The only constituents of 5% glucose are glucose and water. The water moves freely, only one-tenth remaining intravascularly (Webb 1999). This makes 5% glucose useful for intracellular rehydration. But 5% glucose is not a substitute for feeding, each litre containing only 50 grams of glucose; a daily regimen of 3 litres contains about as many calories as a typical chocolate bar. Concentrated glucose solutions, such as 20%, should only be given through a large vein, preferably a central line.

Colloids have larger molecules than crystalloids do, so remain longer intravascularly, sustaining blood pressure for longer. But colloids are more expensive and have more complications. Therefore, crystalloids are normally given unless colloids are specifically indicated.

Blood transfusion infuses living cells. During storage, continued metabolism and lack of oxygen delivery and waste product removal in transfusion bags cause progressive cell damage (minimised, but not prevented, by storing at 4°C). Damage to the sodium–potassium pump in cell membranes allows intracellular potassium to leak into the remaining plasma, increasing plasma potassium concentrations (hyperkalaemia). However, life-threatening hyperkalaemia is unlikely unless ten or more units are transfused (Humphreys 2002).

Diuresis from furosemide, usually given with blood transfusion, removes excess potassium, preventing hyperkalaemia. But as damaged cells recover, plasma potassium is progressively drawn into intracellular fluid, causing potential hypokalaemia 24 hours after transfusion (Isbister 2003). Therefore potassium level should be checked within 24 hours following blood transfusion; if it is low, replacement potassium should be given. Blood and blood products are usually given only if specific components are needed, so are not discussed further here.

The main colloids used for 'filling' are gelatins such as Haemaccel®
and Gelofusine®. Compared with other artificial colloids, gelatins are
relatively cheap and rarely cause reactions. Although gelatin molecules are considerably larger than crystalloids, they are below
renal threshold, limiting their effectiveness to about 90–120 minutes
(Mythen 2003). Therefore, further intravenous fluids may be needed
within a few hours to maintain blood pressure.

Conclusion

The healthy body maintains fluid balance through a number of mechanisms. This balance distributes water across intravascular, interstitial
and intracellular fluid compartments. Acute or chronic disease can
cause imbalances between fluid compartments, resulting in many
complications.

Maintaining hydration is fundamental to life, so practitioners should
encourage or help people to obtain drinks. In acute illness, intravenous fluid replacement may be needed. Although prescribing intravenous fluids remains a medical role, nurses may be the first health care
professionals to assess fluid needs, should understand the effects of
fluids they give, and question inappropriate prescriptions. Crystalloid
fluids provide effective intracellular hydration but, for sustained intravascular 'filling', colloids may be needed.

39 Continence

Lesley Wilson

Despite considerable numbers of older people experiencing continence problems, incontinence is not an inevitable part of ageing. Many health professionals, as well as the general population, believe incontinence to be inevitable with advancing years. This belief endorses the myth of incontinence being part of the ageing process, that very little can be done to relieve symptoms or lead to a cure, with the consequences of negative attitudes and beliefs in our society about older people and incontinence. The truth is that much can be done to relieve symptoms, and in many cases a cure is realistic.

Figures quoted for the number of people with urinary incontinence range between 10 and 70 per cent in adults aged 65 or over (Royal College of Physicians 1995; Fonda et al 1999) but the general health of the older person is a significant factor. For those who live at home, between 5 and 41 per cent have problems whereas of those living in residential accommodation or long-term hospital care, between 25 and 70 per cent are likely to have continence problems (Royal College of Physicians 1995; Roberts et al 1999). The figures for faecal incontinence are not so reliable but Kamm (1998) found that approximately 7 per cent of healthy, independent adults of 65 years or over experienced leakage of stool and a third of those in residential care were likely to be faecally incontinent. Combined urinary and faecal incontinence is thought to be prevalent in 5–9 per cent of older people living at home (Roberts et al 1999) and in about 54 per cent of those in nursing home care (Chiang et al 2000).

The causes of incontinence in healthy older adults are similar to those in younger people but older people are more likely to be affected by risk factors that may influence their continence. These factors can be physiological, pharmacological or psychological (Royal College of Physicians 1995; Fonda et al 1999) and may be directly or indirectly due to the effects of ageing (Table 39.1).

Table 39.1 **Risk factors for incontinence in older people**

Factor	Comment
Renal function	The filtration function of the kidneys reduces with age to approximately 50% by the age of 80. They have reduced ability to absorb sodium and to respond to antidiuretic hormone (ADH).
Bladder function	The capacity of the bladder and urinary flow rates reduce with age. Sensation of the desire to void is often reduced until the bladder is almost full.
Urethral changes	Reduction in oestrogen leads to reduced ability of the urethra to remain closed. There is also a reduction in the muscle composition of the urethral wall.
Lower gastro-intestinal changes	There is a slowing down of activity in the gastrointestinal tract and absorption. Decreased sensation of rectal distension may be present together with reduced ability to distinguish between fluid and flatus in the anal canal.
Neurological changes	Changes in the various micturition centres and nerves can lead to poor co-ordination of the micturition process and, in some cases, urine retention.
Cardiac function	Cardiac dysfunction usually leads to increased blood supply to the kidneys at rest, with the effect of more urine being passed at night.

continued

Table 39.1 (continued)

Factor	Comment
Endocrine factors	Reduced oestrogen levels can cause atrophic vaginitis, but undiagnosed late-onset (type 2) diabetes may be the cause of urinary symptoms.
Impaired functional ability	Reduced mobility, dexterity or cognitive ability can affect continence status.
Drug toxicity and poly-pharmacy	The ageing process affects the absorption and elimination of drugs and, due to reduced renal function, elimination is retarded with the effect of residual quantities being retained. Certain drugs prescribed to older people will affect the bladder.

The increased vulnerability of older people to illness means that the effects of minor illnesses are often more serious and debilitating than would be likely in younger people, with the result that recovery periods are longer. If incontinence occurs due to illness, continence may not always be fully restored on recovery.

Transient (temporary or reversible) incontinence can occur in older people as a result of an illness or traumatic event such as a change in environment or a bereavement (Wilson 2003a) but continence, or at least improvement, should be achievable in many cases. In frail older people, who may be considerably compromised in their abilities, their problems are often complex and more difficult to resolve.

Assessment

Assessment is the key to identifying the cause and determining the most effective methods of managing health problems. Incontinence is a symptom of an underlying condition and the planning of effective treatment and management depends on the information gathered from comprehensive, accurate assessment.

The aims of continence assessment are threefold (Ouslander and Schnelle 1995):

- to identify any reversible factors implicated;
- to determine treatment/management strategies;
- to identify people for whom specialist referral is appropriate.

Urinary and/or faecal incontinence can present in several different ways, depending on the underlying cause, and it is important for the assessor to be familiar with the different types and causes of incontinence (Table 39.2). The process of continence assessment in older people is the same as for younger adults but with more emphasis placed on aspects that are likely to be implicated because of the age of the individual (see Table 39.1).

Table 39.2 **Urinary incontinence – types and causes**

Type of incontinence	Symptoms	Usual causes
Stress	Leaks with coughing, sneezing, exercise or lifting	Weakness in the muscles of the pelvic floor
Urge	Leakage with urgent desire to void. Frequency, nocturia	Overactive bladder (bladder contracts at very slight provocation and is very sensitive)
Mixed stress/ urge	Mixture of symptoms as above	Weakness in pelvic floor muscles and overactive bladder together

continued

Table 39.2 (continued)

Type of incontinence	Symptoms	Usual causes
Dribbling/ Overflow	Frequency, nocturia, passive dribbling, incomplete emptying. Symptoms of urinary tract infection	Outflow obstruction (eg enlarged prostate, constipation) Hypotonic bladder (reduced muscle activity) Detrusor–sphincter dyssynergia (neurological co-ordination dysfunction)
Reflex/ Passive	Bladder empties without warning. No sensation of desire to void	Neuropathic absence of sensation (eg as in paraplegia). May be due to disease or trauma

The process of continence assessment (Nazarko 1999) consists of:

- recording a full and accurate history;
- carrying out simple investigations;
- physical examination;
- diagnosis of the cause/type of incontinence;
- deciding on appropriate treatment/management strategies;
- ongoing reassessment/evaluation of progress.

Assessment should be an ongoing process, and all the relevant information cannot always be obtained on one occasion. The 'full picture' may have to be built up over several occasions as the individual learns to trust their assessor and is able to discuss their problem frankly.

When people have cognitive disorders or learning difficulties, obtaining an accurate history is often difficult, and the assessor will have to depend on information supplied by relatives or carers.

The accuracy of any assessment is only as good as the information given and gathered. But because of the sensitivities relating to incontinence, it is often difficult to obtain accurate information, even from individuals without cognitive difficulties.

It is very important to determine how much the individual is inconvenienced and 'bothered' by their problem – this should be considered when reaching decisions about treatment and management.

The assessment process

History taking

There are many assessment tools or 'forms' available, and most health organisations will have developed their own or adapted an existing tool to be used in their establishments. An example of an assessment tool is given in Box 39.1.

At the initial assessment interview the assessor should aim to obtain specific information from the individual about their problem, including (Getliffe and Dolman 2003):

- their perception of and attitude to the problem;
- urinary and/or faecal symptoms;
- onset date or duration;
- relevant medical, surgical and obstetric history;
- related significant events that could have causative factors;
- current medication;
- functional ability (ie mobility and ability to carry out daily living activities);
- significant environmental factors;
- current management strategies being used (eg continence aids such as pads).

Other essential tools, which should be used in conjunction with the assessment tool to ensure that the information record is accurate, are frequency volume charts, bowel or stool charts and fluid or food diaries. These help determine the causes of an individual's continence problem (Pfister 1999). Ideally, frequency volume charts, stool charts, fluid and food diaries should be recorded by the individual for a week before the assessment interview. This is not always practicable and the length of time these are maintained depends on each individual.

Frequency volume charts indicate the activity of the bladder, *stool charts* record bowel activity, *fluid diaries* record fluid intake and *food diaries* indicate the individual's diet.

Charts may have been developed with assessment tools by health organisations but can also be obtained from many of the companies that manufacture continence aids. However, it is often more effective for the assessor to draw up a chart, using a blank piece of paper, to suit each individual person. For example, many of the charts available are printed with a line for each hour but more accuracy is achieved when the person can add their own times of events.

Frequency volume charts should record:

- how often urine is passed, day and night;
- the amount passed on each occasion;
- the number of incontinent episodes.

If difficulty is experienced in measuring urine – for example, if mobility or dexterity are compromised – recording just frequency will still be a valuable aid to assessing the cause of the problem (Wilson 2003a).

Stool charts should record:

- how often stools are passed;
- stool quantity (approximate);
- stool consistency;
- stool characteristics (eg colour, smell).

The Bristol Stool Form Scale is an excellent tool that can be used to determine stool consistency. Figure 39.1 is a black-and-white version of that chart.

Box 39.1 *An example of a continence assessment tool*

Where applicable please tick boxes

1 Presenting problem as reported by patient/parent/carer:

_____

Duration of present urinary problem:
- [ ] Less than 1 year
- [ ] 3–5 years
- [ ] 1–2 years
- [ ] 5+ years

Micturition pattern before presenting problem:

_____

2 History

a Medical history

- [ ] Recurrent UTI
- [ ] Multiple sclerosis
- [ ] Spinal injury
- [ ] Dementia
- [ ] Diabetes
- [ ] CVA
- [ ] Spinal lesion
- [ ] Parkinson's disease

Other relevant diagnosis

b Surgical history

- [ ] Cystoscopy
- [ ] Bladder neck surgery
- [ ] Abdominal hysterectomy
- [ ] Pelvic floor repair
- [ ] Urethral dilatation
- [ ] Prostatectomy
- [ ] Vaginal hysterectomy
- [ ] None relevant

Other relevant diagnosis _____

c Obstetric history

No. of pregnancies _____ Babies over 3.5 kg (8 lb) _____

d Medical investigation/examination prior to nursing assessment

- [ ] Vaginal examination
- [ ] MSU
- [ ] Previous urodynamics
- [ ] Ultrasound
- [ ] Rectal examination
- [ ] Blood sugar
- [ ] IVP

Has the patient been seen by a doctor or
consultant specifically for incontinence?   ☐   Yes   ☐   No

Name of doctor _____

Date seen _____

Name of consultant_____

Date seen _____

3 Nursing assessment

a   Fluid intake

Number of cups per 24 hours   _____

Number of mugs per 24 hours   _____

Number of litres per 24 hours   _____

b   Urine test results

pH   _____   Specific gravity   _____

Protein   _____   Blood   _____

Glucose   _____   Ketones   _____

c   Micturition (from frequency/volume chart)

Number of urinary voids during day (when up)   _____

Number of urinary voids during night (when in bed)   _____

Maximum volume passed in one void/24hours   _____

Minimum volume passed in one void/24hours   _____

Total urinary output/24hours   _____

Number of incontinence episodes:

Day _____   Night _____

Where applicable:

☐   Primary enuresis   ☐   Secondary enuresis

d Types of urinary incontinence

Symptoms of stress incontinence

Do you leak when you laugh, cough or sneeze? ☐ Yes ☐ No

Do you leak when you get up from a chair/bed? ☐ Yes ☐ No

Symptoms of urge incontinence

How long can you hold on for after you feel the desire to void?

☐ Less than 2 minutes ☐ 2–5 minutes

☐ More than 5 minutes

Is the desire so great that you would be wet if you did not get to the toilet immediately? ☐ Yes ☐ No

Do you feel an urgent desire to void when you hear running water or put your key in the front door? ☐ Yes ☐ No

Symptoms of dribbling/overflow incontinence

Do you know when urine is leaking? ☐ Yes ☐ No

Are you wet all the time? ☐ Yes ☐ No

Do you have hesitancy? ☐ Yes ☐ No

Do you have to strain to pass water? ☐ Yes ☐ No

Is your stream as good as it used to be? ☐ Yes ☐ No

Do you leak immediately after you think your stream has finished (post-micturition dribble)? ☐ Yes ☐ No

Symptoms of reflex/passive incontinence

Does your bladder empty without warning? ☐ Yes ☐ No

Do you sometimes have the sensation of needing to pass urine? ☐ Yes ☐ No

e Diet

☐ Usual (preferred) diet ☐ High-fibre diet ☐ Fluid diet

Please identify usual diet _____

Special diet, please specify _____

f   Defaecation

Do you know when you want to
have your bowels open?   ☐ Yes   ☐ No

Do you know when you are
having your bowels open?   ☐ Yes   ☐ No

Usual bowel habits:

☐ daily   ☐ 3 times a week

☐ 2 times a week   ☐ once a week

☐ less than once a week

Consistency of faeces (see Bristol Stool Form Scale): type _____

g   Faecal incontinence

Number of faecal incontinence episodes during the day_____

Number of faecal episodes during the night _____

Quantity passed in 24 hours:

☐ 30ml   ☐ 30–150ml

☐ 150–200ml   ☐ Over 200ml

h   Drug therapy

☐ Diuretic   ☐ Anticholinergic

☐ Antidepressant   ☐ Hypnotics

☐ Tranquillisers   ☐ Oestrogens

☐ Laxatives

Name of drugs:

_____

_____

i   Skin condition

☐ Healthy   ☐ Groin red and excoriated

☐ Thighs red and excoriated   ☐ Buttocks red and excoriated

j   Mobility

☐ Fully mobile   ☐ Mobile but slow

☐ Walks with an aid   ☐ Walks with physical assistance

☐ Bed-bound

k   Dressing ability

☐ Independent   ☐ Independent but slow

☐ Independent with   ☐ Needs some assistance
  clothing adaptations

☐ Needs total assistance

l   Environment

Is there anything within the patient's environment
that deters them from reaching the toilet?   ☐ Yes   ☐ No

Comments _____

m   Mental awareness of need to eliminate

☐ Fully aware   ☐ Aware but not able to communicate

☐ Needs verbal or physical prompting   ☐ Intermittent awareness

☐ Completely unaware

n   Patient's/carer's attitude

☐ Okay   ☐ Keen to take preventative measures

☐ Anxious and/or afraid ☐ Denial of incontinence problem

☐ Rejection of advice

4   Management plan

☐ Pelvic floor exercises   ☐ Refer to continence adviser

☐ Correct fluid intake   ☐ Refer to GP

☐ Bladder re-training   ☐ Refer to other agencies

☐ Toilet training programme ☐ Intermittent catheterisation

☐ Pads   ☐ Appliances

☐ Buying own pads   ☐ Buying own appliances

*Figure 39.1 **A black-and-white version of the Bristol Stool Form Scale***

Type 1		Separate hard lumps, like nuts (hard to pass)
Type 2		Sausage-shaped but lumpy
Type 3		Like a sausage but with cracks on its surface
Type 4		Like a sausage or snake, smooth and soft
Type 5		Soft blobs with clear-cut edges (passed easily)
Type 6		Fluffy pieces with ragged edges – a mushy stool
Type 7		Water, no solid pieces ENTIRELY LIQUID

Reproduced by kind permission of Dr KW Heaton, Reader in Medicine at the University of Bristol. ©2000 Norgine Ltd

Fluid and food diaries

Drinks or fluid intake may be recorded together with the urinary output (see frequency volume charts discussed on page 382) or may be recorded on a separate chart where more detailed information can be included. They show:

- the amount of fluid drunk by the individual;
- the type of fluid being drunk;
- specific times when drinks are consumed.

Older people are susceptible to dehydration (Fantl et al 1996); it is therefore essential to ensure that fluid intake is adequate. Certain fluids are known to affect bladder activity (Newman 1999), so it is important to identify the type of fluid being consumed in order to advise the person accordingly.

Food diaries record:

- eating times;
- specific foods eaten;
- the quantity of food eaten.

Food diaries, when used in conjunction with stool charts and frequency volume charts, can sometimes help to identify problem foods in the diet.

Simple investigations

- Urinalysis, to exclude urinary tract infection and/or diabetes.
- Mid-stream urine specimen (when urinalysis suggests urinary tract infection is present – see above).
- Residual urine (in/out catheterisation or ultrasound bladder scan).
- Urine flow rate.

Physical examination

- Abdominal examination to identify masses or full bladder/loaded bowel.
- Rectal examination to identify prostate enlargement or faecally loaded rectum.
- Vaginal examination to assess pelvic floor strength or identify masses or prolapse; observation of the lining of the vagina may identify inflammation, or atrophic vaginitis (Ouslander and Schnelle 1995; Getliffe 1996).

Before attempting any physical examination, it is necessary for the patient to consent to the procedure. When caring for the older person, who may be frail or cognitively compromised, it is essential that they are able to understand in order to give informed consent. Performing this type of procedure without real consent may lead, in some circumstances, to allegations of abuse. There is guidance to be found in the literature (McKee 1999; Wallace 2000) or from professional organisations such as the Royal College of Nursing who have published a guidance document on digital rectal examination and manual evacuation of faeces (Royal College of Nursing 2000).

It is also important to determine physical abilities such as hearing, eyesight, mobility and dexterity by observation, and it may be possible to detect cognitive deficit at the assessment interview. These factors could well be determining factors in deciding treatment or management strategies.

It is important to identify and exclude potentially reversible causes of incontinence (transient incontinence). This can be achieved using the mnemonic of DRIP in Box 39.2 (Sander 1998).

Box 39.2 *Transient incontinence*

D Delirium

R Reduced/restricted mobility, acute retention

I Infection, inflammation, impaction of stool

P Pharmaceuticals, polyuria, psychological disorders

After Sander (1998)

Functional assessment

Assessment of functional ability has already been alluded to in this chapter. It is important for any person with continence problems but may be particularly relevant in the case of older adults. Their ability to carry out daily living activities may be compromised, with a resultant effect on their continence status. With appropriate interventions such as the use of equipment or modified clothing, continence can often be restored (Wilson 2003b).

Functional assessment should aim to identify any problems, determine and implement solutions, and continually review progress. Even if incontinence is due to physiological reasons such as overactive bladder (urge incontinence), functional difficulties can affect continence (Williams and Gaylord 1990).

Certain components of functional assessment have already been mentioned; full comprehensive functional assessment falls into four main categories:

- Physical function – mobility, dressing ability, vision and hearing.
- Cognitive function – orientation, mood, the ability to make decisions and understanding.
- Social functioning – activities, relationships, food preparation and shopping.
- Environmental factors – access at home, seating, toileting facilities and bed access.

There are various tools available to assess functional ability, one of the most familiar being the Barthel index. Others include the Katz Activities of Daily Living (ADL) scale, which gives an overview of an individual's dependency (Williams and Gaylord 1990), and the General Health Questionnaire, which is a useful tool to assess the psychological well-being of an incontinent person (Lewis 1999).

Prevention

The prevention of continence problems in older people is, to a great extent, dependent on preventative strategies being used earlier in their lives. With increased general awareness of the causes of incontinence and the risk factors implicated, however, a reduction in its incidence should be possible.

Conclusion

Incontinence should not be considered an inevitable part of getting older, even though large numbers of older adults experience continence problems. The reasons for incontinence in older people are likely to be the same as for younger adults but some factors associated with ageing can increase the risk, especially when illness occurs.

Assessment is the key to identifying the causes of continence problems, and those that are reversible (transient incontinence), in order to plan the most effective treatment or management for each individual. Incontinence can be a devastating experience but in the older person it may mean an early admission to residential care because of their inability to cope at home. Where prevention is successful in reducing or eliminating the incidence of incontinence, independence is assured together with a better quality of life for the older person.

Part 5
Quality of Life

40 Quality of life

Peter Draper

This chapter considers the assessment of the quality of life of older people. It begins by considering some of the ways in which the term 'quality of life' is used. There is then a discussion of various ways in which assessment of the quality of life is described in the literature and the reasons for which such assessments might be made. This helps us to identify a number of principles that guide the assessment of the quality of life. In the final section, these principles are applied to the assessment of the quality of life of older people in practical settings.

What is quality of life?

The assessment of the quality of life has become an industry over the last 20 years, giving rise to an enormous literature in health and social care disciplines such as nursing, social work and medicine. The growth of the literature has been exponential. The first reference to the concept of the quality of life in the medical literature that I have been able to trace was written by Elkington (1966), although the term has a longer history in other disciplines. Since then, the number of papers written has virtually doubled in each five-year period (Draper 1997), about 35,000 having been written during the past five years. The concept is not only found in the professional literature but is also frequently used in a wide range of other contexts. Recently, for example, I have heard a politician promise that his policies will improve people's quality of life; listened to a doctor arguing that a prematurely born infant should be allowed to die because there is no prospect of her having a good quality of life; and driven past a new police station whose sign promises a 'quality of life' approach to policing.

The number and range of references to the quality of life suggest that both professionals and people in the wider community are interested in the concept and seem to find it valuable. However, the fact that it is used in such a wide range of ways may mean that no single satisfactory definition is likely to be appropriate in all circumstances, and this will inevitably have implications for practitioners wishing to assess the quality of life of older people, if we accept that all assessments must reflect some degree of consensus about the nature of the thing being assessed. We will now look at the quality of life literature in a little more detail, and try to tease out from the literature some of the most important principles to guide our assessments of the quality of life of older people.

Thinking about the assessment of quality of life

The first issue to consider is the purpose for which quality of life assessments are made. This is important because different types of assessment are appropriate in different circumstances. In the health and social care literature, quality of life assessments can be placed in three major groups:

- Quality of life as an outcome measure in research.
- Quality of life as a factor in resource allocation.
- Quality of life in the care of individual people.

Quality of life as an outcome measure in research

The earliest systematic attempts to measure the quality of life were made by economists and social psychologists working in the USA in the 1950s and 1960s. Their work was driven by economic and political factors such as the desire to demonstrate that the government was being successful in improving the lives of ordinary people. Their programmes of research considered such issues as the impact of the NASA space programme on North American society. Research of this type may seem a long way removed from the contemporary assessment of older people, but it gave rise to a number of important debates that are still relevant. For example, there is the debate about whether the quality of life is essentially an objective state that can be measured in a scientific way without direct reference to the views of individuals; or whether it is a subjective phenomenon reflecting the unique experiences of each individual, which must be defined afresh in each case. This distinction can still be found in the contemporary literature. Hendry and McVittie (2004) argue that older people's understandings of quality of life are not readily measurable and should be viewed in terms of experience, thereby reflecting the subjective approach. In contrast, the bulk of the literature assumes that the objective measurement of the quality of life is possible, at least in principle (see, for example, Livingston et al 1998). Other researchers employ a combination of quantitative (objective) and qualitative (subjective) approaches.

A large proportion of the medical literature uses measurements of the quality of life as outcome data in clinical trials to compare the effectiveness of different types of medical treatment, and a range of psychometric instruments has been developed for this purpose. Some of these are designed to be applicable to people with a wide range of illnesses and disabilities. These are known as 'generic' instruments, and include the Sickness Impact Profile (Bergner et al 1981) and the SF-36 (Ware et al 1993). Another group of scales enables researchers to assess the quality of life of people with specific diseases such as heart disease or stroke. Many researchers use a combination of generic and disease-specific scales to assess the global and the individual components of a person's condition. As with all scales, it is advisable to ensure that instruments used in quality of life research are both reliable and valid.

Quality of life as a factor in resource allocation

The concept of the quality of life plays an important role in another area of research, where it has been used by health economists and to inform decisions about the allocation of resources. In countries with market-based health services – that is to say, where access to health care is based on the ability of the person or their insurance company to pay – market forces have a significant impact on the allocation of resources. Thus, if the demand for a particular treatment is high but access to the treatment is limited for some reason, perhaps because it involves 'cutting edge' technology that is not commonly available, the price is likely to be high and the resource will be available only to those who have the money to pay for it.

Historically, the National Health Service has not been influenced by market forces in this way, and so other means have had to be found to determine who gets access to relatively scarce resources. One of the ways of allocating resources has been to estimate the effect of a therapy, not only on the physical health of the person but also on their quality of life. The key concept here is the Quality Adjusted Life Year (QALY) (Williams and Kind 1992), which was designed as a generic measure of health benefit, and represented the value attached by members of wider society to different improvements in health, thus enabling systematic and rational comparisons to be made between different treatments. This application of the concept of the quality of life has been subject to sustained criticism from an ethical perspective. Some of the objections have been summarised by Rapley (2003), who argues that QALYs represent a subtle but important change in focus from the quality of lives of individual people to the very abstract, technical concept of the 'life year'.

The concept of the Quality Adjusted Life Year may seem far removed from the day-to-day experience and practice of the health or social care professional, but it raises a number of important issues for all practitioners. As we have seen, the concept of quality of life is not restricted to the pages of academic journals but arises in all sorts of contexts, and it is not uncommon for practitioners to invoke the concept of quality of life in case conferences or meetings that concern resource-allocation decisions on a 'micro' scale such as the continuation or cessation of therapy. The QALY literature is useful in such cases, first because it represents an attempt to be clear about the role that quality of life considerations can play in decision-making and also because it illustrates that the quality of life is not an easily measurable, scientific fact about a person but one that also represents values and assessments of priority, both of which can be contentious.

Quality of life in the care of individual people

The approaches to the quality of life discussed above have a number of common features: they tend towards the objective or scientific end of the scale because they use numbers to represent judgements about individuals and how their health and well-being responds in various circumstances, and they use these measurements to evaluate therapies or the allocation of scarce resources. An important assumption behind such approaches is that there is a degree of consensus about what are the important elements of the quality of life, and that reliable and valid ways can be found to measure these elements, at least in principle.

An alternative approach to the quality of life is based on subjective rather than objective assumptions, and tends to use qualitative rather than quantitative approaches. In this approach the quality of life is not regarded so much as a scientific datum as a value, or an objective of care. Typically, this approach is concerned with creating a social environment in which individuals can fulfil their potential. No prior assumptions need be made about what are the most desirable circumstances for each individual, as these can and will vary from case to case. The relevance of this approach is that it requires and values the views, aspirations and resources of individuals in making decisions about their own circumstances.

Conclusion – assessing the quality of life of older people

Having discussed various approaches to the quality of life, it is now possible to draw out certain principles to guide individual practitioners who might wish to consider the quality of life of older people. I suggest that the first point to consider is the purpose for which the assessment is being made. Assessment methodologies can be placed at a point on a scale ranging between objective and subjective poles. If the purpose of the assessment is to collect formal data for the scientific evaluation of two interventions, it is essential that an objective approach be taken. It will be important to evaluate carefully the psychometric properties of the scale or scales used to ensure reliability and validity, as well as addressing appropriateness, responsiveness, precision, interpretability, acceptability and feasibility (Jenkinson and McGee 1998). A decision must also be made as to whether it is most appropriate to use a disease-specific or a generic indicator, or perhaps a combination of the two.

However, care professionals may have an interest in someone's quality of life that does not arise in the formal context of research. What, for example, is likely to be the impact of a move to residential accommodation, or the introduction of domestic help, on the quality of life of a particular individual? In these circumstances formal scales are likely to be of little use or value because there is no intention to make a comparison and the numbers generated would have little meaning. It may be best to engage in an unstructured interview process where no assumptions are made about what are the most important issues to be considered, but letting the individual concerned express their opinion about the changes they face and the differences they might make to their living situation. In these circumstances, a subjective approach of this kind is more likely to give valid insights into the person's quality of life.

Recent research by Gabriel and Bowling (2004) outlines some of the issues that are likely to emerge as important. Their large-scale study of the quality of life of older people in Britain living in private households points to the importance of having good social relationships, living in a home and a neighbourhood that is safe and pleasant with good access to transport and amenities, having the opportunity to engage in hobbies and leisure activities as well as retaining a role in society, having a positive outlook whilst being able to accept circumstances that cannot be changed, having good health and mobility and enough money to meet basic needs, and remaining independent and in control.

41 Sleep

Sharon Maher

Sleep is a period of diminished responsiveness to external stimuli. It is divided into one rapid eye movement (REM) stage and four non-rapid eye movement (non-REM) stages. Insomnia is the most common sleep problem reported by people over 60 (Avidan 2003). Changes in the sleep patterns of older adults include the non-REM stages taking longer to complete, which in turn leads to a decrease in the amount of REM sleep. As more light stage one and stage two sleep is experienced, an individual will report waking more easily, more frequently and feeling less refreshed.

It is often reported that, as we grow older, our need for sleep grows less. However, it is not the need for sleep but the ability to sleep that diminishes with age. Problems with initiating deep sleep may result from the increase in health problems seen in some older adults, including heart failure, Parkinson's disease, nocturia and sleep apnoea (Maher 2004). Pain from arthritis can impair sleep, as can lowness in mood. By assessing sleep, the practitioner can gain an understanding of the interplay between the seemingly disparate multiple health problems that affect some older adults.

Assessing for negative sleep hygiene

We can assess for changes in sleep associated with ageing – difficulty in falling asleep, frequent awakenings and early morning waking – and need to be attentive to the individual's coping mechanisms. The measures put in place to deal with a perceived sleep problem are called 'sleep hygiene' but, in some older adults, 'inverse' behaviours can lead to an exacerbation of the problem. The individual may:

- spend longer in bed;
- increase daytime napping;
- increase alcohol consumption;
- reduce social activity in favour of earlier bed times.

Alcohol consumption among older adults increases in response to poor sleep. Unfortunately, alcohol consumption in older adults is under-assessed and under-estimated but older women have been known to consume over-the-counter medication and alcohol, regularly mixing both with prescribed medication, being unaware of any health risk.

Dementia

More people are now living with dementia, and this seems to be associated with unique sleep problems (Maher 2004). The symptoms lessen as the disease progresses, but they are distressing symptoms for care-givers. The sleep pattern of a person with dementia should be assessed in the same way as with any other older adult. However, the assessment cannot be done without the input of the main carer or care-givers. Educating the carers of people with dementia about positive sleep hygiene practices, and supporting them while they put into practice what they have learned, greatly improves the sleep behaviours of those they care for (Maher 2004).

Sleeping tablets

When older adults request help with their sleep problems, often what is prescribed is sleeping tablets. Benzodiazepines (temazepam, lorazepam, etc) prescribing is decreasing in favour of non-benzodiazepines (zolpidem, zopiclone). Benzodiazepines should not be taken for longer than two consecutive weeks. After prolonged use, increasing amounts are required, as tolerance can be experienced. Sudden withdrawal of the drug at this stage can be dangerous. Appropriate medical supervision is required to wean people off sleeping tablets, especially the benzodiazepines (Maher 2004).

Other problems linked to benzodiazepines include:

- memory loss;
- increased hospital stays;
- increased risk of pressure sores;
- rebound insomnia;
- increased symptoms of depression;
- hangover effect;
- increased risk of road traffic accidents;
- increased risk of accidents and minor injuries;
- increased incidence of hip fracture;
- can be used as a form of restraint.

Despite these findings, the drugs continue to be prescribed. Dollman and colleagues (2003) state that doctors are encouraged to reduce the prescribing of benzodiazepines but are not given any clear advice on non-drug alternatives; they also state that doctors believe patients will be non-compliant with non-drug options. Perhaps for these reasons, the most common practice has been the reduced prescribing of benzodiazepines and the increased prescribing of non-benzodiazepines. Research suggests that they are less addictive than benzodiazepines but they are not completely free of unwanted effects such as lowering mood, visual hallucinations and impaired reaction times, reasoning and the ability to multitask (Maher 2004).

If your assessment of the person suggests that they are not benefiting from sleeping tablets and, indeed, that their continued use may be harmful, it is important that you explore together the option of stopping them. They may need time and support to think about this option but, given the advantages, it is worth the time and effort.

Sleep hygiene and non-medication treatments

Many older people cope with their sleep problems by putting in place fairly benign but successful practices, such as:

- Warm baths and milky drinks before bed.

- Going to bed at a regular time, getting up at a regular time.
- Filling the day with meaningful activities.
- Exercise. (Wolf et al (2003) found that a programme of tai chi for 'frail' people over 70 reduced the risk of falls by 47.5 per cent and improved perceived quality of sleep.)
- Lavender oil, used in the bath or a few drops on a cloth placed inside a pillowslip, can induce feelings of relaxation.

Possible assessment questions and advice

- *How long have you had a sleep problem?*
  Asking this gives you a clearer idea of how long the person may have been trying to manage their insomnia and whether it was triggered by an event or illness.

- *What is your usual going to bed and waking routine?*
  Are they going to bed earlier and getting up later? Are they 'topping up' lost sleep by sleeping during the day? Napping during the day should be avoided, whilst a single, short period of sleep may help relax the person. Long, uncontrolled periods of 'nodding off' should be avoided. House-bound older people often report being bored. Napping may result from this rather than from genuine tiredness.

- *What treatments have you used for your insomnia? Did you consider them to be successful, or not?*
  People may tell you about what sleeping tablets they have taken or are taking. It may also be useful to ask about any over-the-counter medication, and whether they have used complementary medication or therapies.

- *Do you consume alcohol to help you sleep?*
  You may not get a straight answer to this question; however, it can prove useful to find out how much and how often they use alcohol.

- *What things do you do to help you get to sleep?*
  This will, hopefully, clarify what sleep hygiene they have put in place and whether these practices are helpful or potentially harmful.

- *Do you have difficulty falling asleep and/or do you keep waking in the night?*
  Problems initiating sleep and being easily disturbed are common age-related sleep problems. It is also important to find out what the person does when they wake. People should be discouraged from lying in bed for long periods, waiting for sleep. Relaxation exercises are helpful in gaining control over the vicious circle of worrying about not sleeping and not sleeping because of worrying but, if these do not seem to be working, encourage the person to get out of bed and 'start again'. People get angry when they cannot sleep, and anger is a stimulant.

- *What regular exercise do you get?*
  There is a correlation between increased exercise and improved sleep. The goal is at least 30 minutes of activity a day – not necessarily all in one go! This can be a simple programme of stretch exercises or walking.

- *How much caffeine do you drink?*
  Caffeine is a stimulant, so intake should be reduced during the day and avoided in the evening.

Conclusion

It has been suggested that people do not like to 'bother' their doctor with their sleep problems, believing them to be too busy dealing with ailments more important than insomnia (Dollman et al 2003). Whilst reporting a dislike of sleeping tablets, they are reluctant to ask about alternative treatments because they feel it would take too much of the doctor's time.

It is worth taking the time and trouble to assess sleep thoroughly in the older adult, as this can often 'open a window' onto the person's life and how other health conditions may be affecting them. It is this 'knitting' together of the physical, social and psychological aspects of health that lies at the heart of holistic care.

42 **Pain**

Emma Briggs

Pain can have a detrimental effect on an individual's health, quality of life and recovery from trauma, as a result of its physical, psychological and social consequences. These effects can include depression, anxiety, aggression, suicidal thoughts, and reduced mobility, appetite and cognitive function (American Geriatrics Society 2002). Older adults are more likely to develop acute or chronic conditions that cause pain; an estimated 37–80 per cent of older people experience persistent pain (Ferrell et al 1995; Elliott et al 1999; Allcock et al 2002) but it is not a natural consequence of ageing.

As with any health care intervention, assessment is the cornerstone of management, and this chapter explores the basic principles of assessing older people, including those with cognitive impairment. Care should include frequent pain assessments, based on several principles (similar to those for younger individuals) and tools available for use in practice. Rowlingson (1994) identifies the main aims of assessment:

- To identify what the current pain experience means to the person.
- To lead to a diagnosis of the cause of pain, based on the information collected.
- To provide appropriate therapy.
- Once treatment is being provided, to regularly assess its effectiveness.

Promoting effective communication

Older people may be reluctant to report pain to health care professionals, and sensitive questioning is required to promote effective communication in a trusting relationship. People need to feel that their expression of pain will be listened to, accepted and acted upon (Closs 1994). Consideration also needs to be given to the different terminology older adults use for pain, such as discomfort, hurting or aching (Kamel et al 2001), but employing these terms does not necessarily mean that pain will be less intense or have less impact on a person. If required, communication aids such as glasses, hearing aids and dentures should be in place, and written information or pain assessment tools in large print can be used for aiding memory (Bruce and Kopp 2001).

Providing time

Pain assessment can take a few minutes or up to half an hour. In acute or emergency situations, limited information may be required such as intensity, location and type of pain (although an in-depth assessment should be conducted at a later point; Donovan 1992; McCaffery and Pasero 1999) but persistent pain requires a detailed examination of the cause, effects and factors affecting it. In both scenarios, time and patience are essential to enable the expression of pain and to ensure understanding of the tools used for assessment. Also, Herr and Mobily (1991) suggest that a more reliable and detailed assessment will be obtained if an older person is given privacy rather than discussing pain in a public arena such as a hospital ward or care home.

Assessing pain

As a multidimensional experience influencing an individual's physical, psychological and social well-being, pain requires a multidimensional assessment. McCaffery and Pasero (1999) identify eight areas of initial pain assessment and documentation, discussed below.

Location

Identifying the location of pain is key to diagnosing the cause. Older people may have several sources of pain, each of which needs to be assessed and documented (Closs et al 1993). Body charts, showing the whole or areas of the body, are useful for documenting painful points but do require fine motor movement, co-ordination and visual integrity (Rowlingson 1994).

Intensity

Intensity of pain is most often used to determine the type of analgesic or treatment given. It is important to ask the person to rate intensity of pain using a scale or assessment tool quantifying the subjective experience of pain and evaluating the effectiveness of analgesics. Time is needed to help people understand pain scales, and intensity should be assessed both at rest and during movement and/or coughing.

Verbal rating scales (also referred to as verbal or simple descriptor scales) are designed to assess the intensity of pain by asking the individual to rate their pain using a verbal or written list of adjectives. The most common verbal rating tool uses adjectives such as 'no pain', 'mild', 'moderate', 'severe' or 'very severe'. The tools are easy to use but the adjectives do not necessarily represent equal intervals of pain (Rowlingson 1994) and some people may wish to choose their own list of words. Intensity of pain may also be assessed on a numerical scale from zero to ten, zero being 'no pain' and ten the 'worst pain imaginable'. This scale is extremely easy and quick to administer. Using a visual analogue scale, the person is asked to mark intensity on a 10-cm horizontal or vertical line. The scale has extremes of pain labelled at either end and may include a numerical or verbal scale. Chapman and Syrala (2001) estimate that between 7 and 11 per cent of adults will have difficulty using the scale because of lack of dexterity or visual impairment or simply because they have difficulty representing their experience in this way.

Selecting an appropriate tool for use in practice depends on the individual and clinical area. Research involving younger groups has shown these tools to be valid measures of pain intensity that are generally reliable (they result in consistent measurement; Donovan 1992). The tools can also be easily printed in large or bold type for people with a visual impairment (Herr and Mobily 1991).

Quality

To determine the underlying cause of pain the person should be asked to describe the type or quality of the pain and given pointers such as 'tight', 'stabbing' or 'sharp' pain (McCaffery and Pasero 1999).

Onset, duration, variations and rhythms

A thorough exploration of onset, duration and variation in pain aids diagnosis and planning analgesic administration. McCaffery and Pasero (1999) suggest that the question 'Is the pain better or worse at certain times/hours/day or night?' should also be asked.

Manner of expressing pain

It is necessary to record whether people are able to express their pain verbally. This area is complicated by the wide variations in response to pain and the fact that non-verbal expression is not an indicator of pain intensity. Some studies have found that staff and carers have been unable to judge an individual's pain, under-estimating their suffering (Blomqvist and Hallberg 1999). However, non-verbal expression of pain is particularly important in assessing confused and cognitively impaired adults.

Methods of relieving pain

Some people with persistent pain may have considerable experience in using drug and non-drug methods to relieve their pain. This must be assessed carefully and their continued use encouraged (McCaffery and Pasero 1999).

Factors that cause or increase pain

To determine which activities should be avoided and to plan drug administration, factors causing or increasing pain should be identified and analgesics given at appropriate times (McCaffery and Pasero 1999).

Effects of pain

Pain can have a profound effect on mobility, sleeping pattern, dietary intake, and emotional and cognitive states. It is important that these areas are assessed and the effects minimised.

Multidimensional pain assessment tools

Many multidimensional tools have been developed to assess pain. One of the most widely validated tools in research and practice is the McGill Pain Questionnaire (Melzack and Katz 2001). The questionnaire assesses the sensory dimension (thermal, pressure, shooting), affective dimension (tension, fear) and evaluative dimension of pain (overall intensity). Multidimensional tools are particularly useful in the assessment and treatment of persistent pain but can be lengthy and inappropriate for acute settings.

Frequency of pain assessment

Recommendations for the frequency of pain assessment vary according to the person's situation but a minimum daily pain assessment of all patients has been found to improve pain relief in a Dutch hospital (De Rond et al 1999). In the USA, national guidelines for surgical patients (Agency for Health Care Policy and Research 1992) recommend that pain should be assessed:

- preoperatively;
- routinely at regular intervals as determined by the severity of pain and type of operation;
- with each new report of pain;
- at suitable intervals after each analgesic intervention.

In the UK, acute health care settings are increasingly promoting pain as the 'fifth vital sign' following temperature, pulse, respiration and blood pressure (Pain Society and Royal College of Anaesthetists 2003). Regular assessment ensures that a person in pain will be identified and management plans implemented.

Setting pain management targets

Person-centred goals help health care professionals and patients/ service users work towards a common target. These may be based on a pain-rating scale (for example, for Mrs Smith's pain to be less than two on a scale of zero to ten) or activity-related (for Mrs Smith to be comfortable enough to walk to the shopping centre every day). Discussing goals with people may empower them to be involved in the assessment and management process. The point at which analgesics are required may also be an area for discussion. Some hospital pain documentation includes an 'acceptable pain level' although the term can be difficult for many adults to comprehend and nurses may wish to ask: 'If you have moderate pain now, what would be ideal, no pain or mild pain?'

Assessing pain in people with cognitive impairment

It is a common misconception that pain is perceived differently or cannot be assessed in adults with cognitive impairment, but research examining age-related changes is inconclusive and it is dangerous to assume that perception changes in older adults (American Geriatrics Society 2002). There is also no evidence of people with cognitive impairment exaggerating or fabricating reports of pain (Bruce and Kopp 2001) and, where possible, the experiences of cognitively intact individuals should be used as a surrogate for those with dementia (Morrison and Siu 2000).

Pain in people with mild to moderate impairment

People with mild cognitive impairment are less likely to report pain to carers or nurses but are able to describe their experience accurately when prompted (Feldt et al 1998). Therefore, it is important to be proactive in detecting and assessing pain, and the current experience should be explored rather than the duration or changes in pain due to difficulties in memory (Bruce and Kopp 2001). Sensitive questions should prompt rather than lead, and, if required, be rephrased to ensure understanding. Time should be allowed for the person to answer, as silence does not necessarily mean assent (Simons and Malabar 1995). Finally, creating the right environment is important: the room should be well lit, with any distractions removed (Parke 1998), and the person may need help to get into an upright position to use assessment tools and visual aids.

Using pain assessment scales

Health care professionals may be reluctant to use assessment scales with people who have cognitive impairment but several studies have demonstrated their value. Kamel and colleagues (2001) found that people with mild cognitive impairment were more likely to report pain using assessment tools than if they were simply being asked: 'Do you have any pain?' As a result, staff detected, diagnosed and managed pain more effectively among nursing home residents. Ferrell and colleagues (1995) explored the use of five pain assessment tools with 217 cognitive-impaired nursing home residents and 83 per cent could complete at least one scale. The highest completion rate (65 per cent) was achieved using the Present Pain Index (PPI) that forms part of the McGill Pain Questionnaire (see Box 42.1). Verbal rating scales containing four categories have obtained 97 per cent completion rates in a recent UK study (Closs et al 2004), and this tool may be preferable to the PPI because the terms are more familiar (Feldt et al 1998). Good completion rates have also been reported for the numerical rating scale (Ferrell et al 1995; Closs et al 2004).

Box 42.1 **Pain assessment tools with a high completion rate in older people with mild to moderate cognitive impairment**

Present Pain Index of the McGill Pain Questionnaire (Melzack and Katz 2001)

0 – No pain
1 – Mild
2 – Discomforting
3 – Distressing
4 – Horrible
5 – Excruciating

Verbal rating scale used by Feldt et al (1998)

Slight pain
Mild pain
Moderate pain
Severe pain
Extreme pain
Pain as bad as it could be

Verbal rating scale used by Closs et al (2004)

No pain
Mild pain
Moderate pain
Severe pain

Paediatric 'pain faces' scales – cartoon faces with a range of expressions from happy, 'no pain or hurt', to crying 'as much pain as you can imagine' – have been recommended for use with cognitively impaired older people (Ferrell and Ferrell 1992). However, older adults with and without cognitive impairment have found the tool condescending (Loeb 1999) and research has not established the validity or reliability of this scale with this group of people.

Pain in people with severe impairment

With this group of people, pain assessment becomes more challenging and requires a wide range of nursing skills. Morrison and Siu (2000) examined pain management of patients with hip fractures and advanced dementia; sadly, most patients did not have a regular prescription for pain relief, and cognitively intact older adults received triple the amount of analgesics postoperatively. The main difference between the two groups was a reduced ability to report and describe pain. Attempts to use assessment scales should be made: around a third of nursing home residents with severe cognitive impairment could still use a verbal rating scale (Closs et al 2004). However, assessing pain in people with severe cognitive impairment focuses on detecting the presence of pain and there is less emphasis on other areas such as intensity, location or quality. Astute observational skills are required to detect vocalisations and non-verbal expressions of pain at rest and during movement. Examples of these behaviours are listed in Box 42.2.

Box 42.2 Common behaviours associated with pain

Vocalisations – 'ouch', whimpering, crying out on movement
Grimacing/frowning
Rigid body position
Flinching/guarding or rubbing the painful part
Aggressive behaviour
Restlessness
New repetitive behaviours
Pulling at tubes or clothing (may not be near the painful part)

Hurley and colleagues (1992) developed an assessment tool for detecting discomfort in people with advanced Alzheimer's disease; based on five-minute observations, nine behavioural indicators emerged. These included noisy breathing, negative vocalisations, absence of a look of contentment, looking sad, looking frightened, frowning, absence of a relaxed body posture, looking tense and fidgeting. The usefulness of this tool in practice has not been explored in depth and the authors acknowledge that there are higher levels than discomfort. However, the study does support the use of observation for assessing severely cognitively impaired people. Research by Manfredi and colleagues (2003) also suggests that facial expressions can be used to detect the presence of pain during procedures such as wound dressings, although results do not give an indication of intensity.

People who express their pain through non-verbal behaviours are more likely to receive analgesics (Feldt et al 1998) but behaviours are not always present and facial expressions can be difficult to interpret if someone has Parkinson's disease or has experienced cerebral vascular damage (Simons and Malabar 1995). Family members and carers may be able to provide information on the expression of pain and associated behaviour, and should be encouraged to be part of the assessment process.

The existence of pain may be confirmed through the administration of analgesics that would reduce any pain behaviours or aggression. Efforts should also be made to pre-empt analgesic needs during painful procedures or wound care or after surgery.

Documenting pain assessment for all older people

Documentation formalises the pain assessment process, acknowledges the existence of pain, promotes multidisciplinary communication and has professional and legal implications. The results of an assessment should be documented in nursing records or a specific pain assessment chart or included as part of a routine observation chart. For people with severe cognitive impairment, it is essential that pain behaviours and vocalisations are documented, as this may be the only pain assessment evidence available.

Conclusion

Older people are more likely to experience acute or persistent pain but are less likely to receive analgesics in some health care settings. Nursing practice relies heavily on objective clinical data to validate observations but difficulties arise with the subjective experience of pain (Parke 1998). Assessment of a person in pain is a complex task, based on several principles and requiring many nursing skills. However, assessing pain acknowledges its existence, after which adequate management can be implemented. It is part of the pain management process which ensures that 'freedom from pain [is] a basic human right' (Leibeskind and Melzack 1988).

References

Chapter 1 The health and social care policy context

Challis D. (1999) *Assessment and Care Management: developments since the community care reforms*. Part One of *Community Care and Informal Care*, Research Volume 3, *Royal Commission on Long Term Care*. London: The Stationery Office.

Davis A, Ellis K and Rummery K. (1997) *Access to Assessment: perspectives of practitioners, disabled people and carers*. Bristol: Policy Press (for the Joseph Rowntree Foundation).

Department of Health. (1989) *Caring for People: community care in the next decade and beyond*. London: HMSO.

Department of Health. (1990) *Community Care in the Next Decade and Beyond: policy guidance*. London: HMSO.

Department of Health. (2001) *Valuing People: a new strategy for learning disability for the 21st century. Towards person centred approaches: planning with people – guidance for implementation groups*. London: DoH.

Department of Health/National Statistics. (2004) *Community Care Statistics, 2002–2003: referrals, assessments and packages of care for adults*. London: DoH.

Glasby J and Littlechild R. (2004) *The Health and Social Care Divide: the experiences of older people*, 2nd edition. Bristol: Policy Press.

Means R and Smith R. (1998) *Community Care: policy and practice*, 2nd edition. Basingstoke: Macmillan.

Priestley M. (2004) 'Tragedy strikes again! Why community care still poses a problem for integrated living', in J Swain, S French, C Barnes, C Thomas (eds). *Disabling Barriers: Enabling Environments*, 2nd edition. London: Sage.

Smale G, Tuson G, Biehal N and Marsh P. (1993) *Empowerment, Assessment, Care Management and the Skilled Worker*. London: NISW/ HMSO.

Chapter 2 **The Single Assessment Process**

Baldwin S and Woods PA. (1994) 'Case management and needs assessment: some issues of concern for the caring professions', *Journal of Mental Health* **3**: 311–322.

Baraclough J, Damant M, Metcalfe D and Strehlow M. (1979) *Statement on the Development of Inter-Professional Education and Training for Members of Primary Health Care Teams*. London: Central Council for Education and Training in Social Work (Unpublished paper).

Challis D. *Minimum Data Set – Home Care* Version 2.3. [mail to: PSSRU@man.ac.uk]

Clifford P. *FACE for Older People* Version 3. [www.facecode.com]

Department of Health. (1997a) *Better Services for Vulnerable People*. EL (97) 62. London: DoH.

Department of Health. (1997b) *The New NHS: modern, dependable*. London: The Stationery Office.

Department of Health. (2000a) *The NHS Plan: a plan for investment, a plan for reform*. London: DoH.

Department of Health. (2000b) *A Health Service of all the Talents: developing the NHS workforce*. London: DoH.

Department of Health. (2001) *National Service Framework for Older People: modern standards and service models*. London: DoH.

Department of Health Single Assessment website: www.doh.gov.uk/scg/sap/index.htm

Ellis K. (1993) *Squaring the Circle: user and carer participation in needs assessment*. York: Joseph Rowntree Foundation.

Finch J. (2000) 'Interprofessional education and teamworking: a view from the education providers', *British Medical Journal* **321**: 1138–1140.

Marriott J. *EASYcare* Version 2004. [www.shef.ac.uk/sisa/easycare]

Nolan MR. (1994) 'Geriatric nursing: an idea whose time has gone: a polemic', *Journal of Advanced Nursing* **20:** 989–996.

Nolan M and Caldock K. (1996) 'Assessment: identifying the barriers to good practice', *Health & Social Care in the Community* **4**: 77–85.

Nolan M and Grant G. (1992) 'Mid-range theory building and the nursing theory practice gap: a respite care case study', *Journal of Advanced Nursing* **17**: 217–223.

Rolland JS. (1988) 'A conceptual model of chronic and life threatening illness and its impact on families', in Chilman CS, Nunnally EW and Cox FM (eds). *Chronic Illness and Disabilities*. Families in Trouble series, vol 2. Beverly Hills: Sage.

Runciman P. (1989) 'Health assessment of the elderly at home: the case for shared learning', *Journal of Advanced Nursing* **14**: 111–119.

Stewart K, Challis D, Carpenter I and Dickinson E. (1999) 'Assessment approaches for older people receiving social care: content and coverage', *International Journal of Geriatric Psychiatry* **14**: 147–156.

Twigg J and Atkin K. (1994) *Carers' Perceived: policy and practice in informal care*. Buckingham: Open University Press.

Vanclay L. (1997) *Exploring Inter-professional Education: the advantages and barriers*. Discussion paper for the UKCC Multi-professional Working Group of the Joint Education Committee. London: Centre for the Advancement of Inter-Professional Education.

World Health Organization. (1988) *Learning Together to Work Together for Health*. Report of a WHO Study Group on Multiprofessional Education of Health Personnel: the Team Approach. World Health Organization Technical Report Series, 769:1–72. Geneva.

Zwarenstein M, Reeves S, Barr H, Hammick M, Koppel I and Atkins J. (2004) 'Interprofessional education: effects on professional practice and health care outcomes (Cochrane Review)', in: *The Cochrane Library*, Issue 3. Chichester: John Wiley.

Chapter 3 **Underpinning values**

Agich GJ. (1993) *Autonomy and Long-Term Care*. Oxford: Oxford University Press.

Buchanan AE and Brock DW. (1989) *Deciding For Others: the ethics of surrogate decision making*. Cambridge: Cambridge University Press.

Department of Health. (2001a) *The Single Assessment Process*. London: HMSO. [www.doh.gov.uk/scg/sap/index.htm]

Department of Health [England]. (2001b) *The National Service Framework for Older People*. London: Department of Health.

Department of Health, Social Services and Public Safety. (2001) *Best Practice – Best Care: a framework for setting standards, delivering services and improving monitoring and regulation in the HPSS* [a consultation paper]. Belfast: DHSSPS.

Dewing J. (2002) 'From ritual to relationship: a person-centred approach to consent in qualitative research with older people who have a dementia', *Dementia* **1** (2): 157–171.

Drew P and Heritage J. (1992) *Talk at Work: interaction in institutional settings*. Cambridge: Cambridge University Press.

Goldsmith M. (1996) *Hearing the Voices of People with Dementia: opportunities and obstacles*. London: Jessica Kingsley.

Johnstone MJ. (1989) *Bio Ethics – Nursing Perspective*. London: WB Saunders.

Katz RS. (1990) 'Using our emotional reactions to older clients: a working theory', in B Genevay and RS Katz (eds). *Countertransference and Older Clients*. London: Sage.

Kennedy I. (2001) *Learning from Bristol: the report of the public inquiry into children's heart surgery at the Bristol Royal Infirmary 1984–1995*, Command Paper: CM 5207. London: Department of Health.

Latimer J. (1997) 'Giving patients a future: the constituting of classes in an acute medical unit', *Sociology of Health and Illness* **19**: 160–185.

McCormack B. (2001) *Negotiating Partnerships with Older People: a person-centred approach*. Aldershot: Ashgate Press.

McCormack B. (2002) 'The person of the voice: narrative identities in informed consent', *Nursing Philosophy* **3**: 114–119.

McCormack B and Ford P. (2000) *Warwickshire Health and Social Services/Royal College of Nursing. Multi-agency Assessment Project*. London: Royal College of Nursing.

Moody HR. (1991) 'The meaning of life in old age', in NS Jecker, *Aging and Ethics*. Totowa, NJ: Humana Press.

Nolan M, Keady J and Aveyard B. (2001) 'Relationship-centred care is the next logical step', *British Journal of Nursing* **10** (12): 757.

Ridley J and Jones L. (2002) *User and Public Involvement in Health Services: a literature review*. Edinburgh: Scottish Human Services Trust.

Scottish Executive Health Department. (2001) *Our National Health: a plan for action, a plan for change*. Edinburgh: SEHD.

Thornton P. (2000) *Older People Speaking Out: developing opportunities for influence*. York: Joseph Rowntree Foundation.

Walker E and Dewar B. (2001) 'How do we facilitate carers' involvement in decision making?', *Journal of Advanced Nursing* **34** (3): 329–337.

Chapter 4 **Biographical and developmental approaches**

Baker M, Fardell J and Jones B. (1997) *Disability and Rehabilitation: survey of education needs of health and social service professionals*. Full Report: the Case for Action. London: Disability and Rehabilitation Open Learning Project.

Broadbent I. (1999) 'Using the Biographical Approach', *Nursing Times* **5** (39): 52–54.

Clarke A, Hanson E and Ross H. (2003) 'Seeing the person behind the patient: enhancing the care of older people using the Biographical Approach', *Journal of Clinical Nursing* **12**: 697–706.

Gearing B and Coleman P. (1996) 'Biographical assessment in community care', in Birren JE, Kenyon GM, Ruth JE, Schroots JJF and Svenson T. *Aging and Biography*. New York: Springer.

Johnson M. (1991) 'The meaning of old age', in Redfern SJ (ed). *Nursing Elderly People*, 2nd edition. Edinburgh: Churchill Livingstone.

Kivnick HQ. (1991) *Living with Care, Caring for Life: the inventory of life strengths*. Minneapolis: University of Minnesota: Long-Term Care DECISIONS Resource Center.

Nichols K. (2003) *Psychological Care for Ill and Injured People*. Maidenhead: Open University Press.

Parkes CM and Markus A. (1998) *Coping with Loss*. London: BMJ Publications.

Wells D. (1998) 'Biographical work with older people', in Barnes E, Griffiths P, Ord J and Wells D. *Face to Face with Distress*. Oxford: Butterworth-Heinemann.

Chapter 5 **Cultural and religious needs**

Age Concern (2003) Information and Advice [www.ageconcern.org.uk/ ageconcern/information.htm accessed 03.05.04]

Giger J and Davidhizar R. (1995) *Transcultural Nursing Assessment and Intervention*, 2nd edition. St Louis, MO: Mosby.

Helman C. (2000) *Culture, Health and Illness*, 4th edition. Oxford: Butterworth-Heinemann.

Henley A. and Schott J. (1999) *Culture, Religion and Patient Care in a Multi-ethnic Society. A handbook for professionals*. London: Age Concern Books.

Holland K and Hogg C. (2001) *Cultural Awareness in Nursing and Health Care*. London: Arnold.

Rawlings-Anderson K. (2001) 'Working with older people from minority ethnic groups', *Nursing Older People* **13** (5): 21–26.

Roper N, Logan W and Tierney A. (1980, 1985, 1990, 1996) *The Elements of Nursing*, 1st, 2nd, 3rd & 4th editions. Edinburgh: Churchill Livingstone.

Roper N, Logan W and Tierney A. (2000) *The Roper–Logan–Tierney Model of Nursing: based on activities of living*. Edinburgh: Churchill Livingstone.

Chapter 6 Lifestyle and health promotion

Cattan M. (2001) 'Practical health promotion: what have we learnt so far?', in Chiva A and Stears D (eds). *Promoting the Health of Older People*. Milton Keynes: Open University Press; 11–22.

Davidson K and Arber S. (2003). 'Older men's health: a lifecourse issue?', *Men's Health Journal* **2**: 72–75.

Department of Health (2001). *National Service Framework for Older People*. London: DoH.

Government Actuary's Department. (2001) Vol. London: GAD [www.gad.gov.uk/news/marital_projections.htm]

Hunter W, Jones G, Devereux H, Rutsihauser I and Talley N. (2002) 'Constipation and diet in a community sample of older Australians', *Nutrition & Dietetics* **59**: 253–259.

Kitwood T. (1997) *Dementia Reconsidered: the person comes first*. Milton Keynes: Open University Press.

Nutbeam D. (1999). *Measuring the Effectiveness of Health Promotion*. Brussels: European Commission Report.

Office of National Statistics. (2003) *Population Trends 112, Summer*. London: HMSO.

Schaie KM and Willis SL. (2002). *Adult Development and Aging*. Upper Saddle River, NJ: Prentice Hall.

StatBase. (2002) Vol. [www.statistics.gov.uk/cci/nugget.asp?id=168] National Statistics Online.

Chapter 7 **Coping strategies and sources of support**

Bartlett R and Cheston R. (2003) 'Counselling people with dementia', in Adams T and Manthorpe J (eds). *Dementia Care*. London: Arnold; 86–102.

Cattan M. (2002) *Supporting Older People to Overcome Social Isolation and Loneliness*. London: Help the Aged.

Marriott A. (2003) 'Helping families cope with dementia', in Adams T and Manthorpe J (eds). *Dementia Care*. London: Arnold; 187–202.

Parker J and Bradley G. (2003) *Social Work Practice: assessment, planning, intervention and review.* Exeter: Learning Matters.

Wenger GC. (1992) *Help in Old Age – Facing up to change: a longitudinal network study*. Liverpool: Liverpool University Press.

Wenger GC and Tucker I. (2002) 'Network variation in practice: identification of support network type', *Health and Social Care in the Community* **10** (1): 28–35.

Chapter 8 **Cognitive capacity and consent**

Caulfield H. (1996) 'Legal aspects of nursing', in Kemworthy N, Snowley G and Gilling C. *Common Foundation Studies in Nursing*, 2nd edition. Edinburgh: Churchill Livingstone; 279–294.

Conn V, Taylor S and Miller R. (1994) 'Cognitive impairment and medication adherence', *Journal of Gerontological Nursing* **20** (7): 41–47.

Department for Constitutional Affairs. (2005) *Mental Capacity Act 2005*. [www.dca.gov.uk/menincap/legis.htm) (Accessed 05/08/05).]

Department of Health. (2001a) *12 Key Points on Consent: the law in England*. London: DoH.

Department of Health. (2001b) *Seeking Consent: working with older people*. London: DoH. [www.doh.gov.uk/consent]

Dewing J. (2001) 'Care for older people with a dementia in acute hospital settings', *Nursing Older People* **13** (3): 18–20.

Dewing J. (2002a) 'Older people with confusion: capacity to consent and the administration of medicines', *Nursing Older People* **14** (8): 23–28.

Dewing J. (2002b) 'From ritual to relationship: a person centred approach to consent in qualitative research with older people who have a dementia', *Dementia: The International Journal of Social Research & Practice* **1** (2): 156–171.

Jones RG. (2001) 'The law and dementia: issues in England and Wales', *Ageing and Mental Health* **5**: 329–334.

Meisel A. (1989) *The Right to Die*. New York: John Wiley.

Mezey M, Mitty E and Ramsey G. (1997) 'Assessment of decision making capacity', *Journal of Gerontological Nursing* **23** (2): 28–35.

Mukherjee S and Shah A. (2001) 'The prevalence and correlates of capacity to consent to a geriatric psychiatric admission', *Ageing and Mental Health* **5**: 335–339.

Widdershoven GAM and Berghmans RLP. (2001) 'Advance directives in dementia care; from instructions to instruments', *Patient Education and Counselling* **44**: 179–186.

Wills T and Dewing J. (2001) 'Supporting older people with acute confusion: the contribution of mental health nurses', *Nursing Older People* **13** (1): 17–19.

Chapter 9 Sexuality, intimacy and sexual health

Annon J. (1976) The 'P-LI-SS-IT model: a proposed conceptual scheme for behavioural treatment of sexual problems', *Journal of Sex Education Therapy* **2**: 1–15.

Bancroft J. (1989) *Human Sexuality and its Problems*, 2nd edition. Edinburgh: Churchill Livingstone.

Clifford D. (2000) 'Caring for sexuality in loss', in Wells D. *Caring for Sexuality in Health and Illness*. Edinburgh: Churchill Livingstone; 85–105.

D'Ardenne P and Morrod D. (2003) 'Later life – till death us do part', in *The Counselling of Couples in Healthcare Settings: a handbook for clinicians*. London: Whurr; 105–117.

Hawton K. (1985) *Sex Therapy: a practical guide*. Oxford: Oxford Medical; 56–94.

Rutter M. (2000) 'The impact of illness on sexuality', in Wells D. *Caring for Sexuality in Health and Illness*. Edinburgh: Churchill Livingstone; 207–220.

Searle E. (2002) 'Sexuality and people who are dying', in Heath H and White I (eds). *The Challenge of Sexuality in Health Care.* Oxford: Blackwell Science; 153–166.

Skrine R. (1997) *Blocks and Freedoms in Sexual Life.* Oxford: Radcliffe Medical.

White I. (2001) 'Facilitating sexual expression: challenges for contemporary practice', in Heath H and White I (eds). *The Challenge of Sexuality in Health Care.* Oxford: Blackwell Science; 243–263.

White I and Heath H. (2002) 'Introduction', in Heath H and White I (eds). *The Challenge of Sexuality in Health Care.* Oxford: Blackwell Science; 3–11.

Chapter 10 **Environment**

Association of Social Alarm Providers. (2005) 'What is a telecare service?' [www.asap-uk.org]

Judd S. (1997) 'Technology', in Marshall M (ed). *State of the Art in Dementia Care.* London: Centre for Policy on Ageing; 144–149

Judd S, Marshall M and Phippen P. (1998) *Design for Dementia.* London: Hawker Publications.

Lawton MP and Nahemow L. (1973) 'Press-competence model of person–environment interaction', cited in Matteson MA and McConnell ES (eds). (1988) *Gerontological Nursing: concepts and practice.* Philadelphia: WB Saunders.

Marshall M. (2000) *ASTRID: a social and technological response to meeting the needs of individuals with dementia and their carers.* London: Hawker Publications.

McCormack B. (1996) 'Life transitions', in Ford P and Heath H. *Older People and Nursing: issues of living in a care home.* Oxford: Butterworth-Heinemann; 71–86.

Minns J, Nabhani F and Bamford JS. (2004) 'Can flooring and underlay materials reduce hip fractures in older people?', *Nursing Older People* **16** (5): 16–20.

Morrison J. (1997) 'Is it music to their ears?', *Journal of Dementia Care* **5** (3): 18–19.

Netten A. (1993) *A Positive Environment?: physical and social influences on people with senile dementia in residential care.* Aldershot: Ashgate.

Nightingale F. (1946) *Notes on Nursing*. Philadephia: JB Lippincott.

Phair L and Good V. (1998) *Dementia: a Positive Approach*. London: Whurr.

Schofield I. (1999) 'Environmental safety and security', in Heath H and Schofield I (eds). *Healthy Ageing: nursing older people*. London: Mosby, 297–318.

Chapter 11 Normal ageing

Bellamy D. (1998) 'A biological perspective', in Pathy MSJ (ed). *Principles and Practice of Geriatric Medicine*, 3rd edition, vol 1. London: Wiley, 9–34.

Christiansen JL and Grzybowski JM. (1993) *Biology of Aging*. St Louis: Mosby.

Kirkwood TBL and Wolff SP. (1995) 'The biological basis of ageing', *Age and Ageing* **24**: 167–171.

Peris TT. (1995) 'The oldest old', *Scientific American* **272** (1): 51–55.

Rowe JW and Khan RL. (1997) 'Successful ageing', *The Gerontologist* **37**: 433–440.

Chapter 12 Altered presentation of disease

Davies IB and Sinclair AJ. (1995) 'Physiological and biochemical factors influencing presentation and outcome of disease in elderly people', in Sinclair AJ and Woodhouse KW (eds). *Acute Medical Illness in Old Age*. London: Chapman and Hall Medical; 1–20.

Heath H. (2000) 'Assessing older people', *Elderly Care* **11** (10): 27–28.

Isaacs B. (1981) 'Ageing and the doctor', in Hobman D. *The Impact of Ageing*. London: Croom Helm; 143–157

Somerville K. (1999) 'Laboratory values and implications', in Heath H and Schofield I (eds). *Healthy Ageing: nursing older people*. London: Mosby; 103–118.

Watson R. (1996) 'Mixed medicines: spotting the signs', *Practice Nursing* **7** (20): 32–35.

Watson R. (2000) 'Altered presentation in old age', *Elderly Care* **12** (3): 19–21.

Chapter 13 **Neurological functioning**

Goff S. (1999) 'Pain and comfort', in Health H and Schofield I (eds). *Healthy Ageing*. London. Mosby; 211–226.

Le May A. (1999) 'Sensory and perceptual issues of ageing comfort', in Heath H and Schofield I (eds). *Healthy Ageing*. London: Mosby; 273–296.

Pathy MSJ. (1998) 'Neurological signs and ageing', in Pathy MSJ (ed). *Principles and Practice of Geriatric Medicine*, 3rd edition. London: Wiley; 711–722.

Surman L. (1998) 'Sensory deprivation and the older person', in Marr J and Kershaw B (eds). *Caring for Older People*. London: Arnold; 53–70.

Timiras PS. (1998) 'Ageing in the central nervous system', in Pathy MSJ (ed). *Principles and Practice of Geriatric Medicine*, 3rd edition. London: Wiley; 703–710.

Chapter 14 **Endocrine system function**

Christiansen JL and Grzybowski, J.M. (1993) *Biology of Aging.* St Louis: Mosby.

Goldberg AP, Andres R and Bierman EL. (1984) 'Diabetes mellitus in the elderly', in Andres R, Bierman EL and Hazzard W (eds). *Principles of Geriatric Medicine*. New York: McGraw-Hill; 750–764.

Gould D. (1999) 'Homeostasis', in Watson R (ed). *Essential Science for Nursing Students*. London: Baillière Tindall; 123–144.

Linton AD, Lee P and Matteson MA. (1988) 'Age-related changes in the endocrine system', in Matteson MA and McConnell AS (eds). *Gerontological Nursing,* 2nd edition. New York: WB Saunders; 354–383.

Lipson LG. (1985) *Diabetes Mellitus in the Elderly: special problems, special approaches*. New York: Pfizer.

Reeve PA. (2000) 'Assessing orthostatic hypotension in older people', *Nursing Older People* **12** (7): 27–28.

Schofield I. (1999) 'Biological support needs', in Heath H and Schofield I (eds). *Healthy Ageing*. London: Mosby; 81–101.

Sommerville K. (1999) 'Laboratory values and implications', in Heath H and Schofield I (eds). *Healthy Ageing*. London: Mosby; 103–115.

Chapter 15 **Skin**

Christiansen JL and Grzybowski JM. (1993) *Biology of Aging*. St Louis: Mosby.

Hill V. (2002) 'The skin in the elderly', in Armour D and Cairns C (eds). *Medicines in the Elderly*. London: Pharmaceutical Press; 329–349.

Lyder CH, Clemes-Lowrance C, Davis A, Sullivan L and Zucker A. (1992) 'Structured skin care regimen to prevent perineal dermatitis in the elderly', *Journal of ET Nursing* **19** (1): 12–16.

McGovern M and Kuhn J. (1992) 'Skin assessment of the elderly client', *Journal of Gerontological Nursing* **18** (4): 39–43.

Pedley G. (1999) 'Maintaining healthy skin', in Redfern S and Ross F (eds). *Nursing Older People*. London: Churchill Livingstone; 431–464.

Penzer R and Finch M. (2001) 'Promoting healthy skin in older people', *Nursing Standard* **15** (34): 46–52.

Smoker A. (1999) 'Skin care in old age', *Nursing Standard* **13** (48): 47–53.

Waterlow J. (1988) 'Prevention is cheaper than cure', *Nursing Times* **84** (25): 69–70.

Chapter 16 **Laboratory tests**

Department of Health. (2003) Information from National Service Framework for Diabetes website www.doh.gov.uk/nsf/diabetes/ (Accessed June 2003).

Gibson JM. (1997) 'Focus of nursing in critical and acute care settings', *Intensive and Critical Care Nursing* **13**: 163–166.

Joint European Society of Cardiology/American College of Cardiology Committee. (2000) 'Myocardial infarction redefined – a consensus document of the Joint European Society of Cardiology/American College of Cardiology Committee for the redefinition of myocardial infarction', *European Heart Journal* **21**: 1502–1513.

Jowett NI and Thompson DR. (2003) *Comprehensive Coronary Care*, 3rd edition. London: Baillière Tindall.

Mahon A and Hattersley J. (2002) 'Investigations in renal failure', in Thomas N (ed). *Renal Nursing*, 2nd edition. Edinburgh: Baillière Tindall; 143–170.

Minors DS. (2001) 'Blood cells, haemoglobin, haemostasis and coagulation', *Anaesthesia and Intensive Care Medicine* **2**: 149–154.

Somerville K. (1999) 'Laboratory values and implications', in Heath H and Schofield I (eds). *Healthy Ageing: nursing older people*. London: Mosby; 103–116.

Van Den Berghe G, Wouters P, Weekers F, et al. (2001) 'Intensive insulin therapy in critically ill patients', *New England Journal of Medicine* **345**: 1359–1367.

Wood S. (2000) 'Osteoporosis', *Geriatric Medicine* **30** (9): 35–41.

Chapter 17 **Hearing**

Allen NH, Burns A and Newton V. (2003) 'The effects of improving hearing in dementia', *Age and Ageing* **32**: 189–193.

Boots Healthcare and Hearing Concern. (undated) *Communication with Deaf and Hard of Hearing Patients: a guide for hospital staff*. London: Hearing Concern. [Available from: www.hearingconcern.com/aai_c.html (Accessed on 26 May 2004).]

Clark K, Sowers MF and Wallace RB. (1991) 'The accuracy of self-reported hearing loss in women aged 60–85 years', *American Journal of Epidemiology* **134**: 704–708.

Clinical Guidelines Working Group of the British Tinnitus Association. (2001) 'Helping patients with tinnitus: guidance for nurses', *Nursing Standard* **15** (24): 39–42.

Gilhome Herbst K. (1999) 'Hearing', in Redfern SJ and Ross FM (eds). *Nursing Older People*, 3rd edition. Edinburgh: Churchill Livingstone; 291–302.

Help the Aged. (1996) *Better Hearing*. London: Help the Aged.

Heron R and Wharrad H. (2000) 'Prevalence and nursing staff awareness of hearing impairment in older hospital patients', *Journal of Clinical Nursing* **9**: 834–841.

Hines J. (1997) 'Make the right noises: caring for hearing impaired patients', *Nursing Times* **93** (1): 31–33.

Lavis D. (1997) 'Identification of hearing impairment in people with a learning disability: from questioning to testing', *British Journal of Learning Disabilities* **25**: 493–494.

Le May A. (1999) 'Sensory and perceptual issues of ageing', in Heath H and Schofield I (eds). *Healthy Ageing: nursing older people*. London: Mosby; 273–295.

Lewis-Cullinan C and Janken J. (1990) 'Effect of cerumen removal on the hearing ability of geriatric patients', *Journal of Advanced Nursing* **15**: 595–600.

Lim DP and Stephens SD. (1991) 'Clinical investigation of hearing loss in the elderly', *Clinical Otolaryngology* **16**: 288–293.

Mahoney DF. (1992) 'Hearing loss among nursing home residents', *Clinical Nursing Research* **1**: 317–322.

Mulrow CD and Lichenstein MJ. (1991) 'Screening for hearing impairment in the elderly: rationale and strategy', *Journal of General Internal Medicine* **6**: 249–258.

Mulrow CD, Aigular C, Endicott JE, et al. (1990) 'Association between hearing impairment and quality of life in elderly individuals', *Journal of the American Geriatrics Society* **38**: 45–50.

Nondahl DM, Cruickshanks KJ, Wiley TL, et al. (1998) 'Accuracy of self-reported hearing loss', *Audiology* **37**: 295–301.

Philp I, Lowles RV, Armstrong GK, et al. (2002) 'Repeatability of standardized tests of functional impairment and well-being in older people in a rehabilitation setting', *Disability and Rehabilitation* **24**: 243–249.

Practical Support for Clinical Governance. (2004) PRODIGY Guidance – Earwax [Available from: www.prodigy.nhs/guidance.asp?gt=Earwax (Accessed on 15 September 2004).]

Reuben DB, Walsh K, Moore A, et al. (1998) 'Hearing loss in community dwelling older persons: national prevalence data and identification using simple questions', *Journal of the American Geriatrics Society* **46** (8): 1008–1011.

Royal National Institute for Deaf People. (2004a) *A Simple Cure.* London: RNID.

Royal National Institute for Deaf People. (2004b) Facts and figures on deafness and tinnitus. [Available from www.rnid.org.uk/html/factsheets/general_statistics_on_deafness.htm (Accessed on 28 May 2004).]

Royal National Institute for Deaf People. (2004c) Ear Syringing. [Available from: www/rnid.org.uk/html/factsheets/med_ear_syringing.htm (Accessed 28 May 2004).]

Slaven A. (2003) 'Communication and the hearing-impaired patient', *Nursing Standard* **18** (12): 39–41.

Strawbridge W, Wallhagen W and Sheema S. (2000) 'Negative consequences of hearing impairment in old age: a longitudinal analysis', *Gerontologist* **40**: 320–326.

Swan IR and Browning GG. (1985) 'The whispered voice as a screening test for hearing impairment', *Journal of the Royal College of General Practitioners* **35**: 197.

Tolson D. (1995) An Investigation of the Nursing Care of Hearing-impaired Elderly Hospital Residents, unpublished PhD thesis. Glasgow Caledonian University.

Tolson D. (1997) 'Age-related hearing loss: a case for nursing intervention', *Journal of Advanced Nursing* **26**: 1150–1157.

Tolson D, McIntosh J and Swan I. (1992) 'Hearing impairment in elderly hospital residents', *British Journal of Nursing* **1**: 705–710.

Tomita M, Mann WC and Welch TR. (2001) 'Use of assistive devices to address hearing impairment by older persons with disabilities', *International Journal of Rehabilitation Research* **24L**: 279–289.

Ventry I and Weinstein B. (1982) 'The hearing handicap inventory for the elderly: a new tool', *Ear and Hear* **83**: 128–134.

Wu HY, Chin JJ and Tong HMH. (2004) 'Screening for hearing impairment in a cohort of elderly patients attending a hospital geriatric medicine service', *Singapore Medical Journal* **45**: 79–84.

Resources

Hearing Concern at www.hearingconsern.com (Accessed on 26 May 2004.) [*Provides advice and information about hearing loss and deaf awareness.*]

Help the Aged. (1996) Better Hearing. London: Help the Aged. [*A useful leaflet to give to clients that informs people about age-related hearing loss and the benefits that can be obtained from using a hearing aid. Local health-promotion resource centres usually stock these.*]

Meecham E. (1999) 'Audiology and hearing impairment: improving the quality of care', *Nursing Standard* **13** (43): 42–46. [*Provides an update on the anatomy and physiology of the ear, changes with hearing loss and the role of audiology.*]

RNID. (2004) *Working with a BSL/English interpreter.* [Available from www.rnid.org.uk/html/factsheets/ (Accessed on 28 May 2004).] [*Advice for professionals on how to access and work with a BSL/English interpreter.*]

RNID. (2004) *All About Hearing Aids: a guide for users.* [Available from www.rnid.org.uk/html/factsheets/ (Accessed on 28 May 2004).] [*Also available in Bengali, Chinese, Gujarati, Hindi, Punjabi and Urdu.*]

Chapter 18 **Vision**

Halle C. (2002) 'Achieve new vision screening objectives', *Nurse Practitioner* **27** (3): 15–35.

International Glaucoma Association. (2000) *Glaucoma 2000 Information for Patients.* [Available on www.iga.org.uk]

Kane W. (1999) 'Sight specific', *Nursing Times* **95** (32): 54–55.

Kanski J. (1997) *Clinical Ophthalmology*, 3rd edition. Oxford: Butterworth-Heinemann.

Kelly JS. (1996) 'Eye examination and vision testing', *British Journal of Nursing* **5**: 630–634.

Le May A. (1999) 'Sensory and perceptual issues of ageing', in Heath H and Schofield I (eds). *Healthy Ageing: nursing older people.* London: Mosby.

Macular Disease Society. (2002) www.maculardisease.org.uk

Royal National Institute of the Blind. (1999) *Modernising social services.* [www.rnib.org.uk]

Royal National Institute of the Blind. (2002) www.rnib.org.uk

Sperazza L. (2001) 'Rehabilitation options for patients with low vision', *Rehabilitation Nursing* **26**:148–151.

Chapter 19 **Memory and cognition**

Alexopoulos GS, Abrams RC, Young RC and Shannon CA. (1988) 'Cornell Scale for depression in dementia', *Biological Psychiatry* **23**: 271–284.

Folstein M, Anthony JC, Parhad I, et al. (1985) 'The meaning of cognitive impairment in the elderly', *Journal of the American Geriatrics Society* **33**: 228.

Hayes N and Minardi HA. (2002) 'Psychology and ageing', in Philip Woodrow (ed). *Ageing: issues for physical, psychological and social health.* London: Whurr; 93–114.

Hodkinson HM. (1972) 'Evaluation of a mental test score for assessment of mental impairment in the elderly', *Age and Ageing* **1**: 233–238.

Minardi H and Hayes N. (2003) 'Nursing older people with mental health problems: therapeutic interventions – part 1', *Nursing Older People* **15** (6): 22–28.

Minardi H and Riley M. (1997) *Communication in Health Care: a skills based approach.* Oxford: Butterworth-Heinemann.

Taylor DG and Shah AK. (2001) 'Organic mental disorders', in Melding P and Draper B (eds). *Geriatric Consultation Liaison Psychiatry.* New York: Oxford University Press; 215–244.

Ward HW, Ramsdell JW, Jackson JE, et al. (1990) 'Cognitive function testing in comprehensive geriatric assessment – a comparison of cognitive test performance in residential and clinic settings', *Journal of the American Geriatrics Society* **38**: 1088–1092.

Wiederholt WC, Cahn D, Butters NM, et al. (1993) 'Effects of age, gender and education on selected neuropsychological tests in an elderly community cohort', *Journal of the American Geriatrics Society* **41**: 639–647.

Yesavage JA, Brink TL, Rose TL, et al. (1983) 'Development and validation of a geriatric depression screening scale: a preliminary report', *Journal of Psychiatric Research* **17**: 37–49.

Chapter 20 **Acute confusional states/delirium**

American Psychiatric Association. (1994) *Diagnostic and Statistical Manual of Mental Disorders*, 4th edition. Washington DC: American Psychiatric Association.

American Psychiatric Association. (1999) *Practice Guidelines for the Treatment of Patients with Delirium.* Washington DC: American Psychiatric Association.

Fick D and Foreman M. (2000) 'Consequences of not recognising delirium superimposed on dementia in hospitalised elderly individuals', *Journal of Gerontological Nursing* **26** (1): 30–40.

Hodkinson HM. (1972) 'Evaluation of a mental test score for assessment of mental impairment in the elderly', *Age and Ageing* **1** (23): 308.

Inouye SK. (2000) Prevention of delirium in hospitalized older patients: risk factors and targeted intervention strategies. *Annals of Internal Medicine* **32**: 257–263.

Inouye SK, VanDyck CH, Alessie CA, et al. (1990) 'Clarifying confusion: the Confusion Assessment Method. a new method for detection of delirium', *Annals of Internal Medicine* **113**: 941.

Inouye SK, Bogardus S, Singleton SJ, et al. (1999) 'A multicomponent intervention to prevent delirium in hospitalized older patients', *New England Journal of Medicine* **340**: 669–721.

Johnson J. (1999) 'Identifying and recognizing delirium', *Dementia and Geriatric Cognitive Disorders* **10** (5): 353–358.

Neelon VJ, Champagne MT, Carlson JR, et al. (1996) 'The NEECHAM Confusion Scale: construction, validation and clinical testing', *Nursing Research* **45**: 324–330.

Rapp CG, Mentes JC and Titler MG. (2001) 'Acute confusion/delirium protocol', *Journal of Gerontological Nursing* **28** (28): 21–33.

Royal College of Nursing and Help the Aged. (2000) *Dignity on the Ward: improving the experience of acute hospital care for older people with dementia or confusion. A pocket guide for hospital staff.* London: Help the Aged.

Chapter 21 Communication

Dryden W and Feltham C. (1992) *Brief Counselling.* Buckingham and Philadelphia: Open University Press.

Dryden W and Feltham C. (1994) *Developing the Practice of Counselling.* London: Thousand Oaks.

Forchuk C, Westwell J, Martin M-L, et al. (1998) 'Factors influencing movement of chronic psychiatric patients from the orientation to the working phase of the nurse–client relationship on an inpatient unit', *Perspectives in Psychiatric Care* **34** (1): 36–44.

Geerts E, Bouhuys AL and Boem GM. (1997) 'Nonverbal support-giving induces nonverbal support-seeking in depressed patients', *Journal of Clinical Psychology* **53**: 35–39.

Groom CJ and Pennebaker JW. (2002) 'Words', *Journal of Research in Personality* **36**: 615–621.

Kemper S, Finter-Urczyk A, Ferrell P, Harden T and Billington C. (1998) 'Using Elderspeak with older adults', *Discourse Processes* **25** (1): 55–73.

Lyons F and Minardi H. (1993) Unpublished lecture notes on using counselling skills effectively.

Minardi H and Hayes N. (2003) 'Nursing older people with mental health problems: therapeutic interventions – part 2', *Nursing Older People* **15** (7): 20–24.

Minardi H and Riley M. (1997). *Communication in Health Care: a skills based approach.* Oxford: Butterworth-Heinemann.

Schön DA. (1983) *The Reflective Practitioner: how professionals think in action.* New York: Basic Books.

Scrutton S. (1997) 'Counselling: maintaining mental health in older age', cited in Norman IJ and Redfern SJ (eds). *Mental Health Care for Elderly People.* Edinburgh: Churchill Livingstone; 271–286.

Troisi A and Moles A. (1999) 'Gender differences in depression: an ethological study of nonverbal behaviour during interviews', *Journal of Psychiatric Research* **33**: 243–250.

Troisi A, Belsanti S, Bucci RA, Mosco C, Santi F and Verucci M. (2000) 'Affect regulation in alexithymia: an ethological study of displacement behaviour during psychiatric interviews', *Journal of Nervous and Mental Diseases* **188**: 13–18.

Tschudin V. (1999) *Counselling and Older People.* London: Age Concern England.

Chapter 22 **Rights and risks**

Alaszewski H and Manthorpe J. (2000) 'Finding the balance: older people, nurses and risk', *Education and Ageing* **15**: 195–209.

Cabinet Office. (2002) *Risk: improving the government's capability to handle risk and uncertainty, Strategy Unit Report Cabinet Office.* London: The Stationery Office.

Clarke CL. (2000) 'Risk: construction care and care environments in dementia', *Health Risk and Society* **2**: 83–93.

Clarke C, Gibb C, Williams L, Keady J, Cook A and Wilkinson H. (2004) 'Contemporary risk management in dementia: an organisational survey of practices and inclusion of people with dementia', *Signpost* **9** (1): 27–31.

Department of Health. (2001) *National Service Framework for Older People.* London: DoH.

Harding T and Gould J. (2003) *Memorandum on Older People and Human Rights.* London: Help the Aged.

Langan J and Lindow V. (2004) *Living with Risk.* Bristol: Policy Press.

Moore B. (1996) *Risk Assessments: a practitioner's guide to predicting harmful behaviour.* London: Whiting and Birch.

Reed J, Stanley D and Clarke C. (2004) *Health, Well-being and Older People*. Bristol: Policy Press.

Watson J. (2002) *Something for Everyone*. London: British Institute of Human Rights.

Chapter 23 **Musculoskeletal function**

Christiansen JL and Grzybowski JM. (1993) *Biology of Aging*. St Louis: Mosby.

Matteson MA. (1997) 'Age-related changes in the musculoskeletal system', in Matteson MA, McConnell AS and Linton AD (eds). *Gerontological Nursing*, 2nd edition. New York: WB Saunders; 196–221.

Ryan S. (1999) *Drug Therapy in Rheumatology Nursing*. London: Whurr.

Simpson JM and New E. (1999) 'Promoting safe mobility', in Redfern SJ and Ross FM (eds). *Nursing Older People*, 3rd edition. Edinburgh: Churchill Livingstone; 315–337.

Further reading

Watson R. (2005) *Anatomy and Physiology for Nurses*, 12th edition. London: Baillière Tindall.

Chapter 24 **Risk of falling and hip fracture**

American Geriatrics Society, British Geriatrics Society and the American Academy of Orthopaedic Surgeons Panel on Falls Prevention. (2001) 'Guideline for the prevention of falls in older people', *Journal of the American Geriatrics Society* **49**: 664–672.

Arden NK and Spector TD. (1997) *Osteoporosis Illustrated*. London: Current Medical literature.

Chang JT, Morton SC, Rubenstein LZ, et al. (2004) 'Interventions for the prevention of falls in older adults: systematic review and meta-analysis of randomised controlled trials', *British Medical Journal* **328**: 680–683.

Chapuy MC, Arlot ME, Duboeuf F, et al. (1992) 'Vitamin D_3 and calcium to prevent hip fracture in elderly women', *New England Journal of Medicine* **327**: 1637–1642.

Close J, Ellis M, Hooper R, Glucksman E, Jackson S and Swift C. (1999) 'Prevention of falls in the elderly: a randomised control trial', *Lancet* **353**: 93–97.

Cummings SR, Nevitt MC, Browner WS, et al. (1995) 'Risk factors for hip fracture in white women', *New England Journal of Medicine* **332**: 767–773.

Department of Health. (2001) *National Service Framework for Older People.* London: DoH.

Department of Trade and Industry. (1997) *Home Accident Surveillance System Data.* London: DTI.

Grisso JA, Kelsey JL, Stromb BL, et al. (1991) 'Risk factors for falls as a cause of hip fracture in women', *New England Journal of Medicine* **324**: 1326–1331.

Melton LJ. (1988) 'Epidemiology of fractures', in Riggs BL and Melton LJ (eds). *Osteoporosis: etiology, diagnosis, and management.* Philadelphia: Lippincott–Raven; 133–154.

Nandy S, Parsons S, Cryer C, et al. (2004) 'Development and preliminary examination of the predictive validity of the Falls Risk Assessment Tool (FRAT) for use in primary care', *Journal of Public Health (Oxf.)* **26**: 138–43.

National Institutes of Health, Consensus Development Panel on Osteoporosis. (2001) 'Osteoporosis prevention, diagnosis, and therapy', *Journal of the American Medical Association* **285**: 785–795.

National Osteoporosis Society. (1999) *Accidents, Falls, Fractures and Osteoporosis.* London: NOS.

Royal College of Physicians. (1999) *Osteoporosis: clinical guidelines for prevention and treatment.* London: RCP.

Royal College of Physicians. (2000). *Osteoporosis: clinical guidelines for prevention and treatment. Update on pharmacological interventions and an algorithm for management.* London: RCP.

Rubenstein LK, Josephson KR and Robbins AS. (1994) 'Falls in a nursing home', *Annals of Internal Medicine* **121**: 442–451.

Tinetti ME, Speechley M and Grinter SF. (1988) 'Risk factors for falls among elderly persons living in the community', *New England Journal of Medicine* **319**: 1701–1707.

Tinetti ME, Baker DI, Dutcher J, Vincent JE and Rozett RT. (1997) *Reducing the Risk of Falls among Older Adults in the Community.* Berkeley, CA: Peaceable Kingdom Press.

Chapter 25 **Older people using medication**

Gould D. (1999) 'Drugs and older people', in Redfern S and Ross F (eds). *Nursing Older People*, 3rd edition. Edinburgh: Churchill Livingstone; 233–248.

McConnel ES, Linton AD and Hanlon JT. (1997) 'Pharmacological considerations', in Matteson MA, McConnel ES and Linton AD (eds). *Gerontological Nursing: concepts and practice*, 2nd edition. Philadelphia: Saunders; 738–762.

O'Mahoney D and Martin U. (1999) *Practical Therapeutics for the Older Patient*. London: Wiley.

Swift CG. (1998) 'Clinical pharmacology and therapeutics', in Pathy MSJ. *Principles and Practice of Geriatric Medicine*, 3rd edition. London: Wiley.

Watson R. (1996) 'Mixed medicines: spotting the signs', *Practice Nurse* **7** (20): 32–35.

Chapter 26 **Restraint**

Burton LC, German PS, Rovner BW and Brant LJ. (1992) 'Physical restraint use and cognitive decline among nursing home residents', *Journal of the American Geriatrics Society* **40**: 811–816.

Castle NG, Foge IB and Mor V. (1997) 'Risk factors for physical restraint use in nursing homes: pre- and post-implementation of the Nursing Homes Reform Act', *Gerontologist* **37**: 737–747.

Counsel and Care. (2001) *Residents Taking Risks*. London: Counsel and Care.

Evans LK and Strumpf NK. (1989) 'Tying down the elderly: a review of the literature on physical restraint', *Journal of the American Geriatrics Society* **37:** 65–74.

Evans LK, Strumpf NE, Allen-Taylor L, Capezuti E, Maislin G and Jacobsen B. (1997) 'A clinical trial to reduce restraints in nursing homes', *Journal of the American Geriatrics Society* **45**: 675–681.

Hantikainen V and Käppeli S. (2000) 'Using restraint with nursing home residents: a qualitative study of nursing staff perceptions and decision-making', *Journal of Advanced Nursing* **32**: 1196–1205.

Morse JM and McHutchion E. (1991) 'Releasing restraints: providing safe care for the elderly', *Research in Nursing and Health* **14**: 187–196.

Royal College of Nursing. (1999) *Restraint Revisited – Rights, Risks and Responsibility: guidance for nurses working with older people*. London: RCN.

Strumpf NE, Robinson JP, Wagner JS and Evans LK. (1998) *Restraint-free Care*. New York: Springer.

Watson R. (2001) 'Restraint: its use and misuse in the care of older people', *Nursing Older People* **13** (3): 21–25.

Watson R and Brunton M. (1990) 'Restrain yourself', *Nursing the Elderly* **2** (7): 14–15.

Werner P, Cohen-Mansfield J, Braun J and Marx MS. (1989) 'Physical restraints and agitation in nursing home residents', *Journal of the American Geriatrics Society* **37**: 1122–1126.

Chapter 27 **Preventing and responding to elder abuse**

Community and District Nursing Association. (2004) *Responding to Elder Abuse: guidance notes.* [Available on www.cdna.tvu.ac.uk (accessed 5 July 2004).]

Department of Health. (2000) *No Secrets: guidance on developing and implementing multi-agency policies and procedures to protect vulnerable adults from abuse.* London: DoH.

Health Select Committee. (2004) *Report on Elder Abuse.* London: House of Commons Health Select Committee.

Homer A and Gilleard C. (1990) 'Abuse of elderly people by their carers', *British Medical Journal* **301**: 1359–1362.

Jeary K. (2004) 'The victim's voice: how is it heard? Issues arising from adult protection case conferences', *Journal of Adult Protection* **6** (1): 12–19.

Juklestad O. (2001) 'Institutional care for older people: the dark side', *Journal of Adult Protection* **3** (2): 32–41.

Mathew D, McCreadie C, Askham J, Brown H and Kingston P. (2004) *Protecting Vulnerable Adults from Abuse: investigation of government guidance on local multi-agency systems.* London: Nuffield Foundation.

McCreadie C, Bennett G, Gilthorpe M, Houghton G and Tinker A. (2000) 'Elder abuse: do general practitioners know or care?', *Journal of Royal Society of Medicine* **93**: 67–71.

Pritchard J. (2000) *The Needs of Older Women: services for victims of elder abuse and other abuse.* Bristol: Policy Press.

Taylor K and Lamb L. (2004) 'Recommendations into practice: implementing the results of local research into adult protection', *Journal of Adult Protection* **6**: 20–26.

Resource

Action on Elder Abuse is at Astral House, 1268 London Road, London
SW16 4ER; www.elderabuse.org.uk

Chapter 28 Cardiovascular functioning

British Hypertension Society. (1997) *Management Guidelines in Essential Hypertension*. London: British Hypertension Society.

Fairweather S. (1998) 'The presentation and management of physical disease in older people', in Beales D, Denham M and Tulloch A (eds). *Community Care of Older People*. Oxford: Radcliffe Medical Press; 15–52.

Harrell JS. (1997) 'Age-related changes in the cardiovascular system', in Matteson MA, McConnell AS and Linton AD (eds). *Gerontological Nursing*. New York: WB Saunders; 222–255.

O'Keeffe ST and Lye M. (1999) 'Heart failure', in Pathy MSJ (ed). *Principles and Practice of Geriatric Medicine*, 3rd edition. London: Wiley; 585–598.

Rush S and Schofield I. (1999) 'Biological support needs', in Heath H and Schofield I (eds). *Healthy Ageing: nursing older people*. London: Mosby; 119–159.

Chapter 29 Blood pressure

Asmar R, Darne B, el Assaad M and Topouchian J. (2001) 'Assessment of outcomes other than systolic and diastolic blood pressure: pulse pressure, arterial stiffness and heart rate', *Blood Pressure Monitoring* **6**: 329–333.

Baguet JP, Joseph X, Ormezzano O, Neuder Y, Quesada JL and Mallion JM. (2001) 'Ambulatory blood pressure variation in healthy subjects, hypertensive elderly and type 1 diabetic patients in relation to the sitting or standing position', *Blood Pressure Monitoring* **6**: 191–194.

Beevers G, Lip GYH and O'Brien E. (2001) 'Blood pressure measurement', *British Medical Journal* **322**: 981–985.

Darovic GO. (2002) 'Arterial pressure monitoring', in Darovic GO (ed). *Hemodynamic Monitoring: invasive and noninvasive clinical application*, 3rd edition. Philadelphia: WB Saunders; 133–160.

Franklin SS, Gustin WIV, Wong ND, et al. (1997) 'Hemodynamic patterns of age-related changes in blood pressure: the Framingham Heart Study', *Circulation* **96**: 308–315.

Haider AW, Larson MG, Franklin SS and Levy D. (2003) 'Systolic blood pressure, diastolic blood pressure, and pulse pressure as predictors of risk for congestive heart failure in the Framingham Study', *Annals of Internal Medicine* **138**: 10–16.

Herbert RA. (1999) 'The biology of human ageing', in Redfern SJ and Ross FM (eds). *Nursing Older People*, 3rd edition. Edinburgh: Churchill Livingstone; 55–77.

Jones DW, Appel LJ, Sheps SG, Roccella EJ and Lenfant C. (2003) 'Measuring blood pressure accurately', *Journal of the American Medical Association* **289**: 1027–1030.

Lip GYH. (2003) *Clinical Hypertension in Practice*. London: RSM Press.

Mitchell GF, Moye LM, Braunwald E, et al. (1997) 'Sphygmomanometrically determined pulse pressure is a powerful independent predictor of recurrent events after myocardial infarction in patients with impaired left ventricular function', *Circulation* **96**: 4254–4260.

Nicol M, Bavin C, Bedford-Turner S, Cronin P and Rawlings-Anderson K. (2000) 'Taking blood pressure', *Nursing Standard* **14**: 38, insert.

O'Brien E, Beevers G and Lip GYH. (2001) 'Blood pressure measurement: Part IV – automated sphygmomanometry: self blood pressure measurement', *British Medical Journal* **322**: 1167–1176.

Qui C, Winblad B, Viitanen M and Fartiglioni L. (2003) 'Pulse pressure and risk of Alzheimer disease in persons aged 75 years and older', *Stroke* **34**: 594–599.

Treacher D. (2003) 'Acute heart failure', in Bersten AD and Soni N (eds). *Intensive Care Manual*, 5th edition. Edinburgh: Butterworth-Heinemann; 221–235.

Chapter 30 **Pulse**

Ganong WF. (2001) *Review of Medical Physiology*, 20th edition. New York: Lange Medical Books.

Hart RG, Halperin JL, Pearce LA, et al and Stroke Prevention in Atrial Fibrillation Investigators. (2003) 'Antithrombotic therapy to prevent stroke in patients with atrial fibrillation: a meta-analysis', *Annals of Internal Medicine* **138**: 831–838.

Houghton AR and Gray D. (2003) *Making Sense of the ECG*, 2nd edition. London: Edward Arnold.

Jowett NI and Thompson DR. (2002) *Comprehensive Coronary Care*, 3rd edition. London: Baillière Tindall.

Royal College of Physicians. (1999) 'Atrial fibrillation in hospital and general practice: a consensus statement', *British Journal of Cardiology* **6**: 138–140.

Walraven RG, Hart RG, Singer DE, et al. (2002) 'Oral anticoagulants vs aspirin in nonvalvular atrial fibrillation. An individual meta-analysis', *Journal of the American Medical Association* **188**: 2441–2448.

Chapter 31 **Respiratory functioning**

Barnes PJ, Shapiro SD and Pauwels KA. (2003) 'Chronic obstructive pulmonary disease: molecular and cellular mechanisms', *European Respiratory Journal* **22**: 672–688.

British Thoracic Society. (1997) 'BTS guidelines for the management of chronic obstructive pulmonary disease', *Thorax* **52**: supplement 5.

Caird FI and Judge TG. (1979) *Assessment of the Elderly Patient*. Philadelphia: Lippincott.

Christiansen JL and Grzybowski JM. (1993) *Biology of Aging.* St Louis: Mosby.

Darovic GO. (2002) 'Physical assessment of the pulmonary system', in Darovic GO (ed). *Hemodynamic Monitoring: invasive and noninvasive clinical application*, 3rd edition. Philadelphia: WB Saunders; 43–56.

Frausing E, Jorgen H, Phanareth K, Kok-Jensen A and Dirksen A. (2001) 'Peak flow as predictor of overall mortality in asthma and chronic obstructive pulmonary disease', *American Journal of Respiratory and Critical Care Medicine* **163**: 690–693.

Hall MRP, MacLellan WJ and Lye MDW. (1993) *Medical Care of the Elderly*. London: Wiley.

Harrell JS. (1997) 'Age-related changes in the respiratory system', in Matteson MA and McConnell AS (eds). *Gerontological Nursing*, 2nd edition. New York: WB Saunders; 256–281.

Hayward J. (1975) *Information: a prescription against pain*. London: Royal College of Nursing.

Herbert RA. (1999) 'The biology of human ageing', in Redfern SJ and Ross FM (eds). *Nursing Older People,* 3rd edition. Edinburgh: Churchill Livingstone; 55–77.

Hinds CJ and Watson D. (1996) *Intensive Care: a concise textbook*, 2nd edition. London: WB Saunders.

Intensive Care Society. (2001) *Intensive Care Society Standards Committee. Outreach: a guideline for the introduction of outreach services*. London: ICS.

Kenward G, Hodgetts T and Castle N. (2001) 'Time to put the R back in TPR', *Nursing Times* **97** (40): 32–33.

Martinson BC, O'Connor PJ and Pronk NP. (2001) 'Physical inactivity and short-term all-cause mortality in adults with chronic disease', *Archives of Internal Medicine* **161**: 1175–1180.

Pelkonen M, Notkola IL, Tukianen H, Teruahauta M, Tuomilehto J and Nissinen A. (2001) 'Smoking cessation, decline in pulmonary function and total mortality: a 30 year follow up study among the Finnish cohorts of the Seven Countries Study', *Thorax* **56**: 703–707.

Rush S and Schofield I. (1999) 'Biological support needs', in Heath H and Schofield I (eds). *Healthy Ageing: nursing older people*. London: Mosby; 119–158.

Tolep K and Kelsen SG. (1998) 'The effect of ageing on the respiratory skeletal muscles', in Pathy MSJ (ed). *Principles and Practice of Geriatric Medicine*, 3rd edition. London: Wiley; 647–654.

Watson R. (1999) 'Respiration', in Watson R (ed). *Essential Science for Nursing Students*. London: Baillière Tindall; 199–212.

Chapter 32 **Body temperature**

Bartlett EM. (1996) 'Temperature measurement: why and how in intensive care', *Intensive and Critical Care Nursing* **12**: 50–54.

Clancy J and McVicar J. (2002) *Physiology and Anatomy: a homeostatic approach*, 2nd edition. London: Arnold.

Dowding D, Nimmo S and Wisiewski M. (2002) 'An investigation into the accuracy of different types of thermometers', *Professional Nurse* **18** (3): 166–168.

Eliopoulos C. (2001) *Gerontological Nursing*, 5th edition. Philadelphia: Lippincott.

Ganong WF. (2001) *Review of Medical Physiology*, 20th edition. New York: Lange Medical Books.

Herbert RA and Rowswell M. (1999) 'Maintaining body temperature', in Redfern SJ and Ross FM (eds). *Nursing Older People*, 3rd edition. Edinburgh: Churchill Livingstone; 413–430.

Hinds CJ and Watson D. (1996) *Intensive Care: a concise textbook*, 2nd edition. London: WB Saunders.

Lattavo K, Britt J and Dobal M. (1995) 'Agreement between measures of pulmonary artery and tympanic temperatures', *Research in Nursing and Health* **18**: 365–370.

Manthous CA, Hall JB, Olson D, et al. (1995) 'Effect of cooling on oxygen consumption in febrile critically ill patients', *American Journal of Respiratory and Critical Care Medicine* **151**: 10–14.

Marieb EN. (2004) *Human Anatomy and Physiology*, 6th edition. San Francisco: Pearson/Benjamin Cummings.

Marik PE. (2000) 'Fever in the ICU', *Chest* **117**: 855–869.

Perlino CA. (2001) 'Postoperative fever', *Medical Clinics of North America* **85**: 1141–1149.

Rhoades R and Pflanzer P. (1996) *Human Physiology*, 3rd edition. Fort Worth: Saunders College Publishing.

Rowsey PJ. (1997) 'Pathophysiology of fever. Relooking at cooling interventions', *Dimensions of Critical Care Nursing* **16**: 202–207; **16**: 251–256.

Samples JF, Van-Cott ML, Long C, King IM and Kersenbrock A. (1985) 'Circadian rhythms: basis for screening fever', *Nursing Research* **34**: 377–379.

Schofield I. (1999) 'Environmental safety and security', in Heath H and Schofield I (eds). *Healthy Ageing: nursing older people*. London: Mosby; 297–318.

Watson R. (1993) 'Hypothermia', *Nursing Standard* **5** (6): 41–44.

Watson R. (2000) 'Altered presentation in old age', *Nursing Older People* **12** (3): 19–21.

Weller AS. (2001) 'Body temperature and its regulation', *Anaesthesia and Intensive Care Medicine* **2**: 195–198.

Chapter 33 **Eating and drinking in everyday life**

Chen CC-H, Schilling LS and Lyder CH. (2001) 'A concept analysis of malnutrition in the elderly', *Journal of Advanced Nursing* **36** (1): 131–142.

Eberhardie C. (2002) 'Nutrition and the older adult', *Nursing Older People* **14** (2): 20–25.

Eberhardie C. (2004) 'Assessment and management of eating skills in the older adult', *Professional Nurse* **19**: 318–322.

Edington J, Kon P and Martyn CN. (1996) 'Prevalence of malnutrition in patients in general practice', *Clinical Nutrition* **15**: 60–63.

Great Britain Working Group on the Nutrition of Elderly People. (1992) *The Nutrition of Elderly People*. London: HMSO.

Hamilton K, Spalding D, Steele C and Waldron S. (2002) 'An audit of nutritional care delivered to elderly inpatients in community hospitals', *Journal of Human Nutrition and Dietetics* **15**: 49–58.

Kelly IE, Tessier S, Cahill A, et al. (2000) 'Still hungry in hospital: identifying malnutrition in acute hospital admissions', *Quarterly Journal of Medicine* **93**: 93–98.

King's Fund. (1992) *Nutrition – a positive approach to treatment: report of a working party*. London: King's Fund.

McCormack P. (1997) 'Undernutrition in the elderly population living at home in the community: a review of the literature', *Journal of Advanced Nursing* **26**: 856–863.

McLaren S. (1999) 'Eating and drinking', in Redfern SJ and Ross FM (eds). *Nursing Older People*, 3rd edition. Edinburgh: Churchill Livingstone; 363–394.

McWhirter JP and Pennington CR. (1994) 'The incidence of malnutrition in hospitals', *British Medical Journal* **308**: 945–948.

Perry L and Love CP. (2001) 'Screening for dysphagia and aspiration in acute stroke', *Dysphagia* **16**: 7–18.

Resources

Allison SP. (1999) *Hospital Food as Treatment*. Maidenhead: British Association of Parenteral and Enteral Nutrition.

Bond S. (1998) *A Review of Eating Matters – a resource for improved dietary care in hospitals*. Newcastle upon Tyne: University of Newcastle upon Tyne.

Disabled Living Foundation: www.dlf.org.uk

Fieldhouse P. (1995) *Food and Nutrition: customs and culture*, 2nd edition. London: Chapman & Hall.

Chapter 34 **Oral health**

Adams R. (1996) 'Qualified nurses lack adequate knowledge related to oral health, resulting in inadequate oral care of patients on medical wards', *Journal of Advanced Nursing* **24**: 552–560.

Barnett J. (1991) 'A reassessment of oral healthcare', *Professional Nurse* **6**: 703–708.

British Dental Health Foundation. (2000) *Caring for My Teeth*. Rugby: BDHF.

Clay M. (2000) 'Oral health in older people', *Nursing Older People* **12** (7): 21–26.

Clay M and Nelson D. (2002) 'Assessing oral health in older people', *Nursing Older People* **14** (8): 31–32.

Department of Health. (1994) *An Oral Health Strategy for England*. London: DoH.

Department of Health. (2001) *The Essence of Care: patient-focused benchmarking for healthcare practitioners*. London: DoH.

Evans G. (2001) 'A rationale for oral care', *Nursing Standard* **15** (43): 33–36.

Fahs D. (1981) 'Dental care', *Journal of Gerontological Nursing* **17** (1): 22–25.

Heals M. (1993) 'Tools for mouth care', *Nursing Times* **76** (8): 340–342.

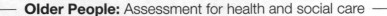

Health Education Authority. (1996) *Handbook of Dental Health for Health Visitors, Midwives and Nurses*, 2nd edition. London: HEA.

Holmes S. (1996) 'Nursing management of oral care in older patients', *Nursing Times* **92** (9): 37–39.

Relatives and Residents Association. (2004) *Dental Care for Older People who live in Care Homes*. London: RaRA. [Available from mail to: info@relres.org]

Roberts J. (2001) 'Oral assessment and intervention', *Nursing Older People* **13** (7): 14–16.

Shepherd A. (2002) 'The impact of oral health on nutritional status', *Nursing Standard* **16** (27): 37–38.

Todd J and Lader D. (1991) *Adult Dental Health in the United Kingdom: 1988*. OPCS Social Survey Division. London: HMSO.

Turner G. (1996) 'Oral care', *Nursing Standard* **10** (28): 51–54.

Xavier G. (2000) 'The importance of mouth care in preventing infection', *Nursing Standard* **14** (18): 47–51.

Resource

British Dental Health Foundation: publishes a range of helpful leaflets; it also has an advice line 0870 333 1188

Chapter 35 **Gastrointestinal tract functioning**

Clinch DP and Hilton DA. (1998) 'Constipation', in Pathy MSJ (ed). *Principles and Practice of Geriatric Medicine*, 3rd edition. London: Wiley; 437–442.

Dew MJ. (1999) 'Diseases of the colon and rectum', in Pathy MSJ (ed). *Principles and Practice of Geriatric Medicine*, 3rd edition. London: Wiley; 395–405.

Ebersole P and Hess P. (1990) *Toward Healthy Aging*. St Louis: Mosby.

Hall MRP, MacLellan WJ and Lye MDW. (1993) *Medical Care of the Elderly*. London: Wiley.

Harari B, Gurwitz JH and Minaker KL. (1993) 'Constipation in the elderly', *Journal of the American Geriatrics Society* **41**: 1130–1140.

Koch T. (1998) 'Older people and laxative use: literature review and pilot study report', *Journal of Clinical Nursing* **9**: 516–525.

Linton AD. (1997) 'Age-related changes in the gastrointestinal system', in Matteson MA and McConnell AS (eds). *Gerontological Nursing*, 2nd edition. New York: WB Saunders; 316–335.

McLaren SM. (1999) 'Eating and drinking', in Redfern SJ and Ross FM (eds). *Nursing Older People*, 3rd edition. Edinburgh: Churchill Livingstone; 363–394.

Molyneux H. (1998) 'Nutrition of older people', in Beales D, Denham M and Tulloch A (eds). *Community Care of Older People*. Oxford: Radcliffe Medical Press; 72–79.

Morris JS. (1998) 'Diseases of the gall-bladder and bile ducts', in Pathy MSJ (ed). *Principles and Practice of Geriatric Medicine*, 3rd edition. London: Wiley; 419–436.

Norton C. (1999) 'Eliminating', in Redfern SJ and Ross FM (eds). *Nursing Older People*, 3rd edition. Edinburgh: Churchill Livingstone; 395–412.

Rush S and Schofield I. (1999) 'Biological support needs', in Heath H and Schofield I (eds). *Healthy Ageing: nursing older people*. London: Mosby; 119–158.

Schofield I. (1999) 'Age related changes', in Heath H and Schofield I (eds). *Healthy Ageing: nursing older people*. London: Mosby; 81–102.

Watson R. (2000a) 'Normal ageing', *Elderly Care* **12** (2): 23–24.

Watson R. (2000b) *Anatomy and Physiology for Nurses*, 11th edition. London: Baillière Tindall.

Watson R. (2000c) 'Assessing gastrointestinal (GI) tract functioning in older people', *Nursing Older People* **12** (2): 27–28.

Chapter 36 **Nutritional status**

Barker HM. (2002) *Nutrition and Dietetics for Healthcare*. Edinburgh: Churchill Livingstone.

Barrocas A, Belcher D, Champagne D and Jastram C. (1995) 'Nutrition assessment: practical approaches', *Clinics in Geriatric Medicine* **11** (4): 675–713.

Baxter JP. (1999) 'Problems of nutritional assessment in the acute setting', *Proceedings of the Nutrition Society* **58**: 39–46.

Bond S. (1997) *Eating Matters*. Newcastle upon Tyne: The Centre for Health Services Research, University of Newcastle upon Tyne.

British Association of Parenteral and Enteral Nutrition. (2003) *Malnutrition Universal Screening Tool (MUST)*. Redditch: BAPEN.

British Dietetic Association. (2003) 'Effective Practice Bulletin issue 32: challenging the use of Body Mass Index (BMI) to assess under-nutrition in older people', *Dietetics Today* **38** (3): 15–19.

Chu L, Eberhardie C, Forte D, et al. (1999) 'An audit of measuring equipment in elderly care', *Professional Nurse* **14** (7): 463–466.

Copeman J. (1999) *Nutritional Care for Older People*. London: Age Concern England.

Department of Health. (1991) *Dietary Reference Values for Food and Nutrients for the United Kingdom*. London: HMSO.

Department of Health. (2001) *National Service Framework for Older People*. London: The Stationery Office.

Detsky AS, McLaughlin JR, Baker JP, et al. (1987) 'What is subjective global assessment of nutritional status?', *Journal of Parenteral and Enteral Nutrition* **11**: 8–13.

Elia M. (2003) *The 'MUST' Report*. Redditch: British Association of Parenteral and Enteral Nutrition.

Finch SA, Doyle W, Lowe C, et al. (1998) *National Diet and Nutrition Survey: people aged 65 years and older*. Volume 1: *Report of the Diet and Nutrition Survey*. London: The Stationery Office.

International Obesity Task Force. (2000) *About Obesity*. Quebec: IOTF [Available at www.iotf.org (accessed 10 March 2004).]

Lennard-Jones JE, Arrowsmith H, Davison C, Denham AF and Micklewright A. (1995) 'Screening by nurses and junior doctors to detect malnutrition when patients are first assessed in hospital', *Clinical Nutrition* **14**: 336–340.

McLaren S and Crawley H. (2000) NT Monographs: *Promoting Nutritional Health in Older Adults*. London: Nursing Times Books.

Micklewright A and Todorovic V. (1997) 'Good old home cooking', *Nursing Times* (supplement) **93** (49): 58–59.

Nutrition Advisory Group for Elderly People. (1994) *Taking Steps to Tackle Eating Problems*. Leeds: NAGE/British Dietetic Association.

Simmons SF and Reuben D. (2000) 'Nutritional intake monitoring for nursing home residents: comparison of staff documentation, direct observation, and photography methods', *Journal of the American Geriatrics Society* **48**: 209–213.

Stratton RJ, Green CJ and Elia M. (2003) *Disease Related Malnutrition: an evidence-based approach to treatment.* Wallingford: CABI.

UKCC. (1997) 'Nurses are responsible for feeding patients', *Register* **20**: 5.

Vellas B, Garry PJ and Guigoz Y. (1999) Nestlé Nutrition Workshop Series Clinical and Performance Programme, Volume 1. *Mini Nutritional Assessment (MNA): research and practice in the elderly.* Basel, Switzerland: Karger.

Webb GP and Copeman J. (1996) *The Nutrition of Older Adults.* London: Arnold.

Chapter 37 **Renal function**

Baker R. (2002) 'Acute tubulointerstitial nephritis', in Glynne P, Allen A and Pusey C (eds). *Acute Renal Failure in Practice.* London: Imperial College Press.

Baylis C. (1997) 'The aging kidney', in Jamison RL and Wilkinson R (eds). *Nephrology.* London: Chapman & Hall; 170–180.

De Zeeuw D, Remuzzi G, Parving H-H, et al. (2004) 'Proteinuria, a target for renprotection with type 2 diabetic nephropathy: lessons from RENAAL'. *Kidney International* **65**: 2309–2320.

Epstein O, Perkin GD, de Bono DP and Cookson J. (2003) *Clinical Examination*, 3rd edition. London: Mosby.

Renal Association. (2002) *Treatment of Adults and Children with Renal Failure: standards and audit measures*, 3rd edition. London: Renal Association & Royal College of Physicians.

Renal Registry Report. (2003) *The Sixth Annual Report UK Renal Registry.* [Available on www.renalreg.com]

Stewart Cameron J and Greger R. (1998) 'Renal function and testing function', in Davison AM, Stewart Cameron J, Grunfeld J-P, et al (eds). *Oxford Textbook of Clinical Nephrology*, 2nd edition. Oxford: Oxford Medical Publishers; 39–69.

Chapter 38 **Fluid balance**

Boldt J. (2000) 'Volume replacement in the surgical patient – does the type of solution make a difference?', *British Journal of Anaesthesia* **84**: 783–793.

Coutts A. (2001) 'Nutrition and the life cycle – 5: nutritional needs of older adults', *British Journal of Nursing* **10**: 603–607.

Deroy R. (2000) 'Crystalloids or colloids for fluid resuscitation – is that the question?', *Current Anaesthesia and Critical Care* **11**: 20–26.

Ganong WF. (2001) *Review of Medical Physiology*, 20th edition. East Norwalk CT: Appleton & Lange.

Haljamae H and Lindgren S. (2000) 'Fluid therapy: present controversies', in Vincent J-L (ed). *Yearbook of Intensive Care and Emergency Medicine*. Berlin: Springer; 429–442.

Heath H. (2000) 'Assessing older people', *Nursing Older People* **11** (10): 27–28.

Humphreys M. (2002) 'Hyperkalaemia: a dangerous electrolyte disturbance', *Connect* **2**: 28–30.

Isbister JP. (2003) 'Blood transfusion', in Bersten AD and Soni N (eds). *Intensive Care Manual*, 5th edition. Edinburgh. Butterworth-Heinemann; 915–926.

Marieb EN. (2004) *Human Anatomy and Physiology*, 6th edition. San Francisco: Pearson/Benjamin Cummings.

Mythen M. (2003) 'Colloids and blood products', in Bersten AD and Soni N (eds). *Intensive Care Manual*, 5th edition. Edinburgh: Butterworth-Heinemann; 927–932.

Webb AR. (1999) 'Fluids', in Webb AR, Shapiro M, Singer M and Suter PM (eds). *Oxford Textbook of Critical Care*. Oxford: Oxford University Press; 1246–1249.

Chapter 39 **Continence**

Chiang L, Ouslander J, Schnelle J and Reuben DB. (2000) 'Dually incontinent nursing home residents: clinical characteristics and treatment differences', *Journal of the American Geriatrics Society* **48**: 673–676.

Fantl JA, Newman DK, Colling J, et al. (1996) *Agency for Health Care Policy and Research (AHCPR) 1996 Clinical Practice Guideline Urinary*

Incontinence in Adults: acute and chronic management. Rockville: US Department of Health and Human Services.

Fonda D, Benvenuti F, Castleden M, et al. (1999) 'Management of incontinence in older people', in Abrams P, Khoury S and Wein A (eds). *Incontinence: 1st International Consultation on Incontinence*. Plymouth: Health Publications; 731–773.

Getliffe K. (1996) 'Urinary incontinence: assessing the problem', *Primary Health Care* **6** (8): 31–38.

Getliffe K and Dolman M. (2003) 'Normal and abnormal bladder function', in Getliffe K and Dolman M (eds). *Promoting Continence: a clinical and research resource*. Edinburgh: Baillière Tindall; 21–51.

Kamm MA. (1998) 'Fortnightly review: faecal incontinence', *British Medical Journal* **316**: 528–531.

Lewis G. (1999) 'Assessing psychological well being of incontinent patients', *Journal of Community Nursing* **13** (9): 40–43.

McKee D. (1999) 'The legal framework for informed consent', *Professional Nurse* **14** (10): 688–690.

Nazarko L. (1999) 'Assess all areas', *Nursing Times* **95** (6): 68–72.

Newman DK. (1999) *The Urinary Incontinence Sourcebook*. Los Angeles: Lowell House; 143–148.

Ouslander JG and Schnelle JF. (1995) 'Incontinence in the nursing home', *Annals of Internal Medicine* **122** (6): 438–449.

Pfister SM. (1999) 'Bladder diaries and voiding patterns in older adults', *Journal of Gerontological Nursing* **25** (3): 36–41.

Roberts RO, Jacobsen SJ, Reilly WT, Pemberton JH, Lieber MM and Talley NJ. (1999) 'Prevalence of combined fecal and urinary incontinence: a community-based study', *Journal of the American Geriatrics Society* **47** (7): 837–841.

Royal College of Nursing. (2000) *Digital Rectal Examination and Manual Removal of Faeces: guidance for nurses*. London: Royal College of Nursing.

Royal College of Physicians. (1995) *Incontinence: causes, management and provision of services.* London: Royal College of Physicians.

Sander R. (1998) 'Promoting urinary continence in residential care', *Elderly Care* **10** (3): 28–32.

Wallace B. (2000) 'Nurses and consent', *Professional Nurse* **15** (11): 727–730.

Williams ME and Gaylord SA. (1990) 'Role of functional assessment in the evaluation of urinary incontinence', *Journal of the American Geriatrics Society* **38**: 296–299.

Wilson L. (2003a) 'Focus on older people', in Getliffe K and Dolman M (eds). *Promoting Continence: a clinical and research resource.* Edinburgh: Baillière Tindall; 135–184.

Wilson L. (2003b) 'Continence and older people: the importance of functional assessment', *Nursing Older People* **15** (4): 22–28.

Chapter 40 **Quality of life**

Bergner M, Bobbitt RA, Carter WB, et al. (1981) 'The Sickness Impact Profile: development and final revision of a health status measure', *Medical Care* **19**: 787–805.

Draper P. (1997) *Nursing Perspectives on Quality of Life.* London: Routledge.

Elkington J. (1966) 'Medicine and the quality of life', *Annals of Internal Medicine* **64** (3): 711–714.

Gabriel Z and Bowling A. (2004) 'Quality of life from the perspectives of older people', *Ageing and Society* **24**: 675–691.

Hendry F and McVittie C. (2004) 'Is quality of life a healthy concept? Measuring and understanding life experiences of older people', *Qualitative Health Research* **14** (7): 961–976.

Jenkinson C and McGee H. (1988) *Health Status Measurement.* Abingdon: Radcliffe Medical Press.

Livingston G, Watkin V, Manela M, Rosser R and Katona C. (1998) 'Quality of life in older people', *Aging and Mental Health* **2** (1); 20–23.

Rapley M. (2003) *Quality of Life Research: a critical introduction.* London: Sage.

Ware J, Snow K, Kosinski M, et al. (1993) *SF-36 Health Survey: manual and interpretation guide.* Boston MA: Health Institute, New England Medical Centre.

Williams A and Kind P. (1992) 'The present state of play about QALYs', in Hopkins A (ed). *Measures of the Quality of Life.* London: Royal College of Physicians of London; 21–34.

Chapter 41 **Sleep**

Avidan A. (2003) 'Insomnia in the geriatric patient', *Clinical Cornerstone* **5** (3): 51–60.

Dollman WB, Le Blanc VT and Roughead EE. (2003) 'Managing insomnia in the elderly – what prevents us using non-drug options?', *Journal of Clinical Pharmacy and Therapeutics* **28**: 485–491.

Maher S. (2004) 'Sleep in the older adult', *Nursing Older People* **16** (9): 30–35.

Wolf SL, Barnhart HX, Kutner NG, McNeely E, Coogler C and Xu T. (2003) 'Reducing frailty in older persons: an investigation of tai chi and computerized balance training', *Journal of the American Geriatrics Society* **51**: 1794–1803.

Chapter 42 **Pain**

Agency for Health Care Policy and Research. (1992) *Acute Pain Management: operative or medical procedures and trauma.* Rockville: US Department of Health and Human Services.

Allcock N, McGarry J and Elkan R. (2002) 'Management of pain in older people within the nursing home: a preliminary study', *Health and Social Care in the Community* **10**: 464–471.

American Geriatrics Society Panel on Persistent Pain in Older Persons. (2002) 'The management of persistent pain in older persons', *Journal of the American Geriatrics Society* **50** (6 Suppl): S205–S224.

Blomqvist K and Hallberg IR. (1999) 'Pain in older adults in sheltered accommodation – agreement between assessments by older adults and staff', *Journal of Clinical Nursing* **8**: 159–169.

Bruce A and Kopp P. (2001) 'Pain experienced by older people', *Professional Nurse* **16**: 1481–1485.

Chapman CR and Syrala KL. (2001) 'Measurement of pain', in Loeser JD, Butler SH, Chapman CR and Turk DC (eds). *Bonica's Management of Pain*, 3rd edition. Philadelphia: Lippincott/Williams & Wilkins; 310–328.

Closs SJ. (1994) 'Pain in the elderly: a neglected phenomenon?', *Journal of Advanced Nursing* **19**: 1072–1081.

Closs SJ, Fairclough HL, Tierney AJ and Curry CT. (1993) 'Pain in elderly orthopaedic patients', *Journal of Clinical Nursing* **2**: 41–45.

Closs SJ, Barr B, Briggs M, Cash K and Seers K. (2004) 'A comparison of five pain assessment scales for nursing home residents with varying degrees of cognitive impairment', *Journal of Pain and Symptom Management* **27**: 196–205.

De Rond M, De Wit R, Van Dam F, et al. (1999) 'Daily pain assessment; value for nurses and patients', *Journal of Advanced Nursing* **29**: 436–444.

Donovan MI. (1992) 'A practical approach to pain assessment', in Watt-Watson JH and Donovan MI (eds). *Pain Management: nursing perspective.* Philadelphia: Mosby; 59–78.

Elliott AM, Smith BH, Penny KI, Smith WC and Chambers WA. (1999) 'The epidemiology of chronic pain in the community', *Lancet* **354**: 1248–1252.

Feldt KS, Ryden MB and Miles S. (1998) 'Treatment of pain in cognitively impaired compared with cognitively intact older patients with hip fracture', *Journal of the American Geriatric Society* **46**: 1079–1085.

Ferrell BA and Ferrell BR. (1992) 'Pain in the elderly', in Watt-Watson JH and Donovan MI (eds). *Pain Management: nursing perspective.* Philadelphia: Mosby; 349–369.

Ferrell BA, Ferrell BR and Rivera L. (1995) 'Pain in cognitively impaired nursing home patients', *Journal of Pain and Symptom Management* **10**: 591–598.

Herr K and Mobily PR. (1991) 'Complexities of pain assessment in the elderly; clinical considerations', *Journal of Gerontological Nursing* **17** (4): 12–19.

Hurley AC, Volicer BJ, Hanrahan PA, Houde S and Volicer L. (1992) 'Assessment of discomfort in advanced Alzheimer patients', *Research in Nursing and Health* **15**: 369–377.

Kamel HK, Phlavan M, Malekgoudarzi B, Gogel P and Morley JE. (2001) 'Utilizing pain assessment scales increases the frequency of diagnosing pain among elderly nursing home residents', *Journal of Pain and Symptom Management* **21** (6): 450–455.

Leibeskind JC and Melzack R. (1988) 'The International Pain Foundation: meeting a need for education in pain management', *Journal of Pain and Symptom Management* **3**: 131–132.

Loeb JL. (1999) 'Pain management in long-term care', *American Journal of Nursing* **99** (2): 48–52.

McCaffery M and Pasero C. (1999) *Pain: clinical manual*, 2nd edition. St Louis: Mosby.

Manfredi PL, Breuer B, Meier DE and Libow L. (2003) 'Pain assessment in elderly patients with severe dementia', *Journal of Pain and Symptom Management* **25**: 48–52.

Melzack R and Katz J. (2001) 'The McGill Pain Questionnaire: appraisal and current status', in Turk DC and Melzack R (eds). *Handbook of Pain Assessment*, 2nd edition. New York: Guildford Press; 35–51.

Morrison RS and Siu AL. (2000) 'A comparison of pain and its treatment in advanced dementia and cognitively intact patients with hip fracture', *Journal of Pain and Symptom Management* **19**: 240–248.

Pain Society and Royal College of Anaesthetists. (2003) *Pain Management Services: good practice*. London: Pain Society.

Parke B. (1998) 'Realizing the presence of pain in cognitively impaired older adults', *Journal of Gerontological Nursing* **24** (6): 21–28.

Rowlingson JC. (1994) 'The assessment of pain in the critically ill', in Puntillo KA (ed). *Pain in the Critically Ill: assessment and management*. Philadelphia: Aspen; 39–52.

Simons W and Malabar R. (1995) 'Assessing pain in elderly patients who cannot respond verbally', *Journal of Advanced Nursing* **22**: 663–669.

Resources

Web resources and further information

American Geriatrics Society	www.americangeriatrics.org/education
British Pain Society	www.britishpainsociety.org
Oxford Pain Internet Site	www.jr2.ox.ac.uk/bandolier/booth/painpag
Pain Relief Foundation	www.painrelieffoundation.org.uk
Pain Talk	www.pain-talk.co.uk

Support groups

Pain Support	www.painsupport.co.uk
Pain Association Scotland	www.chronicpaininfo.org

About Age Concern

Age Concern is the UK's largest organisation working for and with older people to enable them to make more of life. We are a federation of over 400 independent charities that share the same name, values and standards.

We believe that ageing is a normal part of life, and that later life should be fulfilling, enjoyable and productive. We enable older people by providing services and grants, researching their needs and opinions, influencing government and media, and through other innovative and dynamic projects.

Every day we provide vital services, information and support to thousands of older people of all ages and backgrounds.

Age Concern also works with many older people from disadvantaged or marginalised groups, such as those living in rural areas or black and minority ethnic elders.

Age Concern is dependent on donations, covenants and legacies.

Age Concern England
1268 London Road
London SW16 4ER
Tel: 020 8765 7200
Fax: 020 8765 7211
Website:
www.ageconcern.org.uk

Age Concern Scotland
113 Rose Street
Edinburgh EH2 3DT
Tel: 0131 220 3345
Fax: 0131 220 2779
Website:
www.ageconcernscotland.org.uk

Age Concern Cymru
Ty John Pathy
Units 13–14 Neptune Court
Vanguard Way
Cardiff CF24 5PJ
Tel: 029 2043 1555
Fax: 029 2047 1418
Website:
www.accymru.org.uk

Age Concern Northern Ireland
3 Lower Crescent
Belfast BT7 1NR
Tel: 028 9024 5729
Fax: 028 9023 5497
Website:
www.ageconcernni.org

Age Concern Books

To order a book:

- Telephone our hotline: **0870 44 22 120**
  (Opening hours: 9am-7pm Mon to Fri, 9am-5pm Sat and Sun)

- Website: **www.ageconcern.org.uk/bookshop** (secure online bookshop)

- Post: send a cheque or money order to:
  Age Concern Books, Units 5 and 6 Industrial Estate, Brecon, Powys LD3 8LA.
  Fax: 0870 8000 100. Cheques payable to Age Concern England for the appropriate amount plus p&p.

Postage and packing: mainland UK and Northern Ireland: £1.99 for the first book, 75p for each additional book up to a maximum of £7.50. For customers ordering from outside the mainland UK and NI: credit card payment only; please telephone for international postage rates or email sales@ageconcernbooks.co.uk

Bulk order discounts are available on orders totalling 50 or more copies of the same title. For details, please contact Age Concern Books on 0870 44 22 120.

Free service for businesses and organisations: for orders totalling 500 or more copies of the same title, you can have a unique front cover design featuring your organisation's logo and corporate colours, or adding your logo to the current cover design. You can also insert an additional four pages of text for a small additional fee. For full details, please contact Sue Henning, Age Concern Books, Astral House, 1268 London Road, London SW16 4ER. Fax: 020 8765 7211. Email: sue.henning@ace.org.uk

Age Concern Factsheets

Age Concern produces 45 comprehensive factsheets designed to answer many of the questions older people (or those advising them) may have. These include money and benefits, health, community care, leisure and education, and housing. For up to five free factsheets, telephone the information line on 0800 00 99 66 (8am-7pm, seven days a week, every week of the year). Alternatively you may prefer to download them free from our website: www.ageconcern.org.uk

Care Professional Handbook Series

The Care Assistant's Handbook
Helen Howard

Nowadays, people who live in care homes are likely to need more intensive care than in the past, so the role and responsibilities of carers have changed. More specialist and more regular care may be required 24 hours a day. This book is written specifically for care assistants who work in care home settings and who provide this type of care.

£11.99 + p&p   0-86242-288-4

Hearing *and* Sight Loss
Sarah Butler

Although a sensory impairment may not be life-threatening in itself, it can exacerbate other impairments and contribute to a major loss of independence for older people. This in-depth handbook offers a holistic approach, bringing together information on the different sensory impairments (visual, hearing and dual impairment). It explores the ways in which sensory impairment affects older people in the care system, and offers a wide range of ways to support them.

£14.99 + p&p   0-86242-359-7

Money at Home: The home care worker's guide to handling other people's finances and belongings
Pauline Thompson

This guide covers some of the key issues to consider when handling other people's money and belongings. It is essential reading for: home care workers, and staff and volunteers who visit people in their own homes in an official capacity and who may be involved in assisting with some financial matters; home care managers who are responsible for devising procedures on the handling of money and belongings.

£7.99 + p&p   0-86242-293-0

■ This book reflects the law and practice in England.
   However, many of the principles are similar across the UK.

Moving on from Community Care:
The treatment, care and support of older people in England
Lorna Easterbrook

This book gives an overview of the wide range of recent changes within the NHS, local government and the independent sector, relating to health, housing and social care for older people in England. It explores the background to the last decade of change, and explains the more important aspects for older people with ongoing care needs. The book can be read as a whole or used for reference to find areas of key interest.

£14.99 + p&p   0-86242-348-1

Nutritional Care for Older People: A guide to good practice
June Copeman

Food plays a vital role in all of our lives, but can present a particular challenge for those looking after older people. A sound, balanced diet, and appetising meals can have a major impact on their health, well-being, and general motivation. Packed full of practical information and guidance, this book will help staff develop and maintain the very best good practice in all aspects of nutritional care.

£14.99 + p&p   0-86242-284-1

Reminiscence and Recall: A guide to good practice: 2nd edition
Faith Gibson

This edition provides advice and guidance to develop and maintain the very highest standards in reminiscence work, and helps readers to develop the confidence, knowledge, understanding and skills needed to encourage people to value themselves by valuing their past. It also includes guidance on working with people with dementia, international developments and creative communication.

£11.99 + p&p   0-86242-253-1

Other titles for Care Professionals

Alive and Kicking: The carer's guide to exercises for older people
Julie Sobczak

£11.99 + p&p   0-86242-289-2

Counselling and Older People: An introductory guide
Edited by Verena Tschudin

£12.99 + p&p   0-86242-245-0

Their Rights: Advance directives and living wills explored
Kevin Kendrick and Simon Robinson

£9.99 + p&p   0-86242-244-2

Training Packs and Learning Resources

Age Concern currently publishes nine Training Packs and two Learning Resources, which are ideal teaching tools for all care staff involved in the training and support of other staff. Topics include: Accident Prevention; Cross Cultural Care; Reminiscence; Supporting People with Dementia; Understanding Bereavement; and The Successful Activity Co-ordinator.

Training Packs

These packs are ideal teaching tools for all care staff involved in the training and support of other staff. They enable trainers to effectively guide and reinforce staff skills and development by providing all the material necessary to run successful group training sessions. The packs can:

- be used either as an integrated or topic-led course
- be used again and again
- be used by inexperienced trainers
- save time and money

All contain key point overhead transparencies, aims and objectives, teaching plans, group activities, support material and photocopiable handouts.

Accident Prevention in Residential and Nursing Homes
Royal Society for the Prevention of Accidents (RoSPA)

£45 + p&p   0-86242-402-X
                                                                   Ring binder cover

Care Assistant Training Packs
To use with care assistants working in residential and nursing homes
Helen Howard

Volume 1: Setting the Scene   £35 + p&p   0-86242-330-9
Volume 2: The Principles of Care   £35 + p&p   0-86242-335-X
                                                         Ring binder covers

Cross Cultural Care
To use with care assistants working with older people in all care settings
Helen Howard

£35 + p&p   0-86242-355-4
Ring binder cover

Reminiscence Trainer's Pack
For use in health, housing, social care and arts organisations; colleges, libraries and museums; volunteers' and carers agencies
Faith Gibson

£35 + p&p   0-86242-305-8
                                                                   Shrink-wrapped product

Supporting People with Dementia
A training pack to use with care assistants working in care homes
Dementia Voice

£45 + p&p   0-86242-349-X
                                                       Ring binder cover

Trained Nurse's Teaching Packs
For use in the workplace to educate nursing auxiliaries, health care
assistants and social services care staff
Gill Early and Sarah Miller

Volume 1   £35 + p&p   0-86242-357-0
Volume 2   £35 + p&p   0-86242-400-3
                                                       Ring binder covers

Understanding Bereavement Training Pack
A guide for carers working with older people
Toni Battison

£35 + p&p   0-86242-304-X
                                                       Shrink-wrapped product

Learning Resources

These packs serve professional carers and managers as an invaluable resource to
help with day-to-day activities for which they are responsible. They contain aims
and objectives, definitions, action plans/activities, plus a broad range of essential
background information.

The Process of Care
A learning resource for care home managers and senior staff
Neil Blacklock

£25 + p&p   0-86242-246-9
                                                       Ring binder cover

The Successful Activity Co-ordinator
For activity and care staff engaged in developing an active care home
Rosemary Hurtley and Jennifer Wenborn

£25 + p&p   0-86242-390-2
                                                       Ring binder cover

Cross Cultural Care

Culture, Religion and Patient Care in a Multi-Ethnic Society:
A handbook for professionals
Alix Henley and Judith Schott

Meeting cultural and religious needs is an essential part of providing care in a multi-ethnic society. This book describes ways of identifying individual needs and offers sensitive and practical approaches to adapting care to meet them. It is rooted in the experiences and views of people of minority cultural and religious groups.

'...a stimulating and accessible book that is a useful introduction for the healthcare professional to explore how best to meet the healthcare needs of a multi-ethnic society.' **Nursing Standard**

The book is an important and invaluable resource for everyone involved in providing, planning or managing care in hospital, in the community, in residential care, and in hospices. Its wealth of references make it ideal for undergraduate and postgraduate students.

£19.99 + p&p

0-86242-231-0
624 pages

Cross Cultural Care:
A training pack to use with care assistants
working with older people in all care settings
Helen Howard

This pack provides an introduction to the principles of cross cultural care for older people through engaging participants in thinking about their own experience, identity and lifestyles. It will help care providers to meet their responsibilities under the Care Standards Act 2000 to train care staff, and to meet the national minimum standards for their service. A wide range of topics covered include:

■ Racial, ethnic and cultural identity

■ The changing nature of cultures

■ Understanding prejudice and discrimination

■ Issues around touch and privacy

Learning is achieved through interactive methods, including discussion of case studies and small group activities. Each session has support material, including overhead transparencies and photocopiable handouts.

£35 + p&p

0-86242-355-4
Ring binder cover. Contains 74 pages
and 17 key point overhead transparencies

Index

Note Numbers in *italic* refer to pages with illustrations, tables or boxes.

boundary negotiation 48–49, 59–60
communication systems 48
consent issues 49
disengagement 50–51
environmental preparation 47–48
ethical issues 47
reasons for 55
stages 55–58
time commitment 46–47, 59–60
values underpinning 50–51
views representation 50
see also Single Assessment Process (SAP)
phenytoin 254
phlegm 301
phobias *192*
phosphate *164,* 166–167
physical activity 78, 79, 295, 403, 404
pitting oedema 370, 372
pituitary gland 141, *142*
'platelet cover' 160
platelets 159–160
P-LI-SS-IT model 100–103, *101*
pneumonia 132–133
policy context 20–25
independent sector 22
practice and 24–25
of Single Assessment Process 24
statutory regulations 20–21
polypharmacy 150, 251–253, *252,* 372
continence effects *378*
polyurea 369, 370
postal questionnaires 36
postural hypotension *274,* 283
posture 139, 294
potassium 165–166, 371
potassium tests *164,* 355, 360, *362*
presbyacusis 137, 171–173

'presenting need' 38
Present Pain Index (PPI) 411, *412*
'press-competence' model 113
pressure sores 124, 150, 402
assessment tool 152
primary care 20, 127–128
private sector 22
problem-solving approach 56–58
'process consent' 49, 94, 97
professional perspectives 28–30, *29*
professional training/education 28–30
collaborative assessment role 31–32
progesterone 143
propranolol 281
prostate surgery 107
proton-pump inhibitors 318
proxy consent 49
pruritus 150
psychological development 122–123
factors influencing *190*
psychosexual problems *see* sexual problems
pulmonary oedema 301, 374
pulse 284–291
age-related effects 284–285
atrial fibrillation 285, 288–290
bradycardia 284, 286–287
sick sinus syndrome 290
strength 288
tachycardia 285–286, 287
pulse pressure 282–283
purchaser–provider split 23
pyrexia 129, 133, 304–308, 369

Q
Quality Adjusted Life Year (QALY) 397
quality of life 295, 394–399
definitions 394–395